The Xinjiang emergency

Exploring the causes and consequences
of China's mass detention of Uyghurs

Edited by Michael Clarke

Manchester University Press

Copyright © Manchester University Press 2022

While copyright in the volume as a whole is vested in Manchester University Press, copyright in individual chapters belongs to their respective authors, and no chapter may be reproduced wholly or in part without the express permission in writing of both author and publisher.

Published by Manchester University Press
Oxford Road, Manchester M13 9PL

www.manchesteruniversitypress.co.uk

British Library Cataloguing-in-Publication Data
A catalogue record for this book is available from the British Library

ISBN 978 1 5261 5309 8 hardback
ISBN 978 1 5261 5311 1 paperback

First published 2022

The publisher has no responsibility for the persistence or accuracy of URLs for any external or third-party internet websites referred to in this book, and does not guarantee that any content on such websites is, or will remain, accurate or appropriate.

Printed in Great Britain
by TJ Books Ltd, Padstow

The Xinjiang emergency

Manchester University Press

To the Uyghur people – may they soon have a 'road back home'

No road back home

Abdulqadir Jalalidin (Translated by Joshua L. Freeman)

In this forgotten place I have no lover's touch
Each night brings darker dreams, I have no amulet
My life is all I ask, I have no other thirst
These silent thoughts torment, I have no way to hope

Who I once was, what I've become, I cannot know
Who could I tell my heart's desires, I cannot say
My love, the temper of the fates I cannot guess
I long to go to you, I have no strength to move

Through cracks and crevices I've watched the seasons change
For news of you I've looked in vain to buds and flowers
To the marrow of my bones I've ached to be with you
What road led here, why do I have no road back home

Contents

List of figures and tables   *page* ix
List of contributors   x
Acknowledgements   xv

1. Framing the Xinjiang emergency: Colonialism and settler colonialism as pathways to cultural genocide? – Michael Clarke   1

Part I: Context

2. Echoes from the past: Repression in the Uyghur region now and then – Sandrine Catris   35

3. The Kashgar Dangerous House Reform Programme: Social engineering, 'a rebirth of the nation', and a significant building block in China's creeping genocide – Anna Hayes   61

4. Settler colonialism in the name of counterterrorism: Of 'savages' and 'terrorists' – Sean R. Roberts   90

Part II: Discourses and practices of repression

5. Pathology, inducement, and mass incarcerations of Xinjiang's 'targeted population' – Timothy A. Grose and James Leibold   127

6 Two-faced: Turkic Muslim camp workers, subjection, and active witnessing – Darren Byler ... 154

7 Corrective 're-education' as (cultural) genocide: A content analysis of the Uyghur primary school textbook *Til-Ädäbiyat* – Dilmurat Mahmut and Joanne Smith Finley ... 181

8 Predatory biopolitics: Organ harvesting and other means of monetizing Uyghur 'surplus' – Matthew P. Robertson ... 227

Part III: Domestic and international implications

9 'Round-the-clock, three-dimensional control': The evolution and implications of the 'Xinjiang mode' of counterterrorism – Michael Clarke ... 275

10 The effect of Xinjiang's virtual lockdown on the Uyghur diaspora – Ablimit Baki Elterish ... 306

11 'Window of opportunity': The Xinjiang emergency in China's 'new type of international relations' – David Tobin ... 327

Index ... 355

Figures and tables

Figures

3.1 Map showing Kashgar (circled) and its proximity to Middle Eastern and Central Asian capital cities (map data © 2017 Google)   67
3.2 New-Old Kashgar (photo: Anna Hayes)   77
7.1 Textile banner hung outside the Ürümchi No. 1 Primary School, 5 July 2018 (photo: Joanne Smith Finley)   188
7.2 Picture of a group of Uyghur students, featuring deep-set eyes and Uyghur braids (*Til-Ädäbiyat*, 2018, Book 2, Level 6, p. 95)   199
7.3 The same picture as that on p. 95 (see Figure 7.2), but this time depicting a group of Han Chinese students with shallow-set eyes and regular pigtails/ponytails (*Til-Ädäbiyat*, 2018, Book 2, Level 6, cover image)   200

Tables

10.1 Dimensions of collective trauma among the Uyghur diaspora   310

Contributors

Darren Byler is Assistant Professor of International Studies at Simon Fraser University, Vancouver. His first book project, *Terror Capitalism: Uyghur Dispossession and Masculinity in a Chinese City* (Duke University Press, 2021), examines emerging forms of media, infrastructure, economics, and politics in the Uyghur homeland in Chinese Central Asia. It considers how biotechnical surveillance systems can be tied to new forms of control both in China and in sites across the world where these technologies are exported. Prior to joining the University of Colorado, he was a lecturer in anthropology at the University of Washington. Dr Byler has published research articles in the *Asia-Pacific Journal*, *Contemporary Islam*, *Central Asian Survey*, the *Journal of Chinese Contemporary Art*, and contributed essays to volumes on ethnography of Islam in China, transnational Chinese cinema, and travel and representation. He has additionally provided expert testimony on Uyghur human rights issues before the Canadian House of Commons and writes a regular column on these issues for the journal *SupChina*. He also edits the art and politics repository *The Art of Life in Chinese Central Asia*, which is hosted at livingotherwise.com.

Sandrine Catris is an assistant professor at Augusta University. She is a cultural historian of modern China, Chinese Central Asia, colonialism, memory, and gender and sexuality. Dr Catris' current book project explores the Great Proletarian Cultural Revolution as it played out in the Xinjiang Uyghur Autonomous Region.

Contributors

Michael Clarke is a Senior Fellow at the Centre for Defence Research, Australian Defence College, and Visiting Fellow at the Australia-China Relations Institute (ACRI) at the University of Technology Sydney (UTS). His areas of primary research interest lie in the history and politics of the Xinjiang Uyghur Autonomous Region, Chinese foreign policy in Central Asia, Central Asian geopolitics, and great power politics in Asia. He is the author of *Xinjiang and China's Rise in Central Asia: A History* (Routledge, 2011), editor of *China's Frontier Regions: Ethnicity, Economic Integration and Foreign Relations* (I.B. Tauris, 2016), editor (with Anna Hayes) of *Inside Xinjiang: Space, Place and Power in China's Muslim Far Northwest* (Routledge, 2016), editor of *Terrorism and Counterterrorism in China: Domestic and Foreign Policy Dimensions* (Oxford University Press, 2018), and editor (with Matthew Sussex and Nick Bisley) of *The Belt and Road Initiative and the Future of Regional Order in the Indo-Pacific* (Lexington Books, 2020). Dr Clarke also regularly provides media commentary on Uyghur/Xinjiang and Chinese foreign policy-related issues to national and international media and has published commentary with *Foreign Policy*, *Wall Street Journal*, *The National Interest*, CNN, BBC News, *South China Morning Post*, and *The Diplomat* amongst others.

Ablimit Baki Elterish is a senior language tutor of Chinese at the University of Manchester. Dr Elterish also teaches courses related to Uyghur studies at undergraduate and postgraduate levels. His research area is the relationship between languages (Uyghur and Chinese) and society in Xinjiang.

Timothy A. Grose is an assistant professor of China studies at Rose-Hulman Institute of Technology. His research on Uyghur ethno-national identities and their expressions of Islamic piety has been published in the *China Journal*, *Journal of Contemporary China*, and *Foreign Policy* and featured in *The Economist*, *The Atlantic*, and CNN. He is the author of *Negotiating Inseparability in China: The Xinjiang Class and the Dynamics of Uyghur Identity* (Hong Kong University Press, 2019).

Anna Hayes is a senior lecturer in international relations in the College of Arts, Society and Education at James Cook University, Australia. She is also an honorary research fellow at the East Asia Security Centre, a collaborative enterprise between Bond University, China Foreign

Affairs University, and the University of New Haven. Dr Hayes specializes in non-traditional threats to security, with a particular focus on the People's Republic of China. Her research examines the ongoing human insecurity of the Uyghurs in the Xinjiang Uyghur Autonomous Region, including Xinjiang's position within China's Eurasian pivot as part of its Belt and Road Initiative. Dr Hayes is the editor (with Michael Clarke) of *Inside Xinjiang: Space, Place and Power in China's Muslim Far Northwest* (Routledge, 2016).

James Leibold is Professor of Politics and Asian Studies at La Trobe University in Melbourne, Australia, and Head of the Department of Politics, Media and Philosophy and Senior Fellow at the Australian Strategic Policy Institute (ASPI). His research expertise is focused on the politics of ethnicity, race, and national identity in modern Chinese history and society, and he is currently engaged in research on ethnic policymaking and ethnic conflict in contemporary China with a particular focus on Tibetan and Uyghur ethnic minorities. He is the editor (with Thomas Mullaney, Stéphane Gros, and Eric Vanden Bussche) of *Critical Han Studies: The History, Representation, and Identity of China's Majority* (University of California Press, 2012), and author of *Reconfiguring Chinese Nationalism: How the Qing Frontier and Its Indigenes Became Chinese* (Palgrave, 2007). His recent journal articles include 'The Spectre of Insecurity: The CCP's Mass Interment Strategy in Xinjiang', *China Leadership Monitor* 58; 'Surveillance in China's Xinjiang Region: Ethnic Sorting, Coercion, and Inducement', *Journal of Contemporary China* 29; and (with Adrian Zenz) 'Securitizing Xinjiang: Police Recruitment, Informal Policing and Ethnic Minority Co-optation', *The China Quarterly* 242.

Dilmurat Mahmut is a doctoral candidate in the Faculty of Education at McGill University. His research interests include Muslim identity in the West, religion and education, education and violent extremism, and immigrant/refugee integration in Canada and beyond. Currently, he is studying Uyghur immigrants' identity reconstruction experiences in Quebec and English Canada. He is part of the Preventing Extremism through Educational Research (PEER) group at McGill University.

Sean R. Roberts is Director of the International Development Studies programme at the Elliott School of International Affairs, George

Washington University. Dr Roberts is a cultural anthropologist with extensive applied experience in international development work. Having conducted ethnographic fieldwork among the Uyghur people of Central Asia and China during the 1990s, he has published extensively on this community in scholarly journals and collected volumes, as well as producing a documentary film, *Waiting for Uighurstan* (1996). Previously, he worked at the United States Agency for International Development (USAID) in Central Asia on democracy and governance programmes, and was a postdoctoral fellow in Central Asian Affairs at Georgetown University, as well as working on development programmes for a variety of NGOs. He is the author of *The War on the Uyghurs: China's Internal Campaign against a Muslim Minority* (Manchester University Press/Princeton University Press, 2020).

Matthew P. Robertson is a doctoral candidate in the School of Politics and International Relations, Australian National University. He took his Bachelor of Arts (2008) majoring in English and Philosophy from the Australian National University. His doctoral research uses computational methods and process tracing to study the People's Republic of China's (PRC) organ transplantation industry. It focuses on empirical questions, while also using the case to explore the political logic of state control over citizen bodies in the PRC. Matthew has worked as a researcher and translator for non-profit organizations, and has done interpretation (from Chinese) and due diligence for financial services firms and family offices. His research using statistical forensics to demonstrate the falsification of Chinese organ donor registry data was published in the leading journal of medical ethics, *BMC Medical Ethics*. Other peer-reviewed publications he has co-authored have appeared in *BMJ Open* and *The BMJ*.

Joanne Smith Finley is Reader in Chinese Studies in the School of Modern Languages, Newcastle University. Dr Smith Finley's research interests in Xinjiang include evolving Uyghur identities, strategies of symbolic resistance, the gendering of ethno-politics, gender, the Uyghur diaspora in the context of Islamic revival, and PRC counterterrorism as state terror in the era of mass internment camps. Her monograph *The Art of Symbolic Resistance: Uyghur Identities and Uyghur-Han Relations in Contemporary Xinjiang* (Brill, 2013) is an ethnographic study of evolving Uyghur identities and ethnic relations over a period of twenty years (from the 1991 collapse of the Soviet Union through the 1997 Ghulja disturbances and the 2009 Ürümchi riots to 2011). She is also co-editor of two volumes, *Situating the Uyghurs between China and Central Asia* (Ashgate, 2007) and *Language, Education and Uyghur Identity in Urban Xinjiang* (Routledge, 2015), and guest editor of a special issue (2019) for *Central Asian Survey*, titled 'Securitization, Insecurity and Conflict in Contemporary Xinjiang'.

David Tobin is Dr David Tobin is Lecturer in East Asian Studies at the University of Sheffield. He has published on China's ethnic policy, political violence, and Han-Uyghur relations in *China Quarterly, Oxford Bibliographies, Inner Asia,* and *Positions – Asia Critique*. His book with Cambridge University Press, *Securing China's Northwest Frontier: Identity and Insecurity in Xinjiang,* analyses the relationship between identity and security in Chinese policy-making and its impact on Han-Uyghur relations. His current research focuses on explaining China's new ethnic policy and collecting Uyghur diaspora narratives on violence and trauma.

Acknowledgements

This volume is the product of a conference held at the Australian National University (ANU) in September 2019. I would like to warmly thank the ANU China in the World Centre and its director, Professor Jane Golley, and the US State Department Public Affairs grants for providing funding for the conference. This funding enabled me to gather some of the world's leading experts on Xinjiang and the Uyghurs for a focused discussion of the context, causes, and consequences of China's mass repression of Turkic Muslim ethnic minorities.

Michael Clarke

1

Framing the Xinjiang emergency: Colonialism and settler colonialism as pathways to cultural genocide?

Michael Clarke

The Xinjiang Uyghur Autonomous Region (XUAR) is the site of the largest mass repression of an ethnic and/or religious minority in the world today. Researchers estimate that since 2016 at least one million people have been detained without trial in the XUAR (Batke 2019; de Hahn 2019). Analysis based on Chinese government procurement contracts for construction of these centres and Google Earth satellite imaging has revealed the existence of hundreds of large, prison-like facilities throughout Xinjiang (Sudworth 2018; Zenz 2019; Ruser 2020). One of the largest detention centres, Dabancheng near the regional capital, Ürümqi, alone was estimated to have a capacity to hold up to 130,000 people (Sudworth 2018). In the detention centres – framed by Beijing as 'transformation through re-education' centres – these individuals are subjected to deeply invasive forms of surveillance and psychological stress as they are forced to abandon their native language, religious beliefs, and cultural practices, and in some instances sexual abuse (Millward 2019; Hill *et al.* 2021). Outside of the detention centres more than ten million Turkic Muslim minorities in the region exist in a 'carceral state' (Xiaocuo 2019) where they are subjected to a dense network of hi-tech surveillance systems (including key elements of China's 'social credit' system), checkpoints, and interpersonal monitoring which severely limit all forms of personal freedom (Mozur 2019; Grauer 2021).

'How did a revolutionary state', David Brophy has pointedly asked, 'which came to power promising to end all forms of national discrimination, end up resorting to such horrific policies?' (Brophy 2018). This fundamental question has exercised Xinjiang and Uyghur studies scholars since 2016 when information about this repressive apparatus first began to filter out of the region. It is a question that also formed the basis of the conference held at the Australian National University in September 2019 that generated this edited volume. That conference, however – which brought together a group of some of the world's leading scholars on Xinjiang and the Uyghurs – not only sought to identify and explain the causes of this repressive turn in the Chinese Communist Party's (CCP) approach to Xinjiang but also to examine the short- and long-term consequences of CCP policy for Xinjiang, the Uyghur people, and the People's Republic of China (PRC). While the contributors to this volume adopt their own approaches to these core questions there is broad agreement that the causes of the current situation in the XUAR derive from the long history – both under the PRC and its Republican and imperial antecedents – of the Chinese state's efforts to control and assimilate both the territory and the non-Han Chinese peoples of what is now known as the XUAR. While the repressive turn from 2016 onwards has been overseen by CCP Chairman Xi Jinping and XUAR CCP Chairman Chen Quanguo in response to immediate security concerns and ideological imperatives – aspects which are covered in detail by some of this volume's contributors – the broad trajectory of the party-state's governance of the XUAR has been set in train over a matter of decades.

This chapter undertakes two major tasks. First, it attempts to provide a conceptual entry-point into exploring the Xinjiang emergency. It does so by arguing that the trajectory of the party-state's governance of the XUAR has been profoundly shaped by dynamics of colonialism, settler colonialism, and associated state-building that have provided the bases for a transition towards cultural genocide in the XUAR as a means of resolving China's 'Xinjiang problem'. Second, the chapter then provides an overview of the structure of and individual contributions to this volume.

Xinjiang: Colonial past, settler colonial present?

Xinjiang's colonial position vis-à-vis the Chinese state has been increasingly referenced since information about the 're-education' system

Framing the Xinjiang emergency

and the associated apparatuses of surveillance became known from 2016 onwards (Chung 2018; Anand 2019). This chapter seeks to build on such accounts by arguing that while Beijing frames the draconian measures it has adopted in the XUAR as necessary 'counterterrorism' measures, the intersection between concern for the 'welfare' of subject populations and the desire to *eradicate* 'defective' elements of Turkic Muslim cultural identities that is central to the 're-education' system reveals that the objective of the party-state has transitioned to a fundamentally *settler colonial* one: the dissolution of autonomous Uyghur identity and its replacement by one subordinate to the Chinese state. What follows, however, is by no means a definitive explanation as to the ultimate causes and consequences of the CCP's mass repression in the XUAR. Rather it is an attempt to frame and give meaning to it by reference to the history of what we might term the Chinese 'colonial enterprise' in the region and an attempt to identify the intersection of key developments within that enterprise that have resulted in the 'horrific' policies that we now see in contemporary Xinjiang.

Scholars such as Georges Balandier and Jurgen Osterhammel have defined colonialism simply as a 'relationship of domination' characterized by the imposition of an exogenous minority rule over an indigenous majority (Balandier 1966: 54; Osterhammel 1997: 16–17). At first sight such a 'relationship of domination' characterized Xinjiang's position vis-à-vis the Qing Empire (1644–1911). However, within this seemingly straightforward conceptualization of colonialism also lies further distinctions between 'colonies of settlement' and 'colonies of exploitation'. In the former 'the colonising effort is exercised from within the bounds of a settler colonising political entity', while in the latter 'colonialism is driven by an expanding metropole that remains permanently distinct from it' (Veracini 2010: 6). In the Qing 'colonial enterprise' in Xinjiang it is clear that settlement of exogenous populations was largely absent until after the great Turkic Muslim rebellions of the second half of the nineteenth century, while the exploitation of the region's human and material resources remained under-developed (Millward 1998; Perdue 2009; Kinzley 2018).

The unevenness of Qing colonialism has given rise to significant debate and controversy within the school of 'New Qing History' as to the applicability of Western conceptions of colonialism (Millward 1998; Perdue 1998; Crossley 1999; Hostetler 2001; Schneider 2020).

Schneider (2020: 314), for instance, argues that two core components of colonialism – the 'exploitation of human resources and embedding of colonies in global economic structures' and the 'political and institutional differentiation of peoples in and from the center and the peripheries at the expense of the latter' – were in fact 'detectable only partially' in the Qing Empire leaving the 'one main aspect of colonialism' consistent with the Qing experience being 'a colonial discourse that includes tropes of othering and racism as well as a justification of colonialism as a *mission civilisatrice*'. Others such as Di Cosmo (1998), Millward (1998), Crossley (1999), and Perdue (2009), however, suggest a specific 'Altaic model' of colonialism in which the Manchus imposed a system of 'simultaneous rule' whereby Manchu officials monitored and ruled through co-opted 'native' elites in Xinjiang, Tibet, and Mongolia that endured from the mid-seventeenth century to the late nineteenth century.

The significance of this period of Xinjiang's history for the subject at hand is twofold. First, the Qing 'colonial enterprise' in the region was not entirely consistent with the definition of colonialism as a 'relationship of domination' characterized by the imposition of an exogenous minority rule over an indigenous majority nor defined by the settlement of an exogenous population and/or the systematic exploitation of its human and material resources in service of the metropole. Second, the retention of the region by the Qing for much of this time was ultimately 'negotiable' and based on strategic cost-benefit assessment as to its worth. 'Since its conquest in the eighteenth century', Laura Newby notes, 'Xinjiang had been viewed as a bulwark of the empire's defences, control of which was arguably preferable to allowing it to fall prey to petty, squabbling tribes and polities, but ultimately negotiable' (Newby 2014: 323). Both of these dynamics, however, changed as a result of the convergence of internal rebellion and external pressure/imperialism in the nineteenth century (Newby 2005: 232–238; Millward 2007: 135–139). The great Turkic Muslim rebellion of 1866–77 led by Yaqub Beg, in particular, saw the development of far-reaching strategic debate about the future of Qing dominion in the region as both Tsarist Russia (via its annexation of the Ili Valley in 1871) and Great Britain took advantage of Qing weakness to extend their spheres of influence in the region (Kim 2004). With the Qing reconquest of Xinjiang in 1877 and the Qing court's subsequent granting of provincehood to the region in 1884 (including the extension of the *junxian* system of administration applied throughout China proper), the region's relationship to the core of the empire was, at least in theory, transformed. No longer was Xinjiang to remain simply a strategic buffer. It was now conceived of, and to be administered, as any other province of the empire. This, as Millward notes, also signified a 'fundamental shift in the governing principles of the Qing empire as a whole' which revealed a transformation of the relationship between the centre and periphery and the non-Han and Han:

> The late Qing state took an administrative model employed in the agrarian core of its sprawling empire and applied it to the ecologically and culturally different regions of the periphery. The debates over the pragmatics of provincehood thus hinted at deeper issues involving the nature of the empire and the status of the Manchus, Mongols and other Inner Asians in a realm dominated demographically by Han Chinese. Though proponents of provincehood stressed the fiscal savings and reduction of troop numbers to be realised by the reform ... underlying these claims was the *assumption that a Xinjiang that was both demographically and culturally more like China proper would be both easier and cheaper to govern.* (Millward 2007: 138, emphasis added)

It is thus from the late nineteenth century that we can see the beginnings of a pathway that promised to combine the forms of domination inherent in 'colonies of settlement' and 'colonies of exploitation' via the settlement of large numbers of Han Chinese which would demographically, culturally, and politically transform the region. The late Qing bureaucracy, then, opted for what Scott Atran has dubbed 'surrogate colonization' whereby 'another people' – in this instance Han Chinese – would 'colonize the territory for the Empire's sake' (Atran 1989: 720).

While this project was derailed by the collapse of the Qing in 1911 and the weakness of the succeeding Republic of China under Sun Yatsen and then Chiang Kai-shek, it nonetheless established an important precedent for future efforts of the Chinse state to control Xinjiang. In the intervening years between the collapse of the Qing and the establishment of the PRC, Xinjiang experienced 'warlord colonialism' through which a succession of Han Chinese rulers sought to maintain their position of political and economic dominance over the majority Turkic Muslim populations of the region.[1] The region also experienced two significant rebellions in 1933 and 1944–49 that resulted in the establishment of an 'East Turkestan Republic' (ETR) by Uyghur and other Turkic Muslim nationalists. Significantly, each of these rebellions sought to harness a number of transnational intellectual and ideological currents such as the late nineteenth-century reformist *jadidist* movement for the 'local' purposes of defining a modern 'Uyghur' nation *and* defending it from the depredations of Chinese and Russian (and Soviet) colonialism (Brophy 2005; Roberts 2009; Klimeš 2015).

When Xinjiang was 'peacefully liberated' by the People's Liberation Army (PLA) in October 1949 after decades of autonomy from the Qing's Republican successors, the CCP confronted the question of 'how to run an empire without looking like colonialists' (Millward 2019). Its answer – recognition of the region's twelve non-Han Chinese *minzu* (nationality or ethnic group) and implementation of a system of 'national regional autonomy' – in theory, was meant to ensure that under the leadership of the CCP the various *minzu* were to stand as equals, their individual culture, language, and practice of religion respected and protected (Bovingdon 2004). In practice, however, this was accompanied by tight political, social, and cultural control, encouragement of Han Chinese settlement, and state-led economic development, backed by the repression of overt manifestations of opposition and dissent by the security forces (Clarke 2011). This approach stimulated periodic and sometimes violent opposition from the Uyghur population (and other ethnic minorities), who bridled against its major consequences: demographic dilution, political and economic marginalization, and cycles of state interference in the practice of religion (Karrar 2018).

With Mao Zedong's death in 1976, and the ascendancy of Deng Xiaoping's 'reform and opening' agenda by the early 1980s, the means by which the state sought the integration of Xinjiang shifted fundamentally in favour of an approach based on the assumption that delivery of economic development and modernization would ultimately 'buy' if not the loyalty then at least the acquiescence of the Uyghur and other non-Han *minzu* (Clarke 2007). An important outgrowth of this assumption from the late 1990s onwards has been a gradual shift away from the central organizing principles of 'national regional autonomy' towards a 'developmentalist' approach that sees not only economic development/modernization as the key to resolving the Xinjiang issue but also the breakdown of the social, economic, and cultural barriers between non-Han *minzu* and the Han Chinese majority and the development of non-Han *minzu* into 'high-quality' citizens. In this framework, the Han Chinese-dominated party-state is conceived of as *the* transformative and modernizing agent (Barbantseva 2008; Groot 2016; Roberts 2016; Köpke 2019).

This 'developmentalist' turn, also implemented in Tibet and Inner Mongolia, has been most deeply felt in Xinjiang. Here, the Chinese party-state has embarked – through the Great Western Development (GWD) plan (launched in 2000) and the Belt and Road Initiative (BRI) (launched in 2013) – upon a concerted endeavour to achieve the full and complete political, economic, social, and cultural integration of Xinjiang and its non-Han *minzu* into the PRC. Under both of these state-led development plans Xinjiang has been envisaged as an industrial and agricultural base and a trade and energy corridor for the national economy. Central to this developmental agenda has been a focus on a variety of infrastructure 'mega-projects' (e.g. oil and natural gas pipelines) linking Xinjiang with Central and South Asia and the various subregions of Xinjiang with each other and the interior of China.

An important purpose of this channelling of capital and investment into Xinjiang was to 'stabilize' the region by 'reshaping' its 'socio-economic, cultural and political environment' (Cappelletti 2016: 161). Indicative of such 'reshaping' have been major infrastructure projects such as the Xinjiang–Shanghai gas pipeline that physically linked such regions to the centre and the creation of key urban 'hubs', or 'networks' of development, such as Kashgar, Shihezi, and Urumqi in Xinjiang that focused on specific industrial or infrastructural features and opened major border 'ports' such as Alashankou and Khorgos to facilitate trade with Central Asia (Allf 2016). While this has brought economic development it has done so in ways that create a variety of new socio-economic pressures – e.g. encouragement of further Han settlement, rapid urbanization, and environmental degradation – that exacerbate long-standing tensions between the party-state and the region's non-Han *minzu* populations (Chaudhuri 2010; Howell and Fan 2011; Zang 2012; Cao et al. 2018). Indeed, as Sean Roberts and Kilic Bugra Kanat (2013) noted, 'development' may have been raising 'the region's economic potential' but it is also further marginalizing the Uyghurs in their perceived homeland. State projects have destroyed Uyghur communities, displaced thousands, and have brought an influx of Han migrants to the region. They have also been accompanied by aggressive attempts to assimilate Uyghurs into Han culture through targeted educational and work programs that incentivize the learning of Mandarin and integration into the Chinese state's vision of modernization.

It is perhaps not surprising that amidst the Chinese state's 'developmentalist' turn in Xinjiang in the 1990s and 2000s scholars would return to the question as to whether, and in what particular sense, Xinjiang had been or continued to be embedded in a colonial relationship with the Chinese state. Indeed, as the 'developmentalism' noted above proceeded a number of scholars and journalists explicitly framed their analysis by reference to colonialism (Winchester 1997; Gladney 1998, 1998/99; Sautman 2000; Gilley 2001). In particular, Dru C. Gladney, following Michael Hechter (1975), argued that Xinjiang exhibited hallmarks of 'internal colonialism' (Gladney 1998). For Hechter, the relationship of Britain's 'Celtic fringe' (i.e. Scotland, Wales, and Ireland) to the centre was defined by 'hierarchical cultural divisions of labor' that were established as the dominant culture fixed both an unequal distribution of power and resources and cultural boundaries between it and subordinate cultures. Such 'internal colonialism' was a deliberate strategy of domination by a 'superordinate group [that] seeks to stabilize and monopolize its advantages through policies aiming at the institutionalization and perpetuation of the existing stratification' (Hechter 1975: 39). Sautman, while acknowledging that 'several factors' – such as a regional economic strategy based on resource extraction, 'an apparent ethnic division of labour', an inter-ethnic 'income imbalance', an 'ethnic division of political power' favouring the Han Chinese, and a 'migrant influx' – indicated that 'China proper' and 'Xinjiang are like métropole and colony', nonetheless concluded that 'Xinjiang's conditions result from complex historical, geographic and political factors' rather than 'exploitation and ethnic domination' (Sautman 2000: 240–243, 261). For Gladney, however, the factors noted by Sautman combined with the objectification and 'minoritization' of the Uyghurs meant that Xinjiang 'fits the internal colonialism model' (Gladney 1998: 4).

The disagreement between these two scholars in fact highlights the need to explicitly recognize the analytical and functional distinctions

Framing the Xinjiang emergency

between *types* of colonialism. As noted previously, there is a distinction to be made regarding 'colonies of settlement' and 'colonies of exploitation'. In the case of Xinjiang under the PRC there have been elements of Chinese practice that resonate with both, for instance, extraction of the region's natural resources and encouragement of Han Chinese settlement. Yet, as we have seen with Gladney's and Sautman's opposing conclusions, this distinction (i.e. between settlement and exploitation/extraction) is not enough to provide clarity. Rather, and this is something Gladney hints at, the missing piece of the puzzle concerns the subject or indigenous population itself. Recall that for Gladney it is the objectification and 'minoritization' of the Uyghurs that is the key to determining the pathway of the PRC's 'colonial enterprise' in Xinjiang. Objectification, Gladney argues, has resulted in the inculcation of a 'sub-altern status' that is 'subject only to definition by state categories and policies' and 'displaces indigenous prior claims to land and voice in the administration of local affairs' (Gladney 1998: 10).

This process arguably marks the PRC's enterprise in Xinjiang as moving towards settler colonialism as distinct from colonialism. Recall here that in the definition of scholars such as Balandier and Osterhammel noted above, colonialism is a 'relationship of domination' characterized by the imposition of an exogenous minority rule over an indigenous majority. However, with the institution of 'national regional autonomy' in the early 1950s, and its associated identification and categorization of twelve distinct non-Han ethnic 'minorities' in Xinjiang, combined with the 'developmentalism' of the 1990s and 2000s, the party-state has created the conditions under which its rule in the region can no longer simply be categorized as a form of exogenous minority rule based either on settlement or exploitation/extraction *alone*. Rather, the trajectory of Chinese rule in the region has encouraged Han Chinese settlement to the extent that in the 2010 census the Han constituted some 40.48 per cent of the region's population in contrast to the Uyghurs' 45.84 per cent (Toops 2016), while the channelling of investment into industrial and infrastructure development has reshaped the region's economy. Colonizers, as Veracini pointedly notes, 'cease being colonisers if and when they become the majority of the population' and 'indigenous people only need to become a *minority* in order to cease being colonised' (Veracini 2010: 5, emphasis added). The former – i.e. the Han becoming a majority of the XUAR population – may not have occurred as yet but as Toops (2016) suggests demographic trends indicate that the 'Han may be a plurality ... if not a majority' in the near future. Meanwhile, the objectification and 'minoritization' of the Uyghurs has been occurring for decades.

In this situation we may see the fundamental distinction between colonialism and settler colonialism emerging. Veracini (2015: 15) utilizes the metaphor of viruses and bacteria to illustrate the distinction between the two. Although viruses and bacteria, he notes, 'are exogenous elements that often dominate their destination locales', the former need 'living cells to operate' while the latter 'attach to surfaces and may or may not rely on the organisms they encounter'. Colonizers and settler colonizers too are exogenous elements that dominate 'destination locales' but they fundamentally differ in the manner in which they do so: colonialism is 'premised on the presence and subjugation of exploitable Others' whereas settler colonizers 'attach to land but generally do not need indigenous "Others" for their reproduction and operation' (Veracini 2015: 15, 22). Taking the bacteria metaphor further Veracini notes:

> Bacteria also frequently secrete chemicals into their environment in order to transform it to their benefit. This can facilitate the acquisition of nutrients from the surrounding environment ... Similarly settlers routinely and programmatically set out to reorganise the landscapes they encounter and deliberately promote the processes of systematic environmental transformation. (Veracini 2015: 22)

Just such a 'systematic environmental transformation' has been underway in Xinjiang since the 1990s through the state's 'developmentalism' which has reshaped the region's economy, demography, and geography.

The implication for subject or indigenous peoples in a settler colonial situation is stark. 'The primary objective of settler-colonization', Patrick Wolfe remarks, 'is the land itself rather than the surplus value to be derived from mixing native labour with it' and as such the logic of settler colonial projects is 'a sustained institutional tendency to eliminate the Indigenous population' (Wolfe 1999: 163). Where colonialism seeks to institute a relationship of domination and/or material extraction of an exogenous minority over an indigenous minority, settler colonialism, then, 'strives for the dissolution of native societies' and 'erects a new colonial society on the expropriated land base' (Wolfe 2006: 388). The 'general tendency' of settler colonialism with respect to indigenous populations is to perceive them 'as rapidly degrading and/or vanishing', a dynamic that produces the coexistence of assimilationist and genocidal 'impulses' within settler colonial rule (Veracini 2010: 25). The end point of either impulse of course is the same: the cultural or physical removal of the indigenous Other.

'Re-education', cultural genocide, and the logic of settler colonialism

One of the central controversies regarding the CCP's systematic repression of the Uyghurs and other Turkic Muslims concerns the question of intent. What, ultimately, is the party-state attempting to achieve? Is it, as official explanations would have it, protecting Xinjiang (and the PRC) from the potential threat of 'terrorism' by 'inoculating' an 'at risk' population from the perils of 'radicalization' and 'extremism'?[2] Or has it cynically manipulated the global prioritization of 'counterterrorism' as a cover to eliminate the very possibility of future resistance to the party-state in Xinjiang? Or does it seek the dissolution and replacement of the Turkic Muslim Other? One possible answer, as detailed above, is that it is driven by the logic of settler colonialism in which the indigenous Other is culturally or physically removed and a 'new' society erected. As noted in the introduction, a key way in which this logic is expressed in contemporary Xinjiang is through the discourse and practice of 're-education' that emphasizes concern for the 'welfare' of subject populations and the desire to eradicate 'defective' elements of their cultural identities so that 'security' and 'prosperity' may be achieved.

The known practices of the 're-education' facilities clearly resonate with the worst totalitarian precedents of the twentieth century. Not only do many of these facilities resemble prisons complete with hardened security and surveillance features including barbed wire, guard towers, and CCTV cameras but within them detainees experience a regimented daily existence as they are compelled to repeatedly sing 'patriotic' songs praising the benevolence of the CCP and study Mandarin, Confucian texts, and President Xi Jinping's 'thought' (Zenz 2018; Millward 2019). Those detainees that resist or do not make satisfactory progress 'risk solitary confinement, food deprivation, being forced to stand against a wall for extended periods, being shackled to a wall or bolted by wrists and ankles into a rigid "tiger chair", and possibly waterboarding and electric shocks' (Millward 2019). There have also been harrowing testimonies from 're-education' camp survivors of consistent patterns of rape and sexual abuse of detainees and enforced sterilizations, and evidence of forcible removal of Uyghur children to state-run orphanages (Ferris-Rotman 2019; Zenz 2020a; Hill et al. 2021).

However, it is the discourse erected by the party-state around this system that arguably provides insight into its intent. All of these facilities are underpinned by the logic of 'transformation through re-education' (*jiaoyu zhuanhua*) – a concept whose lineage blends elements of traditional Chinese statecraft and state socialism of the Leninist–Stalinist and Maoist variants with the CCP's more recent racialized politics of exclusion. In the first instance, both traditional Chinese statecraft and the major variants of state socialism have held a 'paternalistic approach that pathologizes deviant thought and behavior, and then tries to forcefully transform them' (Leibold 2018). Under Stalin, the Soviet state went to great lengths to propagandize the *gulag* as a transformative 'reforging' of former 'class enemies' into ideologically committed Soviet citizens (Draskozy 2012).[3] Once the CCP had achieved power, it too instituted a system of extrajudicial 'remolding through labor' (*laogai*) and 're-education through labor' (*laojiao*) camps where the goal was to 'transform' the prisoner (usually defined as a 'class enemy') and achieve their 'reform and rehabilitation' (Fu 2005).

By the late 1990s the CCP drew on these precedents to develop the concept of 'transformation through re-education' in response to a series of new political and social challenges such as the rise of the Falun Gong spiritual movement and drug addiction. A key element in the repression of the Falun Gong was the implementation of 'legal education centres' where detainees were 'forced to watch propaganda videos, sing patriotic or pro-Communist Party (CCP) songs, and "repent"', while recalcitrants were 'subject to various forms of physical coercion and torture' and dedicated believers described as 'addicts' (Cook 2019). The key elements of this discourse of 'transformation through re-education' have been central to the current repression in Xinjiang. Of particular note is how the language of pathology has now permeated official statements and rhetoric regarding the purpose of the system. From government officials describing Uyghur 'extremism and terrorism' as a 'tumour' to the equation of religious observance to an 'illness', the CCP's discourse frames central elements of Uyghur identity as pathologies to be 'cured' (Dooley 2018; Roberts 2018; Grose 2019). The speech of a CCP Youth League official in October 2017 explaining the purpose of 're-education' provides one such example of the pathologizing of Uyghur cultural identity and practices:

> The religious extremist ideology is a type of poisonous medicine which confuses the mind of the people. Once they are poisoned by it, some turn into extremists who no longer value even their own lives … If we do not eradicate religious extremism at its roots, the violent terrorist incidents will grow and spread all over like an incurable malignant tumor. Although a certain number of people who have been indoctrinated with extremist ideology have not committed any crimes, they are already infected by the disease. There is always a risk that the illness will manifest itself at any moment, which would cause serious harm to the public. That is why they must be admitted to a re-education hospital in time to treat and cleanse the virus from their brain and restore their normal mind. We must be clear that going into a re-education hospital for treatment is not a way of forcibly arresting people and locking them up for punishment, it is an act that is part of a comprehensive rescue mission to save them. (Radio Free Asia 2018)

This, as Sean Roberts has pointedly noted, presents a racialized conception of threat that conceives of the Uyghurs (and other Turkic Muslims) as a 'virtual biological threat to the body of society'. Such language, as Timothy A. Grose and James Leibold demonstrate in Chapter 5, has now become a defining feature of the discourse and practice of 're-education'.

Part of the 'cure' prescribed by the CCP for such pathologies are stints of varying lengths in 're-education'. Another important part of the prescription has also been the imposition of forms of coerced labour. This is due to the fact that not only does the CCP view key components of Uyghur identity as 'root causes' of 'terrorism' but also 'under-development'. This was made clear in China's White Paper of 16 August 2019 on 'Vocational Education and Training in Xinjiang' (Information Office of the State Council of the PRC 2019). This document asserted that many parts of Xinjiang have remained 'impoverished' as 'terrorists, separatists, and religious extremists have long preached that "religious teachings are superior to state laws", inciting the public to resist learning the standard spoken and written Chinese language, reject modern science, and refuse to improve their vocational skills'. This has caused 'local people' to have 'outdated ideas', 'suffer from poor education and employability', and have 'low employment rates and incomes' (Information Office of the State Council of the PRC 2019).

The provision of 'vocational education and training' for all social classes of Uyghurs, as a number of researchers have demonstrated, points towards what Byler (2019a) describes as an attempted 'proletarianization' of such populations into a 'docile yet productive lumpen class' via a clear linkage between the 're-education' camp system and forced labour (see also Zenz 2020b; Xu et al. 2020). Here, Uyghurs are either compelled to work as low-skilled labour in factories directly connected to 're-education' centres or, upon their 'release', in closely proximate 'industrial parks' where companies from throughout China have been incentivized to relocate to (Rickleton 2019). This is something that China's subsequent White Paper on 'Employment and Labor Rights in Xinjiang' of September 2020 tacitly acknowledged by noting that the state has been actively 'promoting capital, technology and knowledge-intensive advanced manufacturing industries and emerging industries' as well as 'labor-intensive industries such as textiles and garments, shoes and accessories' into Xinjiang to provide 'key groups' such as 'surplus rural labor' (a euphemism for Uyghurs and other Turkic Muslim minorities) with employment (Information Office of the State Council of the PRC 2020).

The practice and discourse of 're-education' potentially provides a means through which the CCP may be in the process of answering the core question posed by settler colonial practices. As noted above, settler colonialism seeks the replacement of the indigenous Other but, as Wolfe (1999: 1–2) notes, the question remains as to what to *do* with such populations: 'what if the natives themselves have been reduced to a small minority whose survival can hardly be seen to furnish the colonizing society with more than remission from ideological embarrassment?' Does 're-education' offer the CCP a pathway through which to achieve its apparent objective of the eradication of 'defective' elements of Uyghur identity and their replacement with qualities that, in the words of Xi Jinping (China.org.cn 2017), are consistent with 'the Chinese nation, Chinese culture, the CCP and socialism with Chinese characteristics' *without* physical elimination – thus saving the CCP from 'ideological embarrassment' and opprobrium reserved for genocidal regimes? While it is impossible to definitively answer this troubling question, it is clear that for the subject population this attempt to reprogramme or 're-engineer' its cultural identity amounts to 'a process of social elimination' as 'being forced to speak the language of the colonizer, prohibited from performing religious practice and compelled to perform secular rituals imposed by the colonizer functions as a form of epistemic violence and structural oppression rather than a liberation of indigenous minds' (Byler 2017: 2).

It is for this reason that many scholars of Xinjiang and the Uyghurs believe that cultural genocide is underway in contemporary Xinjiang (Smith Finley 2020). According to the United Nations (UN) Convention on the Prevention and Punishment of the Crime of Genocide (1948), genocide 'means *any* of the following acts committed with intent to destroy, in whole or in part, a national, ethnical, racial or religious group': '(a) Killing members of the group; (b) Causing serious bodily or mental harm to members of the group; (c) Deliberately inflicting on the group conditions of life calculated to bring about its physical destruction in whole or in part; (d) Imposing measures intended to prevent births within the group; (e) Forcibly transferring children of the group to another group' (United Nations 1948). The CCP has undertaken, as we have already noted, measures in Xinjiang that are clearly consistent with this definition. For example, the practice of 're-education' has involved credible reports of physical and psychological torture and sexual abuse that cause 'serious bodily or mental harm to members of the group', while the removal of Uyghur children to state-run orphanages and forced sterilizations of Uyghur women point towards forcible 'transfer of children of the group to another group' and the imposition of 'measures intended to prevent births within the group'. Beyond such actions the state has also in parallel prohibited the use of Uyghur language, script, and signage, imposed new legal restrictions on religious practice, razed mosques and other religious sites and shrines, encouraged inter-ethnic marriage via monetary inducements, and instituted the concerted persecution of the Uyghur intelligentsia (Byler 2019b, 2019c; Kuo 2019; Ramzy 2019; Zhou 2019; Thum 2020).

More broadly, the Chinese state's actions in Xinjiang are consistent with the meaning of genocide originally conceptualized by Raphael

Lemkin. For Lemkin, genocide has in fact two phases: 'destruction of the national pattern of the oppressed group' and 'the imposition of the national pattern of the oppressor' (Lemkin 2008 [1944]). Elsewhere, Lemkin argued that destruction of the 'national pattern' could occur via physical destruction or through a systematic attempt to destroy what he termed the 'shrines of the soul of a nation' such as its language, traditions, monuments, archives, libraries, and places (Lemkin 2013). In this manner the CCP is arguably seeking to destroy the 'shrines of the soul' of the Uyghur nation so that it may impose its conception of 'Chinese' culture and civilization in its place. This imperative is consistent with the logic of the transition of China's enterprise in Xinjiang from a colonial to a settler colonial one.

Exploring the causes and consequences of China's mass detention of Turkic Muslims

As indicated by the title of this volume, contributors seek to provide a rigorous exploration of the causes and consequences of China's mass repression of Turkic Muslim peoples in Xinjiang. The introductory discussion above has attempted to provide one conceptual lens – that of settler colonialism – through which to understand the cause and consequences of this. However, this is but only one possible means of framing and understanding the causes and consequences of the Xinjiang emergency. As will be demonstrated through the three distinct yet overlapping parts to this volume, contributors bring their own disciplinary and conceptual frameworks to bear on this complex issue.

Part I: Context

Contributors in Part I of the volume – Sandrine Catris, Anna Hayes, and Sean R. Roberts – provide historically informed analyses of the causes of the current situation in Xinjiang. Sandrine Catris (Chapter 2) begins Part I by contextualizing the current repression in the history of previous campaigns of mass repression in Xinjiang. She notes that the current crisis in the XUAR – defined by mass internment and the increasing policing of Uyghur life in and out of the camps via high- and low-tech means – has led many to look to the past for answers. In particular, many see echoes from the Cultural Revolution (CR) in today's Xinjiang. However, she argues that the more apt analogy to understand today's campaign, and imagine an end to it, can be found in a better understanding of the 1957 Anti-Rightist Campaign. Many elements of the current campaign in the Uyghur region are undoubtedly reminiscent of the CR: the attacks on Uyghur cultural expressions and material culture; razing of mosques and Sufi shrines; closing of mosques for religious practice; disappearance of many books from circulation; the quasi-disappearance of veiling and many forms of facial hair; the presence of a Xi cult of personality; and the omnipresence of propaganda. Indeed, during the years from mid-1966 through 1976, Uyghurs had to prove their loyalty to the CCP and the state by displaying images of Mao Zedong and owning the *Little Red Book*. The mosques and Sufi shrines of the region, while not fully destroyed, were damaged, closed, and repurposed. Red Guards, who saw veiling and having a beard as signs of feudalism, attacked and bullied those who sported them.

Yet the differences between the two periods she suggests are too vast to help us imagine what the end could look like. In the last years of the 1960s, there were 'good' Uyghurs who showed loyalty to the party. Today, there is arguably no acceptable way of being Uyghur in Xinjiang. Any Uyghur can be disappeared – even loyal CCP members. Additionally, in the CR nationality (or ethnicity) was *not* the basis for internment and persecution while the party and the government did not really control the repression that occurred during the CR. Catris argues that there are, however, three key parallels with the 1957 Anti-Rightist Campaign. First, the Anti-Rightist Campaign was, just like today's, completely controlled by the party and the government. Second, ethnicity clearly played a major role in the implementation of the Anti-Rightist Campaign in the XUAR, morphing into a campaign against 'local nationalism' that primarily targeted Uyghur cadres and intellectuals. Today, too, Uyghur elites have been targeted for repression with over four hundred Uyghur intellectuals, artists, and businesspeople having been arrested and taken to camps and prisons, accused of being 'two-faced' and fomenting separatist ideas. Finally, after the anti-local nationalism campaign in the XUAR ended, the CCP did not have to disavow its actions despite its disastrous consequences. Catris concludes by suggesting that a similar outcome may in fact take place with respect to the 're-education' campaign: once the current leadership of the CCP concludes that 're-education' has served its purposes there is little to suggest that it will face the consequences of even a symbolic reckoning with the injustices imposed on the Uyghur people.

Anna Hayes (Chapter 3) through an examination of the destruction of Old Kashgar via the Kashgar Dangerous House Reform Programme (KDHRP) demonstrates the 'creeping' nature of cultural genocide in Xinjiang. She argues that the KDHRP was undergirded by desires of social control and social engineering aimed at perceived 'deviant' Uyghurs, with the ultimate goal being the purposeful destruction and eradication of Uyghur culture in the Uyghur heartland. Moreover, her analysis suggests that some of the measures taken under the KDHRP in fact paved the way for the increased surveillance, social control, and the mass incarceration of Uyghurs that has escalated under the presidency of Xi Jinping and the regional leadership of Chen Quanguo. In particular, she notes the consistent manner in which Uyghurs have long been dehumanized via applied collective labels such as being 'backwards' and a 'terrorist collective'. She concludes that the KDHRP can be seen as a building block within a pattern of social engineering across the XUAR that amounts to creeping genocide.

Sean R. Roberts (Chapter 4) closes Part I of the volume with an examination of the relationship between 'counterterrorism' and settler colonialism in Xinjiang. He begins by noting that it has become clear that the destruction of the Uyghurs as a people is part and parcel of the CCP's strategy for developing and resettling the region that Uyghurs view as their homeland. This, Roberts suggests, does not mean that cultural genocide is an inevitable outcome of the long process of modern China's colonization of this region but rather begs the question as to why the PRC has chosen the present moment to hastily and violently exclude the indigenous peoples from this region's development.

He argues that to answer this question we must look at the fundamentally colonial relationship between modern China and the indigenous people of this region that has marked Uyghurs and other native non-Hans since the nineteenth century as inferior and backwards vis-à-vis the ideal of Chinese civilization. While the PRC could work to decolonize this relationship, and arguably has at times in history attempted to do so, Xi Jinping's CCP appears to be establishing a model for modern China, which does not recognize the strategies of decolonization or multiculturalism as options. As a result, the state is embarking on an overall drive to assimilate non-Han peoples into a Han-centric state culture. While this approach to nation-building is articulated through aggressive assimilationist policies targeting the Tibetans, Mongolians, Hui Muslims, and other non-Hans, only in the XUAR has this been articulated through a violent cultural genocide intended to destroy the resident non-Han population.

Significantly, Roberts notes, the PRC has repeatedly suggested that its acts against the Uyghur people and other non-Hans of this region are not motivated by settler colonial ambitions, but are an attempt to mitigate the spread of Islamic 'extremism' and violent 'terrorism' among the Muslims of the XUAR. In a post-9/11 world, however, this, Roberts argues, is a convenient justification for state violence deployed against Muslim citizens. Since 9/11, the label of 'terrorist' has served to dehumanize entire groups of people and allow for the suspension of their human rights with international impunity. In doing so, the label also precludes those to whom it is applied from having any legitimate grievances, instead characterizing their actions as being reflections of irrational and 'extremist' Islamic beliefs. While counterterrorism is more a justification for cultural genocide in the XUAR than it is a motivation for state actions, Roberts argues that it has also facilitated this cultural genocide and has affected the way it has been carried out. The campaign to eradicate 'terrorism' and 'extremism' in the region, which predates 2017, has taken on a life of its own. He concludes that it has been internalized by many state officials and citizens, who now view Uyghurs and related peoples as an existential threat to society and deserving of the violent policies that target them. In this sense, the PRC's 'counterterrorism' justification for its settler colonization of the Uyghur homeland mimics that of the 'civilizing mission' for European settler colonialism in the nineteenth and early twentieth centuries.

Part II: Discourses and practices of repression

Part II shifts our focus from the contextual underpinnings of contemporary mass repression to the more concrete issue of *how* that mass repression is both discursively framed and enacted in Xinjiang. Timothy A. Grose and James Leibold (Chapter 5) begin this part with an examination of the centrality of themes of 'pathology' and 'deviancy' in the party-state's discourse of 're-education'. They note that countless individuals have been identified by the CCP as threats to social order and those who cannot be 'reformed' through first-line treatment – visits from government workers and presentations of state 'care' – are quarantined: forcibly taken from their homes, ripped away from their families, and even separated from their children to endure 're-education' in 'concentrated re-education centres' (*jizhong zhuanhua jiaoyu zhongxin*). While such facilities have been justified by the Chinese state as necessary 'counterterrorism' measures and analogized to 'boarding schools', Grose and Leibold note that this is belied by the highly securitized nature of such facilities and the known practices undertaken within them. Here they make three main arguments. First, the 're-education' centres – contra Chinese government claims – have been established to forcefully and permanently erase meaningful cultural markers (including Islam and native language) from Turkic Muslims, amounting to what experts believe is an intentional act of cultural genocide. Second, the lexicon of 'pathology' has been deployed – likening elements of Turkic Muslim identity to severe mental illness, drug addiction, and communicable diseases – to justify the state's efforts to 'save' Turkic Muslims, especially Uyghurs and Kazakhs, from themselves and their communities. They note that the party's use of phrases such as 'contracting illness' (*ganran bingdu*), 'penetrate like an intravenous needle' (*guanchuan diandi*), and 'cure sickness to save a patient' or 'reform through criticism' (*zhibing jiuren*) exposes a familiar rhetoric: like counter-revolutionaries, prostitutes, and other aberrant populations, Turkic Muslims are deemed unacceptable threats to the social order and thus must be quarantined and then actively reprogrammed. Finally, they argue that although the CCP has long policed social deviance and political disloyalty, the current repression in Xinjiang has lumped an entire ethno-religious group into the same sociopolitical and criminal category as individuals convicted of violent crime, drug addicts, political activists, and mental health patients. Using the pathology metaphor within the context of the 'targeted population' label, the CCP can simultaneously justify repression (i.e. provide a cure), apply this repression to large segments of society (i.e. treat an outbreak), and deflect blame from its own policies (i.e. offer an index case to an epidemiology that originates outside China). They conclude that the CCP's pathologizing of Turkic Muslims is reflective of what James C. Scott (1998: 87–102) identified as 'authoritarian high-modernism', a utopian yet pernicious effort by the state to re-engineer society in its own image and create a perfect social order through science and technology, but one that actually leaves a wake of personal destruction in its path.

Drawing on interviews with former detainees and their relatives, with a special focus on in-depth interviews with a former police contractor and camp instructor, Darren Byler (Chapter 6) shows how the 're-education' system turned Uyghurs and Kazakhs against themselves, making them the human intelligence janitors and interpreters of a colonial system. He finds that because of the ethno-racial devaluation of their social position and the effects of the system of surveillance, Uyghur or Kazakh police contractors felt they had no choice but to work in service to the system of enclosure even as it foreclosed other life-paths for them. Byler notes how this outsourced task, in the most general of terms, was to normalize the dehumanization of other Turkic Muslims. Simultaneously, however, he finds that such Uyghur and Kazakh translators and janitors were confronted with a dehumanized mirroring of their own Turkic Muslim identifications as their own masks of 'trustworthiness' were often not enough to protect them from extreme forms of stress. Byler concludes that as as system of subjectification, the 're-education' process pushed deep forms of trauma onto those who were forced to 'collaborate' with the processes they enacted and observed. Ultimately, for some, these forms of encounter resulted in the active witnessing of the suffering of Turkic Muslim detainees, while for others it produced ongoing forms of dehumanization.

Dilmurat Mahmut and Joanne Smith Finley (Chapter 7) explore the manner in which the CCP's turn towards coercive mass 're-education' has reconstructed the Uyghur body, mind, language, religion, and culture as an existential and biological threat to the Chinese nation. They begin by noting that the 2017 Xinjiang Uyghur Autonomous Region Regulation on De-extremification and related documentation reveals a disturbing concept of 'correction' that is reminiscent of Bradley Campbell's (2009) notion of genocide as social control: a top-down moralistic correction of 'deviant' behaviour by an increasingly powerful and violent state. They demonstrate the practical effects this form of social control via an in-depth case study of the Uyghur literature textbook compiler Yalqun Rozi. Rozi was arrested in 2016 at the age of fifty and later sentenced to fifteen years in prison on charges of 'incitement to subvert state power' and his textbooks from the shelves of state bookstores were removed. The textbooks were subsequently denounced as 'problematic' and 'treasonous', and as having 'poisoned Uyghurs with ideas of splitting China'.

Mahmut and Smith Finley draw upon Campbell's theory to examine the new, revised content in six issues of the second edition of the children's Uyghur-language textbook *Til-Ädäbiyat* (Language and Literature, 2018, Xinjiang Education Press). Their findings suggest that these textbooks were produced in revised form in order to better assimilate Uyghur children into Han Chinese culture and the national polity, which in the 'new era' of Xi Jinping Han-majoritarian assimilationism are intertwined. They note that the content of these books is largely transposed and adapted from the corresponding set of Chinese-medium textbooks, which are highly Han-centric, and thus these new Uyghur textbooks largely feature Han Chinese culture, history, natural and geographical features, and touristic attractions specific to Han-dominated inner China. Although certain Uyghur-specific elements can be found in practice drills, such as Uyghur personal names, place names, idioms, and proverbs, these lack Islamic associations and are insufficient for Uyghur pupils to build a positive and strong self-conception about their own ethnic group. These new textbooks, Mahmut and Smith Finley argue, 'invisibilize' the Uyghurs (and other Turkic Muslim peoples) within the local education system. They note that this 'invisibilization' of Uyghurs and Turkic Muslims in school textbooks mirrors the coercive forms of 'corrective re-education' taking place in the 're-education' centres for adults. As such they conclude that these revised textbooks further expose the ultimate aim of the government's two-decade-old 'War on Terror' rhetoric in Xinjiang to fully erase Uyghur cultural identity – in this case by negating one central means of reproducing Uyghur culture, Uyghur language.

Matthew P. Robertson (Chapter 8) provides a provocative analysis of the potential links between the CCP's mass incarceration and 're-education' of Uyghurs with a growing literature on state predation through organ harvesting. He attempts to theorize the political logic of organ harvesting from vulnerable, primarily prison, populations in China, and then to review the evidence and consider the possibility that Uyghur Muslims are now victims of this activity. Robertson's primary concern is to clear a space for thinking about coercive organ procurement and transplantation in China that is free from the lurid public descriptions it is often couched within. Here, Robertson adopts a biopolitical approach as the most effective lens through which to see the Chinese state's relationship to the bodies of its subjects as this theoretical approach reveals the internal logic of coercive organ procurement in the context of large-scale political violence and the hyper-marketization of contemporary China.

His analysis proceeds in three sections. First, he provides a review of extant research on China's organ transplantation industry, with a particular focus on the claims that the CCP has harvested the organs from political prisoners – such as practitioners of the Falun Gong spiritual movement – before. Second, Robertson examines what we can reasonably infer about China's organ transplantation system at present from this history before reviewing the evidence that is consistent with Uyghurs being victims of coercive organ procurement. Third, he then attempts to 'de-fetishize' organ harvesting by showing that it can be located firmly within two dominant logics and stages of the CCP's ruling legacy: revolutionary governance and what some scholars have termed 'gangster capitalism' (Holmstrom and Smith 2000; Walker 2006). He concludes, utilizing Marx's de-fetishizing critique of capitalism, that there is an exploitative biopolitical logic that sustains organ harvesting – i.e. that while it is the apparently natural character of the commodity form that obscures the forces that created it, it seems that it is the *unnatural* character of organ harvesting that conceals its cold rationality. In Marx's de-fetishizing critique, capital conceals the nature of commodities; in organ harvesting, the state turns its subjects into commodities. Given that the PRC has adopted an instrumental logic towards Uyghur bodies, whether by expropriation of the migrant labour force, settler colonialism, and forced intermarriages, it is plausible that Uyghur organs may now too have become commodities.

Part III: Domestic and international implications

Part III concludes the volume through an exploration of some of the domestic and international effects of the Xinjiang emergency. Michael Clarke (Chapter 9) opens the part with an examination of the intersection of counterterrorism and surveillance in the current repression in Xinjiang. He begins by noting that Xinjiang has been subjected to a dense network of hi-tech surveillance systems (including key elements of China's 'social credit' system), checkpoints, and interpersonal monitoring which severely limit all forms of personal freedom penetrating society to the granular level. The objective, as CCP deputy leader Zhu Hailun asserted in 2017, is to ensure that there are 'no cracks, no blind spots, no gaps' in the state's surveillance of the region. The chapter argues that the CCP has sought this ambitious and dystopian objective through the imposition of the 'Xinjiang mode' of counterterrorism which combines the counter-insurgency (COIN) models adopted by the West (primarily the United States) in its 'War on Terrorism' with China's own 'public security' and 'governance' models to create a counterterrorism strategy defined by militarization, surveillance, and ideological 'remoulding'. The central objective of the 'Xinjiang mode', Clarke concludes, is to not only prevent 'terrorism' before it occurs but rather to pre-empt its very possibility by identifying and 'remoulding' individuals who display 'abnormal' behaviours.

Ablimit Baki Elterish (Chapter 10) then turns our attention to the effects of the system of mass repression in Xinjiang on the Uyghur diaspora. He begins by noting that since 2016 thousands of Uyghurs living outside China have gradually been unable to make contact with their families, relatives, and friends back in Xinjiang. This prolonged loss of communication, he argues, is creating tremendous effects on everyday life, work, studies, and business of Uyghur diaspora communities. Drawing upon the theory of collective trauma Elterish provides an investigation of three dimensions of collective trauma: psychological, family, and social. The data used for this study come from semi-structured interviews with individuals selected from the Uyghur diaspora communities living in Turkey, Canada, the US, Australia, and Europe. The analysis of these data will enable us to have a clearer picture of the effects of the virtual lockdown of Xinjiang on Uyghur diaspora communities.

David Tobin (Chapter 11) concludes the volume with an examination of the interconnections between China's world order politics encapsulated under the official narrative of China's 'Great Revival' and its policies towards ethnic minorities. He begins by noting that following the 19th CCP Congress in November 2017, President Xi Jinping declared that while China will preserve sovereignty as the underlying principle of international relations it remains 'dissatisfied' with a system built by European colonialism and as such China will seek to forge new norms of 'mutual respect, fairness, and justice'. China's foreign policy narratives explicitly highlight Western 'hegemon anxiety' as an opportunity to remake world order by leading a 'new age of socialism with Chinese characteristics' (Xi 2017). However, Xi's emphasis on global 'justice' reflects intertwined cultural anxieties about Western colonial desires to convert China and non-Han peoples' desires for identity recognition.

Tobin argues here that while China's bold pronouncements speak from new global confidence, they also have emerged alongside heightened domestic anxieties, which imagine alternative identities on China's frontiers as threats to the unification and Great Revival (*weida fuxing*, 伟大复兴) of the Chinese race (*Zhonghua minzu*, 中华民族). China's racialized anxieties have thus contributed to ethnic policy shifts to promote racial 'fusion' (*jiaorong*, 交融) with mass education and intensifying extra-legal security measures in Xinjiang; mass internment camps and 'orphanages' to eliminate and transform Uyghur identities. He concludes that the CCP's 'window of opportunity' to transform colonial world order and its 'mission' to unify the 'Chinese race' are mutually constitutive goals in China's Great Revival narrative of inevitable trajectory towards global power and domestic racial unification.

Notes

1 Joseph Lawson (2013) used this phrase to characterize post-imperial Han Chinese elite's attempts to maintain their position of dominance in the Kham region of Tibet through control of corvee labour, transportation routes, and militias.
2 For one official explanation of policy, see Xinhua (2018), in which the head of the XUAR government, Shokar Zakir, details official rationale for 'vocational education and training'.
3 Vyachslav Molotov (one of Stalin's key lieutenants), for example, asserted in 1931 that the gulag 'accustoms them [class enemies] to labor and makes them *useful* members of society' (cited in Vinokour 2018).

References

Allf, Henryk (2016). 'Getting Stuck within Flows: Limited Interaction and Peripheralization at the Kazakhstan–China Border', *Central Asian Survey* 35 (3), 369–386.

Anand, Dibyesh (2019). 'Colonization with Chinese Characteristics: Politics of (In)security in Xinjiang and Tibet', *Central Asian Survey* 38 (1), 129–147.

Atran, Scott (1989). 'The Surrogate Colonization of Palestine, 1917–1939', *American Ethnologist* 16 (4), 719–744.

Balandier, Georges (1966). 'The Colonial Situation: A Theoretical Approach', in Immanuel Wallerstein (ed.), *Social Change: The Colonial Situation* (New York: John Wiley & Sons), 34–61.

Barbantseva, Elena (2008). 'From the Language of Class to the Rhetoric of Development: Discourses of "Nationality" and "Ethnicity" in China', *Journal of Contemporary China* 17 (56), 565–589.

Batke, Jessica (2019). 'Where Did the One Million Figure for Detentions in Xinjiang's Camps Come From?', *China File*, 8 January, www.chinafile.com/reporting-opinion/features/where-did-one-million-figure-detentions-xinjiangs-camps-come (accessed 9 February 2021).

Bovingdon, Gardner (2004). 'Heteronomy and Its Discontents: Minzu Regional Autonomy in Xinjiang', in Morris Rossabi (ed.), *Governing China's Multiethnic Frontiers* (Seattle: University of Washington Press), 117–154.

Brophy, David (2005). 'Taranchis, Kashgaris, and the "Uyghur Question" in Soviet Central Asia', *Inner Asia* 7 (2), 163–184.

Brophy, David (2018). 'China's Uyghur Repression', *Jacobin*, 31 May, www.jacobinmag.com/2018/05/xinjiang-uyghur-china-repression-surveillance-islamophobia (accessed 12 March 2021).

Byler, Darren (2017). 'Imagining Re-engineered Muslims in Northwest China', *Milestones: Commentary on the Islamic World*, 20 April, www.milestonesjournal.net/photo-essays/2017/4/20/imagining-re-engineered-muslims-in-northwest-china (accessed 17 January 2020).

Byler, Darren (2019a). 'How Companies Profit from Forced Labor in Xinjiang', *SupChina*, 4 September, https://supchina.com/2019/09/04/how-companies-profit-from-forced-labor-in-xinjiang/ (accessed 8 October 2019).

Byler, Darren (2019b). 'The "Patriotism" of Not Speaking Uyghur', *SupChina*, 2 January, https://supchina.com/2019/01/02/the-patriotism-of-not-speaking-uyghur/ (accessed 9 April 2019).

Byler, Darren (2019c). 'Uyghur Love in a Time of Inter-ethnic Marriage', *SupChina*, 7 August, https://supchina.com/2019/08/07/uyghur-love-in-a-time-of-interethnic-marriage/ (accessed 10 October 2019).

Campbell, Bradley (2009). 'Genocide as Social Control', *Sociological Theory* 27 (2), 150–152.
Cao, Xun, Haiyan Duan, Chuyu Liu, James A. Piazza, and Yingjie Wei (2018). 'Digging the "Ethnic Violence in China" Database: The Effects of Inter-ethnic Inequality and Natural Resources Exploitation in Xinjiang', *China Review* 18 (2), 121–154.
Cappelletti, Alessandra (2016). 'Socio-economic Disparities and Development in Xinjiang: The Cases of Kashgar and Shihezi', in Michael Clarke and Anna Hayes (eds), *Inside Xinjiang: Space, Place and Power in China's Muslim Far Northwest* (London: Routledge), 151–182.
Chaudhuri, Debasish (2010). 'Minority Economy in Xinjiang: A Source of Uyghur Resentment', *China Report* 46 (1), 9–27.
China.org.cn (2017). 'Xi Calls for Safeguarding Social Stability in Xinjiang', 10 March, www.china.org.cn/china/NPC_CPPCC_2017/2017–03/10/content_40440842.htm (accessed 5 June 2018).
Chung, Chien-peng (2018). 'Evaluating Xinjiang and Tibet as "Internal Colonies" of China: Evidence from Official Data', *Journal of Ethnic and Cultural Studies* 5 (2), 118–139.
Clarke, Michael (2007). 'Xinjiang in the "Reform" Era: The Political and Economic Dynamics of Dengist Integration', *Issues & Studies* 43 (2), 39–92.
Clarke, Michael (2011). *Xinjiang and China's Rise in Central Asia: A History* (London: Routledge).
Cook, Sarah (2019). 'The Learning Curve: How Communist Party Officials Are Applying Lessons from Prior "Transformation" Campaigns to Repression in Xinjiang', *China Brief* 19 (3) (1 February), https://bit.ly/2S1rwSG (accessed 11 November 2019).
Crossley, Pamela (1999). *A Translucent Mirror: History and Identity in Qing Imperial Ideology* (Berkeley: University of California Press).
de Hahn, Patrick (2019). 'More than 1 Million Muslims Are Detained in China: But How Did We Get That Number?', *Quartz*, 5 July, https://qz.com/1599393/how-researchersestimate-1-million-uyghurs-are-detained-in-xinjiang/ (accessed 30 October 2019).
Di Cosmo, Nicola (1998). 'Qing Colonial Administration in Inner Asia', *The International History Review* 20 (2), 287–309.
Dooley, Ben (2018). '"Eradicate the Tumours": Chinese Civilians Drive Xinjiang Crackdown', *Yahoo News*, 26 April, www.yahoo.com/news/eradicate-tumours-chinese-civilians-drive-xinjiang-crackdown-051356550.html (accessed 11 February 2021).
Draskozy, Julie (2012). '"The Put" of Perekovka: Transforming Lives at Stalin's White Sea-Baltic Canal', *The Russian Review* 71 (1), 30–48.

Ferris-Rotman, Amie (2019). 'Abortions, IUDs and Sexual Humiliation: Muslim Women Who Fled China for Kazakhstan Recount Ordeals', *Washington Post*, 5 October, https://wapo.st/3c3JMBG (accessed 15 March 2020).

Fu, Hualing (2005). 'Re-education through Labour in Historical Perspective', *The China Quarterly* 184 (December), 811–830.

Gilley, Bruce (2001). '"Uighurs Need Not Apply"', *Far Eastern Economic Review* 164 (33), 26.

Gladney, Dru C. (1998). 'Internal Colonialism and the Uyghur Nationality: Chinese Nationalism and Its Subaltern Subjects', *Cahiers d'études sur la Méditerranée Orientale et le Monde Turco-Iranien* 25, 1–12.

Gladney, Dru C. (1998/99). 'Whither the Uighur: China's Indigenous Peoples and the Politics of Internal Colonialism', *Harvard Asia Pacific Review* 3 (1), 11–15.

Grauer, Yael (2021). 'Revealed: Mass Chinese Police Database', *The Intercept*, 29 January, https://theintercept.com/2021/01/29/china-uyghur-muslim-surveillance-police/ (accessed 5 March 2021).

Groot, Gerry (2016). 'The Contradictions of Developmentalism and the Chinese Party-state's Goal of Ethnic Harmony: The Case of Xinjiang', in Curtis Andressen (ed.), *China's Changing Economy: Trends, Impacts and the Future* (London: Routledge), 35–49.

Grose, Timothy (2019). '"Once Their Mental State Is Healthy, They Will Be Able to Live Happily in Society": How China's Government Conflates Uighur Identity with Mental Illness', *China File*, 2 August, www.chinafile.com/reporting-opinion/viewpoint/once-their-mental-state-healthy-they-will-be-able-live-happily-society (accessed 19 September 2019).

Hechter, Michael (1975). *Internal Colonialism: The Celtic Fringe in British National Development* (New Brunswick: Transaction Books).

Hill, Matthew, David Campanale, and Joel Gunter (2021). '"Their Goal Is to Destroy Everyone": Uighur Camp Detainees Allege Systematic Rape', BBC News, 2 February, www.bbc.com/news/world-asia-china-55794071 (accessed 5 March 2021).

Holmstrom, N., and R. Smith (2000). 'The Necessity of Gangster Capitalism: Primitive Accumulation in Russia and China', *Monthly Review* 51 (9), 1–15.

Hostetler, Laura (2001). *Qing Colonial Enterprise: Ethnography and Cartography in Early Modern China* (Chicago: University of Chicago Press).

Howell, Anthony, and Cindy Fan (2011). 'Migration and Inequality in Xinjiang: A Survey of Han and Uyghur Migrants in Urumqi', *Eurasian Geography and Economics* 52 (1), 119–139.

Information Office of the State Council of the PRC (2019). 'Vocational Education and Training in Xinjiang', 17 August, http://english.www.gov.cn/

archive/whitepaper/201908/17/content_WS5d57573cc6d0c6695ff7ed6c.html (accessed 25 October 2020).

Information Office of the State Council of the PRC (2020). 'Full Text: Employment and Labor Rights in Xinjiang', 17 September, www.scio.gov.cn/zfbps/32832/Document/1687593/1687593.htm (accessed 25 October 2020).

Karrar, Hasan H. (2018). 'Resistance to State-orchestrated Modernization in Xinjiang: The Genesis of Unrest in the Multiethnic Frontier', *China Information* 32 (2), 183–202.

Kim, Hodong (2004). *Holy War in China: The Muslim Rebellion and State in Chinese Central Asia, 1864–1877* (Stanford: Stanford University Press).

Kinzley, Judd C. (2018). *Natural Resources and the New Frontier: Constructing Modern China's Borderlands* (Chicago: University of Chicago Press).

Klimeš, Ondřej (2015). 'Nationalism and Modernism in the East Turkestan Republic, 1933–34', *Central Asian Survey* 34 (2), 162–176.

Köpke, Soren (2019). 'Territorialising Chinese Inner Asia: The Neo-developmentalist State and Minority Unrest', *International Quarterly for Asian Studies* 50 (1/2), 137–156.

Kuo, Lily (2019). 'Revealed: New Evidence of China's Mission to Raze the Mosques of Xinjiang', *The Guardian*, 7 May, www.theguardian.com/world/2019/may/07/revealed-new-evidence-of-chinas-mission-to-raze-the-mosques-of-xinjiang (accessed 3 July 2019).

Lawson, Joseph D. (2013). 'Warlord Colonialism: State Fragmentation and Chinese Rule in Kham, 1911–1949', *Journal of Asian Studies* 72 (2), 299–318.

Leibold, James (2018). 'Mind Control in China Has a Very Long History', *New York Times*, 28 November, www.nytimes.com/2018/11/28/opinion/china-reeducation-mind-control-xinjiang.html (accessed 7 March 2019).

Lemkin, Raphael (2008 [1944]). *Axis Rule in Occupied Europe: Laws of Occupation, Analysis of Government, Proposals for Redress (Foundations of the Laws of War)*, 2nd ed. (London: The Lawbook Exchange, Ltd.).

Lemkin, Raphael (2013). *Totally Unofficial: The Autobiography of Raphael Lemkin* (New Haven: Yale University Press).

Millward, James (1998). *Beyond the Pass: Economy, Ethnicity and Empire in Qing Central Asia, 1759–1864* (Stanford: Stanford University Press).

Millward, James (2007). *Eurasian Crossroads: A History of Xinjiang Uyghur Autonomous Region* (New York: Columbia University Press).

Millward, James (2019). 'Reeducating Xinjiang's Muslims', *New York Review of Books*, 7 February, www.nybooks.com/articles/2019/02/07/reeducating-xinjiangs-muslims/ (accessed 21 March 2020).

Mozur, Paul (2019). 'One Month, 500,000 Face Scans: How China Is Using A.I. to Profile a Minority', *New York Times*, 14 April, www.nytimes.com/2019/04/14/

technology/china-surveillance-artificial-intelligence-racial-profiling.html (accessed 28 April 2020).
Newby, Laura J. (2005). *The Empire and the Khanate: A Political History of Qing Relations with Khoqand c.1760–1860* (Leiden: Brill).
Newby, Laura J. (2014). 'Evolving Representations of Xinjiang in Chinese Travel Writings', *Studies in Travel Writing* 18 (4), 320–331.
Osterhammel, Jurgen (1997). *Colonialism: A Theoretical Overview* (Princeton: Markus Weiner Publishers).
Perdue, Peter C. (1998). 'Comparing Empires: Manchu Colonialism', *The International History Review* 20 (2), 255–262.
Perdue, Peter C. (2009). 'China and Other Colonial Empires', *Journal of American-East Asian Relations* 16 (1–2), 85–103.
Radio Free Asia (2018). 'Xinjiang Political "Re-education Camps" Treat Uyghurs "Infected by Religious Extremism": CCP Youth League', 8 August, www.rfa.org/english/news/uyghur/infected-08082018173807.html (accessed 5 May 2020).
Ramzy, Austin (2019). 'China Targets Prominent Uighur Intellectuals to Erase an Ethnic Identity', *New York Times*, 5 January, www.nytimes.com/2019/01/05/world/asia/china-xinjiang-uighur-intellectuals.html (accessed 19 August 2020).
Rickleton, Christopher (2019). 'From Camps to Factories: Muslim Detainees Say China Using Forced Labour', AFP, 4 March, https://sg.news.yahoo.com/camps-factories-muslim-detainees-china-using-forced-labour-041047367.html (accessed 25 May 2020).
Roberts, Sean R. (2009). 'Imagining Uyghurstan: Re-evaluating the Birth of the Modern Uyghur Nation', *Central Asian Survey* 28(4), 361–381.
Roberts, Sean R. (2016). 'Development with Chinese Characteristics in Xinjiang: A Solution to Ethnic Tension or Part of the Problem?', in Michael Clarke and Douglas Smith (eds), *China's Frontier Regions: Ethnicity, Economic Integration and Foreign Relations* (London: I.B. Tauris), 22–55.
Roberts, Sean R. (2018). 'The Biopolitics of China's "War on Terror" and the Exclusion of the Uyghurs', *Critical Asian Studies* 50 (2), 232–258.
Roberts, Sean R., and Kilic Bugra Kanat (2013). 'China's Wild West: A Cautionary Tale of Ethnic Conflict and Development', *The Diplomat*, 15 July, https://thediplomat.com/2013/07/chinas-wild-west/ (accessed 29 May 2021).
Ruser, Nathan (2020). 'Documenting Xinjiang's Detention System' (Canberra: Australian Strategic Policy Institute), https://bit.ly/3wJnq0d (accessed 30 March 2021).
Sautman, Barry (2000). 'Is Xinjiang an Internal Colony?', *Inner Asia* 2 (2), 239–271.
Schneider, Julia C. (2020). 'A Non-Western Colonial Power? The Qing Empire in Postcolonial Discourse', *Journal of Asian History* 54 (2), 311–342.

Scott, James C. (1998). *Seeing Like a State: How Certain Schemes to Improve the Human Condition Have Failed* (Princeton: Princeton University Press).

Smith Finley, Joanne (2020). 'Why Scholars and Activists Increasingly Fear a Uyghur Genocide in Xinjiang', *Journal of Genocide Research*, https://doi.org/10.1080/14623528.2020.1848109.

Sudworth, John (2018). 'China's Hidden Camps', BBC News, 24 October, www.bbc.co.uk/news/resources/idt-sh/China_hidden_camps (accessed 27 August 2020).

Thum, Rian (2020). 'The Spatial Cleansing of Xinjiang: Mazar Desecration in Context', *Made in China Journal*, 24 August, https://madeinchinajournal.com/2020/08/24/the-spatial-cleansing-of-xinjiang-mazar-desecration-in-context/ (accessed 30 September 2020).

Toops, Stanley (2016). 'Spatial Results of the 2010 Census in Xinjiang', China Policy Institute Blog, 7 March, https://blogs.nottingham.ac.uk/chinapolicyinstitute/2016/03/07/spatial-results-of-the-2010-census-in-xinjiang/ (accessed 21 March 2021).

United Nations (1948). *Convention on the Prevention and Punishment of the Crime of Genocide* (New York: United Nations), https://bit.ly/3wNZw3E (accessed 27 May 2021).

Veracini, Lorenzo (2010). *Settler Colonialism: A Theoretical Overview* (London: Palgrave).

Veracini, Lorenzo (2015). *The Settler Colonial Present* (London: Palgrave).

Vinokour, Maya (2018). '2+2=5: On the White Sea-Baltic Canal and Totalitarian Pipe Dreams', *Los Angeles Review of Books*, 27 September, https://lareviewofbooks.org/article/225-white-sea-baltic-canal-totalitarian-pipe-dreams/# (accessed 15 February 2020).

Walker, K. L. M. (2006). '"Gangster Capitalism" and Peasant Protest in China: The Last Twenty Years', *The Journal of Peasant Studies*, 1–33.

Winchester, Michael (1997). 'Beijing vs. Islam', *Asiaweek*, 24 October, 30–33.

Wolfe, Patrick (1999). *Settler Colonialism and the Transformation of Anthropology: The Politics and Poetics of an Ethnographic Event* (London: Cassell).

Wolfe, Patrick (2006). 'Settler Colonialism and the Elimination of the Native', *Journal of Genocide Research* 8 (4), 387–409.

Xi, Jinping (2017). 'Report at 19th CPC National Congress', 3 November, www.xinhuanet.com//english/special/2017-11/03/c_136725942.htm (accessed 28 March 2020).

Xiaocuo, Yi (2019). 'Recruiting Loyal Stabilisers: On the Banality of Carceral Colonialism in Xinjiang', *Made in China Journal*, 25 October, https://madeinchinajournal.com/2019/10/25/recruiting-loyal-stabilisers-onthe-banality-of-carceral-colonialism-in-xinjiang/ (accessed 19 February 2020).

Xinhua (2018). 'Full transcript: Interview with Xinjiang Government Chief on Counterterrorism, Vocational Education and Training in Xinjiang',

16 October, www.xinhuanet.com/english/2018-10/16/c_137535821.htm (accessed 16 July 2020).
Xu, Vicky Xiuzhong, Danielle Cave, James Leibold et al. (2020). 'Uyghurs for Sale: "Re-education", Forced Labour and Surveillance beyond Xinjiang', 1 March (Canberra: Australian Strategic Policy Institute), www.aspi.org.au/report/uyghurs-sale (accessed 11 April 2021).
Zang, Xiaowei (2012). 'Scaling the Socioeconomic Ladder: Uyghur Perceptions of Class Status', *Journal of Contemporary China* 21 (78), 1029–1043.
Zenz, Adrian (2018). 'New Evidence for China's Political Re-education Campaign in Xinjiang', *China Brief* 18 (10) (15 May), https://jamestown.org/program/evidence-for-chinas-political-re-education-campaign-in-xinjiang/ (accessed 2 June 2020).
Zenz, Adrian (2019). '"Thoroughly Reforming Them towards a Healthy Heart Attitude": China's Political Re-education Campaign in Xinjiang', *Central Asian Survey* 38 (1), 102–128.
Zenz, Adrian (2020a). 'China's Own Documents Show Potentially Genocidal Sterilization Plans in Xinjiang', *Foreign Policy*, 1 July, https://foreignpolicy.com/2020/07/01/china-documents-uighur-genocidal-sterilization-xinjiang/ (accessed 7 August 2020).
Zenz, Adrian (2020b). 'Coercive Labor in Xinjiang: Labor Transfer and the Mobilization of Ethnic Minorities to Pick Cotton', Center for Global Policy, December, https://cgpolicy.org/briefs/coercive-labor-in-xinjiang-labor-transfer-and-the-mobilization-of-ethnic-minorities-to-pick-cotton/ (accessed 16 March 2021).
Zhou, Zunyou (2019). 'Chinese Strategy for De-radicalization', *Terrorism and Political Violence* 31 (6), 1187–1209.

Part I

Context

2

Echoes from the past: Repression in the Uyghur region now and then

Sandrine Catris

To travel to the Xinjiang Uyghur Autonomous Region (XUAR) in 2018 was to be confronted with the violence and omnipresence of the colonial Chinese party-state and with the successes of development. No matter which part of the region you travelled to, and which parts of the cities you went to, the mass surveillance was ubiquitous. What changed, however, was the aural and visual quality of the experience. In the areas with more Uyghurs, the near silence of the once bustling streets and markets was felt through all of one's senses as a scream of the pain of living in an open-air prison and of having friends and relatives disappeared by the state.[1] The propaganda plastered throughout every corner of the region via multiple media exalting the benevolence of the party-state, and the prosperity under Xi Jinping contrasted sharply with the lives of Uyghurs, Kazakhs, and other Turkic peoples.[2] For the last few years, Turkic peoples in the region have been treated as potential enemies to the country. Those lucky enough not to have been swept up into internment camps – called Vocational Training Internment Centres (VTIC) by Chinese authorities – or into prisons live in constant fear they can be detained by local authorities. The tensions between the state pronouncements of stability and progress, the Han Chinese population mirroring of these, and the lived realities of Uyghurs was tangible. The silence of the population's pain surpassed the loudness of the state's proclamations of success. For Uyghurs and

Kazakhs especially, Xi Jinping's promise that citizens of the People's Republic of China (PRC) would attain the *Zhongguo meng* (China dream) has translated into a Chinese nightmare for those who have not adequately assimilated and become 'Chinese' for they can neither forget nor discard their history and culture.

The current crisis in Xinjiang with the opening of internment camps, forced labour, and the increasing policing of Uyghur life in and out of the camps via high- and low-tech means has led many of us to look to the past for answers and points of comparison. The so-called People's War on Terror campaigns that started in 2014, and expanded under Chen Quanguo, did not come out of the blue, but rather should be seen as part of a long series of campaigns since the founding of the PRC aimed at integrating the region into the PRC more firmly. The current campaigns, however, differ from earlier ones because authorities have taken 'a carpet-bombing approach' (Smith Finley 2018a). This approach may be a reflection of the frustration that after over seventy years of PRC control, despite periods of tolerance and a variety of assimilationist projects, Uyghurs and other Turkic peoples still appear to the state as irredentists in need of reform. In this chapter, I argue that although we see many echoes from the Cultural Revolution in today's Xinjiang, we would benefit from understanding today's campaigns, and perhaps imagine an end to them, by looking at the 1957–58 Anti-Rightist Campaign and its aftermath. The attacks on Uyghur cultural expressions and material culture, with the razing of mosques and Sufi shrines, the closing of mosques for religious practice, the disappearance of many books from circulation, the quasi-disappearance of veiling and many forms of facial hair, the presence of a Xi cult of personality, and the omnipresence of propaganda all bring to mind the Cultural Revolution. Indeed, during the years from mid-1966 through 1976, Uyghurs had to prove their loyalty to the Chinese Communist Party (CCP) and the state by displaying images of Mao Zedong and owning the *Little Red Book*. The mosques and Sufi shrines of the region, while not fully destroyed, were damaged, closed, and repurposed. Red Guards saw veiling and having a beard as signs of feudalism and bullied those who sported them. The repression we see today undeniably echoes the repression of the Cultural Revolution. Yet the differences between the two periods are significant and limit our ability to imagine what the end could look like. In the last years of the 1960s, there were 'good' Uyghurs and 'good' Kazakhs who showed loyalty to the party. Today, there is no acceptable way of being Turkic. Any Uyghur and any other Turkic person can be disappeared despite decades of loyalty as CCP members. In Mao's last campaign, one's *minzu* was not the basis for internment and persecution.[3] Finally, the party and the government did not really control the repression that occurred during this period. So, if we were to compare it to a past campaign, the current situation most resembles the Anti-Rightist Campaign that began in 1957. In the Uyghur region, this campaign, just like today's, was completely controlled by the party and the government. Furthermore, in 1957 ethnicity also became a factor, as the Anti-Rightist Campaign became one against 'local nationalism' that primarily targeted Uyghur cadres and intellectuals. Today, over four hundred Uyghur intellectuals, artists, and businesspeople have been arrested and taken to camps and prisons. These people, just like Uyghurs from the late 1950s, have been accused of being 'two-faced' and fomenting separatist ideas. Let us now turn to the echoes from the Cultural Revolution.

In October 2017, a Uyghur friend said to me 'everyone is saying that it's so much worse now; during the Cultural Revolution, it was bad, but people would attend the rally, participate in the *ziwo piping* sessions, and then they'd go home and do whatever they wanted. Today, even home isn't safe.'[4] This comment was in response not only to the reports that had come out on the internment camps but also to the ramping up of mass surveillance that had exponentially increased by 2017. My friend, let us call her Gulnisa, was neither the first nor the only one to draw parallels between the most recent developments in the Uyghur region and the era of the Cultural Revolution. Members of the Uyghur and the Xinjiang Kazakh diasporas, academics, and journalists have also made the comparison (Klimeš 2018; Smith Finley 2018a, 2018b; Dillon 2020). In part, this chapter explores the validity, but also the limits, of this comparison. Are these echoes from the past that of the Cultural Revolution, or are there other Maoist campaigns that may serve us better in understanding the history of distrust between the Chinese party-state and the Uyghur, Kazakh, and other Turkic peoples of the region? How do the current developments fit in a longue durée understanding of Chinese colonial rule of the region? Using memoirs, party and government documents, but also newspapers and magazines, I argue that the ongoing campaigns of repressions in the XUAR under Chen Quanguo are not an aberration, but rather part of a history of successive campaigns of repression and attempts at assimilation of Turkic peoples.

Many scholars and the CCP have portrayed the Great Proletarian Cultural Revolution as an aberration, and have often classified it as 'ten years of catastrophe' heralded by a power-hungry Mao Zedong for which millions of Chinese citizens suffered (Karl 2020: 141). The notion of a 'clean' resolution to the Cultural Revolution was assisted by the death of Mao Zedong and the subsequent arrest of the infamous 'Gang of Four'. Their much publicized and staged trial enabled the party to place much of the blame for the Cultural Revolution's turmoil on the gang's manipulation of the old and feeble Mao (Cook 2016). Thus the Cultural Revolution in the PRC is not a history that can be told in all its complexities. As many scholars have argued, writers and artists in China have used literature and art to address the pains of this past (Schwarcz 1998; Karl 2020: 139–164). The loud silence of the historical void left by this era would lead many to use it as a tool to understand, criticize, or praise their present circumstances. How, then, do we understand the reform period without understanding what had transpired during the Cultural Revolution? More than fifty years since its beginning the Cultural Revolution has left many vivid examples of injustice and suffering that seem so similar to the pain and suffering of Uyghurs, Kazakhs, and other Turkic peoples throughout the region and in the diaspora.

The Cultural Revolution in many ways started as a struggle about interpretations of the past in the new socialist present. This struggle had existed from the very beginning of the PRC but had become more polarizing and urgent during the Cultural Revolution. Many scholars have dated the beginning of this revolution with the polemic that surrounded the historian and playwright Wu Han over accusations that he had told the past incorrectly and that he was criticizing Mao Zedong indirectly. Questions and debates about Wu Han's play, *Hai Rui Dismissed from Office*, came to populate the pages of the *Xinjiang Daily* with reprints from articles published in the *People's Daily*. The Xinjiang newspaper included many letters sent by residents of Xinjiang of many different *minzu*. These amateur critics and historians all engaged in what was the proper way to criticize the newly alleged counter-revolutionary, Wu Han. They also criticized the Beijing mayor, Peng Zhen – who had failed to criticize Wu Han, and in the logic of the time had therefore revealed himself to be a counter-revolutionary hidden within the ranks of the party. Wu Han had failed to interpret the past correctly (Aihamaiti 1966: 2; Li 1966: 1). Outside of PRC-wide discussion of the 'Chinese' past, there were also many discussions of the Uyghur past that focused on describing pre-PRC Xinjiang as a land where not only Chiang Kai-shek's Kuomintang but also feudal and religious elements had brought untold amount of misery to the 'innocent' commoners whom they duped and hurt. In an article on the state of Xinjiang's literature and art in the *Xinjiang Daily*, a young woman named Tillaqiz, a member of the Xinjiang Dance and Song Theatre Company, praised the good of the new China and explained that in the old China, she would not have had the opportunities to be part of a dance troupe. Tillaqiz, however, seemed most angry with those who 'opposed Han Chinese art in Xinjiang and who pretended they wanted to preserve *minzu fengge*'. Tillaqiz accused them of being Soviet revisionists in disguise (Telakezi 1966: 4). Hers was not the only attack made on people who wanted to promote Uyghur literature or other Uyghur arts. The socialist present in the Cultural Revolution was portrayed as an idealized present that would be even better once all class enemies were rooted out.

In Xinjiang, many party cadres would be rooted out, beaten, humiliated, and imprisoned for alleged crimes of their pasts. Red Guards, of all *minzu*, did not seem to have targeted and singled out specific Turkic cadres. Here, one must acknowledge that the Beijing authorities, mostly represented by Zhou Enlai in Xinjiang, did have some influence in saving certain cadres and condemning others. In transcripts of meetings between Beijing authorities and Red Guards acting within Xinjiang, we see the messiness of this movement mobilized from the top that had become a mass movement. For example, Eziz Saypedin, who had been part of the Eastern Turkestan Republic (ETR) of 1944–49, and was its sole leadership survivor, would be protected on more than one occasion from Red Guards by Zhou Enlai (Cultural Revolution Database 2009a). The less fortunate Burhan Shahidi who had been a bureaucrat in the Nationalist government of Xinjiang, however, would be beaten, humiliated, and imprisoned for about ten years. His crime was his historical ties to the Nationalists, not his present-day actions

(Shahidi 1984). Cadres who bore the brunt of Red Guards, worker, and government violence against them were labelled two-faced officials and cadres. The revolutionary actors accused them of publicly supporting Mao Zedong and of being loyal to the PRC and CCP, but of privately harbouring bourgeois, Soviet revisionist, and separatist ideas.

It is in this example that we hear echoes from the past in Xinjiang. According to many reports, many of the men and women who have suffered extrajudicial arrests since 2017 have been sent to 're-education' centres not for present wrongdoings, but for past actions that at the time had been legal. For example, words posted on social media years ago, books published via state presses, travels to foreign countries, communications with foreigners, the buying of a tent, all done in total legality and transparency years ago, now served as markers of suspicious and illegal activities and as a justification for incarceration. These last few years have given us several examples of such retroactive guilt. Take the example of Iminjan Seydin, a book publisher and an associate professor of history at the Xinjiang Islamic Institute. In May 2017, he disappeared and was reported detained in a camp. After more than a year of detainment, he received a fifteen-year sentence in February 2019. According to the victim database Shahit.biz, the probable cause of his arrest and later sentence was for 'inciting extremism'. The suspected cause according to his daughter and Amnesty International was the fact that he had previously published a book on teaching the Arabic language (Xinjiang Victim Database 2020). When the dictates of what was evidence of loyalty to the party-state changed, the past was combed for evidence of alleged crimes. Furthermore, in many of the most high-profile cases of disappearance resulting in later accusations of separatism and terrorism, formerly loyal Turkic CCP members were accused by China of being two-faced officials like Burhan Shahidi had been (Radio Free Asia 2019).

Some scholars have argued that the Cultural Revolution was the first time since the founding of the PRC that assimilationist tendencies became powerful in Xinjiang (McMillen 1979; Millward and Tursun 2004: 94–98). Although this point may be exaggerated, evidence suggests that ideas about assimilating Uyghurs and other Turkic peoples did play a more obvious part in Red Guards' plan for *nao geming* ('to make revolution') by destroying the 'four olds' (i.e. old ideas, old culture, old custom, old habits). We know that the policies that have been implemented since Chen Quanguo took control of the region in 2016 have had an even stronger assimilationist component. One of the obvious places we find assimilation playing out is in language policies and shifts. During the Cultural Revolution, parts of the Uyghur language became more Sinicized, at least in published material, but also in certain everyday encounters. According to the Uyghur nationalist activist and writer Abdurräshid Haji Kerimi, during the Cultural Revolution he no longer heard the typical Muslim greeting, 'assalamu alaykum' – instead, he heard Uyghurs greet each other with 'Long Live Chairman Mao!' in *putonghua*. He explains that studying them became a necessity during the Cultural Revolution (Kerimi 2006: 9). Indeed, many travellers to the region recently have noted eerily similar linguistic shifts. Uyghurs and other Turkic peoples avoid using traditional greetings, especially those rooted in Islam, and instead prefer to use the more neutral 'Yaxshimusiz' or Chinese-language greetings. This is especially true for anyone born in the 1980s and after. Furthermore, the Chinese language is being pushed as the sole language of the region (Byler 2019a).

The current attempts to transform, and we could say erase, Uyghurs and others, by erasing Uyghur traditions and changing Uyghur bodies, has many parallels in the Cultural Revolution. During the Cultural Revolution, Red Guards and other revolutionaries created an atmosphere of fear that led to sartorial, linguistic, and behavioural changes. In both memoirs and works of historical fiction, Uyghur and Tatar writers from Xinjiang have addressed these attempts. In the novella *Sawaqdashlar* by the Uyghur writer Memtimim Hoshur, there is a wedding scene where Ali – the main protagonist – recalls his wife being upset that people were not allowed to dance to Uyghur-style music at their wedding (Hoshur 2010). This evokes recent reports that for important life celebrations, such as weddings and funerals, a party cadre will have to be present (Kang and Wang 2018). Kerimi also mentions everyone being forced to perform the loyalty dance in public to demonstrate love and loyalty to Chairman Mao. Written works also note that everyone suddenly began to greet each other with 'Mao Zhuxi wansui!'. This aspect is also one of the facts that people readily discuss in Xinjiang. All of these were small, yet nonetheless real forms of violence that imposed a language and a way of behaving that barely had roots in Han Chinese culture, even less in Uyghur culture. Kerimi saw these small acts of cultural violence as a source of dissatisfaction and proof of the colonial nature of Chinese rule (Kerimi 2006: 10). He also describes occasions when Red Guards attacked older Uyghurs for their physical appearances that were deemed counter-revolutionary. For instance, he tells the story of an old Uyghur woman who was walking in the streets of Kashgar, when a group of Red Guards walked up to her and cut off her hair. He explains that she cried and said: 'How am I to return home to my daughter-in-law and grandchildren with my hair cut like this?' (Kerimi 2006: 9).[5] James Leibold and Timothy Grose have written on the 'beautification' campaigns of the 2010s (Leibold and Grose 2016). There were also more recent news reports that younger Turkic women's clothes were being cut in the streets because they were deemed to be signs of Muslim modesty (Radio Free Asia 2018). Several journalists have reported that local authorities have used schools and orphanages to assimilate Uyghur children in the region. Human rights activists and journalists also suspect that the children of parents who have been either sent to the camps or prison have been particularly targeted by assimilationist programmes as they do not even have a home life where Uyghur culture and language can be learned and preserved (Human Rights Watch 2019; Qin 2019).

An important point of similarity between the second half of the 1960s and today lies in the preponderance of violence – both psychological and physical – and fear. We have already discussed the violence of linguistic changes and of some assimilationist actions. Let us take a closer look at the anti-religious atmosphere of both the Cultural Revolution and present-day Xinjiang. In 1966 and 1967, Red Guards, in acts of ritualized violence, ransacked people's homes, libraries, and bookstores to find books and objects deemed counter-revolutionary. During these raids, Red Guards gathered Qur'ans, collections of hadiths, along with books about the culture of Uyghurs and burned them in public displays (Xinjiang Ribao 1966a, 1966b; Kerimi 2006: 17–18). Historians have recorded similar acts by Red Guards throughout the PRC. Red Guards also raided bookstores in search of similarly counter-revolutionary material. In late August 1966, many such stories of Red Guard revolutionary raids were printed in the pages of the *Xinjiang Daily*. For example, Red Guards in Altai visited a Xinhua bookstore allegedly under the approving eyes of its young Kazakh clerk. They took books about *Manas*, the folkloric Äpändi stories, and religion, labelled them poisonous to the people, and presumably destroyed them. We also know that all over China Red Guards carried out house searches, sometimes in the middle of the night. They would ransack the house and seize 'black materials' – incriminating evidence of low ideological adherence to Mao Zedong Thought. Wu Guang, a vice chairman of the CCP from 1963 to 1966, and Kerimi both mentioned seeing, and in the case of Wu, personally experiencing, the house searches. The materials would then be carried out to public spaces where they would be burnt as crowds looked on and Red Guards performed their revolutionary zeal. In Kashgar, Kerimi witnessed Red Guards gathering on the square in front of the Id Kah Mosque, bringing all the books they had seized as being 'poisonous', and burning them (Xinjiang Ribao 1966b; Kerimi 2006: 6–7). Such stories conjure up other historical periods where book burning happened. This also resembles the early journalistic coverage during the current wave of repression that reported police raiding Uyghur homes and seizing their Qur'an and other religious books even when printed by state presses (Radio Free Asia 2017; CECC 2018). Furthermore in 2018, the large Xinhua bookstore in Urumqi that in the past sold many Uyghur-language books covering a variety of subjects including religious ones had a much smaller Uyghur-language section and no books about religion.

Beyond the destruction of religious books and objects, Red Guards also began targeting religious architecture. Historians have written extensively on the destruction of religious sites by Red Guards throughout the PRC. They destroyed and repurposed Buddhist, Confucian, and Daoist temples, and even Christian churches. Similar actions happened in Xinjiang where Red Guards did not stop at the burning of books and began attacking religious sites. In the city of Kashgar, on 18 August 1966, Red Guards from the Kashgar 'Sipen' School (The Kashgar Teachers' School) and the Agricultural Vocational School marched to the Id Kah Mosque – an important religious and historical site for Uyghurs. Red Guards began hitting the part of the dome with the crescent moon. After that, they attempted to damage one of the minarets and damaged its left side. According to the eyewitness, Kerimi, thousands of local Uyghurs watched these youths perform their act of destruction. Many onlookers cried and were clearly upset at the sight of the Red Guards' actions. Some simply came closer to the youths and moaned to Allah. They screamed: 'What kind of work is this?' Of course, they did not try to stop them because they knew too well what could happen if they spoke out. These youths would label them anti-Cultural Revolution and therefore punish them severely all in the name of Mao Zedong and of revolution. Id Kah was allegedly saved from more serious damage by a local party official claiming: 'The Id Kah mosque is one of the select mosque[s] of the autonomous region to be protected, it is not okay to smash it. On this topic, there are documents from the Central Committee [of the CCP]' (Kerimi 2006: 7). The front and back doors of Id Kah were sealed, and the coming and going was restricted. Until the Heyt (Eid) festival of 1968, the mosque's doors were locked, but people used the side door to go in and pray (Bekri 1983). Id Kah, however, was not the only mosque to be attacked. Kerimi claims that in every city of Xinjiang, Red Guards damaged other mosques, and that in rural areas, they even turned them into animal pens, and some even into swine pens, while others were repurposed as storage spaces for production units (Kerimi 2006: 7–8). Although the evidence is scant to give more details on the ways religious architecture fared during this period, these were common stories circulated in hushed tones (Mackerras 1994: 152; Millward and Tursun 2004: 67–102).[6] We know of similar attacks against religious sites in other parts of China, so it is plausible to believe that it happened in Xinjiang as well. The only difference is that in the case of Xinjiang, the stakes of admitting to such disrespect for the local religion are higher than in parts that are more strongly anchored and invested in the Chinese nation-state.

The most recent closing, destruction, and repurposing of religious buildings have been well-documented. During her 2018 visit to the region, Joanne Smith Finley, a contributor to this edited volume (see Chapter 7), documented how a neighbourhood mosque in the Old City of Kashgar has been transformed into a cafe-bar for domestic and foreign tourists named 'Dream of Kashgar' (Smith Finley 2018b). In 2019, Shawn Zhang using Google satellite images showed suspicious scenes that suggested that the almost 800-year-old Keriya Mosque in Xinjiang had probably been demolished (Weber 2019). This happened as historian Rian Thum and journalists have also reported on the destruction of Sufi shrines throughout the region (Kuo 2019). As for the religious buildings that remained in 2018, local authorities had either disfigured them to erase their former function, or adorned them with razor wires, a PRC flag, surveillance cameras, rules about mosque use, and a banner that read 'Love the Party, Love the State'. For example, during my visit to Kashgar, 2–5 June 2018, Id Kah Mosque was the only open mosque. Id Kah also had all the elements mentioned earlier. It functioned, however, more as a touristic historical site than as a religious building of worship. Beyond the doors of the mosque, at least two police officers sat controlling who visited Id Kah. In previous years, before Chen Quanguo, Id Kah and the surrounding areas were always full of local inhabitants and visitors. In 2018, however, there were few visitors and even fewer local people entering the mosque.[7] Going to the mosque, or having a relative who does, has been one of the reasons that local authorities have labelled someone as disloyal and poisoned with religious extremism. For people outside of the camps and prison, proving one's loyalty to the state has been an important task.

During the last ten years of the Maoist period, loyalty was also a major concern. The one book people had to read and keep safe was Mao's *Little Red Book*. Everyone had a picture of Mao in their house. Everyone wanted to appear loyal to the Chairman. Red Guards would enter people's homes and write reports about their 'redness'. Kerimi said that people had to sing the song 'Mao Zedong is our Red Sun' all the time, and dance to it because they had no choice. If they did not participate people would accuse them of having ill will towards Mao. Soyüngül Chanisheff, a Tatar woman from Nanshan now living in Australia, has written about her life during the 1960s and 1970s in Xinjiang. She explains the ways that loyalty to the state was measured. She even discussed attempts at the school before the Cultural Revolution to force Muslim students to eat the same food as Han Chinese and eliminate halal foods (Chanisheff 2018). We see similar patterns at play today. This seems very similar to reports about party cadres and police officers spending time in the homes of Uyghurs to observe evidence of disloyalty and 'religious extremism'. During these visits, according to Darren Byler, the Han visitors bring food and drinks and expect them to be accepted. Refusal to ingest any food brought by the cadres is seen as evidence of disloyalty to the state (Byler 2018). In the 1960s, images of Mao were ubiquitous, but today it is images of Xi Jinping. Darren Byler has reported on several occasions the ways that Uyghur loyalty to the state is being measured by monitoring if they watch state television or private videos. Chinese officials saw staying away from consuming state television as a reason to suspect religious extremism (Byler 2019b).

One of the parallels with the Cultural Revolution that has come up is the ways in which the language of the current campaigns of 'de-extremification' (since Chen and a little before) parallel the language of the Cultural Revolution by using dehumanizing words to justify violence against those deemed enemies. The violent language and rhetoric of the Cultural Revolution has been well-documented by many scholars. This aspect is not unique to China. Indeed, dehumanization of enemies is a common strategy that has a long history in Chinese culture, but also many other societies. During the Cultural Revolution being labelled a spirit or demon could be tantamount to a death sentence. Many scholars of this period have argued that language and rhetoric became spaces for revolutionary struggle. Red Guards, Revolutionary Workers, and other opposing factions used Maos's words to legitimize their actions and agendas at times to terrible ends. Memtimim Hoshur explores the danger of language in his short story 'Yiraqtin Yezilghan Xet' (Letter Written from Afar). He tells the story of a middle-aged man, Nuri, who in 1979 remembers painfully the actions he took as a young revolutionary during the Cultural Revolution. 'I hit him [*jinn-shaytan*, demon] with a leather belt until I was tired. At the end, he was no longer able to endure the pain … I hit his head forcefully with an iron rod, he fell over to one side, and from his wound thick blood oozed out onto the cement … the eyes of the young man still clearly stared at me with absolute disdain' (Hoshur 1987: 11). As we read the story, we feel the guilt of Nuri over his action and the struggle he felt in retrospect that he could kill another human being simply because he had then seen him as a demon.

Reading Red Guard reports from Xinjiang, we find similar words in Chinese provinces that justified attacks on people deemed 'enemies' of Mao Zedong and of the revolution. Epithets such as 'vermin', 'little Khrushchevs', 'traitors', 'capitalist roader', 'cow and snake spirit', 'pile of dog faeces', 'crawling snakes', 'black hand', and 'Soviet revisionists' appear repeatedly in many publications of the time to describe 'enemies of the people' including Red Guard reports, *Xinjiang Youth*, and the *Xinjiang Daily*. For instance, Wu Guang and Burhan Shahidi were both insulted by one of the Red Guard Faction and they called them a number of these terms. Red Guards paraded both through the streets of Urumqi, beaten and insulted. Wu Guang, for example, describes in detail the ways he was left almost to die in the Taklamakan desert after such a public humiliation session (Wu 2000: 56–57). Similar dehumanizing language has been used by Chinese officials to justify the repression of Uyghurs and others in Xinjiang. Officials have compared people they considered as being extremists and terrorists to weeds. As reported in multiple media outlets, a Han official in Kashgar announced: 'You can't uproot all the weeds hidden among the crops in the field one by one. You need to spray chemicals to kill them all' (cited in Forth 2020). Officials have also compared Islam to a dangerous virus that needs to be eradicated. Hence religious belief is seen as a pathology that only the extreme measures taken by Chen Quanguo's administration can cure (Samuel 2018).

The measure that has received the most international coverage since 2017 has been the extrajudicial disappearances of a very large number of Uyghurs, Kazkahs, and other Turkic peoples into what journalists, activists, and Xinjiang scholars have called internment camps. The most compelling evidence of their numbers and presence throughout Xinjiang came from an article by Adrian Zenz, later corroborated by the satellite imagery of Shawn Zhang, and anecdotal evidence from reports from the Uyghur diaspora, journalists, and scholars who travelled to the region between 2017 and 2020 (Zhang 2018; Zenz 2019). Since 2020, new evidence has emerged that shows the link between forced labour and different levels of internment camps. Furthermore, Eugene Bunin has also reported on social media that many of the testimonies that have been submitted between 2019 and 2020 suggest a shift from these extrajudicial internment camps to prisons as relatives of detainees are reporting their family members are receiving long prison sentences after being detained one or two years (Ramzy and Buckley 2018; Bunin 2020). Extrajudicial disappearances, forced labour, and prison sentences are nothing new to the PRC and here again we hear the echoes from the Cultural Revolution. In several testimonies about life in the internment camps by Mihrigul Tursun and ethnically Kazakh camp teacher Sayragul Sauytbay, they both speak of torture, cramped and dirty quarters, medical experiments, and lack of privacy (Hong Kong Free Press 2018; Synovitz *et al.* 2018). When reading Cultural Revolution-era accounts of detention in Xinjiang we see the same patterns at play. Soyüngül Chanisheff spent over three years in a prison in Xinjiang from 1963 to 1966, and then spent time in a forced labour camp during the Cultural Revolution. She writes of the disgusting conditions and of the physical and mental torture she underwent while doing forced labour. She writes that on 20 September 1966, *minbing*s told young Uyghur girls who refused to smoke, 'You silly, backward people, ignorant of the glorious social changes in this country. You are no longer allowed to hold on to your traditional beliefs. You can say no today, but just wait and see: The Party will soon forbid you to wear even your traditional clothes, let alone your traditional way of life and your religion!' (Chanisheff 2018: 242). The words of these young men seem to prophesize what has been happening in the region. Kerimi also writes about his experiences in prison and makes similar observations (Kerimi 2006: 48–49).

The extrajudicial disappearances and the post-facto prison sentences are perhaps not the most salient of comparisons because after all those, in one way or another, have a long history in the PRC, where dissent has often been met with similar tactics. The scale, however, is what makes this current situation exceptional. Mass surveillance and the ability of the state or its agents to penetrate into the private and public lives of its citizens and to transform reality may be what makes the current situation so comparable to the last ten years of the Maoist era. In 2018, police presence, cameras, and spying technologies were ubiquitous. Recent reports, however, have mentioned the beginning of the disappearance of the most obvious elements of mass surveillance. During the Cultural Revolution, mass surveillance became part of the everyday life of most citizens of the PRC, though it was much easier to hide than it would be today, especially for Turkic peoples. Chanisheff writes about the mass surveillance she felt once the Cultural Revolution began. She discusses the ways in which her neighbours kept tabs on her comings and goings. She had to be careful. Red Guards and later *minbing*s could come at any time and ransack people's homes as discussed earlier. She explains how from the moment the Cultural Revolution started and the moment she returned home, everyone in her neighbourhood learned she needed to be watched. She recalls how during a neighbourhood meeting a Kazakh man said, 'I would like to stress again that she [Chanisheff] has been stripped of all of her rights, and she has to do hard labour under the supervision of everyone in the commune.' Rights to privacy or any other protection no longer existed for those who had been labelled like she had, 'a revisionist', 'a direct agent of Khrushchev', and 'a proven counter-revolutionist' (Chanisheff 2018: 228–229).

The comparisons made by so many between the current situation in Xinjiang and the era of the Cultural Revolution are compelling as demonstrated above. There are, however, important differences that prevent us from fully understanding the present. The current situation orchestrated by the Chen Quanguo administration are top-down initiatives approved not only by the highest authority in Xinjiang, but also by the central authorities in Beijing. This is quite significant because Xi Jinping completely supports the actions of the regional authorities. This has been demonstrated not only by his leading role in setting policy for Xinjiang (e.g. through chairing of CCP Xinjiang Work Forums) but also disclosures in leaked CCP documents pertaining to Xinjiang published by the New York Times in 2019 (Ramzy and Buckley 2019). It would be impossible to simply blame a few people. The Cultural Revolution in Xinjiang, however, was not exactly a top-down initiative. Although as mentioned earlier this revolution had been mobilized by the very top, Chairman Mao, this campaign was also a mass movement (Wu 2014; Karl 2020: 139–163).

In Xinjiang, there is a lot of evidence that regional authorities did not want to see this movement take off. They were frightened that the potential unrest of the great link-up of Red Guards coming from other parts of the PRC would destabilize the region, something even more worrisome at the time for both Beijing and Urumqi, as they feared Soviet Union interference. In many telegrams from 1966 and 1967 between the regional and central authorities in Beijing, party cadres, government, and military officials regularly cited concerns that young Red Guards from *neidi* would bring chaos to the region. This can be seen, for example, in a telegram from 4 September 1966. In it, the Central Committee of the CCP sent a telegram to the Party Committee of the Xinjiang CCP that read: 'You particularly want to discourage outside students (*waidi*) from coming in this district [*bianjing* of Yili, Tacheng, and Altai] to link-up (*chuanlian*) and you have to convince the ones already there to leave' (Cultural Revolution Database 2009b). How can we understand this directive from the Central Committee when less than a month earlier Chairman Mao, on 8 August 1966, had called on students to 'bombard the headquarters'? Xinjiang then was simply treated differently from internal Chinese provinces. Once

Red Guards, both local and outsiders, began *nao geming*, regional authorities under the aegis of Wang Enmao did try to control and subdue it by supporting opposing factions. Even then pro-Wang factions were not fully under his control. This led to multiple attempts by Zhou Enlai to intervene. Xinjiang would be the last place where revolutionary committees would be formed. A basic point of difference between then and now is that the regional and national authorities today are not worried that a large influx of Han Chinese, young or old, would bring ethnic instability. In fact, they have encouraged more than ever Han Chinese migration to the region. In part because this last Maoist revolution had become a mass campaign, even with some top-down mobilization and limited control, the attacks on Uyghur traditions and Turkic peoples was ad hoc and unsystematic. Furthermore, perpetrators and victims came from all ethnicities, while today, the victims and survivors are Turkic peoples, with some cases limited to a number of Hui and Han victims. During the Cultural Revolution, some Uyghurs and Kazakhs became model citizens, but today it seems that no Turkic person in the region can be safe from falling victim to the state (Radio Free Asia 2019).

This is an important distinction. Today the repression is top-down and systematic and targets any person of Uyghur and Turkic descent. During the Cultural Revolution, however, this national mass movement had everyone swept up by it regardless of ethnicity. Furthermore, Red Guards, even when supported by regional or indeed national authorities, did not act in any systematic way. Many of the excesses and wrongs of the Cultural Revolution could also easily be blamed on the mental health of Mao Zedong and on the manipulations of his closest comrades in the Gang of Four. But to admit to the wrongs and the immorality of the state project in Xinjiang today would require a condemnation of the CCP, and of all the academic and journalistic justifications created to support it (Xinjiang Documentation Project 2020a). Furthermore, during the Cultural Revolution, many Uyghurs participated, perhaps at times under duress but unlike the current situation, the actors of the mass movements did not think they needed to destroy Uyghurs or any other ethnic groups; they believed they would build a better world where equality would prevail. However, as revealed by the leaked 400 pages of internal documents covered in *The New York Times*, Xi Jinping in a visit to Xinjiang in a private meeting with regional authorities asked them to show 'absolutely no mercy' when dealing with terrorism and separatism. These documents directly link Xi Jinping to the mast internment that would follow once Chen Quanguo became the new Party Chief in Xinjiang in 2016. The goal appears to be cultural genocide, not equality (Ramzy and Buckley 2019).

This difference between the Cultural Revolution and the current crisis is significant. As mentioned earlier we can also learn from the campaigns of the late 1950s. The Anti-Rightist Campaign is not as spectacular and evocative as the Cultural Revolution. It lacks the drama. This may explain why scholars and journalists have not looked at the parallels with the 1957–58 Anti-Rightist Campaign, the way they have looked at the parallels with the last ten years of Maoism. Let us look at the parallels with this historical moment and its long-lasting impact in the Uyghur region. In PRC history, the Anti-Rightist Campaign is already seen as a turning point. Timothy Cheek in a recent special issue of *Twentieth-Century China* has called on historians to revisit that one year, 1957, as a crucible, to appreciate the diversity of the experiences and individual choices made then, and to avoid understanding it from the point of the future Great Leap Forward and Cultural Revolution. It is a year of great significance in the history of Communist China (Cheek 2020: 121–126). This is also true for Xinjiang where the carrying out of this campaign appeared to have solidified the *minzu* problems of this region (Wu 2015). This campaign swept through the country immediately after the Hundred Flowers Campaign (February–June 1957) and played out in distinct ways especially in the PRC's autonomous regions. The Hundred Flowers Campaign, however, represented a moment of hope and possibilities in the history of Communist China, a moment when the PRC could have learned from the Soviet Union's mistakes and taken a different trajectory.

According to Donald McMillen, and other scholars, the Anti-Rightist Campaign in the Uyghur region targeted mostly Uyghur intellectuals and cadres. Han cadres saw most Uyghurs and other Turkic persons with any social and political capital as untrustworthy and with little loyalty to the CCP. Regional authorities argued they allegedly harboured separatist desires. This reveals how early in the history of Communist-controlled Xinjiang these kinds of beliefs about Turkic intellectuals and cadres existed. In Xinjiang, the Anti-Rightist

Campaign would turn quickly into an anti-local nationalism campaign that went on to affect local politics well into the Maoist period. The cadres leading the assault in the region blamed the continuing power of Uyghur nationalism on the party's earlier position against Han chauvinism and its gradual approach towards local traditions, which they found too lenient (McMillen 1979: 91-93). During the Anti-Rightist Campaign, many Uyghur and Turkic cadres were targeted and labelled counter-revolutionary because of their alleged separatism. The historian Zhe Wu – who had access to the XUAR archives – argues that Eziz Saypedin participated in a meeting of the Xinjiang Party Committee to resolve the issue of local nationalism on 16 December 1957. During this meeting, Saypedin allegedly argued that local nationalist tendencies presented the highest danger in the region (Wu 2015: 319). The same would be true during the Cultural Revolution. Today, being labelled a separatist is associated with 'terrorism' and 'religious extremism'; then it was associated with being a counter-revolutionary. The kind of criticism that had come out from the Hundred Flowers Campaign and the impression that Uyghurs should have been happier to be part of the PRC are likely to have played a part in this development.

Joshua Freeman gives a detailed discussion of the anti-local nationalism campaign born out of the Anti-Rightist Campaign (Freeman 2019: 262-266). In Xinjiang, Uyghur and Turkic intellectuals felt invigorated and began criticizing the false autonomy that had come with the creation of the XUAR in 1955. Freeman explains that in Xinjiang, local intellectuals began actively participating in the criticism that Mao had called for. Freeman gives the example of Memetjan Mekhsum, the deputy head of the Xinjiang People's Political Consultative Conference, who called for more non-Han cadres in the local party and government. Mekhsum was not alone to do so (Freeman 2019: 280). Soyüngül Chanisheff discusses the activities during this time among university professors and students. At the time, she was a student at the Xinjiang Medical University. She alleges that during her first year there amidst the Hundred Flowers Campaign, students and professors debated whether Xinjiang should be independent or not using an old text by Mao that said Xinjiang needed to be added to the Republic for its wealth. She then alleges that most students, faculty, and cadres believed that it needed to be the case. They all were in favour of an independent Xinjiang Republic. She also claims that students who did not participate in these public debates were shamed for it. This reveals how popular their independentist calls were. She explains that images of those who would not participate in these debates were put on walls to shame their silence. Although she was afraid, she participated (Chanisheff 2018: 19–20). In her memoir, she writes that during one of these meetings in a reversal of Han stereotypes about Uyghurs, she said: 'since the Chinese have arrived in Xinjiang, there has been a rise in street-crime, and in night-time muggings and murders, which have been committed by Chinese criminals. This anti-social behaviour is disturbing the peaceful lives of the native peoples and if it continues, the consequences for this country will be disastrous.' In her narrative, she also contrasts the ways in which Chinese students were treated with the treatment of Turkic students. On several occasions, she writes about how school authorities tried to force the minority students to eat the same food as the Han students. All of what she saw as repeated insults and injuries to her people led her to want to form an organization that would fight for the independence of Xinjiang. She also uses both terms, East Turkestan and Xinjiang, for the region (Chanisheff 2018: 20).

The clear discontent voiced by non-Han cadres in the region led to the Xinjiang CCP beginning the anti-local nationalism campaign. A parallel with the current situation in Xinjiang is that the authorities fully controlled the campaign. Uyghur and other non-Han cadres and intellectuals, but also Han cadres who had supported them, were punished in various ways, often arrested, and sent to prison and forced-labour camps. The campaign was decidedly an attempt to stamp down Uyghurs and other local intellectuals and cadres who had the social, cultural, and political capital to advocate for more autonomy and knew well their own history of the region. McMillen even mentions that some of the intellectuals noted that autonomy under the Soviet Union would be better than control by the Chinese (McMillen 1979: 91–96). From then on, any criticism of the dubious autonomy of the region would be met with accusations of being a separatist. In fact, many Uyghur intellectuals who had been accused of that crime would be accused again during the Cultural Revolution even if they had managed to get back into the good graces of the party. Before 1957, the overall position of the CCP in Xinjiang was that Han chauvinism represented the largest threat to stability in the region. After 1957, local nationalism and separatism would become the recurring issue in the region to this day. Authorities interpreted any criticism of Han chauvinism in Xinjiang but also any pride in Turkic culture, language, and the practice of Islam as evidence of local nationalism and separatism. This anti-Turkic intellectual trend started in 1957. Today, as mentioned above, being accused of separatism has continued to be one of the most common reasons for extrajudicial disappearances and retroactive charges and sentences to long prison terms. During the last ten years of Mao's life, these kinds of accusations also existed, but it seems that the focus on Turkic intellectuals and others with social capital is something that really links these two periods together. Like the 'People's War on Terror', the Anti-Rightist Campaign in Xinjiang focused almost exclusively on Turkic peoples for both their ethnicity and their religious beliefs. Both periods focused practically exclusively on the lack of loyalty of their non-Han population seeing the most educated as 'two-faced' people.

Conclusion

Although we hear fewer echoes from the Anti-Rightist Campaign in today's Xinjiang, the focus on Turkic intellectuals and officials and the party-state's total control of both may help us imagine what the end of the current crisis may look like. Uyghurs from the diaspora, journalists, and academics have also wondered: What does the future hold for Uyghurs and other Turkic peoples in Xinjiang? How will perpetrators be held accountable for their crime? As many scholars and activists have argued, the current situation in the region is cultural genocide (Smith Finley 2020). The PRC, its party leaders, and its academics have denied that anything wrong is happening in the region. Despite the evidence, the testimonies, and the leaked documents, Chinese authorities keep arguing that their actions in the region are benevolent. They have staged visits to the internment camps for foreign journalists. Using social media and well-crafted propaganda they lie to shape both domestic and global perceptions (Xinjiang Documentation Project 2020b). The recent reports of the dismantling of the visible mass surveillance and the charging of detainees for actual crimes and the sentencing of them to prison terms may be a sign that the PRC is trying to clean up and erase the evidence of its crimes. What will this mean for the local population? Will their cause be forgotten once the cultural genocide appears more respectable? Many problems plague any advocacy for change in Xinjiang. The lack of respect for human rights and the lack of actual political will in many other countries, including the United States and the European Union, weakens any international effort to affect change. Foreign politicians have co-opted the Xinjiang crisis as a tool to fuel their new cold war politics and anti-Chinese sentiments and not much of consequences has come out of any of the resolutions passed.

What does the future hold? Historians cannot answer this question. We can, however, look to the past for patterns. As argued above, while the Cultural Revolution offers us many enticing parallels, the differences between then and now are too vast. Not only was this revolution a nation-wide effort to reshape the present, it was also not a movement fully controlled by the government. Furthermore, after the death of Mao, there were easy scapegoats – the Gang of Four and the enfeebled Mao. The Anti-Rightist Campaign of 1957–58 and its aftermath, on the other hand, offer important points of comparison. Just like the current situation, this campaign was fully organized and orchestrated by local authorities with the support of the party-state. Although it was a nation-wide campaign, in Xinjiang it specifically targeted Turkic intellectuals and cadres, and became an anti-local nationalism campaign. After the anti-local nationalism campaign ended, the CCP did not have to disavow its actions despite its disastrous consequences: perpetuating Han distrust towards Turkic intellectuals and cadres persists to this day and therefore gives fodder to anti-Han sentiment. From where we stand today, this may be about to happen again. As mentioned above leaders of the CCP, especially Xi Jinping and Chen Quanguo, with the help Chinese academics have orchestrated and provided justification for this last wave of repression. Will the PRC move into the next ten years, following the South African example, with a truth and reconciliation type of national grappling for the crimes against Uyghurs and other Turkic peoples? Or will they follow the example of many other countries where nationalism shapes the historical amnesia that hinders an even symbolic reckoning with injustice?

Notes

1. I spent most of my time in urban areas in the cities of Urumqi, Ghulja (Yining), and Kashgar in May–June 2018. Therefore, most of the Turkic population there was Uyghur.
2. The repression today mostly targets people of Turkic descent and anyone who has spoken in their defence. Uyghurs represent most Turkic people in the region. So, for the sake of clarity, I will sometimes write Uyghur when I mean Turkic peoples in general.
3. *Minzu* has been translated as nationality in the Soviet sense of the word or ethnicity in the Western European and American context.
4. Gulnisa, personal discussion with author, Seattle, WA, 7 October 2017.
5. Colin Mackerras (1994: 152) also writes about such attacks on anything seen as traditional Uyghur culture. However, he does not give any sources for this. He is not the only scholar to report on such rumours; see also Millward and Tursun (2004: 101–102).
6. On multiple visits to the Uyghur region between 2007 and 2009, but also during my longer stay in 2010 and 2011, people spoke of these rumours regularly.
7. Personal travel observations, Kashgar, 2–5 June 2018.

References

Aihamaiti, Kazimu (1966). 'Yongkai jiqi de shuang shou qi bi lai zhan dou', *Xinjiang Ribao*, 8 May, 2.

Bekri, Joneyid (1983). 'Qeshqer heytqar jamesining otmushi we haziri', in *Shinjang tarikhi materialliri*, vol. 12 (Urumqi: Shinjang khelk neshriyati).

Bunin, Eugene (2020). 'Victim-Centered Primary Evidence for the Mass Incarcerations and Immense Rights Violations in the Xinjiang Uyghur Autonomous Region', Xinjiang Victims Database, Shahit.biz, www.shahit.biz/primrep.php (accessed 19 July 2021).

Byler, Darren (2018). 'China's Government Has Ordered a Million Citizens to Occupy Uighur Homes: Here's What They Think They're Doing', *China File*, 24 October, www.chinafile.com/reporting-opinion/postcard/million-citizens-occupy-uighur-homes-xinjiang (accessed 9 June 2020).

Byler, Darren (2019a). 'The Patriotism of Not Speaking Uyghur', *SupChina*, 2 January, https://supchina.com/2019/01/02/the-patriotism-of-not-speaking-uyghur/ (accessed 9 June 2020).

Byler, Darren (2019b). 'China's Hi-tech War on Its Muslim Minority', *The Guardian*, 11 April, www.theguardian.com/news/2019/apr/11/china-hi-

tech-war-on-muslim-minority-xinjiang-uighurs-surveillance-face-recognition (accessed 10 June 2020).
CECC (2018). '2018 Congressional-Executive Commission on China Report on Xinjiang', www.cecc.gov/sites/chinacommission.house.gov/files/documents/2018AR_Xinjiang_1.pdf (accessed 10 June 2020).
Chanisheff, Soyüngül (2018). *The Land Drenched in Tears*, trans. Rahima Mahmut (England: Hertfordshire Press).
Cheek, Timothy (2020). 'The Chinese Crucible of 1957', *Twentieth-Century China* 45 (2), 121–126.
Cook, Alexander (2016). *The Cultural Revolution on Trial: Mao and the Gang of Four* (Cambridge: Cambridge University Press).
Cultural Revolution Database (2009a). 'Zhou Enlai guanyu Xinjiang Hong'ersi chao Saifuding jiadeng wenti de zhishi, 1968–05–02', ed. Song Yongyi, http://ccrd.usc.cuhk.edu.hk (accessed 7 December 2009).
Cultural Revolution Database (2009b). 'Zhonggong zhongyang guanyu bianjing diqu wenhua dageming you guan wenti de jueding 1966–09–07', ed. Song Yongyi, http://ccrd.usc.cuhk.edu.hk (accessed 7 December 2009).
Dillon, Michael (2020). 'A Uighurs' History of China: The Repression in China's Xinjiang Region Has Deep Historical Roots', *History Today* 70 (1) (January), www.historytoday.com/archive/behind-times/uighurs%E2%80%99-history-china (accessed 30 June 2020).
Freeman, Joshua (2019). 'Print and Power in the Communist Borderlands: The Rise of Uyghur National Culture' (PhD diss., Harvard University).
Forth, Aidan (2020). 'The Language of the Uighur Holocaust', *The Wire*, 22 January, https://thewire.in/communalism/china-uighur-holocaust (accessed 4 June 2020).
Hong Kong Free Press (2018). 'Video: In Full – Ex-Xinjiang Detainee Mihrigul Tursun's Full Testimony at the US Congressional Hearing', 8 December, https://hongkongfp.com/2018/12/08/video-full-ex-xinjiang-detainee-mihrigul-tursuns-full-testimony-us-congressional-hearing/ (accessed 8 June 2020).
Hoshur, Memtimin (1987). 'Yiraktin Yezilghan xet' [Letter Written from Afar], in *Kona-yengi ishlar: hikayilar* (Beijing: Millatlar nashriyati).
Hoshur, Memtimim (2010). *Sawaqdashlar* [Classmates], in *Qizil Istakan* [The Red Cup], *Memtimim Hoshur eserliridin tallanmu* [Memtimim Hoshur's Selected Works], vol. 3 (Urumqi: Xinjiang Yashlar-Ösmürler neshryati), 206–377.
Human Rights Watch (2019). 'China: Xinjiang Children Separated from Families', 15 September, www.hrw.org/news/2019/09/15/china-xinjiang-children-separated-families (accessed 7 June 2020).

Kang, Dake, and Yanan Wang (2018). 'Party Cadre Xinjiang Attend Wedding Circumcision and Funerals', Emissourian.com, 30 November, https://emissourian.com/news/world/chinese-party-agents-watch-over-uighur-funerals-weddings/article_88f69a88-f4c4-11e8-ae4e-5b82e7be7ecf.html (accessed 10 June 2020).

Karl, Rebecca (2020). *China's Revolutions in the Modern World* (London: Verso).

Kerimi, Abdurräshid Haji (2006). *Qarajüldiki Jäng* [The Battle of Qarajül] (Istanbul: Taklimakan Uyghur Nashriyati, 2006), www.uyghurweb.net/uy/qarajul.pdf (accessed 20 October 2011, no longer available).

Klimeš, Ondřej (2018). 'China's Decimation of Uyghur Minds', *Asia Dialogue*, 25 October, https://theasiadialogue.com/2018/10/25/chinas-decimation-of-uyghur-minds/ (accessed 8 June 2020).

Kuo, Lili (2019). 'Revealed: New Evidence of China's Mission to Raze the Mosques of Xinjiang', *The Guardian*, 6 May, www.theguardian.com/world/2019/may/07/revealed-new-evidence-of-chinas-mission-to-raze-the-mosques-of-xinjiang (accessed 8 June 2020).

Leibold, James, and Timothy Grose (2016). 'Islamic Veiling in Xinjiang: The Political and Societal Struggle to Define Uyghur Female Adornment', *The China Journal* (76) (July), 78–102.

Li, Hong'en (1966). 'Shenme jieji shuo shenme hua', *Xinjiang Daily*, 8 May, 1.

Mackerras, Colin (1994). *China's Minorities: Integration and Modernization in the Twentieth Century* (New York: Oxford University Press).

McMillen, Donald H. (1979). *Chinese Communist Power and Policy in Xinjiang: 1949–1977* (Boulder: Westview Press).

Millward, James, and Nabijan Tursun (2004). 'Political History and Strategies of Control, 1884–1978', in S. Frederick Starr (ed.), *Xinjiang: China's Muslim Borderland* (New York: M. E. Sharpe), 63–98.

Qin, Amy (2019). 'In China's Crackdown on Muslims, Children Have Not Been Spared', *New York Times*, 28 December, www.nytimes.com/2019/12/28/world/asia/china-xinjiang-children-boarding-schools.html (accessed 7 June 2020).

Radio Free Asia (2017). 'Xinjiang's Korla City Seizes Qurans, Prayer Mats from Uyghur Muslims', 2 October, www.rfa.org/english/news/uyghur/qurans-10022017152453.html (accessed 10 June 2020).

Radio Free Asia (2018). 'Uyghurs Deplore China's Unkind Cuts to Local Women's Skirts', 16 July, www.rfa.org/english/news/uyghur/skirts-cut-07162018151636.html (accessed 8 June 2020).

Radio Free Asia (2019). 'Police Chief Detained in Xinjiang after Expressing Concerns over Mass Detention of Fellow Uyghurs', 10 October, www.rfa.org/english/news/uyghur/detained-10212019174917.html (accessed 9 June 2020).

Ramzy, Austin, and Chris Buckley (2018). 'China's Detention Camps for Muslim Turn into Forced Labor Camps', *New York Times*, 16 December, www.nytimes.com/2018/12/16/world/asia/xinjiang-china-forced-labor-camps-uighurs.html (accessed 10 June 2020).

Ramzy, Austin, and Chris Buckley (2019). '"Absolutely No Mercy": Leaked Files Expose How China Organized Mass Detentions of Muslims', *New York Times*, 16 November, www.nytimes.com/interactive/2019/11/16/world/asia/china-xinjiang-documents.html (accessed 9 June 2020).

Samuel, Sigal (2018). 'China Is Treating Islam Like a Mental Illness', *The Atlantic*, 28 August, www.theatlantic.com/international/archive/2018/08/china-pathologizing-uighur-muslims-mental-illness/568525/ (accessed 1 June 2020).

Schwarcz, Vera (1998). 'A Brimming Darkness: The Voice of Memory/the Silence of Pain in China after the Cultural Revolution', *Bulletin of Concerned Asian Scholars* 30 (1), 46–54.

Shahidi, Burhan (1984). *Xinjiang wushi nian* (Beijing: Wen shi zi liao chu ban she).

Smith Finley, Joanne (2018a). 'Islam in Xinjiang: "De-extremification" or Violation of Religious Space?', *Asia Dialogue*, 15 June, https://theasiadialogue.com/2018/06/15/islam-in-xinjiang-de-extremification-or-violation-of-religious-space/ (accessed 8 June 2020).

Smith Finley, Joanne (2018b). '"Now We Don't Talk Anymore": Inside the "Cleansing" of Xinjiang', *China File*, 28 December, www.chinafile.com/reporting-opinion/viewpoint/now-we-dont-talk-anymore (accessed 9 June 2020).

Smith Finley, Joanne (2020). 'Why Scholars and Activists Increasingly Fear a Uyghur Genocide in Xinjiang', *Journal of Genocide Research*, 1–23, https://doi.org/10.1080/14623528.2020.1848109.

Synovitz, Ron, Asylkhan Mamshuly, and Nurtai Lakhanuly (2018). 'Official's Testimony Sheds New Light on Chinese "Reeducation Camps" For Muslim', *Radio Free Europe*, 29 July, www.rferl.org/a/kazakhstan-officials-testimony-chinese-reeducation-camps-muslims/29396709.html (accessed 8 June 2020).

Telakezi (1966). 'Shi zuo shehuizhuyi wenhua dageming jianbing', *Xinjiang Renmin Ribao*, 28 June, 4.

Weber, Peter (2019). 'China May Have Recently Demolished a Uighur Mosque as Old as Notre Dame', *The Week*, 17 April, https://theweek.com/speedreads/835669/china-may-have-recently-demolished-uighur-mosque-old-notre-dame (accessed 9 June 2020).

Wu, Guang (2000). *Bu Shi Meng: Dui 'Wenge' Niandai de Huiyi* (Beijing: Zhong Gong Dang Shi Chu Ban She).

Wu, Yiching (2014). *The Cultural Revolution at the Margins: Chinese Socialism in Crisis* (Cambridge, MA: Harvard University Press).

Wu, Zhe (2015). 'Caught between Opposing Han Chauvinism and Local Nationalism: The Drift toward Ethnic Antagonism in Xinjiang Society, 1952–1963', in Jeremy Brown and Matthew D. Johnson (eds), *Maoism at the Grassroots* (Cambridge, MA: Harvard University Press), 306–339.

Xinjiang Documentation Project (2020a). 'Key Documents', https://xinjiang.sppga.ubc.ca/policy-documents/ (accessed 7 June 2020).

Xinjiang Documentation Project (2020b). 'Chinese Official Media', https://xinjiang.sppga.ubc.ca/media/documentaries/ (accessed 7 June 2020).

Xinjiang Victim Database (2020). 'Iminjan Seydin – Entry #5645', www.shahit.biz/eng/#view (accessed 9 June 2020).

Xinjiang Ribao (1966a). 'Yi chedi geming jingshen, dao po "sijiu" dali "sixin"', 26 August, 2.

Xinjiang Ribao (1966b). 'Dapo zichan jieji "sijiu" dali quchan jieji "sixin"', 31 August, 2.

Zhang, Shawn (2018). 'List of Re-education Camps in Xinjiang', Medium, https://medium.com/@shawnwzhang (accessed 10 June 2020).

Zenz, Adrian (2019). '"Thoroughly Reforming Them towards a Healthy Heart Attitude": China's Political Re-education Campaign in Xinjiang', *Central Asian Survey* 38 (1), 102–128.

3

The Kashgar Dangerous House Reform Programme: Social engineering, 'a rebirth of the nation', and a significant building block in China's creeping genocide

Anna Hayes

The Xinjiang Uyghur Autonomous Region (XUAR) is experiencing a creeping genocide. With between one and two million Uyghurs and other non-Han ethnic groups incarcerated in concentration camps across the region, and the deployment of some former detainees into unfree labour in factories both inside of the XUAR and across the People's Republic of China (PRC), the situation in the XUAR has become increasingly dire (Xu *et al.* 2020).[1] Genocide scholars have argued there are warning signs for genocide, urging that a gradual genocidal process is identifiable inside of genocidal states long before they commit acts of physical genocide. By recognizing these warning signs, actors, both inside and outside of the state, can attempt to prevent the genocidal process, or rather creeping genocide, from escalating. Given what is unfolding in the XUAR, it has become increasingly clear the Chinese state is engaged in creeping genocide against the Uyghurs and other ethnic minorities inside the region.

This chapter focuses on the destruction of Old Kashgar under the Kashgar Dangerous House Reform Programme (KDHRP). It argues this programme was undergirded by desires of social control and social engineering aimed at perceived 'deviant' Uyghurs, with the ultimate goal being the purposeful destruction and eradication of Uyghur culture in the Uyghur heartland. Moreover, it identifies that the measures undertaken during the KDHRP paved the way for the increased surveillance, social control, and the mass incarceration of Uyghurs that has occurred under the presidency of Xi Jinping and the regional leadership of Chen Quanguo. Finally, it argues that Uyghurs have long been dehumanized via applied collective labels such as 'backwards', a 'terrorist collective', and, more recently, 'weeds'. MacGregor and Bowles (2012: 437) have warned: '[t]o prevent genocide, we have to understand its root causes. Genocide and mass killing do not simply erupt spontaneously. They are incremental processes, building blocks, which aggregate and develop into their final form.' This chapter identifies the KDHRP as a building block within a pattern of social engineering across the XUAR that amounts to creeping genocide.[2]

The genocidal process

Davidson defined cultural genocide as seeking the withering away or severe impairment of the enemy culture. He argued that cultural genocide is evident in the 'purposeful destructive targeting of out-group cultures so as to destroy or weaken them in the process of conquest or domination' (Davidson 2012: 1). He linked cultural genocide to the phenomenon of natural localness, that is, the cultural paradigm of the locale, which distinguishes difference or coherence depending on the individual. This phenomenon causes the individual or the group to be so inward focused that they become ignorant of those outside of the locale, manifesting in emotions of exclusiveness, often presenting as suspicion and dislike of outsiders (the Other). Therefore, natural localness is spurred on by a lack of critical thinking by a population and the inability of rational thought.

Davidson further explained that due to the lack of domain knowledge necessary for critical thinking, a population becomes more reliant on experts to counteract their ignorance. However, the experts are themselves constrained by their own stereotypes and other agendas, so they use manipulation to stylize news of the world outside of the locale to suit their purposes. This can result in artificial views of whole communities of people, which can lead to a thought collective that can be 'mobilised to act collectively against alleged enemies' (Davidson 2012: 18). Hence, natural localness provides the key rationale for actors to regard the 'destruction of the basis for identity and culture' to be a viable tactic in conflict (Davidson 2012: 19). Given the Nazi Genocide evokes an abhorrence of the act of physical genocide, Davidson argued that it is not easily undertaken in the post-Holocaust world (although it certainly still does occur). Instead, genocidal actors often pursue cultural genocide in its place as part of a gradualist approach. However, cultural genocide, warned Davidson, may signal intent for physical genocide so it should not occupy a lesser place when theorizing about genocide and genocidal intent.

For Levine, analyses of genocide must recognize the existence of a 'genocidal process' that incorporates repressive state strategies targeting a perceived 'problem' population such as 'marginalisation, forced assimilation, deportation and even massacre' (Levine 1999: 342). Levine argued the UN Convention definition for genocide is inadequate due to its limited scope.[3] Citing Raphael Lemkin's more encompassing definition for genocide, he argued that the point of mass systematic annihilation (physical genocide) cannot be isolated from the years and decades of calculated events preceding the physical genocide. Moreover, Lemkin (2005 [1944]: 79) identified genocide as a coordinated plan intended to cause 'the disintegration of the political and social institutions of the group', and can include the 'destruction of the personal security, liberty, health, dignity, and even the lives of the individuals belonging to such groups'. This is the genocidal process, or creeping genocide, which may or may not result in a physical genocide occurring, depending on further choices made by the state. According to Levine (1999: 343), states make a calculated decision as to whether or not to engage in physical genocide largely depending on their 'developmental interests' to do so. This argument deliberately shifts away from many viewpoints of genocide as an act of madness or evil. Such viewpoints do not adequately examine the underpinning social dimensions that both contribute to and facilitate the occurrence of physical genocide.

Feierstein (2014: 67) identified 'Genocide [a]s cold-blooded, rational policy, with social and political effects that go beyond the disappearance of the victims, no matter how many are killed'. His examination of the link between social policies as 'reorganising genocide' is significant to the XUAR as is his identification of social engineering and concentration camps as evidence of a genocide in progress. Campbell (2009: 150) also deliberately moves away from approaches to genocide that try to unpack the psychology of the act or equate the act with evil or madness, identifying that 'most genocide is also social control'. He too drew upon the broader definition of genocide by Lemkin, arguing the definition of genocide should engage more deeply with understandings of social life and social control, by which he means how people define and respond to behaviour perceived as deviant. Campbell defined genocide as involving mass killing that is organized, unilateral, and directed against ethnic groups. He identified that some degree of cultural distance is necessary in order for ethnic distinctions to exist. Moreover, he argued that most genocide is moralistic, identifying that perpetrated acts typically follow acts of resistance by the Other to acts of predatory behaviour from the perpetrator, with such resistance deemed 'deviant behaviour' and in need of correction via retaliation.

Campbell believed social structure is the key factor in whether or not a conflict becomes genocidal. Therefore, while ethnic conflict might exist, it is how people define and respond to deviant behaviour from an ethnic Other that sets the parameters for the scale of violence. He identified explanatory variables such as immobility, the extent of cultural distance between the groups, relational distance, the degree of intermarriage between groups, functional independence of groups, and inequality as being key determinants for the likelihood and severity of genocide in a conflict. Further, he warned that 'as states become more elevated in status – when they become more extensive – they become more violent' with totalitarian regimes more violent than authoritarian ones, and authoritarian regimes more violent than democracies (Campbell 2009: 167). Therefore, according to Campbell, genocide arises when 'conflict structures associated with extreme collective liability, extreme violence, organisation, and unilateralism' are present, along with killing of the Other being regarded a moralistic and appropriate response to perceived deviant behaviour (Campbell 2009: 167).

In their discussion of genocide prevention, MacGregor and Bowles (2012: 436) identified there is much scholarly attention focused on the 'downstream' factors that serve as the spark for imminent genocide because they tip 'an already troubled nation or region into committing atrocities'. While downstream factors are important, MacGregor and Bowles argued that the 'upstream' factors such as 'poverty, lack of freedom, education and health care, and environmental degradation and resource scarcity' require more focused analysis because it is these structural factors that contribute to the development of the 'troubled nation' in the first instance, making the state vulnerable to genocide (MacGregor and Bowles 2012: 436). Further, they asserted that because uneven economic growth can worsen tensions, the implementation of economic policies requires careful planning and should aim to increase trust between different groups, reduce intergroup tensions and conflict, and produce a more prosperous and peaceful society for all. Overall, these scholarly works demonstrate that physical genocide is the culmination of a genocidal process (creeping genocide) that can be years or decades in the making.

Background information on the XUAR and Kashgar

While the official view from Beijing (Information of the State Council 2003) is that the XUAR has been 'an inseparable part of the unitary multi-ethnic Chinese nation' since the Han dynasty (202 BC – AD 220), scholarly historical accounts demonstrate the region has been a site of many rulers, battles, invasions, and rebellions involving competing regional and extra-territorial forces.[4] Self-governance and localized resistance, therefore, has long been a feature of the region (Millward and Perdue 2004). Focusing on just the last century, a locally governed East Turkistan Republic operated within the region on two separate occasions, first centred in Kashgar (1933–34) and then in the northern districts of Ili, Tarbaghatai, and Altai (1944–49). There were also a number of autonomous Kazakh groups in some mountainous regions (Millward and Tursun 2004). For the Chinese Communist Party (CCP), these more recent periods of self-rule constitute deviant behaviour by the ethnic minorities of the XUAR. Periods of self-rule also complicate CCP versions of 'correct' regional history, something Millward (2009a: 71) identified as having backed Chinese historians and ideologues 'into a corner'. Officials situate the East Turkistan Republics as involving 'separatists and religious extremists' who they claim were influenced by 'the international trend of religious extremism and national chauvinism' (Information of the State Council 2003). Moreover, officials blame these deviant acts on 'outside forces' in this instance, the unnamed 'old colonialists' (Information of the State Council 2003). Hence, the CCP operates under a type of (Han) natural localness, whereby the region's indigenous ethnic minorities are viewed with suspicion, treated as outsiders, experience Othering, and are largely absent in official versions of regional history.

Located in the south-western corner of the XUAR, Kashgar is a gateway to Central Asia and the Middle East. It is closer to Islamabad, Kabul, Bishkek, Dushanbe, and Tashkent than it is to Beijing (see Figure 3.1). Once an important hub city on the old Silk Roads, Kashgar has a history of over 2,000 years (Millward 2007; Steenberg 2014). In the thirteenth century, Marco Polo visited Kashgar and he described it as 'the greatest and finest' town in the region, replete with 'beautiful gardens and vineyards, and fine estates', an area of cotton growing, and that it was a staging post where 'many merchants go forth about the world on trading journeys' (Polo and Da Pisa 2004). Islam arrived in Kashgar by 950 CE and following local conversion the architecture and layout of the city was influenced by the Islamic traditions. Rudelson (1997: 26) identified that 'Kashgar remains the Islamic heartland of XUAR' and the Uyghur Human Rights Project (2012: 3) highlighted that Uyghurs have long regarded Kashgar City as 'the spiritual heart of their culture' and the 'cradle of Uyghur civilisation that is fundamental to their Uyghur identity'. It was a city that held deep historical, cultural, and religious importance to the Uyghurs.

Between 1949 and the 1980s, Kashgar was virtually off-limits to most non-Chinese nationals due to domestic and international sensitivities related to the region (Dillon 2014). In addition, relatively few Han Chinese migrated to Kashgar during the same period. As a result, the cultural heritage of the city was largely quarantined from development projects, even as other parts of the XUAR and wider China underwent large-scale demolition of historic buildings and important sites of antiquity. Until 2008, Kashgar's Old City was a fusion of the Turkic and Islamic cultural traditions of the Uyghur people. Houses, mosques, and shops were typically mud-brick constructions, one or two storeys high, and set around an internal courtyard that provided relief from the heat and allowed Uyghur women to walk around unveiled.[5] George Michell et al. (2008: 79) declared Kashgar to be 'the best-preserved example of a traditional Islamic city to be found anywhere in Central Asia'. At this time, the local population was still predominantly Uyghur, numbering at 82.8 per cent of the total population of Kashgar, many of whom lived in the Old City (Steenberg 2014: 173).

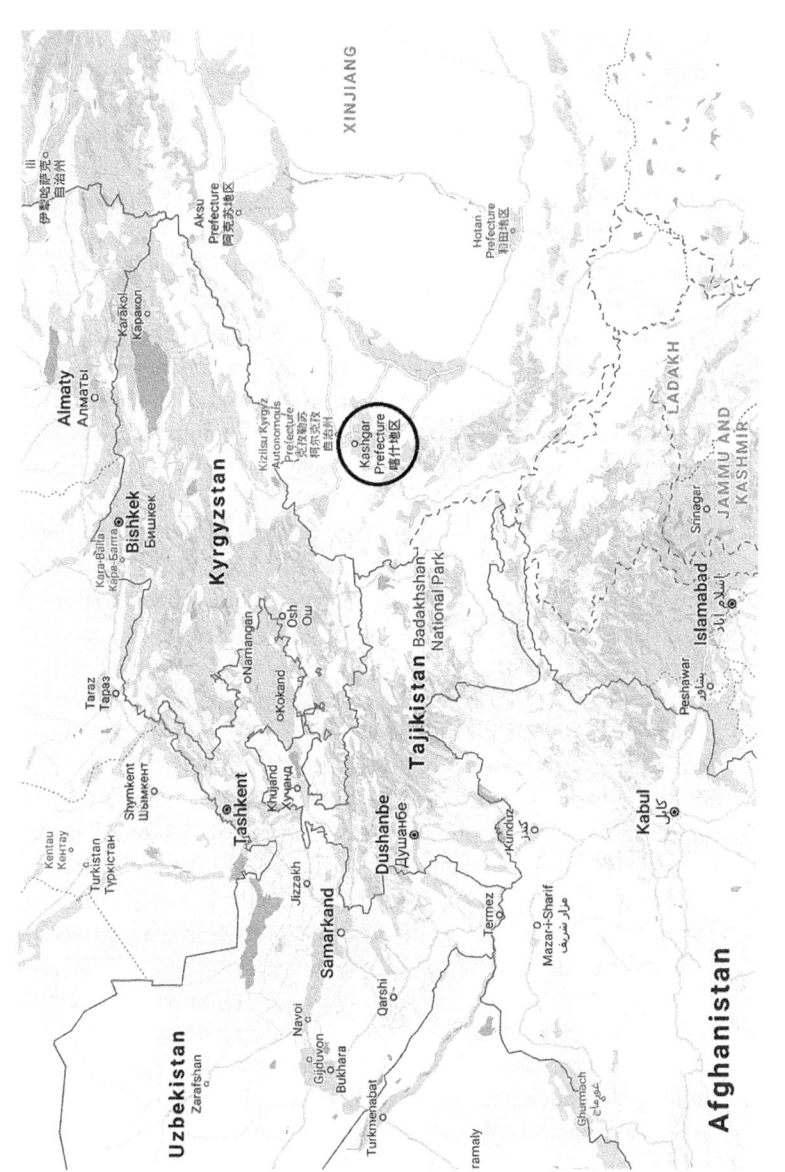

Figure 3.1 Map showing Kashgar (circled) and its proximity to Middle Eastern and Central Asian capital cities

The Old City under threat: Redevelopment and sinification

In the early 1980s, Kashgar was earmarked to become a Western version of Shenzhen, a future bustling metropolis and economic centre in China's remote western region. To achieve this goal, in May 2010 Beijing announced that Kashgar had been granted special economic zone (SEZ) status.[6] Due to its previous role as a hub city linking East China to Central Asia and the Middle East, the city became an integral part of China's unfolding Belt and Road Initiative (BRI).[7] The BRI built upon the previous Great Western Development Strategy (GWDS) or the 'Open Up the North' campaign, which had evolved gradually from the 1980s until its formal announcement as a policy strategy in 1999, and even the long-term and ongoing presence of the Xinjiang Production and Construction Corp (XPCC) demonstrates Beijing's attempts to occupy, control, and ultimately pacify this frontier region (Holbig 2004; Millward 2007).[8]

Beijing's economic aspirations for Kashgar are contained within the 大喀什 梦想 (Great Kashgar Dream) (Liu 2010). This dream incorporates rapid economic development and modernization of Kashgar, making it a 重心 (centre of gravity) in China's economic arteries that extend throughout Central Asia and the Middle East (Liu 2010). It also incorporates the more than doubling of Kashgar's population, hoped to eventually number over one million people, with more than 100 square kilometres of planned construction (Liu 2010). Great Kashgar also incorporates the "九大基地"和"一个中心城市" (the 'nine major bases' and 'one central city') approach, with Kashgar the central city and the nine major bases including textiles; a large-scale metallurgical industrial base; a petrochemical base; a processing base for agricultural and sideline products; an export commodity processing and manufacturing base for neighbouring countries; a halal food production and supply base for Muslim countries; a building materials base for neighbouring countries; a trade logistics base; as well as Kashgar being an international tourist destination (Liu 2010). These plans for rapid and expanded development for Kashgar build on earlier small-scale redevelopments of Kasghar city that began in 2000, when Kashgar's quarantine from modernization abruptly ended.

According to Liu and Yuan (2019), the first significant redevelopment of Kashgar occurred between 2000 and 2006. This initial redevelopment involved the expansion of the square in front of Id Kah Mosque, during which shops and some 5,000 households near the mosque were demolished (Millward 2007: 305). The purpose of this redevelopment was to make Kashgar more appealing and user-friendly for visiting tourists (with tourism constituting one of the nine bases for the Great Kashgar Dream).[9] Liu and Yuan (2019) argued the state planned to use Kashgar's Old City as a tool for ethnic integration and stability maintenance. Despite its impacts on affected Uyghurs, and the layout of the Id Kah Mosque neighbourhood, the scope of the first programme was fairly limited compared to the demolition and redevelopment undertaken as part of the KDHRP.

In March 2009, local authorities launched the KDHRP. Since its inception, this programme has seen a gradual relocation of an estimated 220,000 Uyghurs from their homes in the Old City to government apartment buildings on the outskirts of Kashgar (Zhang 2011; Skinner 2016). An estimated 65,000 homes and an undetermined number of mosques across the Old City have been demolished in the process (Zhang 2011; Skinner 2016). When referring to the goals of the KDHRP, authorities have described it as '社会工程' (social engineering), also identifying that '老城改造，不过是这个民族重生的起点' (the transformation of the Old City is just the starting point for the *rebirth* of this [Uyghur] nation) (Zhang 2011, emphasis added). According to Feierstein (2014: 1), social engineering is 'an important but relatively neglected aspect of genocidal processes', and so the social engineering aspects of the KDHRP command attention. Hitherto, much of the concern and criticism of the KDHRP (and earlier redevelopment) have centred upon the resultant heritage destruction rather than recognition of how this project of social engineering was a significant building block in China's creeping genocide against the Uyghurs.

In 2004, a United Nations Educational, Scientific and Cultural Organization (UNESCO) mission went to China to identify suitable Silk Road sites for nomination for heritage protection. In considering Kashgar, the UNESCO mission concluded that Kashgar 'still has a significant and relatively large, authentic core', making it a suitable site for nomination (Feng and Van Oers 2004: 24). However, they warned that without adopting a suitable Conservation Management Plan, infrastructural interventions proposed by the Kashgar Municipal Government 'would severely fragment the remaining authentic heart of this ancient city of mud brick houses and narrow alleyways. They also warned this would create serious difficulties in identifying a site of proper proportions with related authenticity issues that would merit inscription on the World Heritage List' (Feng and Van Oers 2004: 25). The UNESCO mission urged caution and recommended further consultations be undertaken with the Municipal Government to prevent such a damaging outcome.

Di Castro, a member of the Monash Asia Institute delegation that conducted field research in the region in 2005, reached similar conclusions about Old Kashgar. He stated: 'the study of the Kashgar oasis, therefore, *stands in urgent need of attention* – especially because the archaeological sites in this area may shed light on the earliest arrival of Buddhist and Islamic Cultures in Western China' (Di Castro 2008: 258, emphasis added). Di Castro valued the Kashgar oasis because of its intact nature and due to the many sites of antiquity dotted throughout the city. Vicziany, another member of the Monash Asia Institute team, identified the arbitrary nature of demolitions already taking place. One such demolition was only uncovered when the curator of the Xinjiang Silk Road Museum invited the Monash team to visit one of the *Tim* watchtowers located in Kashgar city, only to realize it had been demolished without his knowledge. According to Vicziany (2005: 15), 'He declared with great consternation that the *Tim* had suddenly and inexplicably been demolished during the last year. It was shocking to realise that whatever demolition was taking place, was occurring without the knowledge of the curator charged with the responsibility of developing the local museum as a major tourist destination.' In another example, sections of the Old City walls were bulldozed and the earth from the wall was loaded into a nearby truck. Again, the curator had not been consulted and there had been no archaeological surveying of the site prior to demolition (Vicziany 2005: 15). When China submitted its list of potential Silk Road heritage sites, the only site in Kashgar city nominated was the Mehmud Qeshqeri Tomb (State Administration of Cultural Heritage 2008). The Old City was not included on the list.

In June 2009, the International Council on Monuments and Sites (ICOMOS) and International Scientific Committee on Earthen Architectural Heritage (ISCEAH) wrote an open letter to the Chinese government offering their assistance in identifying viable alternatives to the KDHRP. They urged authorities to 'preserve the heritage and improve living conditions without resorting to complete rebuilding', noting similar conservation success in Shibam, Yemen (ICOMOS-ISCEAH 2009: 49).[10] The president of the ICOMOS, Gustavo Araoz, also wrote in June 2009 to the president of the ICOMOS in China, Tong Mingkang, expressing his concerns over past and planned demolition of the Old City. He stated that '[n]ews of the demolition of the old city of Kashgar is in and of itself highly worrisome' and he urged that if the 'renovation' was related to 'issues of fire and earthquake safety ... *various solutions have been effectively implemented in other historic settings throughout the world*' (ICOMOS-ISCEAH 2009: 50–51, emphasis added). In Tong's response to Araoz's letter, dated August 2009, he situated the site as having only been built in 1902, following a severe earthquake in the region that he claimed had left Kashgar in 'ruins' (ICOMOS-ISCEAH 2009: 51). Hence, Uyghur accounts of the ages of their homes were disregarded by the Municipal Government.

While in 1902, a sizeable earthquake hit the region, killing approximately 600 people, it was not Kashgar that was left in ruins. Instead, it was the quake's epicentre, the village of Artush (45 kilometres north of Kashgar), and surrounding villages that were destroyed (*New Zealand Herald* 1902; Merzbacher 1905; Skrine and Nightingale 1973). The National Oceanic and Atmospheric Administration (NOAA) (n.d.) identified that the 22 August 1902 Artush earthquake was at a magnitude of 7.7 and that in Karajul, Ahu, Songtake, Artux (Artush), Small Artux (Artush), and Tijiankule 'all earth-timber structure houses collapsed'. In its discussion of specific damage to Kashgar, the NOAA identified some damage, but not widespread destruction as is suggested in Tong's letter. The NOAA reported 'Fissures occurred at the north gate and its vicinity of Kashi [Kashgar] city. Some walls at the north city gate and a tower (upper part) in a mosque collapsed. Historic sites such as Xiangfei Tomb partly collapsed or cracked. A number of civilian houses toppled. About 50 persons were killed or injured' (National Oceanic and Atmospheric Administration n.d.). Gottfried Merzbacher, the German geographer, explorer, and mountaineer, who was on expedition in the region at the time, also confirmed that the location of the most serious damage resulting from the earthquake was not in Kashgar city. Upon arriving in Artush, his personal account stated: 'In August 1902, not long before our arrival [18 October 1902], earthquakes had almost utterly ruined both this [Artush village] and the other group, collectively known as Altyn-Artysh, which lies farther east of the southern border of the tertiary range, and was likewise visited by us. These places, now lying in ruins, presented a sad spectacle' (Merzbacher 1905: 103). Merzbacher also wrote that his team observed the 'almost complete destruction of from ten to twelve populous villages' before discussing his arrival in Kashgar city. Regarding Kashgar he stated that the 'earthquake waves ... [had] made themselves felt even in the city of Kashgar and its environs' and reported that his team 'took up its winter quarters' in Kashgar and experienced several aftershocks (Merzbacher 1905: 103). However, at no point does Merzbacher describe a scene of destruction in Kashgar that would support Tong's claim that Kashgar city had also been 'ruined' by the 1902 earthquake, with all homes destroyed.

Therefore, official claims that all the homes in Kashgar were destroyed by the 1902 earthquake, thereby diminishing their antiquity and heritage value, appear erroneous. Moreover, these sources lend support to Uyghur accounts of the age of their Old City homes, which range from over 150 years to over 400 years. Tong's claim in his reply to Araoz that planning for the renovation was 'based on residents' opinions and experts' studies' is also problematic, a point this chapter will return to shortly (ICOMOS-ISCEAH 2009: 51). He also rejected Araoz's suggestion that the Old City be included in World Heritage nomination. Finally, Tong's assessment of the buildings being 'old and dilapidated' further implied the buildings were not worthy of conservation (ICOMOS-ISCEAH 2009: 51).

KDHRP: Social engineering and creeping genocide

Feierstein (2014: 12) has argued that 'the distinguishing features of modern genocide are the ways in which it is legitimized as well as its consequences not only for the targeted groups but also for the perpetrators, the witnesses, and society as a whole'. Beijing has long considered the XUAR and the Uyghurs as 'backwards', a dehumanizing term and a significant reflection of the social geometry of the region where the Han are advanced and superior ('big brothers') while the Uyghurs are backwards and inferior ('little brothers'). It has also been

The Kashgar Dangerous House Reform Programme

used to legitimize state violence against Uyghurs throughout PRC history. During the Great Leap Forward (GLF), which began in 1958, ethnicity and religion were singled out as both 'obstacles to progress' and 'backwards custom' (Bovingdon 2004: 19). During the Cultural Revolution (CR), any cultures that did not meet CCP parameters for correct Chinese culture, were again identified across China as being backwards and a danger to the state. Minority nationalities were again subjected to widespread cultural and religious insults and human rights abuses (Millward 2007). In the XUAR, this led to targeted ethnic violence by predominantly Han cadres and activists against the minority nationalities and further demonstrated the depth of the cultural divide between Han and Uyghur. Violent acts included the large-scale destruction of mosques, which in Kashgar District went from approximately 5,500 in 1966 to just 392 by the early 1970s, Qur'ans were burnt, ethnic dress was banned, women's long hair was cut off, Imams and Muslim intellectuals were publicly humiliated, the remaining mosques, mazars (shrines), and madrasas (educational institutions) were closed and desecrated, and many Uyghurs, including Imams, were forced to do things that were religiously prohibited such as raising pigs. Some mosques were even converted into pigsties (Bovingdon 2004; Millward 2007). Bovingdon concluded that like the GLF, the CR was another 'attempt to engineer rapid and thorough assimilation', but it also demonstrated the extreme efforts individual and state actors have deployed to 'correct' the 'deviant' and 'backwards' Uyghur Others in every facet of their social, cultural, and religious life through a process of social engineering (Bovingdon 2004: 20). To consider the Old City as backwards is to continue a long pattern of state-legitimized repression.

In 2009, *The New York Times* reported that at least one expert had voiced concerns over the plans to demolish Kashgar's Old City. Wu Lili, the managing director of the Beijing Cultural Protection Centre, indicated his complete disagreement with the plan, also identifying its likely impact on affected Uyghurs. He stated: 'From a cultural and historical perspective, this plan of theirs is stupid. From the perspective of the locals [Uyghurs], it's cruel' (cited in Wines 2009). Another expert, a professor of regional planning from the Beijing Normal University, who had conducted field research in Kashgar in 2008, was similarly critical of the proposed demolition plans for the Old City.

He recognized the unique quality of the Old City's historic, raw-earth buildings and argued:

> The buildings are very scientific. They are warm in winter and cold in summer. The technology used saves material and is environmentally protective ... The old town also reflects the Muslim culture of the Uighurs very well – it has the original taste and flavor without any changes. Here, *Uighur culture is attached to those raw earth buildings. If they are torn down, the affiliated culture will be destroyed.* (Cited in Fan 2009, emphasis added)

In their responses, Wu Lili and Wu Dianting recognized both the tangible loss of heritage and the cultural loss Uyghurs would experience. As Davidson (2012) identified, one method of cultural genocide is the purposeful destruction of the out-group culture in order to weaken them, which allows such groups to be dominated. Such purposeful destruction is often rationalized via the opinions of experts, which, as Davidson warned, are frequently based on stereotypes and manipulated information. Tong's cited experts, who supported the purposeful destruction of the Old City, fit such a categorization. More independent views, such as those expressed above by Lili and Dianting, demonstrate more considered approaches that do not seek purposeful destruction of the out-group culture. However, these views were overlooked in the process.

By 2009, concerns over the KDHRP were being voiced by affected Uyghurs who already identified both cultural loss and the elements of assimilation and social control it entailed. According to journalist Maureen Fan, one resident stated: 'They want us to live like Chinese people but we will never agree. If we move into the government apartments, there are no courtyards and no sun. Women will need to cover up to go outside and we will have to spend money to finish decorating our rooms. This is our land. We have not bought it from the government' (cited in Fan 2009).[11] Another journalist, Stephen McDonell, found similar views expressed by Uyghurs he interviewed. They were distrustful of government intentions, but felt they had little choice in the matter. One woman concluded: 'We don't want to move but if the government forces us, we don't have any option' (cited in ABC 2009). Another man interviewed expressed similar thoughts. He stated: 'If the government gives me money, I will go. Everybody is unhappy about this, but government is government, we can do nothing' (cited in Fan 2009). To persuade the Uyghurs to comply with the KDHRP and to move without resistance, nightly television propaganda showed a stream of compliant ('good') Uyghurs, packing their belongings and moving out of the Old City.

For Uyghurs who moved during the earliest stages of the KDHRP, the impact of the social and cultural disruptions was apparent in their responses to journalists. In particular, the disruptions relocation had caused their community and neighbourly connections were intense. One man stated: 'Our lives in Kashgar city were good. With our neighbours, we sent regards to each other. We cried the deaths of our relatives together. We blessed each other at weddings but here we don't know each other' (cited in Fan 2009). According to Feierstein (2014: 1), social engineering 'creates, destroys, or reorganizes relationships within a given society' so these accounts demonstrate the unfolding reorganizing genocide resulting from the mass relocation of Uyghurs. The KDHRP constituted social engineering on a massive scale.

One woman who had moved from the Old City into one of the apartment blocks, now resigned to her fate, told McDonell: 'It's no use getting angry now. We'll just make ourselves sick if we worry too much. Of course, if we were allowed to move back to our old houses … it would be good – but this is not going to happen. We're living here now. Maybe it will get better' (cited in ABC 2009). Not only have Uyghurs lost their generational homes, but also the social connections and sense of community that went alongside life in the Old City.[12] The loss of cultural inheritance has likewise been significant. For Uyghurs like Hajji and his wife, living in the Old City provided them with a guaranteed home for themselves and their children. In an interview with journalist Michael Wines, the couple raised concerns about the likely lifespan of the government apartment they had been allocated. They stated their previous home in the Old City was dated at around 500 years, but the lifespan of their new apartment was likely to be just fifty to seventy years (Wines 2009). They were deeply concerned by the inadequate inheritance their children would likely receive from them (Wines 2009). Moreover, traditional Uyghur neighbourhoods have been supplanted by high-rise apartment blocks 'resonant of eastern China' (Uyghur Human Rights Project 2012: 3). Given Kashgar was a source of both cultural and nationalistic pride for the Uyghurs, and an anathema to the PRC, this has been an all-encompassing and purposeful destruction of Uyghur social and cultural institutions, seeking to weaken Uyghurs both individually and collectively.[13]

Another outcome of the KDHRP is that the panoramic vista of Old Kashgar has been forever changed and is now sinified. Countless urban structures across the city have been destroyed, alongside the 'neighbourhoods that have perpetuated Uyghur customs for generations in Kashgar' (Uyghur Human Rights Project 2012: 55). Most households were multigenerational, an important feature of Uyghur society (Wines 2009). Hence, Uyghur homes in the Old City provided more than just housing. They were an important cultural asset necessary for the continuation of Uyghur community and religious life, society, and identity. The age of the buildings also provided an important connection between past and present. When accessing sites of the Old City undergoing demolition in 2012, I observed many visible reminders of the rich culture and structures that have been lost in this process. Beautiful wall panels alluded to the former glory of building interiors and large, deserted, dusty spaces identified the locations of Old City neighbourhoods now razed to the ground. The importance of Islam within the community was also visible when orienting oneself to the layout of the Old City, as Old Kashgar fanned out from Id Kah Mosque, the main mosque in the city. Uyghurs relocated to the government apartments have now been dislocated from Id Kah Mosque, thereby affecting their religious life and practices (Uyghur Human Rights Project 2012: 56).

Some parts of the demolished Old City have been reconstructed in a neo-traditional style, which has an inauthentic 'theme-park' feel.[14] These officially sanctioned buildings and neighbourhoods are a construct of the PRC, serving the purpose of the state as a tourist drawcard (see Figure 3.2). While Steenberg (2014: 181) found that some Kashgar residents consider the new buildings 'aesthetically *acceptable*', he identified a key problem with New-Old Kashgar was that Uyghurs who wanted to return to rebuild sections of the Old City have been priced out of the market and neighbourhood plots had been sold to an investor from Zhejiang. Therefore, most of the 220,000 displaced Old City residents will not be in a financial position to return, resulting in a successful gentrification of the inner sections of Kashgar city (Steenberg 2014: 181). New-Old Kashgar also has

Figure 3.2 New-Old Kashgar

much wider roadways than the Old City, more easily accessible to large vehicles, and the PRC flag is on high display. The installation of numerous security cameras has also allowed surveillance of residents.[15] McDonell observed similar surveillance capacities in the government apartments (ABC 2009). This level of surveillance was not a feature of the Old City, nor would it have been easily achieved.

Surveillance efforts across the XUAR have pushed boundaries with high-tech strategies including face and voice recognition, iris scanners, DNA sampling, and 3D identification imagery of Uyghurs (Chin and Bürge 2017). These measures, or digital authoritarianism, control the movement of people at train stations and on roads in and out of locales, and track the activities of people in banks, shopping centres, hotels, and at petrol stations (Chin and Bürge 2017). The appointment of Chen Quanguo as XUAR Party Chief has led to this increase in surveillance and control across the region. His previous appointment was in the Tibet Autonomous Region (TAR), where he increased repression through similar tight controls and surveillance of Tibetans. There have been more than 7,000 newly built police stations across the XUAR under Chen's leadership and surveillance spending has had a significant boost (Feng 2018). In 2015, Beijing spent US$27 million for the whole year on surveillance in the XUAR but in the first quarter of 2017 alone, surveillance spending was just over US$1 billion (Chin and Bürge 2017). Total surveillance spending across the XUAR for 2017 was US$9.1 billion (mainly on technology-based surveillance), which was an increase of 92 per cent from the previous year's total (Shichor 2019). There are now over 35,000 cameras monitoring mosques, schools, and streets all across the XUAR. In addition, part of this spending was used to install surveillance systems within the region's increasing number of concentration camps. Kashgar has been a key target for digital authoritarianism (Cave *et al.* 2019). This has made Kashgar a special surveillance zone alongside its status as a special economic zone.

Islamophobia, thought collectives, and the ongoing dehumanization of the Uyghurs

As Campbell (2009) identified, state attempts at social control intensifies after the oppressed Other engages in acts of resistance to the predatory behaviour of the dominant group. Following the onset of the KDHRP, Kashgar prefecture experienced increased violence. Most notable was the 2014 stabbing murder of the Imam of Id Kah Mosque who was alleged to have been 'pro-China' (Grammaticas 2014). The Imam's murder followed deadly attacks in Kashgar just days earlier, which reportedly led to the deaths of 'dozens' of Han and Uyghur civilians (Grammaticas 2014). Between 2013 and 2014, more people died as a result of violent incidents in Kashgar prefecture than any other location in the XUAR with 327 fatalities recorded during this short time period (Uyghur Human Rights Project 2015: 2). The increasing repression experienced in Kashgar appears to have fuelled local grievances and resistance, and was a trigger for violent incidents.

Roberts (2018) identified the onset of the Global War on Terror (GWOT) as having significantly influenced Beijing's contemporary thought collective towards the Uyghurs. Since its onset, Uyghurs have been recast as a terrorist collective with a guilty-until-proven-innocent status. Moreover, it has been used by the CCP to position the Uyghurs 'as a biological threat to the social order, quarantined so as to not infect the population of the country as a whole' (Roberts 2018: 234). Furthermore, Beijing now recasts any act of grievance or resistance by the Uyghurs as an 'act of terror', closing avenues for Uyghurs to air legitimate grievances (Roberts 2018: 234). This has led to ongoing dehumanization of the Muslim minorities, and Uyghurs in particular, who are automatically labelled as terrorists and committed acts are framed as a deviant behaviour by an enemy culture, rather than being recognized as the outcome of decades of bad government policies and increasing repression. This has resulted in legitimate Uyghur grievances going unresolved. Moreover, rising Islamophobia by Beijing has allowed the further penetration by the state into religious affairs across China. In the XUAR, this form of social control is achieved via the monitoring and control of mosques, direct state involvement in the approval process for Imams, the issuing of state-sanctioned Qur'ans, and the CCP has attempted to transform religious teachings and belief into versions of the faith that project the CCP worldview (Zhou 2019).

While the GWOT has resulted in a rapid rise of Islamophobia globally, in China, Islamophobia has seen prior distinctions between 'good' and 'bad' Uyghurs disappear and the CCP now identifies religion (Islam) as an aggressor.[16] It has also legitimized state violence against Uyghurs among individuals and state actors. This domain knowledge now also legitimizes the widespread arbitrary detention of the Muslim minorities, via pre-emptive policing as described by Smith Finley (2018: 86). She argued pre-emptive policing had become 'increasingly indiscriminate' post-2001, was particularly pronounced following the July unrest in Urumqi in 2009, and has involved mass round-ups of Uyghurs into arbitrary detention (Smith Finley 2018: 86).[17] Smith Finley also argued pre-emptive policing has conflated Uyghur culture and Islamic identity with separatism and terrorism, resulting in an 'over-reaction' by the state to legitimate acts of grievance and a framing of all Uyghurs as potential separatists and terrorists, thereby dehumanizing Uyghurs (Smith Finley 2018: 86). In his declaration of a 'People's War on Terror', Xi Jinping declared terrorists should become 'like rats scurrying across a street, with everybody shouting "beat them"' (cited in Clarke 2014; Wan 2014). As identified by Feierstein (2014: 60, emphasis in the original), 'reorganizing genocide … aims to destroy both materially and symbolically "the enemy within". The Others to be exterminated are … construed as both exotic and inferior. … the Others have to be eliminated because they are *dangerous*'. As already indicated, the domain knowledge of the Chinese state is that Uyghurs are dangerous, an enemy within, and that they are inferior to their Han counterparts.

Zenz (2019: 122) has argued Beijing now sees large-scale detention as the 'cure' for deviant behaviour by Uyghurs. Remembering Campbell (2009) identified that social control measures enacted by genocidal states were centred upon concepts such as the collective liability of the Other, and that there is a perceived need for a moral and responsible state response to deviant behaviour, the findings by Zenz are worrisome. Additionally, Feierstein (2014: 6) has argued that in examinations of the Nazi Genocide, given the first concentration camps in Germany were opened in 1933 when the Nazi Party came to power 'the role played by concentration camps as stepping-stones to genocide' has not received 'adequate' attention by historians. Therefore, the concentration camps in the XUAR further signal the escalation of the genocidal process. A Han official included in Zenz's analysis attempted to rationalize the concentration camps by explaining their role in the re-education of Uyghurs. He stated: 'You can't uproot all the weeds hidden among the crops. … You need to spray chemicals to kill them all. … Re-educating these people is like spraying chemicals on the crops, that is why it is a general re-education, not limited to a few people' (cited in Zenz 2019: 122). His further dehumanization of the Uyghurs, identifying them as weeds that need to be sprayed, and his belief that collective punishment and mass detention of the Uyghur people is warranted, is deeply alarming. Concentration camps are one of a range of structural elements of genocide aimed at 'destroying and reorganising social relations' (Feierstein 2014: 46–48). Their use in the XUAR must be recognized as part of a genocidal process.

Another element of the KDHRP and Beijing's Great Kashgar Dream was the 'zero-24' policy. During its initial evaluation phase, metal signs were put on the doors of individual homes providing important signals to local authorities about the inhabitants. One such sign indicated the presence of a zero-employment family, which meant that no family member in that household had employment. The 'zero-24' policy sought to put at least one family member of the household into employment within twenty-four hours (Zhang 2011; Chaudhuri 2018). While not unique to the XUAR, this strategy may have paved the way for the proliferation of unfree or forced labour of Uyghurs across the XUAR and mainland China due to its coercive top-down approach to connecting Uyghurs to employment. Thereby, it too should be recognized as part of the genocidal process. Sectors using unfree Uyghur labour are linked to the nine industrial bases identified as part of the Great Kashgar Dream. Forced Uyghur labour has been linked to companies such as 'Apple, BMW, Gap, Huawei, Nike, Samsung, Sony and Volkswagen' (Xu *et al.* 2020: 3). Forced labourers in these factories live under constant surveillance in segregated dormitories, they are prevented from enacting their religious faith, they are required to attend Mandarin and ideological instruction outside of work hours, and they are assigned minders, meaning freedom of movement is severely constrained (Xu *et al.* 2020: 3). Their labour has increasingly become part of the global supply chain. Hence, proliferation of the concentration camps across the XUAR, many of which are co-located with factories, demonstrates they are integral to the Great Kashgar Dream and the nine bases approach. However, given the importance of the factories to global corporations state and non-state actors outside of the PRC can play a critical role in stopping this particular element of the creeping genocide taking place inside of the XUAR.[18]

Conclusion

Genocide scholars are in agreement that there is a process to genocide and there are warning signs. Socio-economic cleavage, heightened human insecurity of a targeted group, and cultural distance between the perpetrating and the victim group all increase the risk of physical genocide breaking out. Levine warned that, just like war, states make a calculated decision to commit genocide. For the PRC, the Muslim minorities constitute a 'problem' population and they have experienced increased repression since the mid-1990s. Before the commencement of the KDHRP, Kashgar was a largely intact cultural asset of the Uyghurs and a site of immense cultural heritage and antiquity. It showcased the fusion of Turkic and Islamic influences that make up Uyghur culture. The existence of such a symbol of the Uyghur periphery, an

Islamic symbol at that, was problematic to the non-Uyghur, largely non-Islamic core of mainland China.

There are many factors inside of the XUAR that warrant concern: increased authoritarianism; significant cultural distance between Han and Uyghur; targeted planning by Beijing to disintegrate political and social institutions of the Uyghurs; purposeful destruction of out-group culture; attempts to weaken Uyghurs in the process of continued conquest and domination; expert opinions being shaped around stereotypes and manipulated information; artificial views of an entire community of people, forming a thought collective; and an increasingly entrenched belief in the morally correct, justified, and necessary correction of behaviour exhibited by a perceived inferior group determined to be deviant. All indicate the presence of a creeping genocide inside of the XUAR, and the cultural genocide and social engineering enacted via the KDHRP are crucial building blocks in a pattern of genocide. This unfolding genocide also demonstrates the need for the United Nations definition of genocide to be expanded, reflecting the original parameters proposed by Raphael Lemkin, so that the earliest stages of the genocidal process are more easily recognized as such, thereby halting its progression.

Notes

1 While Beijing has stated the centres are for 'vocational training', the Congressional-Executive Commission on China (2018) characterized them as 'political re-education' centres, citing evidence of multiple human rights violations including sleep deprivation, inadequate clothing for conditions, and other forms of abuse taking place in the centres. It is estimated that over 100 Uyghur intellectuals, including university professors, writers, poets, and journalists, are among those incarcerated in such centres, calling into serious question Beijing's claim that the centres seek to foster employment opportunities for low socio-economic status Uyghurs. Moreover, the CECC report identified detention-related deaths and even the incarceration of citizens from other states in such centres, predominantly citizens of Kazakhstan. In 2018, Australia's Department of Foreign Affairs and Trade confirmed Australian citizens have been incarcerated in the centres while visiting relatives in the XUAR (Robertson and Dziedzic 2018). There are also reports that Uyghur children have

been sent to orphanages, both in the XUAR and in the eastern parts of China, due to their status as a 'double-detained family', meaning both parents have been incarcerated in the centres (Radio Free Asia 2017).
2 Scholarship drawing attention to other programmes and policies that constitute creeping genocide throughout the region include Clarke (2015), Roberts (2018), Smith Finley (2018), and Zenz (2019).
3 See also Tatz (1997).
4 See, for example, Clarke (2007), Dillon (2004), and Millward (2007, 2009b).
5 Due to its authentic nature and layout, in 2006 the Old City was selected as a filming location for *The Kite Runner*, a movie set in 1970s Afghanistan. See Holdstock (2015).
6 'Special economic zones' in China enjoy economic benefits to promote economic activity and direct investment into the zone.
7 See Hayes (2020).
8 The XPCC has a dual role in Xinjiang, best articulated by Zhang Qinli, who was XPCC commander in 2004. He stated: '[i]n peacetime the farming role becomes more important, and in times of tension the security role is more important. These two roles are inseparable' (cited in Kerr and Swinton 2008: 120). The presence of the XPCC in Xinjiang ensures that separatism is not achievable, while their farming role sees them 'opening up the west' for Han economic gain.
9 This redevelopment involved the forcible removal of some affected residents from the Old City, who were not adequately compensated. See Zhang (2011).
10 The Old Walled City of Shibam in Yemen is protected under the Antiquities Law of 1997 and Building Law of 2002. The General Organization for the Preservation of Historic Cities in Yemen manages its preservation. Since 2000, 98 per cent of the traditional homes in Shibam have been documented and more than 60 per cent have been rehabilitated (UNESCO World Heritage Centre 2017).
11 The interviews conducted by Maureen Fan, Stephen McDonell, and Michael Wines occurred when the KDHRP was first enacted and when affected Uyghurs more openly voiced their opposition. Where relevant, I have drawn on their published interview data in order to provide some scope for the Uyghur voice in this research. My own field research was primarily participant observation in order to avoid any potential endangerment of Uyghurs. Interviews were not conducted. My research has been influenced, however, by itinerant ethnography methods employed during the field research. This methodology provides scope for everyday conversations with local Uyghurs to become a source of more general information about space and place inside of Xinjiang. Itinerant ethnography was used by

Louisa Schein during her field research in minority nationality regions in southern China. See Schein (2003: 28).

12   When I visited Kashgar in 2012, even during the most general of conversations, Uyghurs would invariably say to me at some point: 'If only you had come to our city a couple of years ago, you would have been able to see our beautiful Old City. It was not modern like this. Those buildings [action: pointing at the modern high-rise buildings] didn't exist.' This was a persistent sentiment and while it was not necessarily critical of the modernization programme, it reflected a genuine remorse for what had been lost and a strong sense of nostalgia for the Old City's past glory.

13   Similar arguments can also be made with regards to the destruction of Lhasa in Tibet, which Davidson (2012) identified as an act of cultural genocide.

14   'New-Old Kashgar' is a term used by the author to refer specifically to the newly rebuilt areas of the city constructed in the neo-traditional style of the Old City.

15   Field research observations, 6–11 September 2012.

16   Islamophobia is not limited to China. For accounts of the rise of Islamophobia in the Australian context, see Aly (2012), Brown (2012), and Mansouri (2013).

17   The CCP viewed the Urumqi unrest in 2009 as an act of terror. However, the violence occurred due to heavy-handedness by the police against protesting Uyghurs. Their protests centred on perceived government inaction over the beating murders of Uyghur factory workers by ethnic Han co-workers in a toy factory in Shaoguan. The Urumqi unrest, or 5/7 incident, led to officials adopting a viewpoint that previous attempts at moderating Islam in the XUAR have failed. It also deepened the mistrust between ethnic Han and Uyghurs, and it magnified the growing domain knowledge among Han Chinese of a collective guilt among all Uyghurs. Both Roberts (2018) and Smith Finley (2018) identified the Urumqi riots as a watershed moment for Han–Uyghur relations and Uyghur–state relations.

18   See full list of recommendations for foreign governments and consumers and civil society groups in Xu *et al.* (2020: 29–30).

References

ABC (2009). 'The Uighur Dilemma', *Foreign Correspondent*, television programme, 28 July.

Aly, Anne (2012). 'Fear Online: Seeking Sanctuary in Online Forums', in Anna Hayes and Robert Mason (eds), *Cultures in Refuge: Seeking Sanctuary in Modern Australia* (Farnham: Ashgate), 163–178.

Bovingdon, Gardner (2004). 'Autonomy in Xinjiang Uyghur Autonomous Region: Han Nationalist Imperatives and Uyghur Discontent', *Policy Studies* 11 (Washington, DC: East-West Center).

Brown, Malcolm (2012). 'Institutional Islamophobia in the Cases of Ahmed Zaoui and Mohamed Haneef', in Anna Hayes and Robert Mason (eds), *Cultures in Refuge: Seeking Sanctuary in Modern Australia* (Farnham: Ashgate), 149–161.

Campbell, Bradley (2009). 'Genocide as Social Control', *Sociological Theory* 27 (2), 150–152.

Cave, Danielle, Samantha Hoffman, Alex Joske et al. (2019). 'Mapping China's Technology Giants' (Canberra: Australian Strategic Policy Institute), www.aspi.org.au/report/mapping-chinas-tech-giants (accessed 20 January 2020).

Chaudhuri, Debasisch (2018). *Xinjiang and the Chinese State: Violence in the Reform Era* (Oxon: Routledge).

Chin, Josh, and Clément Bürge (2017). 'Twelve Days in Xinjiang: How China's Surveillance State Overwhelms Daily Life', *Wall Street Journal*, 19 December, www.wsj.com/articles/twelve-days-in-xinjiang-how-chinas-surveillance-state-overwhelms-daily-life-1513700355 (accessed 30 March 2019).

Clarke, Michael (2007). 'The Problematic Progress of "Integration" in the Chinese State's Approach to XUAR, 1759–2005', *Asian Ethnicity* 8 (3), 261–289.

Clarke, Michael (2014). 'Xinjiang and Terrorism (Part 2): The New Threat of ISIS', *The Interpreter*, 3 October, www.lowyinstitute.org/the-interpreter/xinjiang-and-terrorism-part-2-new-threat-isis (accessed 25 March 2020).

Clarke, Michael (2015). 'China and the Uyghurs: The "Palestinization" of Xinjiang?', *Middle East Policy* 22 (3), 127–146.

Congressional-Executive Commission on China (2018). *Annual Report 2018*, 10 October, www.cecc.gov/sites/chinacommission.house.gov/files/Annual%20Report%202018.pdf (accessed 24 January 2019).

Davidson, Lawrence (2012). *Cultural Genocide* (London: Rutgers University Press).

Di Castro, Angelo Andrea (2008). 'The Mori Tim Stupa Complex in the Kashgar Oasis', *East and West* 58 (1), 257–281.

Dillon, Michael (2004). *Xinjiang Uyghur Autonomous Region: China's Muslim Far Northwest* (New York: Routledge).

Dillon, Michael (2014). *Xinjiang Uyghur Autonomous Region and the Expansion of Chinese Communist Power: Kashgar in the Early Twentieth Century* (Oxon: Routledge).

Fan, Maureen (2009). 'An Ancient Culture, Bulldozed Away', *Washington Post*, 24 March, www.washingtonpost.com/wp-dyn/content/article/2009/03/23/AR2009032302935.html (accessed 13 August 2016).

Feierstein, Daniel (2014). *Genocide as Social Practice: Reorganizing Society under the Nazis and Argentina's Military Juntas*, trans. Douglas Andrew Town (New Jersey: Rutgers University Press).

Feng, Emily (2018). 'Security Spending Ramped Up in China's Restive Xinjiang Region', *Financial Times*, 13 March, www.ft.com/content/aa4465aa-2349-11e8-ae48-60d3531b7d11 (accessed 24 January 2019).

Feng, Jin, and Ron Van Oers (2004). *The Chinese Silk Road as World Cultural Heritage Route: A Systematic Approach towards Identification and Nomination*, United Nations Educational, Scientific and Cultural Organization, Paris, May, http://unesdoc.unesco.org/images/0013/001381/138161eo.pdf (accessed 1 April 2017).

Grammaticas, Damien (2014). 'Imam of China's Largest Mosque Killed in XUAR', BBC News, 31 July, www.bbc.com/news/world-asia-china-28586426 (24 January 2019).

Hayes, Anna (2020). '"Interwoven 'Destinies": The Significance of Xinjiang to the China Dream, the Belt and Road Initiative, and the Xi Jinping Legacy', *Journal of Contemporary China* 29 (121), 31–45.

Holbig, Heike (2004). 'The Emergence of the Campaign to Open Up the West: Ideological Formation, Central Decision-making and the Role of the Provinces', *The China Quarterly* 178, 335–357.

Holdstock, Nick (2015). *China's Forgotten People: Xinjiang Uyghur Autonomous Region, Terror and the Chinese State* (London: I.B. Tauris).

ICOMOS-ISCEAH (2009). 'Heritage in the Aftermath of the Sichuan Earthquake', in Christoph Machat, Michael Petzet, and John Ziesemer (eds), *Heritage at Risk: ICOMOS World Report 2008-2010 on Monuments and Sites in Danger* (Berlin: Verlag), 46–51, www.icomos.org/images/HR_2008-2010_final.pdf (accessed 1 April 2017).

Information of the State Council (2003). 'White Paper on History and Development of XUAR', *People's Daily*, 26 May, http://en.people.cn/200305/26/eng20030526_117240.shtml (accessed 4 September 2011).

Kerr, David, and Laura Swinton (2008). 'China, Xinjiang, and the Transnational Security of Central Asia', *Critical Asian Studies* 40 (1), 113–142.

Lemkin, Raphael (2005 [1944]). *Axis Rule in Occupied Europe: Laws of Occupation, Analysis of Government, Proposals for Redress*, new introduction by Samantha Power (New Jersey: Lawbook Exchange).

Levine, Mark (1999). 'The Chittagong Hill Tracts: A Case Study in the Political Economy of "Creeping Genocide"', *Third World Quarterly* 20 (2), 339–369.

Liu, Hongpeng (2010). 'Special Zone: Kashgar', *National Financial Weekly*, 2 August, http://finance.ifeng.com/news/special/xjjjxlt/20100802/2467810.shtml (accessed 25 July 2019).

Liu, Tianyang, and Zhenjie Yuan (2019). 'Making a Safer Space? Rethinking Space and Securitization in the Old Town Redevelopment Project of Kashgar, China', *Political Geography* 69 (March), 30–42.

MacGregor, Isabelle, and Devin Bowles (2012). 'Looking Upstream: Increasing Options to Prevent Genocide', in Colin Tatz (ed.), *Genocide Perspectives IV: Essays on Holocaust and Genocide* (Haymarket: University of Technology Sydney Press), 436–464.

Mansouri, Fethi (2013). 'Transnational Practices, Social Inclusion, and Muslim Migrant Integration in the West', in Niklaus Steiner, Robert Mason, and Anna Hayes (eds), *Migration and Insecurity: Citizenship and Social Inclusion in a Transnational Era* (Oxon: Routledge), 127–145.

Merzbacher, Gottfried (1905). *The Central Tian-Shan Mountains, 1902–1903* (London: Royal Geographic Society), https://archive.org/details/centraltianshanm00merz (accessed 2 April 2017).

Michell, George, Marika Vicziany, and Hu Tsui Yen, with John Gollings (2008). *Kashgar: Oasis City on China's Old Silk Road* (London: Frances Lincoln).

Millward, James (2007). *Eurasian Crossroads: A History of Xinjiang Uyghur Autonomous Region* (New York: Columbia University Press).

Millward, James (2009a). 'Positioning Xinjiang in Eurasian and Chinese History: Differing Visions of the "Silk Road"', in Colin Mackerras and Michael Clarke (eds), *China, Xinjiang and Central Asia: History, Transition and Crossborder Interaction into the 21st Century* (Oxon: Routledge), 55–74.

Millward, James (2009b). 'Introduction: Does the 2009 Urumchi Violence Mark a Turning Point?', *Central Asian Survey* 28 (4), 347–360.

Millward, James, and Peter Perdue (2004). 'Political and Cultural History of the Xinjiang Uyghur Autonomous Region through the Late Nineteenth Century', in S. Frederick Starr (ed.), *Xinjiang: China's Muslim Borderland* (New York: M. E. Sharpe), 27–62.

Millward, James, and Nabijan Tursun (2004). 'Political History and Strategies of Control, 1884–1978', in S. Frederick Starr (ed.), *Xinjiang: China's Muslim Borderland* (New York: M. E. Sharpe), 63–98.

National Oceanic and Atmospheric Administration (n.d.). 'Significant Earthquake: China, Xinjiang, Turkestan 22 August 1902', www.ngdc.noaa.gov/nndc/struts/results?eq_0=2631&t=101650&s=13&d=22,26,13,12&nd=display (accessed 2 April 2017).

New Zealand Herald (1902). 'The Kashgar Earthquake', 29 September, 39 (12082), https://paperspast.natlib.govt.nz/newspapers/NZH19020929.2.42 (accessed 2 April 2017).

Polo, Marco, and Rustichello Da Pisa (2004). *The Travels of Marco Polo: The Complete Yule-Cordier Edition: Including the Unabridged Third Edition (1903) of Henry Yule's Annotated Translation*, rev. Henri Cordier, 1993, www.gutenberg.org/cache/epub/10636/pg10636.html (accessed 21 June 2021).

Radio Free Asia (2017). 'Children of Detained Uyghurs Face "Terrible Conditions" in Overcrowded Xinjiang Orphanages', 18 October, www.rfa.org/english/news/uyghur/children-10182017144425.html (accessed 24 January 2019).

Roberts, Sean R. (2018). 'The Biopolitics of China's "War on Terror" and the Exclusion of the Uyghurs', *Critical Asian Studies* 50, 232–258.

Robertson, Holly, and Stephen Dziedzic (2018). 'Three Australians Were Detained in China's Re-education Camps in the Past Year, DFAT Reports', Australian Broadcasting Commission, 25 October, www.abc.net.au/news/2018-10-25/three-australians-were-detained-in-chinas-xinjiang-camps/10429116 (accessed 21 June 2021).

Rudelson, Justin Jon (1997). *Oasis Identities: Uyghur Nationalism along China's Silk Road* (New York: Columbia University Press).

Schein, Louisa (2003). *Minority Rules: The Miao and the Feminine in China's Cultural Politics* (Durham, NC: Duke University Press).

Shichor, Yitzhak (2019). 'Handling China's Internal Security: Division of Labor among Armed Forces in Xinjiang', *Journal of Contemporary China* 28 (119), 813–830.

Skinner, Tomás (2016). 'Urban Heritage of the Silk Road', *International Institute for Asian Studies: The Newsletter* 74 (Summer), http://uhrp.org/uhrp-news-featured-articles/urban-heritage-silk-road (accessed 1 April 2017).

Skrine, Clarmont P., and Pamela Nightingale (1973). *Macartney in Kashgar* (London: Routledge).

Smith Finley, Joanne (2018). 'The Wang Lixiong Prophecy: "Palestinization" in Xinjiang and the Consequences of Chinese State Securitization of Religion', *Central Asian Survey* 38 (1), 81–101.

State Administration of Cultural Heritage (2008). 'Chinese Section of the Silk Road: Land Routes in Henan Province, Shaanxi Province, Gansu Province, Qinghai Province, Ningxia Hui Autonomous Region, and Xinjiang Uygur Autonomous Region; Sea Routes in Ningbo City, Zhejiang Province and Quanzhou City, Fujian Province – from Western-Han Dynasty to Qing Dynasty', UNESCO World Heritage Centre, 28 March, Reference: 5335, http://whc.unesco.org/en/tentativelists/5335/ (accessed 13 August 2016).

Steenberg, Rune (2014). 'Transforming Houses: The Changing Concept of the House in Kashgar', *Internationales Asienforum* 45 (1–2), 171–191.

Tatz, Colin (1997). 'Genocide and the Politics of Memory', in Colin Tatz (ed.), *Genocide Perspectives I: Essays in Comparative Genocide* (Sydney: Centre for Comparative Genocide Studies).

UNESCO World Heritage Centre (2017). 'Old Walled City of Shibam', http://whc.unesco.org/en/list/192 (accessed 1 April 2017).

Uyghur Human Rights Project (2012). *Living on the Margins: The Chinese State's Demolition of Uyghur Communities* (Washington, DC: Uyghur American Association), http://docs.uyghuramerican.org/3-30-Living-on-the-Margins.pdf (accessed 1 January 2014).

Uyghur Human Rights Project (2015). *Legitimizing Repression: China's 'War on Terror' under Xi Jinping and State Policy in East Turkestan* (Washington, DC: Uyghur American Association), http://docs.uyghuramerican.org/pdf/Legitimizing-Repression.pdf (accessed 1 April 2017).

Vicziany, Marika A. (2005). 'Ethics, Archaeology and the Engineering Profession in Developing Countries', in Z. J. Pudlowski (ed.), *Proceedings of the 4th Asia-Pacific Forum on Engineering & Technology Education*, 1 January (Melbourne: UNESCO International Centre for Engineering Education), 13–16.

Wan, William (2014). 'Train Station Attack in Restive Region of China Kills 3', *Washington Post*, 1 May, https://wapo.st/3zs7rps (accessed 25 March 2020).

Wines, Michael (2009). 'To Protect an Ancient City, China Moves to Raze It', *New York Times*, May 27, www.nytimes.com/2009/05/28/world/asia/28kashgar.html?_r=0 (accessed 14 August 2016).

Xu, Vicky Xiuzhong, Danielle Cave, James Leibold et al. (2020). 'Uyghurs for Sale: "Re-education", Forced Labour and Surveillance beyond Xinjiang', 1 March (Canberra: Australian Strategic Policy Institute), www.aspi.org.au/report/uyghurs-sale (accessed 5 March 2020).

Zenz, Adrian (2019). '"Thoroughly Reforming Them towards a Healthy Heart Attitude": China's Political Re-education Campaign in Xinjiang', *Central Asian Survey* 38 (1), 102–128.

Zhang, Chi (2011). 'Old Town Rebirth: 2.0 Version of Kashgar Reconstruction', *Phoenix Weekly*, 7 July, http://news.ifeng.com/fhzk/detail_2011_07/07/7492499_0.shtml (accessed 24 July 2019).

Zhou, Zunyou (2019). 'Chinese Strategies for De-radicalization', *Terrorism and Political Violence* 31 (6), 1187–1209.

4

Settler colonialism in the name of counterterrorism: Of 'savages' and 'terrorists'

Sean R. Roberts

I refer to the Chinese government's repressive actions since 2017 against the Uyghurs and other indigenous peoples in the Xinjiang Uyghur Autonomous Region (XUAR) as 'cultural genocide'. I use this term as it appears in academic literature to describe the destruction of indigenous people in the context of settler colonialism (Davidson 2012; Altman 2018; Luck 2020). It is a term that is as much about territory as it is about people since its goal is to sever a deep bond between a given people and a territory, usually with the aim of mostly removing the people from that territory and breaking their group identity, way of life, and solidarity to prevent further resistance. This is not a legal term that is recognized by international law, and much of the literature on the topic bemoans this fact, but it also is not meant as a designation that precludes international courts from making a determination of 'genocide' (Van Kreiken 2004; Short 2010; Kingston 2015; Bilsky and Klagburn 2018). It is noteworthy, for example, that the acts this term describes clearly fit the definition of genocide as originally imagined by Raphael Lemkin (1944) and, in many cases, align with the criteria in the UN Convention on Genocide (United Nations 1948).

I do not use this term to argue for or against the international recognition that the mass human rights abuses being perpetrated against Uyghurs and related peoples inside China constitute genocide. That question should be reserved for the international legal community, which has the power, credibility, and authority to make such a designation. I use this term because it helps elucidate the reasons for the Chinese state's actions, which I believe are related to its settler colonial ambitions in the Uyghur homeland. As this crisis continues to unfold, it has become clear that the destruction of the Uyghurs as a people is part and parcel of Chinese Communist Party (CCP) strategy for developing and resettling the region that Uyghurs view as their homeland and that the People's Republic of China (PRC) calls the XUAR. This does not suggest that cultural genocide is an inevitable outcome of the long process of modern China's colonization of this region. In fact, in the history of modern China, the state has at different times tried to integrate this region more solidly into the PRC in ways that were far more inclusive of Uyghurs and other indigenous peoples of the region. However, since 2017, the state has appeared to consider the native peoples of this region to be at best superfluous and at worst an obstacle to the region's development.

This begs the question of why the PRC has chosen the present moment to hastily and violently exclude the indigenous peoples from this region's development. There are likely multiple answers to that question. First, there are clear economic reasons to rapidly develop this region. The increased capacity of the state and its export-oriented economy since the 1990s has shifted its thinking about this region, from imagining it as a frontier in need of containment to viewing it as an object of settlement that can play an important role in projecting China's economy outwards through the Belt and Road Initiative (Roberts 2016). Additionally, China's expanding economy now needs constant development to generate more jobs and capital, and the XUAR offers a fertile field for this economic expansion. However, these factors do not explain why the development of this region should require the destruction of the indigenous population rather than their inclusion.

To answer this question, one must look at the fundamentally colonial relationship between modern China and the indigenous people of this region that has marked Uyghurs and other native non-Hans since the nineteenth century as inferior and backwards vis-à-vis the ideal of Chinese civilization. While the PRC could work to decolonize this relationship, and arguably has at times in history attempted to do so, Xi Jinping's CCP appears to be establishing a model for modern China, which does not recognize the strategies of decolonization or multiculturalism as options. As James Leibold (2019) has convincingly suggested, Xi Jinping has embraced an inherently assimilationist approach to nation-building in today's PRC that is based on fusing Han culture with the entire nation of the PRC. As a result, the state is embarking on an overall drive to assimilate non-Han peoples into a Han-centric state culture. While this approach to nation-building is articulated through aggressive assimilationist policies targeting the Tibetans, Mongolians, Hui Muslims, and other non-Hans, only in the XUAR has this been articulated through a violent cultural genocide intended to destroy the resident non-Han population. The violent and destructive manner in which this vision is implemented in the XUAR may be partly due to the potential economic value of the region to the PRC and the perceived urgency to develop it, but it is also a by-product of how the state justifies what it is doing in the region.

The PRC has repeatedly suggested that its acts against the Uyghur people and other non-Hans of this region are not motivated by settler colonial ambitions, but are an attempt to mitigate the spread of Islamic 'extremism' and violent 'terrorism' among the Muslims of the XUAR (CGTN 2019, 2021). In a post-9/11 world, this is a convenient justification for state violence deployed against Muslim citizens. Since 9/11, the label of 'terrorist' has served to dehumanize entire groups of people and allow for the suspension of their human rights with international impunity. In doing so, the label also precludes those to whom it is applied from having any legitimate grievances, instead characterizing their actions as being reflections of irrational and 'extremist' Islamic beliefs. While counterterrorism is more a justification for cultural genocide in the XUAR than it is a motivation for state actions, I would argue it also has facilitated this cultural genocide and has affected the way it has been carried out. The campaign to eradicate 'terrorism' and 'extremism' in the region, which predates 2017, has taken on a life of its own. It has been internalized by many state officials and citizens, who now view Uyghurs and related peoples as an existential threat to society and deserving of the violent policies that target them.

In this sense, the PRC's 'counterterrorism' justification for its settler colonization of the Uyghur homeland mimics that of the 'civilizing mission' for European settler colonialism in the nineteenth and early twentieth centuries (Liebersohn 2016; Tricoire 2017). In the Americas and Australasia, for example, European colonists characterized indigenous resistance to colonization as 'savagery', not motivated by a desire to preserve a way of life or to maintain control over homelands, but by the indigenous peoples' inherent characteristics as 'uncivilized', 'irrational', and 'dangerous'. Thus, colonists not only felt they needed to conquer these people and remove them from their native land, but they also needed to pacify them to ensure they could not pose a continuing threat to new European-led settlements. This included dismantling their group solidarity, reducing their numbers, and 'civilizing' (or assimilating to European culture) those who remained as marginalized others subject to the Eurocentric norms of colonial society. For European settler colonists who internalized the logic of this 'civilizing mission', they believed their actions were benevolent and in the best interests of those whose land they had usurped, even justifying their conquest of those lands in the name of the assumed superiority of European ideals of progress. In other words, the 'civilizing mission' offered more than an excuse for colonization; it was inextricably linked with colonization itself.

In the case of the Uyghur cultural genocide, 'counterterrorism' and 'de-radicalization' play very similar roles to that of the 'civilizing mission' that justified and propelled the cultural genocides perpetrated by European settler colonists in the nineteenth and early twentieth centuries. The PRC has branded any indigenous resistance to the development and settlement of the XUAR as being not motivated by opposition to state policies, but by an irrational ideology that emerges from Islamic 'extremism'. If the PRC initially reserved that judgement for Uyghurs who openly resisted state policies, since 2017, it has been extended to the entire indigenous Muslim population, whose very culture is assumed to have been 'infected' by this alleged irrational 'extremist' ideology. Thus, the PRC is breaking the indigenous population's solidarity, reducing its demographic footprint, and forcibly transforming the culture of those who remain in the name of 'de-radicalization'. It should be assumed that, like European settler colonists who had internalized the logic of their 'civilizing mission', many Chinese state officials implementing the brutal policies in the Uyghur region today believe that they are actually fighting 'terrorism' and saving the region's people from 'extremism' rather than making way for mass development and Han settlement.

In this sense, the cultural genocide in the Uyghur homeland is very much a product of the twenty-first century and the stigma that has become associated with 'terrorism' since 9/11. However, at the same time, it shares many commonalities with cultural genocides from a century or more earlier, suggesting that one cannot ignore the obvious role that settler colonization plays in its motivations. For this reason, I view what is happening to the Uyghurs as cultural genocide in the name of counterterrorism. To make the case for this conceptualization, the chapter first looks at China's gradual colonization of the Uyghur homeland, using a comparison with the United States' settler colonization of its western frontier. In doing so, it suggests that the shared motivations of settling and developing new lands to fuel an expanding economy in both cases result in eerily similar fates for the respective indigenous peoples of those lands. This is followed by an examination of how the PRC's labelling of Uyghurs as a 'terrorist threat' in the aftermath of 9/11 accelerated this process and provided justification for its violent implementation in the form of cultural genocide. Finally, in conclusion, the chapter examines the question of whether the dehumanizing power of the label of 'terrorist', akin to that of the nineteenth-century colonial usage of 'savages', is allowing for a rebirth of settler colonialism and cultural genocide in the twenty-first century.

Frontiers and settler colonies

When most people think about settler colonialism, the examples that come to mind are those in the Americas and Australasia where European colonists conquered and settled new lands in order to build new modern states. In these examples, the colonists depopulated the indigenous peoples, broke their solidarity and connection with the land, and destroyed their identities and culture. These actions vis-à-vis indigenous peoples are hallmarks of settler colonialism. As Lorenzo Veracini (2014) has suggested, the fate of indigenous peoples is qualitatively different in instances of settler colonialism than it is in that of other forms of colonialism. Veracini notes that while standard forms of colonialism seek to subjugate and exploit the indigenous population (particularly their labour), who are usually located far from the imperial metropole, settler colonialism sees the indigenous peoples as an obstacle to the colonial project, which envisions the new settlers staying on the colonized land. For this reason, he argues that settler colonialism usually prefers territory that is sparsely populated by indigenous peoples, and when settler colonial regimes must deal with an indigenous population, it becomes necessary 'to execute the transfer/removal of the indigenous peoples they encounter' (Veracini 2014: 623).

Modern China's colonization of the Uyghur homeland is a particular type of settler colonialism that is characterized by its conquest, development, and settlement of a territory that it is contiguous to the colonizing power. In such instances, there is an ambiguity between the region being a frontier and it serving as a settler colony. As historian Benjamin D. Hopkins (2020) has suggested, frontiers have a logic of their own that invites a certain mode of governmentality that employs one or a combination of three strategies with regards to the indigenous peoples inhabiting them. The indigenous people, who are imagined as 'uncivilized' and often 'dangerous', can be 'remade, civilized, and assimilated', they can be eliminated, or they can be contained along with the land that they inhabit (Hopkins 2020: 4). I would argue that an empire or state can conquer such a region and integrate it into its polity while it remains a frontier, employing strategies of containment, but once the state's relationship with that territory becomes that of outright settler colonialism, it inevitably relies on strategies of elimination and forced assimilation to deal with the resident indigenous population.

To illustrate this point, it is useful to compare China's colonization of the Uyghur region with the actions of another modern state that was built on contiguous colonialism: the United States, particularly during its period of western expansion in the nineteenth and early twentieth centuries. In both of these cases, territories obtained at the western reaches of the state went through a gradual transformation from frontier to settler colonialism. Also in both cases, this transformation was driven by economic growth that required the state to develop and exploit new lands. While this comparison necessarily only briefly covers key moments in the history of US colonization of the west, it highlights the ways that a shift from the governmentality of the frontier to settler colonialism can be devastating for indigenous peoples.

Colonizing the American West

The US western expansion in the nineteenth century offers a somewhat unique example of contiguous colonialism since the whole of the

American continent had already long been the site of settler colonialism from afar. Throughout the Americas, the establishment of settler colonies since the seventeenth century had already devastated many indigenous communities through displacement, violence, and disease. However, the expansive land of what Europeans called 'the new world' had allowed for at least a modicum of segregated cohabitation between indigenous peoples and colonists in North America into the nineteenth century. That began to change about fifty years into the establishment of the United States.

As the United States became stronger and more focused on the development of its economy in the 1820s, its desire to obtain and develop new land expanded. This led to a series of territorial conflicts with other colonial powers including France and Spain, but it also spurred violent conflicts with indigenous peoples that ended in agreements forcing Native Americans to yield more and more land to the new state. By 1830, the United States would controversially adopt legislation calling for the 'removal' of Native Americans in the eastern United States and their assignment to less inhabited land further west (Ostler 2019). This forced removal, which mandated that many Native Americans embark by foot and horse to newly assigned land via the infamous 'trail of tears', not only resulted in the displacement of indigenous peoples from their homelands, but in substantial loss of life as well.

By 1849, the entire territory within the present borders of the continental United States had been established as US territory. However, it would be decades until this land would be thoroughly developed and settled by US citizens. As settlement and development took place over the next several decades, it led to more violent conflict with Native Americans over land, leading to additional native losses of land and lives. As a result, over the span of a few decades, the Native American population had dwindled substantially and their access to lands shrunk considerably. However, this trend would continue for many decades to come as the US west was gradually transformed from the western frontier of an expanding United States to an integral part of the state and nation.

Native resistance to settler encroachment on lands continued into the later 1800s. Thus, in 1887, the United States passed legislation known as the Dawes General Allotment Act, which formalized attempts to further break up lands and group solidarity among the native peoples. This legislation transferred about 60 per cent of the lands inhabited by Native Americans to the state for inhabitation by settlers between 1887 and 1934 and forcibly separated tribal groups (Newcomb 2013: 15). The Dawes Act essentially formalized the Native American reservations that exist in the United States today and serve to isolate Native Americans on small tracts of land where they have a limited level of sovereignty. Furthermore, to ensure that the remaining Native American population would not continue to resist the fate it had been dealt by the US government, the state instituted a series of assimilation policies that sought ways to forcibly integrate the dwindling and marginalized Native American population into the European-based population of the American state. These efforts included a state-sponsored programme of boarding schools, which aimed to assimilate Native Americans 'into dominant Anglo-Protestant society through education … by waging war upon Native American identities and cultural memories' (Bloom 2000: xii). In these schools, native children were separated from their families and cultures, converted to Christianity, and taught English and vocational trades that would integrate them into society. As the superintendent of one of the most famous of these boarding schools, the Carlisle Indian Industrial School, articulated his school's mission, 'all the Indian there is in the race should be dead; kill the Indian in him, and save the man' (Stuart 2020: 296).

This brief sketch of the US destruction of Native Americans does not do justice to the identities it obliterated or to the suffering of those who were not killed outright, but it does highlight how the transition from frontier governmentality to a logic of settler colonialism is ultimately devastating to a territory's indigenous peoples. The primary acts that facilitated this destruction go back at least a century, but many scholars have since categorized them as genocidal, using a term that would only later emerge (Davidson 2012; Alvarez 2014; Ostler 2019). While it was the thirst for economic expansion that drove these genocidal acts, they were also facilitated by a narrative of 'progress' and a 'civilizing mission'. As Lawrence Davidson suggests, 'all of this was possible because the prevailing thought collective of White Americans associated their expansion across the continent with "progress"; this expansion was irresistible and inevitable' (Davidson 2012: 35). In the context of this 'civilizing mission', it was also assumed that the Native American nature was that of 'savages', whether imagined as 'bloody savages' who posed a threat or 'noble savages' who represented an historical anachronism. While within American society, there were those who believed that these 'savages' could be remade into the image of European civilization, others favoured their overall extermination.

In the 'cultural genocide' experienced by Native Americans, one can see many parallels to what is happening to the indigenous peoples of the Uyghur homeland today. Like in the US destruction of the Native Americans, China's efforts to erase the Uyghur people are driven by economic expansionism and justified through a discourse that dehumanizes the indigenous peoples. Also as was the case in the United States, China's cultural genocide in the Uyghur homeland has been a gradual process that only came to an apex centuries after the region was first colonized and as it transitioned from a frontier to a site of settlement. Finally, China's actions against Uyghurs involve many of the same tactics as those employed by the United States against Native Americans – breaking the indigenous peoples' solidarity, destroying their cultures, reducing their demographic footprint, removing them from their native lands, and pacifying them so as to prevent all forms of future resistance.

There are, of course, other ways in which these two cultural genocides differ considerably, largely as outcomes of the respective time periods when they have taken place. Unlike in late nineteenth- and early twentieth-century America, in twenty-first-century China, the state's genocidal acts involve sophisticated surveillance technology, massive modern labour complexes, advanced forms of psychological torture, and the ability to quickly transform a territory through infrastructure and industrial development. Furthermore, in the twenty-first century, it is no longer acceptable to dehumanize people as 'savages' without access to civilization as was done to Native Americans, but it has become acceptable to dehumanize them, if they are Muslims, by labelling them as 'terrorists'. This is precisely what is being done to Uyghurs.

Modern China's colonization of the Uyghur homeland

Like the US settlement of its western frontier, modern China's settler colonization of the Uyghur region has been gradual, going through an evolution from frontier to settlement. For much of the region's colonial history, it remained mostly a frontier in the Chinese imagination that was in need of being controlled, and sometimes 'civilized', but not completely integrated into the core of the state. This frontier governmentality at times included assimilationist campaigns and some Han settlement, but ultimately the indigenous peoples were able to maintain their social capital and identities. However, in recent years, modern China's colonization of the Uyghur homeland has moved into a stage of outright settler colonialism and cultural genocide, seeking to 'remove' the indigenous people from the territory, break their solidarity, depopulate them, and destroy their culture. While this process is reminiscent of the experience of the US destruction of its Native American peoples, it is important to note that the indigenous peoples of the Uyghur homeland were never as isolated as were the Native Americans from peoples and regions outside their homeland. The Uyghur homeland had long been at the crossroads of different empires historically. This situation made this region's incorporation into modern China especially contested, as it remained a battleground of geopolitics and a place where the indigenous peoples had substantial interaction with other peoples and states both before and after its absorption into modern China. It may also explain why the Chinese state must employ more draconian and blatantly violent tactics in the Uyghur homeland than even those employed by the United States against Native Americans.

The Manchu-led Qing Empire, which modern China claims as its immediate predecessor, conquered the Uyghurs' homeland in the mid-eighteenth century, killing almost the entire army of the Zunghar Mongolian Empire, which had controlled the region at the time (Paine 1996). With the Zunghars gone, the Qing Empire controlled the region for the next hundred years in much the same way as had the Zunghars before it. Historian Rian Thum has characterized the Qing Empire's rule of the region at this time as more like that of a frontier 'dependency' than a colonial territory (Thum 2018: 4). While it maintained modest control of the region and took tribute from the local population, the Qing allowed local elites to govern everyday life among the indigenous population while it established segregated military encampments that had limited interaction with local peoples (Millward 1998).

After local revolts had driven the Qing out of the region for about two decades, the empire took control of it again in the 1880s. In doing so, it also sought to make the region a more integral part of the empire, declaring it an Imperial Province named 'Xinjiang' or 'new frontier'. This drive to integrate the region into the Qing Empire also predictably had its own 'civilizing mission' that sought to transform the local Muslim population 'according to their [the colonizers'] own vision of an ideal Confucian society' (Schluessel 2020: 1). While these efforts were aggressive and sought to impose both the Chinese language and culture on the local populations, they were largely a failure. According to Eric Schluessel (2020), whose recently published book examines this period in the north-east oasis of Turpan, this assimilationist campaign likely only served to harden the lines of differentiation between the Han and the region's local Muslims.

With the fall of the Qing Empire in 1911, the nascent Chinese nation-state of the Republican era inherited this region as a colonial appendage. As historian Justin Jacobs (2016: 9) has suggested, this was less a transition from 'empire to nation-state' as it was a transition to a 'national empire'. During this period, the region was largely ruled by Han governors who had only tenuous relations with the central government, returning the region to a frontier status within China even more than had been the case during the late Qing period (Forbes 1986; Jacobs 2016). In addition, influences from outside China would further undermine the power of central Chinese authorities to control the region and its people. At numerous points during the Republican era, the Soviet Union had more influence on events in the region than did central authorities in China (Hasiotis 1987; Brophy 2016; Jacobs 2016). Likewise, the local population would be influenced by their interactions with the Soviets as well as with the Muslim world. Among other things, these interactions precipitated an increase in a variety of anti-colonial ideologies that would inspire local rebellions against Chinese rule and result in two independent regional states run by indigenous Muslims, both called the Eastern Turkistan Republic (ETR). If the first ETR in the south of the region in 1933–34 was inspired by anti-colonial ideas from the Muslim world (Brophy 2016: 244–247), the second in the north in 1944–49 was more inspired by Soviet anti-imperialism and was largely sponsored by the Soviet Union (Hasiotis 1987; Wang 1996; Barmin 1999).

In this context, the relationship between modern China and this region remained tenuous throughout the Republican period, and it could have very well become a separate state prior to 1949 in the mould of the neighbouring Mongolian People's Republic. Perhaps more importantly, by the late 1940s, the indigenous population of the region had entered into a model of shared governance with the modern Chinese state, suggesting a path forwards where the native peoples of the region could become a part of modern China on their own terms (Benson 1990: 97–109). The hope for such a decolonization of the relationship between the region's people and modern China was further extended during the first years of Communist rule after 1949. The CCP heavily recruited from the local population, particularly those who had been aligned with the pro-Soviet second ETR government and placed them in positions of importance in the government (McMillan 1979). Then, in 1955, the state declared the region to be the XUAR, suggesting that the PRC was adopting the same faintly postcolonial model of ethno-national federation for its state as had the USSR.

However, it became clear by 1957 that the PRC's model for governing ethnic or national minority populations was distinctly different from that of the Soviet Union. During the Anti-Rightist Campaign, most indigenous party cadres were purged and punished as nationalists, and by 1959, the CCP had adopted a party line on the history of the region suggesting that the Uyghur homeland had always been a constituent part of China since time immemorial (Millward 2007: 257–259). These acts were a precursor of more assimilationist state policies that were implemented during the Great Leap Forward and the Cultural Revolution. The Great Leap Forward's collectivization did immeasurable damage to the culture of the indigenous peoples by breaking up traditional community structures in villages and herding groups while the Cultural Revolution launched destructive campaigns against religion and expressions of traditional culture (McMillan 1979: 196; Thum 2018: 12). These social engineering campaigns were also coupled with state-led efforts to settle Han from inner China in the region to help pacify what was still very much a frontier of Chinese Communist power. As a result, if in 1953 the proportion of the Han population in the region was only 6 per cent, by the end of the Cultural Revolution it was already 40 per cent (Toops 2004: 1).

Despite the severity of these social engineering campaigns and state-led demographic alterations, the assimilation of the indigenous peoples of the Uyghur region during this time was limited by the fact that the XUAR remained a frontier of the PRC. The Han settlers who had come to the region remained largely segregated from indigenous communities, primarily living in the north and barely penetrating the overwhelmingly Uyghur majority south (Toops 2004: 18–23). Furthermore, social engineering campaigns in the region arguably had less reach into the population than elsewhere in inner China given its distance from Beijing and the party's limited access to local knowledge (Roberts 2020: 49–50). Thus, after the dust had settled from the Cultural Revolution, few Uyghurs, Kazakhs, or other indigenous peoples in the region had been substantially transformed, and many held on to their traditional livelihoods and cultural expressions.

Thus, when a wave of liberalism hit the region in the 1980s, an indigenous cultural renaissance took place as the indigenous population built mosques, schools returned to teaching the Uyghur language, and intellectuals and religious leaders were let out of prisons. At the time, the CCP even considered enhancing ethnic autonomy in regions like the XUAR, providing the indigenous peoples increased self-governance (Bovingdon 2010: 52–53). If the PRC had followed through with such plans in the 1980s, the situation in the region would be much different today. It would have likely remained a frontier supplying the state with valuable natural resources where many of the indigenous people could continue to practise their own cultural traditions and ways of life. However, several factors prevented such a trajectory. First, by the late 1980s, the extent of China's liberalization was being curtailed by more conservative forces in the party, a process that would end all steps towards political liberalism after the crackdown on student protestors in Tiananmen Square in 1989. Second, the fall of the Soviet Union in 1991 led the CCP to rethink its own governance model, and many in the party viewed ethnic autonomy as having contributed to the dissolution of the USSR.

In this context, it is likely that the PRC already began contemplating the transformation of the XUAR's role in greater China in the early 1990s, seeking to integrate it more into a unified state and to limit any concept of ethnic autonomy. In doing so, it would gradually alter its policies from those appropriate for a frontier to ones that reflected outright settler colonialism. Initially, this shift in policies focused on building up the infrastructure of the region to ready it for more substantive economic contributions and eventual settlement, incentivizing Uyghurs and other indigenous peoples to assimilate into a Han-dominant society, and severely punishing any signs of dissent or disloyalty to the state, which were usually characterized as signs of 'separatism'. This strategy for developing the region and controlling its indigenous population created conflict throughout the 1990s as Uyghurs sought to assert their resistance to state policies, which law enforcement sought to punish as 'separatism' (Millward 2007: 322-334). In one such instance at the end of the decade, Uyghurs in the northern town of Kuldja held a protest against state restrictions on religious practices that became violent as security forces suppressed it (Roberts 1998; Dautcher 2009). This led to a massive crackdown as the state increased its search for 'separatists', arresting hundreds and executing scores of Uyghurs, and it accelerated incentivized assimilation programmes for Uyghur youth (Smith Finley 2013: 235-293).

This was the situation in the region at the turn of the millennium. The PRC appeared poised to develop this region with little regard to the wishes of its inhabitants, transforming it from a frontier into an integral part of the Chinese state and nation. It assumed that it could do so by encouraging assimilation among those indigenous peoples who wished to become part of a rising China while brutally suppressing those who did not. It is difficult to know whether this could have been accomplished without extensive violence. State policies continued to treat Uyghurs and other local Muslim peoples as inferior to the Han, suggesting that assimilation would be accompanied with a racialized glass ceiling. Given the state's ambitions for this region and its inability to imagine integrating the region on the terms of its indigenous population as it had contemplated during the 1980s, a genocidal outcome like that in the west of the United States may have been inevitable, but it is more likely that the PRC would have continued to employ a carrot-and-stick approach that enforced substantial consequences for those who resisted state-led development and settlement. However, I would argue that an event that altered the geopolitical and human rights environment globally early in the twenty-first century ensured and accelerated the pace of outright settler colonization and facilitated the outcome of cultural genocide in the

Uyghur homeland. That event was the 11 September 2001 attack on the United States.

The Global War on Terror and the Uyghur cultural genocide

When planes struck the twin towers of the World Trade Center on 11 September 2001, the United States had been enjoying a decade of unprecedented hegemony in world affairs since the early 1990s. With the fall of Soviet Communism, many US foreign policymakers believed that the global community was headed towards a liberal world order where democracy would become the dominant, if not only, form of governance in the future (Fukuyama 1989). As the self-proclaimed leader of this new world order, the United States also demonstrated hubris by frequently asserting its exceptional status to escape accountability for violating human rights throughout the 1990s. However, I would argue that such evocation of American exceptionalism remained contained to a level tolerated by other states during the decade, but the events of 9/11 would change this status quo substantially. In the Global War on Terror (GWOT) that responded to those attacks, the United States more frequently and openly violated human rights than anytime during the 1990s, setting a precedent for its selective application globally that has done great damage to the ideal of a rights-based world order.

In particular, the GWOT set the precedent that it was justified to suspend the human rights of those classified as 'terrorists'. 'Terrorists' were characterized as being opposed to modern civilization, as irrational, and as less than human, much like the 'savages' of European colonies in the nineteenth century (Bush 2003: 10–11). As such, the United States did not afford them even the rights extended to enemies in war. Alleged 'terrorists' were arbitrarily and indefinitely interned at Guantanamo Bay detention center and denied status as prisoners of war, others were detained in undisclosed locations and subjected to torture, and scores were assassinated using precision bombing techniques (Zizek 2002: 92–94). Furthermore, since the war was presumably launched against all 'terrorists' inspired by 'extremist' Islam, it inevitably led to a suspension of some rights for all Muslims. To this day, the United States employs unprecedented racial profiling of Muslim peoples in order to find those suspected of having sympathy for 'terrorist' groups, violating their privacy rights on a regular basis both inside and outside the country (Alimahomed-Wilson 2019).

These precedents are especially problematic because the concept of 'terrorism' has no universally accepted definition, allowing states to subjectively label a 'terrorist' threat on their own terms (Laqueur 1977: 179). As a result, the GWOT has become more than a war; it has become a narrative, a tool in the hands of states everywhere, that justifies state attacks on a variety of Muslim actors without regard for human rights. The United States also set a precedent for instrumentally using the GWOT to attack unrelated opponents when it justified its invasion of Iraq in 2003 by suggesting that the country had weapons of mass destruction it could give to 'terrorists'. As a result, the narrative of the GWOT has since also been used by many states to attack domestic opponents, if they are Muslim. We have witnessed both Muslim-majority states using the GWOT to criminalize domestic political opponents as alleged 'terrorists' and countries with Muslim minorities using the GWOT to demonize entire ethnic groups as alleged 'terrorists'. The PRC did the latter as it began to alter its approach to governing the XUAR after the US declaration of the GWOT. In doing so, the Chinese government would all but ensure that its settler colonization of the Uyghur homeland could involve large-scale cultural genocide with international impunity.

Making 'separatists' into 'terrorists'

Almost immediately after 9/11, the PRC sought ways to connect Uyghur resistance to its agenda of developing and settling the Uyghur homeland to the international 'terrorist' threat that had caught the imagination of the world in late 2001. During the late 1990s, the PRC had already secured the co-operation of the Central Asian states, Pakistan, and, to a certain extent, Afghanistan in ensuring that Uyghur resistance to the state's plans for their homeland could be contained (Roberts 2004). The declaration of the GWOT appeared to be the perfect opportunity to secure co-operation with Western states and the United Nations as well by linking Uyghurs to al-Qaeda and Osama bin Laden.

As a result, within weeks of the attacks on the United States in late November 2001, the Permanent Mission of the PRC to the UN released a statement that sought to make exactly this argument. It suggested that it faced a grave Uyghur 'terrorist' threat with which it had been fighting throughout the 1990s, and this threat was connected with and funded by Osama bin Laden (PMPRCUN 2001). Furthermore, this statement accused a litany of over forty Uyghur diaspora organizations of being part of this 'terrorist' threat, including groups in Europe advocating for Uyghurs' human rights, and provided a list of illustrative violent acts undertaken by this group during the 1990s (PMPRCUN 2001). Subsequently, this statement would begin an extensive international lobbying campaign by the PRC, which I describe in more depth elsewhere (Roberts 2020: 69–75), to have Uyghurs identified as a core part of the al-Qaeda terrorist threat. This effort included the release of a more detailed White Paper on the alleged threat in 2002 that claimed that this expansive Uyghur 'terrorist' network had carried out 200 terrorist attacks inside the Uyghur homeland during the 1990s, including many events that clearly should not be characterized as 'terrorism' (SCIOPRC 2002). Initially, this campaign bore little fruit as most other countries dismissed these claims about the alleged Uyghur 'terrorist' threat. The United States in particular directly pushed back on this issue, suggesting that the PRC's conflict with Uyghurs was more related to state-led human rights abuses than to an international 'terrorist' threat (Kan 2004: 12).

However, the stance of the United States suddenly changed in the summer of 2002 when the US State Department recognized one little-known Uyghur group in Afghanistan, allegedly called the Eastern Turkistan Islamic Movement (ETIM), as a terrorist group (Pan 2002). In doing so, it largely mimicked the allegations from Chinese state documents, including the recognition of the 200 violent incidents claimed by the PRC to be terrorist attacks and blaming them all on the ETIM rather than on a large network of different Uyghur groups as had the PRC (Bovingdon 2010: 136). Subsequently, the United States also assisted the PRC to get the ETIM recognized on the UN Security Council's consolidated list of 'terrorist' organizations in September 2002 (DeYoung 2002). The US State Department never gave a satisfactory answer to why its policy towards the alleged Uyghur 'terrorist' threat had changed so suddenly, but it would later be viewed as being instrumental in getting the PRC not to block the US invasion of Iraq in 2003 (Dao 2002; DeYoung 2002; Eckholm 2002). More recently, the US Deputy Assistant Secretary of State for South and

Central Asian Affairs at the time, Richard Boucher, told a journalist plainly that the decision had been taken 'to help gain China's support for invading Iraq' (Magnier 2021). While, as I have demonstrated elsewhere (Roberts 2020: 100–116), the group identified as the ETIM in Afghanistan neither would be proven to have carried out any violence anywhere in the world nor to have received support from Osama bin Laden, its international recognition as a 'terrorist' organization would have lasting impact on the Uyghurs and, over time, on state policy towards the Uyghur homeland.

Development and counterterrorism, 2002–9

Initially, this international recognition of an alleged Uyghur 'terrorist' threat had little direct ramifications for the Uyghurs' homeland. PRC policies in the region during most of the first decade of the new millennium were largely a continuation of those it had pursued during the 1990s, albeit implemented at a gradually accelerated rate. The state continued incentivizing Uyghurs to assimilate into a Han-dominated society while severely punishing resistance to assimilation, which was now framed as a manifestation of 'extremism' and 'terrorism' rather than of 'separatism'. While this discursive shift led to somewhat more aggressive attempts to incentivize assimilation and punish opposition, counterterrorism would not be the central concern of the state in the region during this time. The PRC's primary objective in the region during the early 2000s was development, and this was pursued with much more zeal than in the 1990s.

In 2000, the PRC had launched a grand campaign called 'Develop the West', which targeted the XUAR in addition to Tibet and other western frontiers of the state (Ma and Summers 2009). This campaign focused primarily on infrastructure development, but it also included urban renewal in cities around the region. Among the most publicized part of this development was the destruction of Kashgar's Old City, which was viewed by many Uyghurs as the best-preserved example of traditional Uyghur urban culture in the world (UNESCO 2003). This period's combination of state-led development, assimilationist goals, and severe punishment of disloyal Uyghurs in the name of counterterrorism was a sign of the direction in which PRC governance of the region was headed. However, before this mixture of policies would transform into outright settler colonization of the Uyghur homeland and blatant genocidal acts, it was inevitable that conflict would transpire.

Cultivating conflict, 2008–9

After six years during which there had been almost no reports of violence in the XUAR, the state once again raised concerns about the alleged Uyghur 'terrorist' threat in the run-up to the 2008 Beijing Olympics. This was precipitated by the first sign of Uyghurs abroad being entangled in Jihadist groups since the US and UN recognition of the ETIM as a 'terrorist' organization. In the months preceding the Olympics, a group calling itself the Turkistan Islamic Party (TIP) issued a series of videos threatening the games (TIP 2008). As a result, the PRC immediately began a massive counterterrorism effort targeting Uyghurs, and Uyghurs became marked as a 'dangerous' people in the Han public imagination. Subsequently, Uyghurs were removed from Beijing, and the region of their homeland was virtually locked down by security forces (York 2008). These forces put Uyghurs, especially in the south, under strict surveillance and limited their movements. While there were two minor violent incidents in the region during the Olympics, it is difficult to know if they were politically motivated or merely responses to the tight security that had blanketed the region for the duration of the games (Wong 2008; Hastings 2011).

Regardless, inter-ethnic relations in the region had become increasingly tense and not only due to the state's heavy-handed treatment of Uyghurs during the Olympics. Simultaneously, development projects were transforming the region's Uyghur character, particularly in Kashgar's Old City, and bringing new Han workers and entrepreneurs to the region. The visible development of the region's capital city of Urumqi also attracted many impoverished Uyghurs from the south who came to seek economic opportunity and to escape the intense pressure from police in their home regions. This situation was destined to explode into conflict, and that is what happened in the summer of 2009 in Urumqi.

In early July 2009, Uyghur students gathered to hold a large protest in response to news that several Uyghur men had been killed at a factory in south China after a rumour had spread that Uyghur workers had raped a Han woman (Branigan 2009; Ryono and Galway 2015). While protests like this were often met with concessions from local authorities elsewhere in China, in the XUAR, they have almost always been violently suppressed as far back as the 1990s. Once security forces suppressed this protest, it flared into street violence that took on a life of its own. Uyghurs and Han attacked each other in fighting that continued for almost three days with many Uyghurs suggesting that police were assisting Han vigilante groups that had formed throughout the city (Macartney 2009).

When the dust had settled on the violence, the state blamed the Uyghurs, especially those migrant labourers who had come from the south to the city. In the following months, the region was cut off from international communications and the Internet shut down for close to a year as security in the XUAR was substantially bolstered (UHRP 2010: 19). In the south of the region, security forces searched villages for those to detain for participation in the violence, leading to hundreds of arrests and scores of disappearances (Human Rights Watch 2009). Thomas Cliff has suggested that this response to the riots was largely an attempt by the regional government to demonstrate to the growing Han population that it could protect them from the region's non-Hans (Cliff 2012). Regardless of whether this is accurate, the response certainly did not encourage inter-ethnic reconciliation. Instead, it drove a deeper wedge between Uyghurs and Han in the region. Furthermore, while the ethnic violence that had transpired was evidently spontaneous and had nothing to do with 'terrorism', the state used it to justify a sharp intensification of counterterrorism measures, especially in Uyghur-majority areas of the south.

While international communications and Internet access in the region were renewed in 2010, the racially profiled security policies initiated after the riots that targeted Uyghurs continued, especially in the south of the Uyghur homeland. Additionally, the state doubled down on development in the aftermath of the Urumqi events of 2009. At the CCP's First Xinjiang Work Forum in May 2010, party leadership proclaimed that the answer to the unrest was 'expediated development', especially in the Uyghur-majority south of the region (Wei and Cuifen 2010). As part of this increased development, the CCP implemented a novel public–private partnership model for this area that matched municipalities outside the region in China proper with specific parts of the XUAR for investment and development projects (Jia 2010). This programme raised the settler colonization of the region to a new level as it also brought an influx of Han-led companies with their capital and their Han workers. As Cliff suggests, the goals of this development in the region were to 'drive the progression from ... a "frontier of defense" (military occupation) to a "frontier of settlement" (Han civilian occupation)' (Cliff 2012: 82). To complement these measures, the Work Forum also initiated increased assimilationist policies, including a drive to educate local children only in the Chinese language and restrictions on clothing and grooming deemed to be associated with 'extremist' Islam (UHRP 2012). This mixture of rapid development, Han in-migration, assimilationist policies, and tightened security in the south of the Uyghur homeland would create a pressure cooker that would inevitably become increasingly violent.

The security response was particularly intense and reached into the village level throughout the south of the region. In my interviews with Uyghur refugees in Turkey in 2016, numerous villagers had suggested that the tense security environment drove them to flee the country and endure dangerous human trafficking routes. They described a situation akin to house arrest where they were under constant surveillance and their homes were frequently searched by police. As a result, there are numerous reports of violent clashes between Uyghurs and police in the south of the region during this time, particularly in rural villages. While most of these clashes were likely inevitable and spontaneous outcomes of tension between law enforcement and civilians, when Chinese media reported on these incidents, they were always framed as 'terrorist' attacks.

Furthermore, the TIP, the small Uyghur militant group in Waziristan that had made videos threatening the 2008 Olympics, continued to make videos that celebrated this violence when Chinese media reported it, congratulating the Uyghurs involved and framing their actions as part of a jihad against the Chinese state. My research on the TIP in Waziristan at this time suggests that it only consisted of a handful of Uyghurs who were connected with Jihadist groups in the region and that they had no capacity to carry out violence in China. As one terrorism expert has said of the group at this time, the TIP 'appeared to be more of a propaganda group with a militant wing than a militant group with a propaganda wing' (Zenn 2018). While it was possible that some Uyghurs were able to access these videos, it is unlikely that many did given the security environment and controls on the Internet. Furthermore, even if some did see the videos, there is no evidence that they were able to communicate with the TIP or were inspired by it. Rather, the TIP's videos celebrating violence primarily gave the state an additional excuse to suggest that any violence involving Uyghurs in the region was an act of 'terrorism' and, subsequently, to increase local security measures.

Over the next four years, this situation spiralled into an escalating cycle of repression–resistance–repression as the security in the south of the region increased with every violent incident. Since the police and security forces viewed this violence through a 'counterterrorism' lens, they assumed it emanated from the local population's religious 'extremism' rather than any particular grievances. As a result, their actions particularly targeted Uyghurs who partook in religious practices as suspected 'terrorists', under the assumption that any Islamic religiosity was a manifestation of 'extremism' and a demonstration of inclination towards 'terrorism'. However, until 2013, none of this violence appeared to be 'terrorist' acts targeting civilians. Furthermore, there was no evidence that this violence was associated with any organized group, most of it erupting spontaneously when police interacted violently with the local population.

The self-fulfilling prophecy, 2013–14

By 2013, the situation in the south of the Uyghur homeland became increasingly tense between citizens and the police/security forces. At the same time, the state was becoming increasingly forceful in its efforts to attack signs of religiosity. In February 2013, the party deployed 200,000 cadres to Uyghur villages in the south, requesting that they intermingle with the local community and promote the values of the party (Leibold 2020). This effort, which was a precursor to an even larger effort in place now, essentially amounted to the establishment of an army of behaviour police that could monitor and seek to alter the religious behaviour of Uyghur villagers. The CCP's 'Project Beauty' campaign launched that same year likewise sought to get Uyghurs to forsake any clothing or grooming habits that the party had associated with religiosity (Traywick 2013). These measures reflected the party's continued attempt to connect Uyghur dissent or disloyalty to signs of religiosity, interpreted as 'extremism'. In line with these policies, the CCP allegedly also began work on a document to assist cadres in identifying the visible traits of those 'extremists' who should be the object of their surveillance (Zhou 2019). Not surprisingly, these intensified measures to regulate and control religious behaviour and appearance in the south of the region led to increased clashes between security organs and Uyghur civilians, which once again resulted in vocal claims from the PRC that it faced a grave 'terrorist' threat from within the Uyghur population.

However, the incident in 2013 that emboldened the PRC to reiterate these claims on a global scale took place in October on Tiananmen Square in Beijing. Allegedly, a family of Uyghurs deliberately drove an SUV into the square, hitting several people and catching fire (Wan 2013). Although only two people died in addition to those in the vehicle, the incident attracted far more attention than any of the violent clashes inside the Uyghur homeland because this was the first time that violence had spilled into inner China. While the TIP in Waziristan once again issued a video celebrating this incident, it did not claim credit, and there is no evidence that the event had anything to do with this small group of Uyghur militants in Pakistan (TIP 2013).

Following this event, not only did the state establish an even stronger counterterrorism regime in the Uyghur region, but it also became more vocal internationally in defending its assertion that it faced a grave Uyghur 'terrorist threat'. In doing so, it also took advantage of the appearance of TIP fighting forces in the Syrian civil war. As I have discussed in more depth elsewhere (Roberts 2020: 187–194), a faction of the TIP mysteriously appeared in Syria in 2012–13, bolstered by new recruits from Uyghur refugees who had fled China to Turkey since the crackdown of 2009. While it is unclear who finances this more recent iteration of the TIP, it appears to have links with both al-Qaeda and perhaps the Turkish government (Roberts 2020: 187–194). My interviews with some of the Uyghurs who had been with the TIP in Syria suggest that many of them came to Syria merely out of necessity seeking shelter, food, and schooling for their families while others were told they would receive training for a future national liberation struggle against China in their homeland. Regardless of their motivations, there is no evidence that this group of Uyghur foreign fighters in Syria has any capacity to attack China or has any presence in the XUAR. However, like other marginal Uyghur groups who have become entangled with global Jihadism since 2001, their existence allowed the PRC to further propagate its accusations of a dangerous 'terrorist threat' within China's own Uyghur population.

As the state violently sought out this alleged 'terrorist threat' from within the Uyghur population, particularly in the rural south, the violent resistance of Uyghurs only intensified and began appearing more like 'terrorism' in its targeting of civilians. In March 2014, a group of Uyghurs, who were fleeing police after being discovered trying to leave the country illegally, entered the Kunming train station in Yunnan Province and allegedly killed thirty-one civilians with knives and machetes (Branigan and Kaiman 2014; Hoshur 2014). While the details of this incident remain unclear, it elicited an even stronger response from the state in its pursuit of the alleged Uyghur 'terrorist threat' inside the XUAR. It also precipitated Xi Jinping's first trip to the region since becoming party chairman. At the end of this trip, which was meant to send a message of stability, another incident occurred at the Urumqi train station as a bomb blew up among a crowd of people (Beech 2014). Similarly, a few weeks later, Uyghurs allegedly drove two SUVs into a market in Urumqi striking salespeople and others, allegedly killing forty-three people (Denyer 2014). While there is no evidence that these events were explicitly premeditated acts of political violence, their seemingly deliberate targeting of civilians made them appear much more like terrorism than anything involving Uyghurs previously.

The CCP's response was swift. As the party called for another Xinjiang Work Forum, the XUAR's party secretary declared a 'People's War on Terror' that aimed to once and for all weed out the alleged 'terrorist' elements within the Uyghur population (Xinhua 2014). The Second Xinjiang Work Forum, unlike its predecessor, was much more focused on issues of security than on development (Leibold 2014). This did not mean that the state slowed down its development efforts, which in fact only increased in the following years. However, it did mean that this development was now accompanied by an intensely increased effort to identify and punish alleged 'terrorists' within the Uyghur population and to attack the Muslim faith in the region. While this campaign focused primarily on Uyghur-majority regions in the XUAR, especially in rural areas, and primarily targeted religious Uyghurs, it was accompanied by increased scrutiny of secular intellectuals as well. In September 2014, for example, the PRC convicted a prominent and outspoken Uyghur professor in Beijing, Ilham Tohti, of 'separatism' and gave him a life sentence (Wong 2014). In reality, Tohti had been a proponent of the XUAR being an integral part of the PRC, but his primary crime had been arguing for a path of development for the region that gave more agency to the region's indigenous peoples (Tohti 2015).

Perhaps more ominously, the 'People's War on Terror' also served as a means to set up the infrastructure that would soon be employed for an aggressive 'cultural genocide' in the region. It was at this time, for example, that the PRC started the procurement for the massive electronic surveillance and tracking system known as the 'Integrated Joint Operations Platform' (IJOP) (Oster 2016). This system had the capability to establish electronic files on every individual Uyghur, which could be viewed when the person was identified at one of the many checkpoints in the region. In the coming years, this system would also be used to determine the level of 'extremism' of individual Uyghurs in deciding who should be subjected to mass internment. Similarly, the party piloted a variety of re-education methods during the 'People's War' (Zenz 2019: 105). Starting in 2014, these methods would be deployed as a means of punishing those whose behaviours, dress, and grooming were interpreted as signs of 'extremism'.

During this time, the situation for Uyghurs in rural regions was already dire, and many rural Uyghurs may have felt as if they were already experiencing a cultural genocide. Uyghurs in rural areas were under constant watch and subjected to regular house searches. However, the PRC appeared to still view its 'Uyghur problem' as being limited to an isolated group of 'bad Uyghurs' who had fallen prey to what it considered an 'extremist' version of Islam. At the same time, the CCP was courting elite Uyghurs with secular sensibilities, particularly if they operated fluently in the Chinese language. One Uyghur businessman from Urumqi even told me that he had more access to party members than ever before during this time and that they welcomed his co-operation in organizing Uyghur cultural events that downplayed religious aspects of their culture. However, this situation apparently changed suddenly in 2016 as the distinction between 'bad Uyghurs' and 'good Uyghurs' would begin breaking down.

Cultural genocide

At the end of August 2016, Chen Quanguo was made the Regional Party Secretary of the XUAR after having served five years as Party Secretary in the Tibet Autonomous Region (TAR) (Zenz and Leibold 2017). Quanguo's appointment in the XUAR ushered in a new period of repression in the region almost immediately. In fact, the transformation was so rapid that it is difficult to believe that Chen's new appointment was the only factor in the changes. Certain changes did reflect a continuation of Chen's policies in Tibet, such as the establishment of satellite police stations throughout urban areas (Zenz and Leibold 2017), but others, such as the IJOP and the new re-education programmes for 'extremists', had been in preparation since 2014. Furthermore, within a month of Chen's appointment, a substantial and coordinated campaign against Uyghur intellectuals began. This included a purge of those Uyghurs involved in creating textbooks for Uyghur language schools, which led to the detainment of four high-profile intellectuals already in September and October 2016 (Hoshur 2018; CGTN 2021). By early 2017, the arrests of intellectuals involved in textbook production expanded to a larger campaign that targeted 'two-faced' party officials who were accused of sympathizing with and/or assisting alleged Uyghur 'terrorists' (Reuters 2017). By the timeline of events, it is likely that plans had been made since the beginning of the 'People's War on Terror' to begin attacking the Uyghur people as a whole as 'dangerous' and 'subversive', a sign that impending genocidal intentions were now being put into action by 2017.

Subsequently, the state started procuring the construction of mass internment camps that would almost randomly intern upwards of 10 per cent of the population and subject them to re-education measures in prison-like conditions by the end of 2017 (Zenz 2019). This would be the beginning of a full-out assault on the Uyghur people and culture, seeking to break their will and solidarity. Additionally, the state also targeted other Muslim ethnic groups in the region, including Kazakhs, Kyrgyz, and Uzbeks. Other chapters in this volume provide more details on the system that has facilitated this violent assault on the indigenous population of the region, but it is noteworthy here to mention, as I have detailed elsewhere (Roberts 2020: 199–235), that this system entails a complex of policies of which the mass internment and comprehensive surveillance systems are only the centrepiece, serving to make resistance to other state policies virtually unimaginable. Other policies include the coerced export of labour to residential factories in other parts of China, the forced participation in Chinese-language boarding schools, the destruction of mosques, pilgrimage sites, and other cultural landmarks, the destruction of traditional villages, a coerced miscegenation programme, forced sterilization, and coerced participation in Chinese cultural holidays. In short, this complex of policies appears intent on separating families, reducing the Uyghur population both in its entirety and in their homeland, and overall obliterating any sense of Uyghur identity, solidarity, and culture.

In many ways, the widespread, calculated, and coercive implementation of these policies resembles a twenty-first-century version of the US assault on Native Americans, adapted for present-day norms and benefiting from new technologies of repression. Notably, the motivations for these two cultural genocides emerge from a similar history of gradual settler colonialism, and they both appear intended to completely pacify and destroy the collective identity of those they target in order to exclude them from their lands. It is difficult to imagine that such a blatant act of cultural genocide, which is reminiscent of the nineteenth century and very well may be in violation of the UN Convention on Genocide, could occur in the twenty-first century. Theoretically, such actions have been universally condemned as reprehensible and as relics from the age of nineteenth-century colonialism and cultural evolutionism. Today, it is assumed that we live in a postcolonial world where concepts of 'savages' and 'civilized' can no longer serve as justification for mass atrocities and social engineering. However, the framing of the cultural genocide in the Uyghur homeland as an effort at 'counterterrorism' and 'countering extremism' provides its implementation with a logic that is unique to the twenty-first century. It is a logic that recognizes alleged 'terrorists' as akin to the 'savages' of the nineteenth century, to which the norms of the civilized world do not apply.

Conclusion: Of 'savages' and 'terrorists'

This chapter has sought to highlight both the motivations and justifications for the PRC's full-out assault on the indigenous peoples of the XUAR, elucidating how motivations and justifications cannot be entirely separated in understanding a state's capacity to carry out mass atrocities. Looking at the region of the Uyghur homeland over time, it appears that the PRC's actions against its indigenous peoples are part of a long-term goal of developing this region as an integral part of modern China, a process that had been gradually ongoing for at least 140 years. In many ways, the parallels to what the United States did to Native Americans and what the PRC is doing to the indigenous peoples of the Uyghur region are striking. The PRC is steadily breaking the solidarity of the Uyghur and related peoples by attacking familial and village ties, it is removing them from their native villages, it is steadily reducing their demographic footprint, and it is destroying their culture and religion. It is shocking to see a state so deliberately and so violently destroy entire peoples in the twenty-first century, particularly when that state is the world's second largest economy and a leading global power. Unlike other recent genocides, this is not occurring in the context of an active conflict; rather, like at the peak of the European colonial era, it is a calculated assault on an indigenous people in the interests of economic expansion. How could this occur in a post-war global order that has sworn to prevent the naked colonial aggression of the past?

Scholars of genocide largely agree that mass atrocities require a dehumanization of their victims (Alvarez 1997; Stanton 1998; Kressel 2002; Blatman 2011). This is especially pronounced when the genocide involves mass killing, such as in the Holocaust, but it is equally true in cases without substantial efforts to physically exterminate a people, but with the goal of breaking their will, solidarity, genealogy, and way of life. In such cases, the perpetrators of genocide must believe that the people they are making suffer are less than human and can only be made human through destroying everything they held dear in their former lives. In the discourse of European colonialism, this was accomplished through defining their victims as 'savages', less than human, and unacquainted with civilization. In the case of the indigenous peoples of the Uyghur homeland, the label of 'Islamic terrorist' fulfills a similar purpose. The Global War on Terror set a precedent for the dehumanizing power of the label of 'Islamic terrorists'. In the aftermath of the 9/11 attacks on the United States, the world adopted a crude and dehumanizing impression of those who had carried out the attacks. It was assumed that they were less than human and opposed to civilized life and rationality. As such, these people posed an existential threat to the world as we know it, and it was proclaimed that they should be exterminated or, in some instances, de-programmed and made into full humans.

I would argue that this is the manner in which the PRC has come to view Uyghurs and related peoples in the XUAR. Its attack on these peoples has gradually escalated from viewing those who resist state policies as 'terrorists' to labelling all those publicly expressing piety as 'terrorists' and finally to considering the entirety of these peoples, by virtue of their identity, to be 'terrorists', or at least 'extremists' prone to 'terrorism'. This blanket characterization of these peoples allows for their wholesale dehumanization in the eyes of those implementing policies. As a result, it is understandable how the PRC has mobilized large numbers of functionaries and large swaths of the Chinese population to support policies that would be considered reprehensible if applied to others because these people are not considered fully human. Those who are deemed incapable of rehabilitation must be destroyed or indefinitely imprisoned, and those who can be reformed must be completely remade as inferior Others who will be allowed to participate on the margins in the fruits of the PRC's overall development. To paraphrase the infamous quote from the director of the Carlisle Indian Industrial School in the United States, 'all the Uyghur there is in the race should be dead; kill the Uyghur in him, and save the man.'

References

Alimahomed-Wilson, Sabrina (2019). 'When the FBI Knocks: Racialized State Surveillance of Muslims', *Criminal Sociology* 45 (6), 871–887.

Altman, Jon (2018). 'Raphael Lemkin in Remote Australia: The Logic of Cultural Genocide and the Homelands', *Ocenia* 88 (3), 336–359.

Alvarez, Alexander (1997). 'Adjusting to Genocide: The Techniques of Neutralization and the Holocaust', *Social Science History* 21 (2), 139–178.

Alvarez, Alexander (2014). *Native America and the Question of Genocide* (New York: Rowan and Littlefield).

Barmin, V. A. (1999). *Sinziyan v Sovetsko-Kitayskikh Otnosheniyakh 1941–1949gg* (Barnaul, Russia: Barnaul'skii Gosudarstvenniy Pedagogicheskii Universitet).

Beech, Hannah (2014). 'In China, Deadly Bomb and Knife Attack Rocks Xinjiang Capital', *Time*, 30 April, https://time.com/83727/in-china-deadly-bomb-and-knife-attack-rocks-xinjiang-capital/ (accessed 16 July 2021).

Benson, Linda (1990). *The Ili Rebellion: The Moslem Challenge to Chinese Authority in Xinjiang, 1944–1949* (New York: M. E. Sharpe).

Bilsky, Leora, and Rachel Klagburn (2018). 'The Return of Cultural Genocide?', *European Journal of International Law* 29 (2), 373–396.

Blatman, Daniel (2011). *The Death Marches: The Final Phase of Nazi Genocide* (Cambridge, MA: The Belknap Press of Harvard University Press).

Bloom, John (2000). *To Show What an Indian Can Do: Sports at Native American Boarding Schools* (Minneapolis: University of Minnesota Press).

Bovingdon, Gardner (2010). *The Uyghurs: Strangers in Their Own Land* (New York: Colombia University Press).

Branigan, Tania (2009). 'Ethnic Violence in China Leaves 140 Dead', *The Guardian*, 6 July, www.theguardian.com/world/2009/jul/06/china-riots-uighur-xinjiang (accessed 15 December 2019).

Branigan, Tania, and Jonathan Kaiman (2014). 'Kunming Knife Attack: Xinjiang Separatists Blamed for "Chinese 9/11"', *The Guardian*, 2 March, www.theguardian.com/world/2014/mar/02/kunming-knife-attack-muslim-separatists-xinjiang-china (accessed 16 July 2021).

Brophy, David (2016). *Uyghur Nation: Reform and Revolution on the Russia-China Frontier* (Cambridge, MA: Harvard University Press).

Bush, George W. (2003). 'Address to a Joint Session of Congress (September 20, 2001)', *Our Mission and Our Moment: Speeches since the Attacks of September 11* (Washington, DC: White House).

CGTN (2019). 'The Black Hand: ETIM and Terrorism in Xinjiang', 7 December, https://news.cgtn.com/news/2019-12-07/The-black-hand-ETIM-and-terrorism-in-Xinjiang-MepKpOPAKA/index.html (accessed 16 July 2021).

CGTN (2021). 'War in the Shadows: Challenges of Fighting Terrorism in Xinjiang', 2 April, https://news.cgtn.com/news/2021-04-02/The-war-in-the-shadows-Challenges-of-fighting-terrorism-in-Xinjiang-Z7AhMWRPy0/index.html (accessed 16 July 2021).

Cliff, Thomas (2012). 'The Partnership of Stability in Xinjiang: State–Society Interactions following the July 2009 Unrest', *The China Journal* (68), 79–105.

Dao, James (2002). 'Threats and Responses: Diplomacy; Closer Ties with China May Help U.S. on Iraq', *New York Times*, 4 October, www.nytimes.com/2002/10/04/world/threats-and-responses-diplomacy-closer-ties-with-china-may-help-us-on-iraq.html (accessed 16 July 2021).

Dautcher, Jay (2009). 'Down a Narrow Road: Identity and Masculinity in a Uyghur Community in Xinjiang, China' (PhD diss., Harvard University Asia Center).

Davidson, Lawrence (2012). *Cultural Genocide* (New York: Rutgers University Press).

Denyer, Simon (2014). 'Terrorist Attack on Market in China's Restive Xinjiang Region Kills More than 30', *Washington Post*, 22 May, https://wapo.st/3vHkS1H (accessed 16 July 2021).

DeYoung, Karen (2002). 'U.S. and China Ask UN to List Separatists as Terror Group', *Washington Post*, 11 September, www.washingtonpost.com/archive/politics/2002/09/11/us-and-china-ask-un-to-list-separatists-as-terror-group/a3adaa3e-2cd3-4861-b544-eac800757255/ (accessed 16 July 2021).

Eckholm, Erik (2002). 'U.S. Labeling of Group in China as Terrorist Is Criticized', *New York Times*, 13 September, www.nytimes.com/2002/09/13/world/us-labeling-of-group-in-china-as-terrorist-is-criticized.html (accessed 16 July 2021).

Forbes, Andrew (1986). *Warlords and Muslims in Chinese Central Asia: A Political History of Republican Sinkiang, 1911–1949* (Cambridge: Cambridge University Press).

Fukuyama, Francis (1989). 'The End of History?', *The National Interest* 16 (Summer), 3–18.

Hasiotis, Arthur C. Jr (1987). *Soviet Political, Economic and Military Involvement in Sinkiang from 1928 to 1949* (New York: Garland).

Hastings, Justin V. (2011). 'Charting the Course of Uyghur Unrest', *The China Quarterly* 208, 893–912.

Hopkins, Benjamin D. (2020). *Ruling the Savage Periphery: Frontier Governance and the Making of the Modern State* (Cambridge, MA: Harvard University Press).

Hoshur, Shohret (2014). 'China Train Station Attackers May Have Acted "in Desperation"', Radio Free Asia, 3 March, www.rfa.org/english/news/uyghur/desperate-03032014224353.html (accessed 16 July 2021).

Hoshur, Shohret (2018). 'Three Uyghur Intellectuals Jailed for Separatism, Political Study Film Reveals', Radio Free Asia, 10 October, www.rfa.org/english/news/uyghur/intellectuals-jailed-10102018172605.html (accessed 16 July 2021).

Human Rights Watch (2009). 'Enforced Disappearances in the Wake of Xinjiang's Protests', 20 October, www.hrw.org/report/2009/10/20/we-are-afraid-even-look-them/enforced-disappearances-wake-xinjiangs-protests (accessed 16 July 2021).

Jacobs, Justin M. (2016). *Xinjiang and the Modern Chinese State* (Seattle: University of Washington Press).

Jia, Cui (2010). 'Xinjiang Takes a Leaf Out of Sichuan's Book', *China Daily*, 21 May, www.chinadaily.com.cn/china/2010-05/21/content_9875137.htm (accessed 16 July 2021).

Kan, Shirley (2004). 'U.S.-China Counter-terrorism Cooperation: Issues for U.S. Policy', Report for Congress, RS21995 (Washington, DC: Congressional Research Service).

Kingston, Lindsey (2015). 'The Destruction of Identity: Cultural Identity and Indigenous Peoples', *Journal of Human Rights* 14 (1), 63–83.

Kressel, Neil (2002). *Mass Hate: The Global Rise of Genocide and Terror* (New York: Westview Press).

Laqueur, Walter (1977). *Terrorism* (London: Weidenfeld and Nicolson).

Leibold, James (2014). 'Xinjiang Forum Marks New Policy of "Ethnic Mingling"', *China Brief* 14 (12), https://jamestown.org/program/xinjiang-work-forum-marks-new-policy-of-ethnic-mingling/ (accessed 16 July 2021).

Leibold, James (2019). 'Planting the Seed: Ethnic Policy in Xi Jinping's New Era of Cultural Nationalism', *China Brief* 19 (22), https://jamestown.org/program/planting-the-seed-ethnic-policy-in-xi-jinpings-new-era-of-cultural-nationalism/ (accessed 16 July 2021).

Leibold, James (2020). 'Surveillance in China's Xinjiang Region: Ethnic Sorting, Coercion, and Inducement', *Journal of Contemporary China* 26 (121), 46–60.

Lemkin, Raphael (1944). *Axis Rule in Occupied Europe: Laws of Occupation, Analysis of Government, Proposals for Redress* (New York: Columbia University Press).

Liebersohn, Harry (ed.) (2016). 'Special Issue: Preaching the Civilizing Mission and Modern Cultural Encounters', *Journal of World History* 27 (3).

Luck, Edward C. (2020). *Cultural Genocide and the Protection of Cultural Heritage* (Washington, DC: Getty Publications).

Ma, Doris, and Tim Summers (2009). 'Is China's Growth Moving Inland? A Decade of "Develop the West"', Asia Programme Paper: ASP PP 2009/02 (London: Chatham House).

Macartney, Jane (2009). 'Hundreds Die in Bloodiest Clashes since Tiananmen Crackdown', *The Times*, 7 July.

Magnier, Mark (2021). '9/11, 20 years later: How China used the attacks to its strategic advantage', *South China Morning Post*. 2 September.

McMillan, Donald H. (1979). *Chinese Communist Power and Policy in Xinjiang, 1949–1977* (Boulder: Westview Press).

Millward, James (1998). *Beyond the Pass: Economy, Ethnicity, and Empire in Qing Central Asia, 1759–1864* (Stanford: Stanford University Press).

Millward, James (2007). *Eurasian Crossroads: A History of Xinjiang* (New York: Columbia University Press).

Newcomb, Steven (2013). 'Dawes Act', *Encyclopedia of Race and Racism* (Detroit: Macmillan Reference).

Oster, Shai (2016). 'China Tries Its Hand at Pre-crime', *Bloomberg Businessweek*, 3 March, www.bloomberg.com/news/articles/2016-03-03/china-tries-its-hand-at-pre-crime (accessed 16 July 2021).

Ostler, Jeffrey (2019). *Surviving Genocide: Native Nations and the United States from the American Revolution to Bleeding Kansas* (New Haven: Yale University Press).

Paine, S. C. M. (1996). *Imperial Rivals: China, Russia, and Their Disputed Frontiers* (New York: M. E. Sharpe).

Pan, Philipp (2002). 'U.S. Warns of Plot by Group in W. China', *Washington Post*, 29 August, www.washingtonpost.com/archive/politics/2002/08/29/us-warns-of-plot-by-group-in-w-china/5607dd9b-9d70-419a-8bac-1f3b39e12bc9/ (accessed 16 July 2021).

PMPRCUN (Permanent Mission of the PRC to the UN) (2001). 'Terrorist Activities Perpetrated by "Eastern Turkistan" Organizations and Their Links with Osama bin Laden and the Taliban', 29 November.

Reuters (2017). 'Uyghurs Should Be Aware of "Two-Faced" People in Separatism Fight, Official Says', 10 April, www.reuters.com/article/us-china-xinjiang-security-idUSKBN17C0HJ (accessed 16 July 2021).

Roberts, Sean R. (1998). 'Negotiating Locality, Islam, and National Culture in a Changing Borderlands: The Revival of the *Mashrap* Ritual among Young Uyghur Men in the Ili Valley', *Central Asian Survey* 17 (4), 673–700.

Roberts, Sean R. (2004). 'A Land of Borderlands: Implications of Xinjiang's Trans-border Interactions', in S. Frederick Starr (ed.), *Xinjiang: China's Muslim Borderlands* (New York: M. E. Sharpe), 216–237.

Roberts, Sean R. (2016). 'Development with Chinese Characteristics in Xinjiang: A Solution to Ethnic Tension or Part of the Problem?', in Michael Clarke and Douglas Smith (eds), *China's Frontier Regions: Ethnicity, Economic Integration and Foreign Relations* (London: I.B. Tauris), 22–55.

Roberts, Sean R. (2020). *The War on the Uyghurs: China's Internal Campaign against a Muslim Minority* (Princeton: Princeton University Press).

Ryono, Angel, and Matthew Galway (2015). 'Xinjiang under China: Reflections on the Multiple Dimensions of the 2009 Urumqi Uprising', *Asian Ethnicity* 16 (2), 235–255.

Schluessel, Eric (2020). *Land of Strangers: The Civilizing Project in Qing Central Asia* (New York: Columbia University Press).

SCIOPRC (State Council Information Office of the PRC) (2002). '"East Turkistan" Terrorist Forces Cannot Get Away with Impunity', China.org, 21 January, www.china.org.cn/english/2002/Jan/25582.htm (accessed 16 July 2021).

Short, Damien (2010). 'Cultural Genocide and Indigenous Peoples: A Sociological Approach', *International Journal of Human Rights* 14 (6), 833–848.

Smith Finley, Joanne (2013). *The Art of Symbolic Resistance: Uyghur Identities and Uyghur-Han Relations in Contemporary Xinjiang* (Leiden: Brill).

Stanton, Gregory (1998). 'The 8 Stages of Genocide', Genocide Watch, http://genocidewatch.net/2013/03/14/the-8-stages-of-genocide/ (accessed 6 April 2021).

Stuart, Paul H. (2020). 'Interventions in Native American Communities during an Era of Assimilation', *Journal of Community Practice* 27 (4), 296–308.

Thum, Rian (2018). 'The Uyghurs in Modern China', *Oxford Encyclopedia of Asian History* (Oxford: Oxford University Press), https://doi.org/10.1093/acrefore/9780190277727.013.160.

TIP (Turkistan Islamic Party) (2008). Untitled [Abdul Haq's statement on the Olympics], March.

TIP (Turkistan Islamic Party) (2013). *Beijing Tiänänmen Mäydanda Elip Berilghan Jihadi Ämäliyät Toghrisida Bayanat*, November.

Tohti, Ilham (2015). 'Present-Day Ethnic Problems in Xinjiang Uighur Autonomous Region: Overview and Recommendations', China Change, 22 April (trans. Cindy Carter), https://chinachange.org/2015/04/22/present-day-ethnic-problems-in-xinjiang-uighur-autonomous-region-overview-and-recommendations-1/ (accessed 16 July 2021).

Toops, Stanley (2004). 'Demographics and Development in Xinjiang after 1949', *East-West Center Washington Working Papers* 1 (Washington, DC: East-West Center), www.eastwestcenter.org/publications/demographics-and-development-xinjiang-after-1949 (accessed 16 July 2021).

Traywick, Catherine (2013). 'Chinese Officials Ask Muslim Women to Unveil in the Name of Beauty', *Foreign Policy*, 26 November, https://foreignpolicy.com/2013/11/26/chinese-officials-ask-muslim-women-to-unveil-in-the-name-of-beauty/ (accessed 16 July 2021).

Tricoire, Damien (ed.) (2017). *Enlightened Colonialism: Civilization Narratives and Imperial Politics in the Age of Reason* (New York: Palgrave Macmillan).

UHRP (Uyghur Human Rights Project) (2010). 'Can Anyone Hear Us? Voices from the 2009 Unrest in Urumqi', 1 July, https://uhrp.org/report/can-anyone-hear-us-voices-2009-unrest-urumchi/ (accessed 16 July 2021).

UHRP (Uyghur Human Rights Project) (2012). 'Uyghur Homeland, Chinese Frontier: The Xinjiang Work Forum', 27 July, https://uhrp.org/report/new-report-uhrp-uyghur-homeland-chinese-frontier-xinjiang-work-forum-and-centrally-led/ (accessed 16 July 2021).

UNESCO (2003). 'Mission Report: A Systematic Approach to Identification and Nomination', Mission to the Chinese Silk Road as World Cultural Heritage Route.

United Nations (1948). *Convention on the Prevention and Punishment of the Crime of Genocide* (New York: United Nations), https://bit.ly/35wbW4V (accessed 16 July 2021).

Van Kreiken, Robert (2004). 'Rethinking Cultural Genocide: Aboriginal Child Removal and Settler-Colonial State Formation', *Ocenia* 75 (2), 125–151.

Veracini, Lorenzo (2014). 'Understanding Colonialism and Settler Colonialism as Distinct Formations', *Interventions* 16 (5), 615–633.

Wan, William (2013). 'Chinese Police Say Tiananmen Square Crash Was "Premeditated, Violent, Terrorist Attack"', *Washington Post*, 30 October, https://wapo.st/3xslV7d (accessed 16 July 2021).

Wang, David (1996). 'The USSR and the Establishment of the Eastern Turkestan Republic in Xinjiang', *Journal of Institute of Modern History, Academia Sinica, Taipei* 25, 337–378.

Wei, Shan, and Weng Cuifen (2010). 'China's New Policy in Xinjiang and Its Challenges', *East Asian Policy* 2 (3), 58–66.

Wong, Edward (2008). 'Doubt Arises in Account of an Attack in China', *New York Times*, 29 September, www.nytimes.com/2008/09/29/world/asia/29kashgar.html (accessed 16 July 2021).

Wong, Edward (2014). 'China Sentences Uighur Scholar to Life', *New York Times*, 24 September, www.nytimes.com/2014/09/24/world/asia/china-court-sentences-uighur-scholar-to-life-in-separatism-case.html (accessed 16 July 2021).

Xinhua (2014). 'Xinjiang's Party Chief Wages "People's War" against Terrorism', *China Daily*, 26 May, www.chinadaily.com.cn/china/2014-05/26/content_17541318.htm (accessed 16 July 2021).

York, Geoffrey (2008). 'Beijing Busy Welcoming the World as It Turns Away Its Ethnic Minorities', *The Globe and Mail*, 18 July, www.theglobeandmail.com/news/world/beijing-busy-welcoming-the-world-as-it-turns-away-its-ethnic-minorities/article656845/ (accessed 16 July 2021).

Zenn, Jacob (2018). 'The Turkistan Islamic Party in Double-Exile: Geographic and Organizational Divisions in Uighur Jihadism', *Terrorism Monitor* 16 (17), 8–11.

Zenz, Adrian (2019). '"Thoroughly Reforming Them towards a Healthy Heart Attitude": China's Political Re-education Campaign in Xinjiang', *Central Asian Survey* 38 (1), 102–128.

Zenz, Adrian, and James Leibold (2017). 'Chen Quanguo: The Strongman behind Beijing's Securitization Strategy in Tibet and Xinjiang', *China Brief* 17 (12), 16–24.

Zhou, Zunyou (2019). 'Chinese Strategy for De-radicalization', *Terrorism and Political Violence* 31 (6), 1187–1209.

Zizek, Slavoj (2002). *Welcome to the Desert of the Real* (London: Verso Press).

Part II

Discourses and practices of repression

5

Pathology, inducement, and mass incarcerations of Xinjiang's 'targeted population'

Timothy A. Grose and James Leibold

Even the neatly staged scene inside one of the Xinjiang Uyghur Autonomous Region's (XUAR) 'vocational training centres' was unnerving. An unidentified young Uyghur woman dressed in a red-and-black tracksuit spoke to a Reuters reporter as dozens of other Uyghurs donning the same uniform wrote feverishly behind schoolhouse-style desks. Her eyes nervously shifted on- and off-camera. She recalled suffering from extremist thoughts, which had invaded her brain after she listened to several religious sermons delivered by a non-state-employed imam. Authorities in her hometown quickly intervened. They told the young woman her actions violated state law and 'recommended' she enter a new government programme to overcome her deviance (Blanchard 2019).

If her incarceration follows the pattern of others, she will remain in 'school' until authorities 'let her out' (Bunin 2019) and grant her permission to be transferred to a factory or other forms of acceptable vocation or detention. She is what Chinese Communist Party (CCP) authorities call a 'targeted person' (Ch. *zhongdian renyuan*): an individual who is deemed to pose a threat to social stability but does not merit formal legal prosecution; rather they must be closely monitored and are often required to undergo 'transformation through education' (Ch. *jiaoyu zhuanhua*) (Pan 2020: 3). Through an evasive process of decontamination, the party believes she can be literally overhauled – made 'lighter', 'brighter', and more 'lively' in the words of Chinese propagandists (CCTV 2019) – and recast in the image of the Han ethnic majority and its chiefly male CCP officials.

In Xinjiang, the Chinese administrative region encompassing the Uyghur homeland, countless individuals have been identified by the CCP as threats to social order. Those who cannot be reformed through first-line treatment – visits from government workers (Byler 2018) and presentations of state 'care' – are quarantined: forcibly taken from their homes (Batke 2019), ripped away from their families, and even separated from their children (Zenz 2019a) to undergo treatment in 'concentrated re-education centers' (Ch. *jizhong zhuanhua jiaoyu zhongxin*) (Sudworth 2018). This term encompasses a broad taxonomy of incarceration, from detention centres (Ch. *kanshousuo*), prisons (Ch. *jianyu*), to what the government dubs 'professional skills education training centres' (Ch. *zhiye jineng jiaoyu peixun zhongxin*). Publicly, the CCP insists these latter facilities are 'the same as boarding schools' (Martina 2019): a curious gloss – even for party officials – considering many of their grounds are fortified with steel barricades, barbed wire fences, and security guards (Ruser 2020).

Yet, satellite imagery, government tender documents, and survivor testimonies present a harrowing reality inside these centres (*Foreign Policy* 2018; Samuel 2018a; Zenz 2018; Ruser 2020). This evidence undermines the CCP's attempts to justify and humanize what it claims are necessary counterterrorism and de-extremization measures (Klimeš 2018; *Global Times* 2019). These re-education centres have been established to forcefully and permanently erase meaningful cultural markers (including Islam and native language) from Turkic Muslims, and amount to what experts believe is an intentional act of cultural genocide (Leibold 2019a). Internees are not students but rather patients and prisoners.

Their therapy reflects long-standing Chinese practices for the treatment of those with severe mental illness (Samuel 2018b), drug addiction (Human Rights Watch 2002), and communicable diseases. In fact, CCP officials in the region have recently returned to the lexicon of pathology in their efforts to 'save' scores of Turkic Muslims, especially Uyghurs and Kazakhs, from themselves and their communities. The party's use of phrases such as 'contracting illness' (Ch. *ganran bingdu*) (Hetian lingjuli 2017), 'penetrate like an intravenous needle' (Ch.

guanchuan diandi) (Tian Shan Net 2015), and 'cure sickness to save a patient' or 'reform through criticism' (Ch. *zhibing jiuren*) (XUAR Reform and Development Commission 2018) exposes a familiar rhetoric: like counter-revolutionaries, prostitutes, and other aberrant populations before them, Turkic Muslims are now deemed unacceptable threats to the social order and thus must be quarantined and then actively reprogrammed. Indeed, the party has adapted and expanded its usage of Mao-era terms like 'targeted population' (Ch. *zhongdian renkou*) and 'poisonous weeds' (Ch. *ducao*) in order to apply them to Xinjiang's Turkic Muslims, whom officials consider to be existential threats to social stability and a roadblock to realizing Xi Jinping's Belt and Road Initiative (Agence France-Presse 2019) and the 'China dream' (Hillman 2018).

The CCP has long policed social deviance and political disloyalty, with Xinjiang's Muslim population the latest target of its repressive intervention into the lives, thoughts, and behaviours of its citizens. But here an entire ethno-religious community is lumped together in the same sociopolitical and criminal category as individuals convicted of violent crime, drug addicts, political activists, and mental health patients. Using the pathology metaphor within the context of the 'targeted population' label, the CCP can simultaneously justify repression (i.e. provide a cure), apply this repression to large segments of society (i.e. treat an outbreak), and deflect blame from its own policies (i.e. offer an index case to an epidemiology that originates outside China). In this chapter, we interrogate the CCP's pathologizing of a culture and a people in China, and demonstrate how it reflects what James C. Scott (1998: 87–102) identifies as 'authoritarian high-modernism', a utopian yet pernicious effort by the state to re-engineer society in its own image and create a perfect social order through science and technology, but one that actually leaves a wake of personal destruction in its path.

Curing social deviants

The CCP has applied the language of pathology and to great utility on deviant populations – beggars, prostitutes, rightists, criminals, and even unemployed Han men (Yang 2010) – in order to justify the use of state violence and transformative methodologies. In fact, 'thought work' (Ch. *sixiang gongzuo*) or 'thought reform' (Ch. *sixiang gaizao*) is foundational to Chinese political culture and emerged as the modus operandi of the CCP. 'Thought work' can be understood as the collection of the party's vast resources and agents for spreading its political messages to the masses. This massive enterprise includes large-scale institutions such as media, schooling, entertainment (Brady 2009), and penal facilities, but also more personalized interventions between officials and individuals such as one-on-one talks (Ch. *tanxin*) and group meetings (Ch. *tanxinhui*) (He 2015). Like the teeth of a giant gear, these institutions are supposed to operate in unison in order to transmit a 'singular' and 'correct' view of the world to its citizens.

The CCP first experimented with a 'scientific' model of thought control before coming to power. As early as 1942, its leader, Mao Zedong, stated that 'our object in exposing errors and criticizing shortcoming is like that of a doctor curing a disease' (Sheres and Springer 1973: 381). During the Yan'an Rectification Campaign (Ch. *Yanan zhengfeng yundong*, 1943–44), Mao and his supporters set about systematically detaining political opponents after taking control of the party during the Long March (1934–35) (Cheng 2009: 59–70). Starting with the writing of Mao and other top party leaders, cadres were encouraged to admit mistakes and shortcomings in small study groups, and through 'self-criticism' and 'exegetical bonding' arrive at a new plane of collective understanding and discourse. Any recalcitrants were 'rescued' from themselves through an intense public and private inquisition of rebuke, confession, and cathartic cleansing. The results were nothing short of remarkable in Yan'an, leading to what Apter and Saich call a 'total restructuring of mind and outlook in accordance with principles and precepts laid down by Mao' (Apter and Saich 1994: 263).

Often times, officials also identified these 'shortcomings' when examining ethnic and religious cultures, which the CCP and mainstream Han society consider 'backward' and in need of rectification (Gladney 1994). For example, 'unscientific' Tibetan medicine was the target of Mao-era campaigns that sought to promote specifically Chinese treatments (Hofer 2018). In one poster from this era, visibly Han doctors in lab coats are treating *chuba*-wearing Tibetan patients on the steppe (Dong c. 1970). The scientific laws of historical materialism meant some cultures and peoples were more socially advanced than others, and the superior ethnic majority in China assumed the 'Han man's burden' of pulling and prodding the weak and uncouth Uyghurs, Tibetans, and other ethnic minority communities towards the light of modernity (Leibold 2007).

Yet, Mao viewed the 'masses' of both majority and minority groups as equally 'poor and blank', and thus pliable for moulding. 'On a blank sheet of paper free from any mark,' he wrote in 1958, 'the freshest and most beautiful characters can be written, the freshest and most beautiful pictures can be painted' (Mao 1966: 36). Still, any sign of deviance or resistance was also a 'poisonous weed', in Mao's words, and 'like all ghosts and monsters, must be subjected to criticism; in no circumstance should they be allowed to spread unchecked' (Mao 1966: 19). Here cognitive and physical rehabilitation of aberrant populations functions like a 'moral orthopaedic' (Foucault 1977: 32) wiping clean stains or blemishes through an intense process of disciplining and decontamination.

Therefore, Mao insisted on controlling and containing society's brambles by pre-emptively identifying sprouting and invasive 'weeds'. These dissents are known as 'targeted populations' or 'focus personnel' (Ch. *zhongdian renkou*) in party-speak. In 1953, the term – used only in tightly-knit law enforcement circles – replaced and extended the state's blacklist system. Initially, the label identified 'non-repentant family members of counter-revolutionaries, landlords in exile, various types of "class enemies", and "suspicious" people from outside China' (Wang 2004: 127). The CCP continues to employ this designation today – replete with political rubrics that classify citizens into an unofficial social hierarchy – to pan for delinquent citizens. Officials believe careful surveillance of the targeted population will 'prevent, discover, and fight unlawful criminal activity; [and] educate, manage, and save those in unlawful activity, in order to maintain social safety' (Pan 2020: 87).

In greater China, or *neidi* (interior) in Chinese, the targeted population includes (1) citizens deemed risks to national security; (2) individuals suspected of serious crimes; (3) individuals who have exhibited behaviours suggesting early signs of violence; (4) ex-convicts; and (5) narcotics users (Wang 2004: 131–132). Citizens branded with this label are subjected to greater surveillance scrutiny by police and party officials. For example, local *hukou* (residential permit) officers routinely monitor the basic information and current behaviour of *all* citizens registered at a local police station (Ch. *paichusuo*); however, officials must keep up-to-date records and frequent checks of the 'targeted populations', including details like current behaviour, family members, financial status, interpersonal relationships, physical features, speech characteristics such as slang or dialect, personality, and daily activities (Wang 2004: 124–129).

The party believes it can prevent the germination of 'targeted people' – and avoid conflict – if it cultivates an environment conducive for the breeding and rearing of 'high-quality' individuals. In the eyes of CCP officials, the masses possess varying degrees of personal quality or *suzhi* (embodied quality) (Lin 2017). As the term gained popularity in the 1970s, it was often contrasted with *suyang* (素养) or learned behaviours (Kipnis 2006: 297). The term took on new life during sweeping birth control and education campaigns of the 1980s as policymakers believed limited births and state schooling could improve the 'quality' of China's population. *Suzhi* transformed into an attainable virtue (Kipnis 2006: 298–301) – not unlike the Confucian pursuit towards the ideal 'gentleman' (Ch. *junzi*) – which could be realized through discipline and self-cultivation (Ch. *xiuxinyangxing*) (Gardner 2014: 16–32). To be sure, *suzhi* has retained some of its original essence. Since environment shapes *suzhi*, physical surroundings produce divergent levels or what may be understood as quality 'potential'. In other words, individuals raised in desolate and remote villages with poor schooling, few employment opportunities, and poor hygiene practices will likely cultivate inferior quality (Ch. *suzhi di*). On the other hand, urban centres – with their neat and orderly environment – can refine *suzhi* through access to education, health care, and other modern amenities.

Therefore, the CCP's efforts to increase education levels, urbanize rural populations, alleviate poverty, and otherwise 'assist' its citizenry is as much about elevating *suzhi* – and thus maintaining stability – as it is about economic development. Jennifer Pan has persuasively argued that during the initial decades of the Reform Era (1978–) social stability was the means for achieving a robust and modern economy; however, at present, social stability is now the end goal in itself. In a process Pan calls 'seepage', all CCP policies are now shaped by the party's insistence on stability (Pan 2020: 4–8). For example, local governments throughout China are tasked with building 'civilized cities' (Ch. *wenming chengshi*). Construction is often at the heart of these projects because new housing and office spaces can quickly and dramatically impact on the interconnected concepts of material (Ch. *wuzhi*)/spiritual (Ch. *jingshen*) civilization (Cliff 2016: 34), and at an individual level can help to boost one's *suzhi*. As such, the party-state's construction of high-rise apartments replete with modern amenities – instead of dusty and dishevelled courtyard dwellings – can nudge all communities towards the nation's 'epistemological center of civilization': the self-disciplined Han urbanite (Moreno 2018: 28–29). 'Civilized living' – with its proper hygiene, disciplined behaviour, ritualized manners, good education, fluency in the national language, and most important wealth and political loyalty – yields high *suzhi* (Anagnost 2004: 193; Moreno 2018: 33–34).

Meanwhile, this civilizing project – as a 'gift' from the party to the masses – entangles citizens in a social bond forged from material and emotional debt and repayment, or what the Chinese call 'human feelings' (Ch. *renqing*) (Yang 1994: 68). Although *renqing* operates within the complex realm of – largely Confucian-defined – interpersonal ethics, it can be unpacked by analysing the dynamics of gift-giving. In her canonical book on social relationships in China, Mayfair Yang explains, 'Gifts require reciprocity, and so do relationships; therefore the ethics of gift-giving are extended to all human relationships' (Yang 1994: 70). In other words, the material gifts of high *suzhi* are commodified objects of the CCP's compassion (Yang 2013: 106–110) and forms of 'repressive assistance' because the recipients become increasingly dependent on patrimonial provisions allocated by the party-state (Pan 2020: 126–127). The party seeks to literally buy stability, which it hopes will lead to individual self-regulation, mutual monitoring of behaviour by urban communities, and a fully visible and ordered set of national spaces (Bray 2008).

A tried-and-true method

Individuals who slip through society's cracks and become 'targets' for attention require a far more invasive and coercive set of interventions. Following the establishment of the PRC, Communist authorities constructed a vast network of prison labour camps (Ch. *laodong gaizao*), or *laogai* for short, where convicted 'criminals' were detained and required to seek 'reform' through forced labour and re-education. The CCP also created a parallel, extrajudicial form of detention and educational transformation for 'minor offences', including those who exhibited 'abnormal' (Ch. *feizhengchang*) thoughts and behaviour. Known as 're-education through labour' (Ch. *laodong jiaoyang, laojiao,* or RTL), this 'non-criminal administrative sanction' was authorized by a 1955 Central Committee directive and ratified by the National People's Congress in 1957, where it was promoted as a more effective method for dealing with internal, non-antagonistic contradictions among the people (Wu 1992: 81–107; Dutton and Zhangrun 2005: 122ff.; Su 2016: 48). China built over three hundred *laojiao* facilities, with estimates of the number of people subjected to RTL varying widely, from hundreds of thousands, to four million, or even twenty million people over the last sixty years (Wu 1992: 18; Su 2016: 47; Noakes 2018: 200).

These extrajudicial labour camps sought to reform 'ideological undesirables' outside the formal legal and penal systems. Inspired by Soviet theories about gulags and Marxist–Leninist beliefs that labour was materially transformative and cognitively liberating, the CCP required detainees to work as a part of their rehabilitation. In the post-Mao period, the party-state also turned to civilizational justification for its coercive programme of transformation through education. As the Confucian concept of 'harmonious society' re-entered popular political discourse (Spencer 2005), the party looked to the ancient sages for the conceptual underpinnings of 're-education'. According to Confucian classics, a benevolent and enlightened state has a moral obligation to shape the thought and behaviour of its subjects and recast them in its own image. This is what the third-century BCE philosopher Xunzi called the planning of 'crooked timber' and modern Chinese officials term *ganhua* (感化), the reformation of vile character traits through moral exemplar: a transformative ethos that is central to education, penal incarceration, and even alliance building in China today (Dutton and Zhangrun 2005: 111–114; Cheng 2009: 49).

Through collective, large-scale work and study sessions, detainees are expected to arrive at a new collective consciousness. *Laojiao* was not considered judicial punishment or the deprivation of liberty, but rather 'administrative disciplinary action' (Ch. *xingzheng chu fen*). Detainees could be held for three years (with a one-year extension) without due process or legal recourse; although in theory, those who exhibited 'good behaviour' were permitted holidays and regular family visitation. That said, we now have many examples of abuses within the system, with citizens subjected to arbitrary detention, ill-treatment, and even torture. Many died or were driven to suicide inside the system (Wang 2017). Yet there was also a great deal of variation in how *laojiao* was implemented and used by local officials (Seymour and Anderson 1998: 9).

To be sure, re-education is best thought of as a fluid set of utopian processes rather than an Orwellian gulag from which there is no escape (Dutton and Zhangrun 2005: 106). The RTL camps evolved during the 1950s, only to decline during the chaos of the Cultural Revolution. They were reinvented and institutionalized during the 1980s as a tool of social governance and stability maintenance (Ch. *weiwen*) (Yu and Mosher 2010), and appear to have even survived RTL's formal disbanding in 2013 (Noakes 2018: 211–214). The forced labour of inmates formed an important part of the system's political economy, albeit never fully subsidizing the institution with detainees paid 40 per cent of an average worker's wage (Wu 1992: 99). Despite its internal dynamics, the purpose of *laojiao* was always ideological remoulding and social transformation rather than incarceration, the rehabilitation of aberrant populations through work, study, and disciplining.

Under domestic and international pressure, the National People's Congress formally abolished the system of re-education through labour in 2013; yet the arbitrary detention of deviant populations continues in China today, with officials now using so-called black jails, psychiatric facilities, detoxification centres, legal education classes, and custody and education centres to subject citizens to extrajudicial thought reform (Amnesty International 2013; Dui Hua Foundation 2013; Li 2015; Noakes 2018: 199–216). Forced labour, in theory, has been removed from the process, with more focus on skills and vocational training as a pathway to employment; although there is little volition with the party-state determining individual worth and how it should be deployed (Byler 2019a). Without any clear and consistent legal guidelines, these revised methods of social transformation encourage a more nimble, customized, and responsive form of governance according to Stephen Noakes (2018: 215), one that is far more hidden and potentially repressive.

Re-education in Xinjiang

Due to its remoteness, Xinjiang has a long history of housing Han criminals and political exiles (Dutton 1992: 249–290; Seymour and Anderson 1998: 8–12). Under the CCP some of these individuals were mobilized into the Xinjiang Production and Construction Corps (or Bingtuan, 兵团, for short) during the early 1950s, and tasked with colonizing and developing China's 'new frontier' (新疆). The Bingtuan also established a network of labour prisons (Ch. *laogai*) which came to house some of the most serious Han prisoners (both political and criminal) from other provinces. A parallel stream of labour-re-education (Ch. *laojiao*) existed both inside the Bingtuan as well as at the regional level. The labour camps in Xinjiang were notorious for their poor conditions, corrupt management, and inhumane treatment (Seymour and Anderson 1998: 44–127). Yet because of its dominant focus on *laogai*, the *laojiao* system was smaller than other regions in China, and chiefly focused on local criminals and drug addicts, especially among the ethnic minority population (Seymour and Anderson 1998: 75). One official Xinjiang source put the number of RTL detainees at 'more than 1,000 people' across ten different centres in 2000, with a 90 per cent reformation rate among the nearly 60,000 detainees since the establishment of the XUAR in 1955 (Zhang 2000: 22). By the time the *laojiao* system celebrated its fiftieth anniversary in Xinjiang in 2007, officials claimed that more than 100,000 'transgressors' had been 'successfully saved through education and persuasion' (Pan 2007).

As sporadic unrest increased in Xinjiang during the 1990s (Bovingdon 2010: 105–134), the *laojiao* system was used to detain, and in theory, transform Uyghur 'hooligans', 'religious extremists', and 'separatists'. While 'ringleaders' were charged and sentenced with 'endangering state security', many of their friends, followers, and family members were either subjected to *laojiao* or classified as a 'targeted population' or 'special groups' (Ch. *teshu renquan*) requiring extra surveillance (Fu 2005: 828–829).

Official sources reveal that in 2001 half of the RTL population in Xinjiang were accused of belonging to an illegal religious organization or engaging in illegal religious activities, and 85 per cent were between the ages of eighteen and thirty years old. The camps were 'jam-packed' due to a 'sharply upward trend' in the number of people sentence to RTL (Human Rights Watch 2002). Like elsewhere in China, drug addicts and Falun Gong practitioners in Xinjiang were also subjected to re-education proceedings, with Human Rights Watch estimating in 2002 that some 10,000 practitioners were detained in *laojiao* camps across China (Human Rights Watch 2002). Following the 7 July 2009 ethnic riots in the regional capital of Urumqi, hundreds (if not thousands) of Uyghurs and other participants were subjected to RTL (Qin 2011).

In Xinjiang, like elsewhere, the guiding principles of RTL are 'education, transformation through persuasion, and redemption' (Ch. *jiaoyu, ganhua, wanjiu*), with a dense web of individual and group disciplining processes. Many of the methods pioneered by Mao in Yan'an are still employed in Xinjiang today. One *laojiao* official in Xinjiang outlined a five-step process in 2002 with detainees first made to reflect on their situation through group study and collective labour; they are next encouraged to recognize their guilt and mistakes; then, they are required to declare a firm break with any splittist groups or illegal religious activities; finally, they are required to publicly repent and sign a formal written guarantee not to reoffend. Inducements are used to coax the reluctant inmate along the path to redemption. And if persuasion fails, more forceful methods are warranted: 'Regarding those who are incorrigible, persist with a reactionary stance, and resist transformation,' a judicial official in Xinjiang wrote in 2002, 'we must correctly employ coercive methods to carry out stern punishment' (Yang 2002: 18–19).

Yet under Xi Jinping's self-proclaimed 'new era' (Ch. *Xinshidai*) of CCP power, there is a new sense of urgency and danger as China 'moves to centre stage and makes greater contributions to mankind' (Economy 2018). The party-state seeks to assert Chinese power abroad while guarding against 'hostile' foreign forces and ideas domestically. Xinjiang is now viewed as one of the 'front lines' of this ideological and political battle, with the 'import' of religious extremism and terrorism viewed as an existential threat to stability. Officials believe that the agentive potential of economic development alone will not increase minority *suzhi* and solve the 'ethnic problem' (Ch. *minzu wenti*). To strengthen ethnic unity and identification with the 'Chinese nation/race' (Ch. *Zhonghua minzu*) among ethnic groups, the party must actively forge it through regular intervention. During a September 2019 speech, Xi Jinping urged party officials 'to plant the seed of love for Zhonghua deep in the soul of each and every child' (Xinhua 2019). 'Culture,' Xi told a gathering of ethnic role models, 'is the soul of every nation and cultural identity is the root artery of national unity.' In fact, the narrow focus on economic development in the past left China vulnerable to outside meddling, according to Zhu Weiqun, with 'hostile foreign forces' exploiting ethnic sentiments and differences in order to weaken and ultimately disintegrate China (Leibold 2019b).

Consequently, the *ganhua* possess is culturally degrading in Xinjiang by design. It requires the unlearning and discarding of 'backward' (Ch. *luohou*) and 'low-quality' (Ch. *di suzhi*) habits, customs, and cultural traits, central to what Stevan Harrell has identified as the CCP's 'civilizing project' in the borderlands (Harrell 1995). Education, whether forced or voluntary, is viewed as salvation from barbarism. While the pace of change differs with each group, the ultimate goal is complete homogeneity under the banner of Han-centric nationalism. Indeed, material and public recognition in Xinjiang is closely tied to the adoption of Han linguistic and cultural norms. Failure to move in this direction risks a 'deviant' designation or being assigned the enigmatic label of 'targeted population' or 'special groups' who are earmarked for special 'assistance, education and management work' (Ch. *bangjiaoguan gongzuo*) (Zhi 2014: 25–26).

In Xinjiang today, Uyghurs – regardless of their level of education, party affiliation, and socio-economic status – can find themselves arbitrarily and pre-emptively deemed a 'targeted population'. If those who express their loyalty to the party in public could secretly be untrustworthy 'two-faced people' (Ch. *liangmian ren*) who seek to undermine the nation and its stability in private, no one can be trusted. Uyghurs have been targets of racial profiling and arbitrary detention long before the 2009 Ürümchi riots (Wong 2009), but authorities did not formally reinterpret the targeted population designation until then Xinjiang Party Secretary Zhang Chunxian announced a 'People's War on Terror' in 2014 (Xinhua 2014). The first notable expansion of the

Pathology, inducement, and mass incarcerations 139

'targeted population' was packaged in the region-wide 'five types of people' (BBC News 2014) and 'Project Beauty' campaigns – a five-year, US$8 million multimedia initiative that promotes 'modern' (i.e. secular) female fashion and educates women to discard their veils – which culminated in legislation introduced in 2015 (Leibold and Grose 2016). The 'five types of people' referred to women who donned *ḥijāb*, *lichäk*, *chumbäl*, and *jilbāb*, young men who groomed 'abnormally long' beards, and individuals who wore clothing featuring star-and-moon insignia in any public area.

Law enforcement in Xinjiang then expanded the 'targeted population' designation again in 2016. Under this revision, Xinjiang's 'targeted population' included the 'five grades' (Ch. *wuji*) and 'ten types of people' (Ch. *shi lei renyuan*). 'Five grades' people included:

(1) those who possess a real threat to society;
(2) have a tendency (Ch. *qingxiang*) to possess a real threat to society;
(3) are ideologically stubborn (Ch. *wanggu*);
(4) are ideologically or emotionally unstable; and
(5) commoners (*lao baixing*). (Li 2016)

Meanwhile, the 'ten types of people' referred to those individuals who:

(1) engaged in 'three evil forces' groups but did not commit a crime;
(2) harboured (Ch. *baobi*), organized, or funded terrorist activities, but have not been convicted of a crime;
(3) committed acts that threatened national security, but were already released from prison;
(4) engaged in activities that threaten state security, including released criminals who had committed common crimes;
(5) engaged in crimes against state security;
(6) disseminated (on the Internet or otherwise) opinions (Ch. *yanlun*) about ethnic separatism and religious extremism;
(7) took advantage of social disorder to create rumours that influence social order;
(8) engaged in 'illegal religious activities' such as delivering unsanctioned *khuṭba*s, or sermons, organized religious gatherings, and operated or attended private religious schools;

(9) printed, sold, distributed, or transported illegal religious articles, especially those who are repeat offenders; and
(10) expressed dissatisfaction with society and may pose a threat to national security or others. (Li 2016)

By expanding and reinterpretating the 'targeted population' classification, the CCP blurs the already hazy legal parameters of 'terrorism' (Zhou 2015) and 'extremism' – defined by the CCP as 'propositions and conduct using distortion of religious teachings or other means to incite hatred or discrimination and advocate violence' (China Law Translate 2017) – with acts of political activism, civil disobedience, or even simple ethno-cultural pride. In fact, the 'targeted population' designation now comprises five main categories – threats to national security, suspects of serious crimes, those capable of creating instability (including the mentally ill), ex-convicts, and narcotics users – and dozens of subcategories which are open to broad interpretation (Pan 2020: 88–89). Under this definition of 'targeted population', an individual who does not possess the correct ideological outlook or mental disposition receives the same scrutiny from law enforcement as someone plotting a violent attack, protesting Xinjiang's veiling ban, or sharing 'illegal' religious texts with a friend.

The criteria defining Xinjiang's 'targeted population' were expanded once again in 2017 when officials introduced a new social taxonomy that labels each citizen as either 'safe' (Ch. *fangxin*), 'normal' (Ch. *yiban*), or 'unsafe' (Ch. *bu fangxin*) (Chin and Bürge 2017). In 2016, law enforcement personnel assigned to urban neighbourhood communities (Ch. *shequ*) were responsible for labelling every adult with one of these three terms (Byler 2019b). While implementation varies locally, party officials use a range of metrics (such as age, ethnicity, religious practices, foreign contacts, and travel abroad) to 'scientifically' quantify an individual's risk profile and social worth. Freedom of movement (both physical and virtual) and access to government entitlements are now determined by this point system (Meduza 2018). According to one account, individuals are initially provided with a 100-point base score (Zand 2018) but then penalized points for such things as having relatives abroad, praying, criticizing the government, or even owning a compass (Greer 2018). Individuals whose scores fall below the 60-point threshold are deemed 'unsafe' and risk detainment (Zand 2018).

Unsurprisingly, given these metrics of classification, Uyghurs and other Turkic Muslims find themselves disproportionally deemed unsafe in Xinjiang, and, as a result, possibly a million or more have been arbitrarily detained in a new archipelago of re-education camps since 2017. Yet, ultimately, Xinjiang's surveillance taxonomy transcends and often transgresses ethnic boundaries. In other words, surveillance is not solely about distinguishing Uyghurs from Han and Hui from Uyghurs. Rather there are other factors at play, such as class, gender, religion, culture, quality (Ch. *suzhi*), and spatial residency, that determine how the party-state watches, sorts, and disciplines its domestic population. Here we must confront the gap between a Mandarin-speaking, secular Uyghur party official in Ürümchi (such as XUAR Chairman Shöhrät Zakir) and a deeply religious, Turkic-speaking Uyghur framer in rural Kashgar prefecture, but also different shades of intermediateness. The ultimate goal of monitoring in Xinjiang is to nudge all residents – Han, Kazakh, Hui, Uyghurs, etc. – in a more compliant direction in order to standardize and normalize behaviour and eliminate any opposition to party rule.

Eradicating tumours

Xinjiang's version of the 'social credit system' and ad hoc applications of the label 'targeted population' place large numbers of Turkic Muslims, especially Uyghurs, under tight surveillance and at a great risk for detention. In Turpan city, for example, 2,764 individuals were identified in 2014 as requiring close surveillance and re-education, and graded by assumed risk, with '16 A category individuals (high level of real harm in the near future), 54 B category individuals (possibility of real harm in the near future), and 2,694 C category individuals (basically no harm in the near future); local officials claimed a nearly 100 per cent re-education rate' (Tulufan diqu gongzuo weiyuanhui 2014).

Meanwhile in Atush County, according to the Party Committee of Xinjiang's Department of Agriculture, one-third of its 200,000 residents (66,000) were affixed a 'targeted population' label and subjected to some form of 're-education' (Xinjiang Nongye Xinxi wang 2016). A Han cadre sent to Azihan village in Atush described her duties as visiting and closely monitoring each individual identified as a 'targeted person'. Many refused to say much, according to the cadre, but she kept detailed records of these interviews anyway. One man who was sentenced to twelve years in prison for committing a crime that threatened state security simply said he hoped to live life honestly (Ch. *tatashishi*) (Xinjiang linguo techan youxian gongsi 2014). Indeed, any individual suspected of not adopting the correct ideology or not faithfully obeying government policy, which the cadre reviewed at the end of each visit, would likely face some sort of 're-education'. The form and intensity of this re-education – one-on-one chats, government homestays, 'vocational' schools, or internment – is determined by 'the severity of the ideological infection' (Zhonggong Yining xian wei 2016).

For reasons that are not entirely clear, in early 2017 Xinjiang authorities began rounding up Muslim men and women for mass internment in purpose-built facilities, as party officials stepped up their efforts to 'eradicate malignant tumours' (Ch. *chu duliu*) and 'permanently cure' any aberrant behaviour (Liu 2017; Leibold 2019c). These extrajudicial institutions are officially known as 'counter-extremism' or 'de-radicalization' training centres, although they often go by more generic, palpable labels such as 'education and transformation training centres' (Ch. *jiaoyu zhuanhua peixun zhongxin*) or 'vocational training centres' (Ch. *zhiye jineng jiaoyu peixun zhongxin*) (Yulixian 2015; Human Rights Watch 2017). Once members of the 'targeted population' are removed from society they can begin a lengthy process of political, mental, and cultural rehabilitation.

Inside these camps, detainees are subjected to forced indoctrination and 'skills' sessions; some survivors have spoken about enduring coercive methods (including both psychological and physical torture) aimed at altering 'deviant' thought and deportment (Zenz 2019b). Those who submit and reform are promised freedom while those who refuse to yield are subjected to additional 're-education', or ultimately sentenced and imprisoned. Some detainees are required to study Mandarin, sing patriotic songs, watch 'Red' movies, and attend classes about correct ideology and permissible religious practices. According to the 12 November 2018 edition of the Uyghur-language *Xinjiang Daily*, the most widely circulated minority-language newspaper in Xinjiang, internees at a camp in Khotan engage in a three-tiered sequence of courses. First, they study the common language (Putonghua), before advancing onto law, and, upon satisfactory completion of these courses, they may engage in a trade, such as baking, cosmetology, hair-cutting, alterations, and agronomics (Uy. *yéza iqtisadi*). If detainees study these trades well, there are other opportunities available such as print-making and painting (Shinjang Géziti 2018a).

However, a rigid curriculum alone will not remedy what the CCP believes are deeply rooted problems shared by thousands (Chen 2015). In a Chinese–Uyghur bilingual article entitled 'Re-education Classes Are a Type of Free Hospital Stay for People with Ideological Illnesses' the author insists:

> Being 'infected' (Ch. *ganran*) by religious extremism and violent terrorist ideology but not receiving immediate 're-education' is similar to contracting an illness but not seeking a cure, or becoming a drug addict but refusing treatment. It is wishful thinking (Ch. *jiaoxing xinli*) to believe [you] will not be affected or shaken by [these thoughts]. (Hetian lingjuli 2017)

State media recycles the language of pathology when describing the region's concentration re-education centres. A January 2015 Tian Shan report describes these programmes as methods to 'penetrate' (Ch. *guanchuan*) detainees like an 'intravenous needle' (Tian Shan Net 2015). Similarly, a woman named Patigül interviewed by *Xinjiang Daily* remarked: 'Because my husband, Mämtimin, was infected (Uy. *yuqumlanghachq*a) by extremism, I never dressed up, and he didn't let me make my own money ... Now [through re-education], he dresses well, his hair and teeth are clean, and he has even influenced my own grooming habits' (Shinjang Géziti 2018a).

But allusions to pathology are not merely metaphorical: 're-education' often requires detainees to undergo psychological treatment. During a 16 October 2018 interview with Xinhua, Shohrat Zakir, chairman of the XUAR government, praises the 'professional psychological counseling services' provided to detainees (Xinhua 2018). These 'services' take the form of invasive psychological evaluations. In fact, officials in Hejing County hosted a clinical psychologist to conduct one-on-one screenings with all detainees. At the conclusion of their psychological evaluation, detainees were provided a course of treatment that will correct (or literally 'exorcise', Ch. *quxie fuzheng*) their harmful thoughts and ensure they resist extremism (Bayin guoleng fazhi qu 2017).

One mental health counsellor, himself Uyghur, told Chinese reporters: 'I think we are doing a really sacred (Uy. *muqäddäs*) thing [by working at a training centre]. We are saving the masses (Uy. *bir kishlär topi*] and a generation of people. Once they study well and their mental state is healthy, they will be able to live happily in society' (Shinjang Géziti 2018b). Indeed, CCP officials have not coincidently adopted the language of pathology to describe so-called extremist Turkic Muslims. Rather, the adaptation and expansion of the term 'targeted population' in the context of 're-education' conveniently places violent crimes, religious practices, addiction, political activism, and mental illness in the same sociopolitical and criminal category, virtually quarantining thousands of Uyghurs as potential malignant tumours. Likewise, this decision emboldens the CCP to administer an apoptosis approach to Turkic Muslims simply for asserting their ethno-religious identities. Yet the CCP's therapeutic intervention is ill-advised: it is destroying social trust while spurring cultural erasure and decades of systemic violence.

Conclusion: The hidden dangers of eradicating viruses

In late January 2020, Chinese state media provided the world with another surreal scene. Instead of a classroom and uniformed students singing gleefully, the report featured medical technicians dressed in hazmat suits, an empty metro station, and visibly ill patients isolated in intensive care units (Xinhua 2020a). COVID-19 had swept through most of central China, but the CCP was mobilizing its resources to contain the epidemic. Battalions of frontline workers were swiftly dispatched throughout the country and worked around the clock 'combing through communities' (Xinhua 2020b) to identify the infected, place the sick in quarantine, and treat them for the novel coronavirus. By early May, the *Global Times* announced that the party had 'contained' the epidemic as it was sweeping across the globe (*Global Times* 2020), setting off a discursive war of recrimination and misinformation about what went wrong and who was to blame (Mills 2020).

The same 'high modernist' mentality on visibility and control is driving the party to identify 'spiritually' and 'mentally' ill Uyghurs in Xinjiang. Indeed, officials believe that 'extremism' has spread throughout Xinjiang, and Uyghurs are inherently predisposed to its harms. The party's strategies for eliminating this social vice are similar to its responses to the COVID-19 outbreak. Potential hosts were identified as vulnerable 'targeted personnel' and then subjected to intense surveillance and corrective treatment. In Xinjiang, the most dangerous cases were isolated from society in concentrated re-education camps, where they were exposed to political indoctrination, forced labour, and, in some cases, corporal punishment as a form of 'treatment'. Elsewhere in China, entire neighbourhoods and even cities were locked down in response to the coronavirus. Those who tested positive were placed in quarantine for treatment while a state surveillance app determined who is safe and free to move about, and those that authorities think are a potential danger to themselves and thus must be closely monitored (*Japan Times* 2020). Ultimately, in both cases, the party claims victory – no new terror attacks in Xinjiang nor virus cases in China – but must remain in a constant state of vigilance for a possible 'second wave' or new outbreaks of instability.

In the case of Xinjiang, it is not only the 'infected' that are targeted but an entire ethno-national group. Today the Uyghurs and other Turkic Muslims are pre-emptively deemed unsafe regardless of their actual exposure to a 'virus' of extremism, instability, or COVID-19. The simple fact of being Uyghur is now enough to be a target of party-state suspicion. The Muslim madman must be saved from himself before his disease spreads and inflects others. 'The "three evil forces" are not some magical panacea for an ethnic group's strong muscles,' one Uyghur party leader told his co-ethnics, 'but rather a cancerous cell which is harmful to an ethnic group's healthy development' (Maituaong 2017). Yet the pathologizing of an entire ethnic and religious population erodes social cohesion and political legitimacy and cannot be conducive to the long-term health of Chinese society under President Xi Jinping. In the meantime, the CCP's mass internment strategy in Xinjiang is doing irreparable damage to the culture and lives of its Muslim populations.

References

Agence France-Presse (2019). 'Xinjiang Crackdown at the Heart of China's Belt and Road', 3 May, www.france24.com/en/20190503-xinjiang-crackdown-heart-chinas-belt-road (accessed 19 January 2020).

Amnesty International (2013). *Changing the Soup But Not the Medicine?* (London: Amnesty International Publications).

Anagnost, Ann (2004). 'The Corporeal Politics of Quality (*Suzhi*)', *Public Culture* 16 (2), 189–208.

Apter, David E., and Tony Saich (1994). *Revolutionary Discourse in Mao's Republic* (Cambridge, MA: Harvard University Press).

Batke, Jessica (2019). 'Where Did the One Million Figure for Detentions in Xinjiang's Camps Come From?', *China File*, 8 January, www.chinafile.com/reporting-opinion/features/where-did-one-million-figure-detentions-xinjiangs-camps-come (accessed 5 August 2019).

Bayin guoleng fazhi qu [Bayingholin Oblasti Law] (2017). 'Hejing xian juban "qu jiduanhua" jiaoyu zhuanhua jizhong peixun ban' [Heijing County Holds a 'De-extremification' Transformation Re-education Concentration Training Class], 18 September, www.9ask.cn/bayinguoleng/lvxie/120820.html (accessed 17 January 2019, no longer available).

BBC News (2014). 'Xinjiang City Bans Islamic Dress on Public Transport', 6 August, www.bbc.com/news/world-asia-china-28670719 (accessed 5 August 2019).

Blanchard, Ben (2019). 'Inside China's Xinjiang "Re-education Camps"', Reuters, 8 January, www.youtube.com/watch?v=QDtJ5-tYcfA (accessed 10 January 2019).

Bovingdon, Gardner (2010). *The Uyghurs: Strangers in Their Own Land* (New York: Columbia University Press).

Brady, Anne-Marie (2009). *Marketing Dictatorship: Propaganda and Thought Work in Contemporary China* (Lanham: Rowman & Littlefield).

Bray, David (2008). 'Designing to Govern: Space and Power in Two Wuhan Communities', *Built Environment* 34 (4), 392–407.

Bunin, Eugene (2019). 'Detainees Are Trickling Out of Xinjiang's Camps', *Foreign Policy*, 18 January, https://foreignpolicy.com/2019/01/18/detainees-are-trickling-out-of-xinjiangs-camps/ (accessed 26 June 2020).

Byler, Darren (2018). 'China's Government Has Ordered a Million Citizens to Occupy Uighur Homes: Here's What They Think They're Doing', *China File*, 24 October, www.chinafile.com/reporting-opinion/postcard/million-citizens-occupy-uighur-homes-xinjiang (accessed 5 August 2019).

Byler, Darren (2019a). 'How Companies Profit from Forced Labor in Xinjiang', *SupChina*, 4 September, https://supchina.com/2019/09/04/how-companies-profit-from-forced-labor-in-xinjiang/ (accessed 26 June 2020).

Byler, Darren (2019b). '方便 Fangbian: Convenience', China Made, 2 August, https://chinamadeproject.net/%E6%96%B9%E4%BE%BF-fangbian/ (accessed 5 August 2019).

CCTV (2019). 'Xinjiang de fankong qu jiduanhua douzheng' [Xinjiang's Anti-terrorism and De-radicalization Struggle], YouTube, 19 March, www.youtube.com/watch?v=3xyMloesl58&bpctr=1592955547 (accessed 3 July 2019).

Chen, Fang (2015). 'Xinjiang qu jiduanhua diaocha' [An Investigation on Extremism in Xinjiang], Fenghuang Wang [Phoenix Television Online],

12 October, http://news.ifeng.com/mainland/special/xjqjdh/?from=timeli ne&isappinstalled=0 (accessed 5 August 2019).

Cheng, Yinghong (2009). *Creating the 'New Man': From Enlightenment Ideals to Socialist Realities* (Honolulu: University of Hawaii Press).

Chin, Josh, and Clément Bürge (2017). 'Twelve Days in Xinjiang: How China's Surveillance State Overwhelms Daily Life', *Wall Street Journal*, 19 December, www.wsj.com/articles/twelve-days-in-xinjiang-how-chinas-surveillance-state-overwhelms-daily-life-1513700355 (accessed 29 March 2020).

China Law Translate (2017). 'Xinjiang Uyghur Autonomous Region Regulation on De-extremification', 30 March, www.chinalawtranslate.com/en/xinjiang-uyghur-autonomous-region-regulation-on-de-extremification/ (accessed 14 June 2020).

Cliff, Tom (2016). *Oil and Water: Being Han in Xinjiang* (Chicago and London: University of Chicago Press).

Dong, Zhonghui (c. 1970). 'Guanhuai' [Showing Loving Care], Gansu renmin chubanshe [Gansu People's Publishing House], Chinese Posters, https://chineseposters.net/posters/e15-264 (accessed 22 July 2021).

Dui Hua Foundation (2013). 'Legal Education', Dui Hua Reference Materials, 2 April, www.duihuaresearch.org/2013/04/legal-education-arbitrary-detention.html (accessed 14 June 2020).

Dutton, Michael (1992). *Policing and Punishment in China* (Cambridge: Cambridge University Press).

Dutton, Michael, and Xu Zhangrun (2005). 'A Question of Difference: The Theory and Practice of the Chinese Prison', in Børge Bakken (ed.), *Crime, Punishment, and Policing in China* (Lanham: Rowman & Littlefield), 103–140.

Economy, Elizabeth (2018). *The Third Revolution: Xi Jinping and the New Chinese State* (Oxford: Oxford University Press).

Foreign Policy (2018). 'A Summer Vacation in China's Muslim Gulag', 28 February, https://foreignpolicy.com/2018/02/28/a-summer-vacation-in-chinas-muslim-gulag/ (accessed 5 August 2019).

Foucault, Michel (1977). *Discipline and Punish* (New York: Vintage Books).

Fu, Hauling (2005). 'Re-education through Labour in Historical Perspective', *The China Quarterly* 184, 811–830.

Gardner, David (2014). *Confucianism: A Very Short Introduction* (Oxford: Oxford University Press).

Gladney, Dru C. (1994). 'Representing Nationality in China: Refiguring Majority/Minority Identities', *Journal of Asian Studies* 53 (1), 92–123.

Global Times (2019). 'Xinjiang Must Maintain Long-Term Stability', 6 May, www.globaltimes.cn/content/1148676.shtml (accessed 5 August 2019).

Global Times (2020). 'China's Achievement of Covid-19 Fight Is Obvious', 10 May, www.globaltimes.cn/content/1187938.shtml (accessed 5 August 2020).

Greer, Tanner (2018). '48 Ways to Get Sent to a Chinese Concentration Camp', *Foreign Policy*, 13 September, https://foreignpolicy.com/2018/09/13/48-ways-to-get-sent-to-a-chinese-concentration-camp/ (accessed 8 October 2018).

Harrell, Stevan (1995). 'Introduction', in Stevan Harrell (ed.), *Cultural Encounters on China's Ethnic Frontiers* (Seattle: University of Washington Press).

He, Henry Y. (2015). *Dictionary of the Political Thought of the People's Republic of China* (New York: Routledge).

Hetian lingjuli [Zero Distance Khotan] (2017). 'Dao jiaoyu zhuanhua ban xuexi shi dui sixiang huanbing qunzhong de yi ci mianfei zhuyuan zhiliao' [Re-education Classes Are a Type of Free Hospital Stay for People with Ideological Illnesses], 10 April, http://m.3gv.ifeng.com/lady/vnzq/news?ch=rj_mr&ou=p%3D3&aid=121028259&mid=3UbyLG&all=1&p=3 (accessed 16 February 2018, no longer available).

Hillman, Ben (2018). 'Xinjiang and the "Chinese Dream"', East Asia Forum, 24 October, www.eastasiaforum.org/2018/10/24/xinjiang-and-the-chinese-dream/ (accessed 1 March 2020).

Hofer, Theresia (2018). *Medicine and Memory in Tibet: Amchi Physicians in the Age of Reform* (Seattle: University of Washington Press).

Human Rights Watch (2002). 'Dangerous Meditation: China's Campaign against Falungong', www.hrw.org/reports/2002/china/index.htm#TopOfPage (accessed 15 April 2020).

Human Rights Watch (2017). 'Free Xinjiang "Political Education" Detainees', 10 September, www.hrw.org/news/2017/09/10/china-free-xinjiang-political-education-detainees 2017 (accessed 5 April 2020).

Japan Times (2020). 'Green or Red Light: China Coronavirus App Is Ticket to Everywhere', 13 May, www.japantimes.co.jp/news/2020/05/13/asia-pacific/china-coronavirus-app/ (accessed 16 May 2020).

Kipnis, Andrew (2006). '*Suzhi*: A Keyword Approach', *The China Quarterly* 186 (June), 295–313.

Klimeš, Ondřej (2018). 'Advancing "Ethnic Unity" and "De-extremization": Ideational Governance in Xinjiang under "New Circumstances" (2012–2017)', *Journal of Chinese Political Science* 23, 413–436.

Leibold, James (2007). *Reconfiguring Chinese Nationalism: How the Qing Frontier and Its Indigenes Became Chinese* (New York: Palgrave Macmillan).

Leibold, James (2019a). 'Despite China's Denials, Its Treatment of the Uyghurs Should Be Called What It Is: Cultural Genocide', The Conversation, 24 July, https://theconversation.com/despite-chinas-denials-its-treatment-of-the-uyghurs-should-be-called-what-it-is-cultural-genocide-120654 (accessed 5 March 2020).

Leibold, James (2019b). 'Planting the Seed: Ethnic Unity Policy in Xi Jinping's New Era of Cultural Nationalism', *China Brief* 19 (22), https://jamestown.org/

program/planting-the-seed-ethnic-policy-in-xi-jinpings-new-era-of-cultural-nationalism/ (accessed 15 April 2020).

Leibold, James (2019c). 'The Spectre of Insecurity', *China Leadership Monitor* 59 (Spring), www.prcleader.org/leibold (accessed 6 April 2018).

Leibold, James, and Timothy Grose (2016). 'Islamic Veiling in Xinjiang: The Political and Societal Struggle to Define Uyghur Female Adornment', *The China Journal* 76, 78–102.

Li, Enshen (2015). 'China's Community Corrections: An Actuarial Mmodel of Punishment', *Crime Law and Social Change* 64, 1–22.

Li, Xinting (2016). 'Fankong beijing xia Xinjiang jiceng paichusuo xinxihua shouduan yingyong ji sikao' [The Application and Discourse of the Xinjiang's Basic-Level Police Stations' Informatization within the Context of Antiterrorism], *Journal of Wuhan Public Security Cadre's College* 4, 57–61.

Lin, Delia (2017). *Civilising Citizens in Post-Mao China: Understanding the Rhetoric of Suzhi* (London: Routledge).

Liu, Donglai (2017). 'Zhengfu bangzhu wo zoushang "huijia" lu' [The Government Helped Me to Stand Up and Walk the 'Road Home'], Xinjiang Ribao, 5 April, www.xinjiangyaou.com/xinjiang/002/1455513.shtml (accessed 5 August 2019, no longer available).

Maituaong, Wubulikamu (2017). 'Zhi Weiwu'er zu tongbao juexing shu' [Letter to Awaken My Uyghur Compatriots], Xinjiang Ribao, 25 March, http://news.ts.cn/content/2017–03/25/content_12572141.htm (accessed 11 April 2018).

Mao, Zedong (1966). *Quotations from Chairman Mao Tse-tung* (Peking: Foreign Languages Press).

Martina, Michael (2019). 'China Says Xinjiang Has "Boarding Schools", Not "Concentration Camps"', Reuters, 12 March, https://reut.rs/3zZdNgo (accessed 5 August 2019).

Meduza (2018). 'An Internment Camp for 10 Million Uyghurs: Meduza Visits China's Dystopian Police State', 1 October, https://meduza.io/en/feature/2018/10/01/an-internment-camp-for-10-million-uyghurs (accessed 21 January 2021).

Mills, Doug (2020). 'From "Respect" to "Sick and Twisted": How the Coronavirus Hit U.S.-China Ties', *New York Times*, 15 May, www.nytimes.com/2020/05/15/world/asia/coronavirus-china-united-states-cold-war.html (accessed 1 October 2020).

Moreno, Aran Romero (2018). 'From Process of Civilization to Policy of Civilization: A Holistic View of the Chinese Concept *Wenming*', *(Con)textos: Revista d'Antropologia i Investigació Social* 8, 23–36.

Noakes, Stephen (2018). 'A Disappearing Act: The Evolution of China's Administrative Detention System', *Journal of Chinese Political Science* 23 (2), 199–216.

Pan, Congwu (2007). 'Xinjiang jinian laojiao zhidue chuanli 50 zhounian' [Xinjiang's RTL System Celebrates Its 50th Year Anniversary], *Fazhi ribao*, 30 July.

Pan, Jennifer (2020). *Welfare for Autocrats: How Social Assistance in China Cares for Its Rulers* (Oxford: Oxford University Press).

Qin, Liping (2011). 'Shilun laojiao (xing du) gongzuo zai weihu shehui zhi'an tiaoling de zhongyaoxing' [The Importance of *Laojiao* (Detoxification) Work in Upholding Regulations on Social Order], Xinjiang Rectify Net, 21 April, www.xjjz.gov.cn/ljj_news.asp?id=7562 (accessed 1 March 2020).

Ruser, Nathan (2020). 'Documenting Xinjiang's Detention System', September, Australian Strategic Policy Institute, https://bit.ly/3qtWBv9 (accessed 26 October 2020).

Samuel, Sigal (2018a). 'Internet Sleuths Are Hunting for China's Secret Internment Camps for Muslims', *The Atlantic*, 15 September, www.theatlantic.com/international/archive/2018/09/china-internment-camps-muslim-uighurs-satellite/569878/ (accessed 5 August 2019).

Samuel, Sigal (2018b). 'China Is Treating Islam like a Mental Illness', *The Atlantic*, 28 August, www.theatlantic.com/international/archive/2018/08/china-pathologizing-uighur-muslims-mental-illness/568525/ (accessed 5 August 2019).

Scott, James C. (1998). *Seeing like a State: How Certain Schemes to Improve the Human Condition Have Failed* (Princeton: Princeton University Press).

Seymour, James D., and Richard Anderson (1998). *New Ghosts, Old Ghosts: Prisons and Labor Reform Camps in China* (New York: M. E. Sharpe).

Sheres, Ita, and Arthur Springer (1973). 'Moses, Mao, and the Messiah: The Prophets of Redemption', *The Centennial Review* 17 (4), 379–399.

Shinjang Géziti (2018a). 'Tärbiyäläp qutquzush, qayta yolgha chiqish' [Training, Rescuing, and Getting Back on Track], 12 November, http://uyghur.xjdaily.com/59/63315.html (accessed 15 November 2018, no longer available).

Shinjang Géziti (2018b). 'Illiqliq ösüp yetilish yoligha hämrah boldi' [Maturing in Warmth and Becoming Life Companions], 13 November, http://uyghur.xjdaily.com/59/63340.html (accessed 15 November 2018, no longer available).

Spencer, Richard (2005). 'China Rediscovers Confucius in Drive for Social Harmony', *The Telegraph*, 16 March, www.telegraph.co.uk/news/worldnews/asia/china/1485772/China-rediscovers-Confucius-in-drive-for-social-harmony.html (accessed 5 August 2019).

Su, Jiang (2016). 'Punishment without Trial: The Past, Present and Future of Reeducation through Labor in China', *Peking University Law Journal* 4 (1), 45–78.

Sudworth, John (2018). 'China's Hidden Camps', BBC News, 24 October, www.bbc.co.uk/news/resources/idt-sh/China_hidden_camps (accessed 5 August 2019).

Tian Shan Net (2015). 'Yining xian: goujian qu zongjiao jiduanhua da geju' [Yining County: Build a Large Framework for Eliminating Religious Extremification], 14 August, http://web.archive.org/web/20180929143434/http:/news.163.com/15/0114/10/AFTNJ4BJ00014AED.html (accessed 5 August 2019).

Tulufan diqu gongzuo weiyuanhui [Turfan Prefectural Work Committee] (2014). 'Tulufan diqu gongzuo weiyuanhui, Guanyu dui luoshi "weihu wending 21 tiao jinling" he zhongdian renqun teshu qunti "qujihuahua" jiaoyu zhuanhua gongzuo zhuanti diaoyan de baogao' [Report regarding the Implementation of '21 Bans to Safeguard Stability' and Special Investigation into 'Extremism' Transformation through Education among Targeted and Special Populations], Tulufan diqu renda, 19 August, http://8gecn.com/html/index..info545870952.html (accessed 14 March 2015, no longer available).

Wang, Fei Lin (2004). 'Reformed Migration and New Targeted People: China's Hukou System in the 2000s', *The China Quarterly* 177, 115–132.

Wang, Ning (2017). *Banished to the Great Northern Wilderness* (Ithaca: Cornell University Press).

Wong, Edward (2009). 'Riots in Western China amid Ethnic Tension', *New York Times*, 5 July, www.nytimes.com/2009/07/06/world/asia/06china.html (accessed 5 August 2019).

Wu, Hongda Harry (1992). *Laogai: The Chinese Gulag* (London: Routledge).

Xinhua (2014). 'Xinjiang's Party Chief Wages "People's War" against Terrorism', 26 May, www.chinadaily.com.cn/china/2014-05/26/content_17541318.htm (accessed 5 August 2019).

Xinhua (2018). 'Full Transcript: Interview with Xinjiang Government Chief on Counterterrorism, Vocational Education and Training in Xinjiang', 16 October, www.xinhuanet.com/english/2018-10/16/c_137535821.htm (accessed 23 February 2020).

Xinhua (2019). 'Xi Jinping: zai quanguo minzu tuanjie jinbu biaozhang dahui shang de jianghua' [Xi Jinping: Speech to the National Conference for Recognizing Progress in Ethnic Unity], 27 September, www.xinhuanet.com/politics/leaders/2019-09/27/c_1125049000.htm (accessed 23 February 2020).

Xinhua (2020a). 'The Latest: China Reports 1,287 Confirmed Cases of New Coronavirus Pneumonia, Ramping Up Quarantine Measures on Public Transport', 25 January, www.xinhuanet.com/english/2020-01/25/c_138733331.htm (accessed 26 June 2020).

Xinhua (2020b). 'Wuhan Combs Communities to Leave No Coronavirus Patient Unattended', 7 February, www.xinhuanet.com/english/2020-02/07/c_138764071.htm (accessed 26 June 2020).

Xinjiang linguo techan youxian gongsi [Xinjiang Forest Fruit Specialty Product Company Ltd.] (2014). 'Xinjiang ganbu zhucun rizhi (5yue 26ri) zhongdian renkou' [Journal Entry for 26 May of Xinjiang Cadre Assigned to Villages: The Targeted Population], 27 May, http://blog.sina.com.cn/s/blog_130e9b5190101ta9v.html (accessed 26 June 2020, no longer available).

Xinjiang nongye xinxi wang [Xinjiang Agricultural Information Web] (2016). '"Liangxue yizuo" jianbao' [Briefing on the 'Two Studies, One Action'], 4 August, https://web.archive.org/web/20170315215532/http://www.xj-agri.gov.cn/sysszl/28298.jhtml (accessed 9 February 2019).

XUAR Reform and Development Commission (2018). Xinjiang Weiwu'er zizhi qu fazhan he gaige weiyuanhui zhuban [The Autonomous Region's Standing Committee], 'Zizhiqu dangwei changwei Zhang Chunlin yu fan xiang daxuesheng hudong jiaoliu' [Member Zhang Chunlin Meets with University Students Who Have Returned Home], 26 February, https://web.archive.org/web/20180621163558/http:/www.xj.cei.gov.cn/info/10947/363114.htm (accessed 21 June 2018).

Yang, Jie (2010). 'The Crisis of Masculinity: Class, Gender, and Kindly Power in Post-Mao China', *American Ethnologist* 37, 550–562.

Yang, Jie (2013). '*Song wennuan*, "Sending Warmth": Unemployment, New Urban Poverty, and the Affective State in China', *Ethnography* 14, 104–125.

Yang, Mayfair Mei Hui (1994). *Gifts, Favors, and Banquets: The Art of Social Relationships in China* (Ithaca and London: Cornell University Press).

Yang, Xueli (2002). '"Sanlei" laojiao renyuan jiaoyu gaizao gongzuo de sikao' [Considering the Education and Reform Work among the 'Three Types' of RTL Personnel], *Judicature of China*, 18–19.

Yu, Jianrong, and Stacey Mosher (2010). 'From Tool of Political Struggle to Means of Social Governance: The Two Stages of the Re-education through Labour System', *China Perspectives* 82, 66–72.

Yulixian (2015). 'Yulixian juxing "qu jiduanhua" jiaoyu zhuanhua zhongxin jiepai yishi' [Ceremony Opening Yuli County's 'De-radicalization' Educational Transformation Centre], Yulixian zhengfu wang, 9 June, www.yuli.gov.cn/Item/71624.aspx (accessed 15 March 2017, no longer available).

Zand, Von Bernhard (2018). 'A Surveillance State unlike Any the World Has Even Seen', Spiegel, 26 July, www.spiegel.de/international/world/china-s-xinjiang-province-a-surveillance-state-unlike-any-the-world-has-ever-seen-a-1220174.html (accessed 5 August 2019).

Zenz, Adrian (2018). 'New Evidence for China's Political Re-education Campaign in Xinjiang', *China Brief* 18 (10), https://jamestown.org/program/evidence-for-chinas-political-re-education-campaign-in-xinjiang/ (accessed 5 August 2019).

Zenz, Adrian (2019a). 'Break Their Roots: Evidence for China's Parent-Child Separation Campaign in Xinjiang', *Journal of Political Risk* 7 (7).

Zenz, Adrian (2019b). '"Thoroughly Reforming Them towards a Healthy Heart Attitude": China's Political Re-education Campaign in Xinjiang', *Central Asian Survey* 38 (1), 102–128.

Zhang, Xiao (2000). 'Xinjiang laojiao suxie' [Sketch of Xinjiang's RTL], *Zhongguo sifa* 3 (22).

Zhi, Zhonghe (2014). 'Xinjiang bianmin lianxi ka zhidu' [Convenient Linking Card System in Xinjiang], Beijing Aizhixing Yanjiusuo, 15 December, www.aizhi.co/download/ziliao/2014/12/15/20141215(1).pdf (accessed 5 August 2019, no longer available).

Zhonggong Yining Xian Wei [Yining County Party Committee] (2016). 'Shishi "si da huodong" tuijin "qu jiduanhua" gongzuo' [Implement the Four Big Campaigns and Promote De-extremification Work], *Zhonguo dangzheng ganbu tanlun* 4, 98–100.

Zhou, Zhonyou (2015). 'How China Defines Terrorism', *The Diplomat*, 13 February, https://thediplomat.com/2015/02/how-china-defines-terrorism/ (accessed 5 August 2019).

6

Two-faced: Turkic Muslim camp workers, subjection, and active witnessing

Darren Byler

The re-education system in Northwest China attempts to produce Turkic Muslims who are subject, or bound, to a Chinese system of control. The overlaid programming of the campaign combined with the profiling gaze of human surveillance technicians attempts to assure the flow of power over life. The campaign strives to assure the movement and security of those whose lives are valued by the system, controlling and transforming those who are devalued. As I observed during a research trip to the Xinjiang Uyghur Autonomous Region (XUAR) in 2018, for Turkic Muslims, checkpoints, home inspections, and political education performances have become a primary way they are addressed by the state. These actions reinforce and enact a pervasive belief that they belong to a category of suspicion. Through these regular, often daily, processes they come to internalize how they are viewed by non-Muslims and what it takes to perform 'trustworthiness'.

This new form of contemporary colonialism should not be seen as a smooth system in which the interrogations run automatically to the programming of surveillance technology and evaluation forms. Rather the whole-of-society 'People's War' compels hundreds of thousands of Uyghurs and Kazakhs to collaborate in the subjection of their own Turkic Muslim neighbours. In the words of the party secretary of the region, fulfilling the goals of the system demands that local authorities 'round up those who needed to be rounded up' (Ramzy and Buckley

2019). In order for that to be accomplished, Turkic Muslims have to be coerced into policing themselves. This chapter examines this process of subjection from the perspective of Turkic Muslim police contractors and camp instructors.

As the ethnographer Lilly Irani (2015) has noted, cutting-edge technology systems everywhere in the world are nearly always trained by low-wage technicians. In European and North American contexts much of this work is done through platforms like the Amazon-hosted contractor network Mechanical Turk. Many of these 'data janitors', as Irani refers to them, are tasked with training AI algorithms to recognize and digitize material objects, behaviours, and people. Often they are forced by class, race, gender devaluation, and citizenship status into these jobs (Amrute 2016). Once in these positions it is often difficult to opt out or demand better work conditions. As anthropologists of policing and prisons have shown, in most contexts the same holds true for low-level prison and policing work (Rhodes 2004; Fassin 2013). Often those who enforce state violence come from ethno-racial minority and lower-class positions. They are in fact placed in service to what Chandan Reddy describes as practices of subjectification, or subject-making, in which ethno-racially heterogeneous workers are mobilized by state proxies to build new frontiers of capital accumulation and state power (Reddy 2011). In Northwest China, Turkic Muslim young people, the most deeply vulnerable population in the re-education project, are coerced through economic and policing pressure into 'freely' contracting with surveillance system employers that enact the general enclosure system over their own societies. Other Turkic Muslims are placed in positions of interpretation and instruction in village committees and 're-education' camps.

Since 2018 I have interviewed over a dozen former detainees who recently fled across the border from Xinjiang to Kazakhstan and elsewhere. These former detainees, as well as dozens of former inhabitants of the region, told me that Turkic Muslim teachers and contractors often become the voice and face of the re-education process. They occupy a primary site of human encounter with other Turkic Muslims who have been dehumanized by party-state power, ethno-racialization, and the ordinary functioning of the camp system. In the end, the surveillance work these Turkic Muslim police contractors and coerced teachers do is a process of converting Turkic Muslim populations into parsed categories, deeming them 'untrustworthy', making them available for assessment, removal, and dehumanization.

Drawing on interviews with former detainees and their relatives, with a special focus on in-depth interviews with a former police contractor and camp instructor, this chapter shows how the re-education system turned Uyghurs and Kazakhs against themselves, making them the human intelligence janitors and interpreters of a colonial system. Because of the ethno-racial devaluation of their social position police contractors such as Baimurat, whose account I will analyse in detail below, felt they had no choice but to work in service to the system of enclosure even as it foreclosed other life-paths for them. As I will describe, former elementary school teachers such as Risalet were pressed by the extreme forms of violence they witnessed in the camps and the effectiveness of the overlaid forms of surveillance to carry out their assignment. This chapter argues that this outsourced task, in the most general of terms, was to normalize the dehumanization of other Turkic Muslims. Yet, as the translators and janitors were confronted with a dehumanized mirroring of their own Turkic Muslim identifications, their own masks of 'trustworthiness' were often not enough to protect them from extreme forms of stress. As a system of subjectification, the re-education process pushed deep forms of trauma onto those who were forced to 'collaborate' with the processes they enacted and observed. Ultimately, for some, these forms of encounter resulted in the active witnessing of the suffering of Turkic Muslim detainees, while for others it produced ongoing forms of dehumanization.

Subjectification through interrogation

In an ethnography of policing systems and social order in France, the anthropologist Didier Fassin describes the way young black and brown men are interpellated or interrogated by the police (Fassin 2013). Drawing on Louis Althusser's famous example he describes the way police hail individuals with the command: 'Hey, you there!' and how the hailed individual turns around and through this becomes a subject (Fassin 2013: 6; Althusser 2014). The behaviour itself of the individual demonstrates that they have recognized themselves as citizens, subject to the power of the state, and that they may be guilty of something or targeted because of their deviance from the normative social order.

By turning around, the person accepts the terms of the state as having authority. Fassin notes that this act is an elementary structure of ordinary state power, 'which consists, paradoxically, in forcing individuals to submit freely to the law and hence to become subjects' (Fassin 2013: 7). In this sense, subject formation includes the 'freely' chosen act of obeying the mandates of state authorities. The very freedom of this act of obedience normalizes the legitimacy of everyday state power. It is through this process that states transform individuals into subjects who recognize themselves both subject to conditions imposed on them and as actors who chose to submit.

As Chandan Reddy and others have shown, the legitimacy of citizen subject behaviour rests on these dueling power relations (Reddy 2011). On the one hand, it proceeds through the submission of the individual to state authority, in this case that of the police, through a form of *subjection*. On the other hand, by claiming agency in the matter, the individual constructs their self and seizes a measure of protection by demonstrating their *subjectification* – on the side of state authority. As Reddy makes clear, for ethno-racial minorities this 'freedom with violence' often amounts to policing ethno-racial minorities in support of state authority and on behalf of ethno-racial majorities (Reddy 2011: 34–35).

This is particularly the case in colonial contexts where civil and human rights are less assured. In a recent essay the scholar Dibyesh Anand has shown the way that the Chinese project 'of occupying, minoritizing and securitizing different ethno-national peoples of Central Asia ... is a colonial project' (Anand 2019: 129). He argues that this form of contemporary colonialism is accomplished by identifying colonized subjects as a source of instability in need of re-education. Through a process of dividing and sorting different populations of Turkic Muslims, state power subjects Uyghurs and Kazakhs to profound forms of insecurity. In order to protect themselves, many Turkic Muslims have been forced to find ways of proving their 'trustworthiness'. Often they do this by working within the re-education system as low-level technicians, instructors, and interpreters.

In the past Uyghurs who were pushed into this process of proving their 'trustworthiness', through their affinity to Chinese language and political ideology, were at times described by other Uyghurs as *collaborators* or race 'traitors' (Smith Finley 2007). During the mass internment campaign this position was reinscribed by state authorities as 'two-faced', meaning that they were secretly on the side of Turkic Muslim 'separatism, extremism, or terrorism' while pretending to support state power (Ala 2018). While such terms carry with them an individualized moral connotation, Reddy makes clear that these forms of boundary policing result from historical conditions of possibility and thus are not simply a result of individual moral failing (Reddy 2011). Instead disidentification with others in the same social position in hopes of finding protections from state violence is an outcome of the way states maintain and extend their power to protect the interests of those with wealth and power in the society. As Homi Bhabha has shown, in colonial contexts mimicry as carried out by collaborators is 'one of the most effective strategies of colonial power and knowledge', but because of the ambivalence that ethno-racialized collaborators carry with them it is nevertheless unstable (Bhabha 1995: 85). If conditions of everyday institutionalized pressure are lifted, the loyalty of collaborators to state power may be revealed for what it is: a mimicry of the colonizer produced through subjugation.

In contemporary Northwest China, Uyghurs and Kazakhs are interrogated by state proxies on a daily basis. In a literal sense, this is expressed through forms of interrogation where they are stopped, identified, detained, and interrogated. Most often these encounters are brief, with very few words exchanged. Instead their digital history contained in their smartphone, the biometric tracking of their travel through time and space, speaks for them. If this speech is flagged by the system it may result in more formal interrogation at a People's Convenience Police Station or higher-level precincts. This questioning happens elsewhere too. On Mondays their political knowledge and loyalty is examined at flag raising ceremonies and interactive political education sessions. At work their behaviour is observed, tasks are asked of them. They are always on guard. These processes result in a second, politically engaged sense of interrogation through which they internalize the way they are at the mercy of the discretion of police contractors and their co-workers. As Fassin puts it, through these types of encounters ethno-racialized subjects are told: 'Become what you are!' (Fassin 2013: 8).

The ethno-racism that is being produced through these practices of racialization is unique to the particular contemporary moment and place in Northwest China. It is nonetheless important to name such processes as ethno-racial, rather than *simply* ethnic or cultural, because it enables us to see how colonial power produces differences among groups through practices of subject-making. Naming this process as racialization centres the way colonial exploitation and domination is embodied. Individual inner characteristics are framed by legal, economic, and educational institutions 'through their skin color, dress, language, smell, accent, hairstyle, way of walking, facial expressions, and behavior' (Amrute 2016: 14). While Sareeta Amrute is writing about a culturalist form of new racism directed towards Indian tech workers in Germany, her argument for why difference should be read as racial rather than simply or only ethnic holds for Turkic Muslims as well. Their bodies – the way they dress, their intimate relations, personal hygiene, their accent, their diet, facial expressions, physical and virtual behaviour, and language use – are the primary object of human face-to-face profiling and surveillance. Their skin colour, eye shape, nose structure, hairstyles as represented in face-scanning checkpoints and in social media are primary markers used in algorithmic assessments of the 'terrorist' body. As such Uyghurs are subject to a particular form of racialization, driven by Han desires for security from abstract threats and discomfort, Chinese state capital, algorithmic assessment tools, and re-education workers. Under such circumstances the bodies of Turkic Muslims are no longer their own, they are always read as potentially untrustworthy (Ch. *bu fangxin*). The slightest misstep can be read as confirmation of their inherent criminality. In one of my interviews, a Uyghur man recalled a dispute he had with a Han petrol station technician. While he was waiting to have his ID checked so he could drive his car into the petrol station, a Han taxi driver cut in line in front of him. When he protested, the Han petrol station worker threatened to call the police contractors. He told the Uyghur customer, 'I'm not afraid of you. You should be afraid of me. I could have you arrested whenever I want.' In the mind of this Uyghur rural-to-urban migrant, this encounter drove home the point that his potential criminality always proceeded him.

Writing about ethno-racial minorities in France, Fassin notes, 'they understand that it is not enough to be innocent in order not to be deemed guilty … They become aware that what is happening to them is related not to what they have done, but to what they represent'

(Fassin 2013: 7). It is through this process of subjection that Turkic Muslims understand that in a time of re-education they are subject to the gaze of others. Anyone can be an informant, no one is a guaranteed ally. In this context, for ethno-racial minorities there appears to be no space that is fully outside state power. This is confirmed on a daily basis by the checkpoints and fear of their relatives, neighbours, and friends. Ultimately, for Turkic Muslims who are assigned to work within the system, it is confirmed by the treatment of those who have been deemed 'untrustworthy' (Famularo 2018; Smith Finley 2019). The dehumanizing effects of the camps and social conditions that construct it make clear that any Turkic Muslim can be assigned this label. Once the untrustworthy label is fully attached, the person's life is no longer valued as rights-bearing. Seeing this ordinary state violence enacted on a daily basis drives home the point that dehumanization is not carried out fully at random, but in fact related to what Turkic Muslims represent in the eyes of state authorities and the Han population the authorities support.

A history of using Turkic Muslims in Xinjiang

There is, of course, a history of using ethnic minorities against each other in the context of the XUAR. As historians have noted since the founding of the People's Republic of China in 1949, state authorities developed a system of nested autonomous areas such as counties and prefectures controlled by Kazakhs, Kirghiz, Hui, Mongols, Tajiks and Sibe within the larger autonomous region (Millward 2007; Brophy 2016). Importantly, however, in each of these autonomous areas multiple nationalities were under-represented and 'in only twelve of the twenty-seven autonomous units did the eponymous nationality constitute a majority. Moreover, the power of any one minority group is further limited by the nesting of autonomous counties of one nationality within prefectures of another' (Millward 2007: 245). By 1957, this party-state system of power was further codified through purges of 'local nationalism' which resulted in the removal of ethnic minority leaders who favoured greater forms of self-determination apart from state mandates (Brophy 2017).

In practice the system pitted minorities against each other, while at the same time subordinating them to ranking Han party members. In effect, elites from each minority were competing with each other for positions whose flows of power were directed by the central authorities and were forced to conform to standards imposed from above. The system also created 'model minorities' by placing Mongols, Kazakhs and Kyrgyz in 'autonomous' control of significant portions of the Uyghur population and territory. For instance, when Bayangolin Mongol Autonomous Prefecture was made a Mongol area in 1960 it was an 'almost purely' Uyghur region that made up nearly one-third of the Xinjiang region (Atwood 2004: 39; Bovingdon 2010: 46). As a result leaders from a population of less than 50,000 Mongols have been placed in nominal representative control of a population of close to half a million Uyghurs (though Mongols too have been subordinated to nearly one million Han settlers who have arrived in the prefecture since the 1960s).

Relative to Uyghurs nearly all minorities in the region were given favourable treatment, when it came to placement in schools, permission to travel, and policing. In fact, as I found through years of fieldwork in the region in 2011 and 2015, among many Kazakhs and Mongols there was a good deal of resentment towards Uyghurs whom they perceived to be 'backwards' (Ch. *luohou*) and responsible for creating a negative image of Islam and Xinjiang in general. As numerous ethnographers have noted, the ethno-nationalities of the region often constructed their identities in opposition to each other rather than in shared solidarity as minorities who were being subjugated by a state colonial project (Gladney 1996; Smith Finley 2013).

Turkic Muslim identities are further divided by urban versus rural residency, which often correlates with exposure to Chinese-language education (Li 2015). Turkic Muslims educated in Chinese, often referred to as *minkaohan*, are at times described as an ethnic group of their own because of their facility in Chinese, their urban residency, and their work within the Chinese state apparatus (Smith Finley 2007: 229). As Joanne Smith Finley has noted, many within this group feel 'a lack of belonging, either to the Chinese social world to which they were expected to assimilate, or to their own people among whom they felt themselves "fakes"' (Smith Finley 2018: 10). While some chose to send their children to Chinese medium schools because they believed it would provide their children better opportunities within the urban Chinese economy, these choices were themselves limited by the overriding constraints of state-directed subjugation, which privileged

Chinese political ideologies, Han cultural values, and capitalist modes of production. At the same time, many found that no matter how hard they strove to succeed within this social order, 'they were considered neither (wholly) Uyghur by *minkaomin* (Uyghurs educated in Uyghur) nor wholly Chinese by the Han' (Smith Finley 2018: 10).

Instead a sense of 'double consciousness', a term that William E. B. Du Bois ([1903] 1994) uses to describe the way racialized minorities are always forced to see themselves from the perspective of the police and the population that is supported by the police, became more acute. Because of their everyday exposure to urban Han-majority society, many *minkaohan* attempted to code-switch and take on majoritarian Han behaviour and speech. Yet, in the midst of this they were also often called on to perform their Uyghurness as a demonstration of the benevolence of ordinary state power and Han-valorized socialist multiculturalism. When the re-education campaign built to its greatest intensity in 2017, the symbolic violence of double consciousness – now responding to the demonized 'two-faced' epithet – was heightened as it was even more fully 'institutionalised and staged by the state through the coercive threat of an extrajudicial internment' (Anderson and Byler 2019: 18).

Putting Uyghurs and Kazakhs to work in the re-education system

The new technological surveillance and internment system that was introduced in the 2010s required a great deal of human labour (Human Rights Watch 2019). Data needed to be input into the system through manual scans and data entry. The parameters of the system needed to be honed. Most importantly the re-education camps needed to be populated with 'untrustworthy' people (Smith Finley 2019). In order to assist in this effort over 90,000 new police, many of whom were low-level contractors (Ch. *xiejing*), were hired (Zenz and Leibold 2020). These new contractors, along with neighbourhood watch unit employees and police, were tasked with building a database of individualized profiles. All inhabitants of the region were required to go to the local police station and submit fingerprints, blood, and DNA samples (Human Rights Watch 2019). Often they had their voice signature recorded, and their irises and faces scanned.

The lowest-level police contractors were hired primarily from Muslim-minority populations. Their job was to perform spot checks, which centred on actively profiling passers-by, stopping Turkic young people, and demanding that they provide their state-issued ID and open their phone for automated inspection via spyware apps and external scanning devices. Policing contractors were also responsible to monitor face-scanning machines and metal detectors at fixed checkpoints. Turkic Muslims were required to carry a smartphone if they had registered a SIM card in the past. At checkpoints the phone was matched to the ID of the carrier allowing systems to perform a hard reset of individual movement in real time and space multiple times per day (Human Rights Watch 2019). All of these activities assured that Uyghurs and Kazakhs continued to build the dataset of the system, making extremism assessment algorithms more and more precise.

Higher-level officers and 'older brother and sister volunteers', most of whom were Han, were given the job of conducting qualitative assessments of the Muslim population as a whole – providing the more complex interview-based survey data for the integrated platform (Byler 2018). Neighbourhood police officers, contractors, and 'relative' assistants assessed the Muslim-minority people to determine if they should be given the rating of 'trustworthy', 'normal', or 'untrustworthy' (Smith Finley 2019). They determined this by categorizing the person using ten or more categories: whether or not the person was of military age, if they were Uyghur, if they were under-employed, if they prayed regularly, if they possessed unauthorized religious knowledge, if they had a passport, if they had travelled to one of twenty-six Muslim-majority countries, if they had overstayed their visa, if they had an immediate relative living abroad, or if they had taught their children about Islam in their home. Those that were determined to be 'untrustworthy' were then sent to detention facilities where they were interrogated, asked to confess their pre-crime violations, and name others who were also 'untrustworthy'. In this manner, and with the help of tech-enabled cyber violation detections, the parameters of the techno-political system determined which individuals should be slotted for the 'transformation through education' internment camps.

One of the police contractors who conducted these checks was a young Kazakh man named Baimurat. He was in one of the first groups of contractors who were hired from across the region in late 2016. In an interview he said that because he was a college graduate he was 'considered very well qualified'. As a result he was given the highest level salary available to contractors, around 6,000 yuan per month, which is far above the minimum wage of around 1,800 yuan. Others in his cohort, who were considered less qualified because of their education background, were paid closer to 2,500 yuan. For Baimurat, who had struggled to find work for which he was qualified in the past, taking the job was a choice he felt he could not refuse. Not only would he be able to provide for his family, but he would also be able to protect them from the re-education system. 'We were given uniforms,' he said. 'Then we started doing different kinds of training. It was really strict, as if we were planning for a war.'

Around this time, the Public Security Bureau started building People's Convenience Police Stations, a type of surveillance hub that was built every several hundred metres in Muslim-majority areas. Then the security company that had hired them divided the contractors up and stationed them at one of the eighty-nine stations that were built in Baimurat's home county. He said:

> We sat facing the TV monitors, and you could see the places where the cameras were pointed. We had to sit there monitoring them all the time. If we failed to notice an alert, or stopped looking, we would be punished.

Over time, the kind of surveillance labour they did began to shift. First the contractors were sorted based on their Chinese-language ability and other proofs of their loyalty and knowledge of the 'extremism' parameters of the re-education system. Baimurat said:

> They made us do other exercises like reciting rules about participating in the camp system. We had to recite things related to law. There were quotes from Xi Jinping on the walls of the station. We had to learn these by heart. We were not allowed to go outside for the patrol until we successfully recited the quotes from Xi Jinping.

Then, around the middle of 2017, the contractors were tasked with actively fine-tuning the programming of the system using assessment tools that scanned through files which were hidden on smartphones. Baimurat continued:

> I worked there for six months. Then they handed out devices to check pedestrians and car drivers. When we scanned their ID card and phone

we got information about whether or not the person had worn a veil, had installed WhatsApp, had travelled to Kazakhstan, all sorts of things like that. We could stop every car on the street and check them. When we stopped them we asked the people inside to show their phones and ID cards. If there was something suspicious, like I mentioned before, we needed to inform the leaders.

Around this time, Baimurat learned that although he was a contingent worker, hired on a contract basis, he was not free to quit. 'If we were tired and wanted to quit, they would tell us if you are exhausted, you can take a rest, but then you must come back. If you quit the job, then you will end up in the "re-education camps" too.' Interviews with another Muslim-minority police contractor and the relatives of other police contractors whom I interviewed in the region in 2018 confirmed this policy.

Camps as subjectification spaces

Initially Baimurat and his co-workers felt that despite the long hours and the confrontational positions they were placed in, being a police contractor 'was a good job' with a steady pay cheque and security from police harassment. They saw themselves as on the side of the 'good guys'. This began to change around the time that they received the smartphone scanning equipment. He said:

> I learned then that they had sent the children from the Kazakh Number 3 Middle School in the county seat to the Han school. They built an iron gate, high electric fence, and four watchtowers around the Kazakh school. If we found anyone suspicious through the ID checks, they would send them to the Kazakh school. They had suddenly turned it into a prison. They forced all of the people who had been visiting mosques, praying, and wearing headscarves to go to that school.

Initially, it seemed to him, that it was just people who had been actively pious in their religious practice who were sent to the new 'prison' school. It was close to six months before he fully realized the implications of the 'rounding up those that need to be rounded up' policy.

> While I was working one day we had a meeting. It was in early 2018. In the meeting we were told we had to transfer some detainees from the prison (Kz. *turme*; Ch. *kanshousuo*) to the school. We had so many manacles. When we got there we saw that they had caught around 600

people. There were rooms inside the building that were like cells. I saw very young women, very old women, and men with beards (over the age of fifty-five) among the detainees. They were mainly minorities, the majority were Uyghurs, then a few Kazakhs, and some Hui people. I don't think there were Han people. Maybe one or two, but not more than that. We handcuffed and shackled them and then we gave blankets to them, whether they could hold them or not, and we told them to get on the bus. I had to handcuff one person that I had a feeling I had seen before. Then I realized he had worked as a police contractor as well. I had seen him before while I was working. I didn't remember his name but I knew him. I really wanted to ask what happened to him, but because there were cameras I didn't ask any questions. I thought maybe I could ask later. But I never found a chance.

In the interview, Baimurat spoke in a quiet voice without much expression on his face. This began to change as he discussed this moment of encounter. He held his hands out in front of him showing the way the detainees were shackled and how they threw the blankets on their bound hands.

Then we started transporting women. I suddenly heard really sharp sounds. I saw an old woman in her eighties whose hair was completely white. She screamed when she was shackled and handcuffed because her leg was injured. They just dragged her to the bus. When I witnessed this, I felt terribly bad. I wanted to quit. I regretted being a police [contractor] with every fibre of my being. I was crying on the inside.

His eyes welling up, Baimurat placed his hand over his heart.

Continuing he explained that sometime later when he felt it was safe he asked another Kazakh police contractor about the man he had recognized among the detainees. His co-worker told him, 'He came from a village and didn't understand how the CCTV cameras worked. While he was working in the prison, he saw a paper on the floor which said "get me out of here". He didn't report it, but the camera saw it, so he was taken "to study".' Hearing this, Baimurat said that for the first time he fully realized that any Kazakh or Uyghur could be sent to the camp. No one was safe, no matter how hard they tried to work within the system. He said:

I felt very bad about [being part of the system]. There were so many people who made very tiny mistakes and ended up there. As police, we had tasks we must fulfil. Some days the leaders said do this, other days they said do that. Each day we had to do what they said.

His fears regarding arbitrary detention were confirmed over and over. His cousin was taken to the camp because he had bought a second-hand smartphone which someone had used to download a video of violence in Ürümchi in 2009. Baimurat's cousin had no way of knowing that the phone had been used for this before he bought it. Others were taken away because they failed to show 'absolutely no mercy' – a sign of being 'two-faced' (Ramzy and Buckley 2019):

> Another one of my co-workers was a twenty-four-year-old [Kazakh] who graduated from Tianjin University. He owned a car and was the only child in his family. He was assigned as a staff member there [in the prison school]. He had to monitor ten Uyghurs who were detained because of [their] religion. One of the Uyghurs asked for a cigarette at midnight. He thought it would not be a big deal so he gave him one. Just as the Uyghur detainee was finishing it, a higher-level police [contractor] came and took my co-worker away. We never saw him again.

Over time the pressure wore on Baimurat. He said, 'We couldn't sleep. We were crying all the time, my wife and I. We didn't show other people that we were crying, because they might think we were dangerous and might inform on us.'

In February 2017, as the re-education camp system swung into motion and Baimurat began his work as a contractor, schoolteachers from across the region were pressed into service as camp instructors. One of these instructors was a *minkaohan* woman named Risalet,[1] who taught Chinese to fifth graders in a primary school in Ürümchi. The daughter of Uyghur and Uzbek government officials, Risalet's parents recognized the relative privilege of being identified as a non-Uyghur so they registered her as an Uzbek on her ID card. After graduating from Xinjiang Teacher's College, Risalet taught at the primary school for twenty-eight years. Because of her experience, she achieved a position of administrative responsibility in the functioning of the school.

She was surprised when she received a new assignment after the winter break for the spring festival. She said:

> On 26 February 2017, we started a new semester. Students were required to report to the school and start their new semester. During that time

we had two days to prepare for class. The principal called me to his office and told me that I needed to go to a meeting at 1.30 p.m. at the city district-level education bureau office. I asked about what would be discussed at this meeting, because I had been to similar meetings many times before and every time I needed to bring documents relevant to the meeting. He didn't respond to my question and just told me not to be late. So at 1.30 p.m., I arrived at the office. There were four Han workers, three female bureau directors and a Uyghur young man. The secretary of the district party office didn't offer much detail and just told us that they had gathered a group of uneducated people and it was our responsibility to teach them Chinese. The 'students' were located on the mountain near a police station at the edge of the district. We were required to teach them for six months. After the meeting, they gave us four or five documents to sign. I did not pay too much attention to them, but one of them I remember was called a 'letter of commitment'. It said we wouldn't say anything about what we saw and heard during our work at the re-education centre. If information was leaked, we must be willing to take all responsibility and the requisite punishment. They emphasized that this was a political assignment and that we cannot refuse this assignment or ask for leave. Otherwise, we would be punished. I didn't say anything about the meeting to the principal, but the next day when I left the elementary school my teaching responsibilities had already been assigned to other people.

Based on Risalet's experience, and those of other former teachers, it was clear from the behaviour of others in their home institution that re-education camp assignments superseded all other responsibilities. Even before she arrived in the camp, Risalet knew that she was embarking on something serious.

In fact, already in 2015 Risalet, like nearly all Uyghurs throughout the region, had heard about what she referred to as 'uneducated migrant Uyghurs' who had been sent to re-education camps. When she first heard about them, she thought it sounded terrible, but she thought it had little to do with her, an urban *minkaohan* woman with a secure Uzbek identification.

> One of the teachers in our school was a woman from Awat County in Aqsu Prefecture in rural southern Xinjiang. She had studied in Ürümchi and stayed after graduating from school. She went back to her home village every summer vacation. In 2015, when she returned, she was very sad and cried in the office for two hours while we talked. The

detention system had begun in her home village. People who prayed regularly, who wore long dresses, or who were imams, were being detained. Awat is a big county, and has one of the largest Uyghur populations. But, she said, you won't find any male Uyghurs on the streets anymore. She had three older brothers, all of them were taken. One brother was taken because he was devout in his Islamic practice, one brother was taken because someone accused him of going to Friday prayers at a mosque, and one was also taken for some other reason. According to my colleague, they gathered all of them in a big hall. The police were carrying weapons. People's names were called, their crimes were declared, and a sentence was given. Police then took that person away with a black plastic bag over their head. When she said this, we cried with her. But, later, we went back to life as normal. We felt shock, but over time I forgot about the conversation. I thought Ürümchi will never be like that. So [in 2017] when the officials said they had gathered a group of uneducated people, I thought again about what my colleague said [two years before]. I thought it must be something similar because they kept saying over and over that it was a political assignment and that we were not allowed to tell anyone about it. If we told anyone, we would receive a punishment, such as losing our jobs and negative effects on our relatives. So I wondered if I was going to the kind of place that my colleague mentioned before, but I tried very hard to push this thought out of my mind.

The next day when Risalet was taken to the camp, she recognized it for what it was.

When I arrived at the building, I felt I had come to a prison. It was a four-storey building surrounded by razor wire. We entered the gate by swiping our ID card. When we passed through the grounds of the compound, I felt very nervous. The yard was guarded by Han police and soldiers with assault rifles. I thought to myself that I had to be very careful and make a good impression on them. After I finished registering, I looked around and noticed the slogan on the wall that said, 'Fight against the religious extremist thought, and prevent religious ideas from entering.' When I entered the building, on the right, there were four police officers and a stair to the second floor. On the left, there were seven or eight offices. Among them was a police command centre, a dorm room for police, a nurse's medical office, and an office for staff from the neighbourhood watch units (Ch. *shequ*). Ten young women from the neighbourhood watch units came to assist in the camp work in shifts. After five of them finished a shift, another five would take over their responsibilities. Their responsibilities included dispensing steamed buns to the detainees and documenting their behaviour.

As Risalet took in the atmosphere of the re-education camp, her own instruction as Turkic Muslim interpreter began. Other Turkic Muslim workers in the camp began to show her how to perform to the standards of the system.

> A police officer brought me to their office. There I met a Uyghur officer named Mahira. She told me that she knew me, that her child was a student at my school. I tried to ask for more information from this woman, but she implied that I should not ask for more. She told me, 'Look up.' And I found that there were cameras pointed at my face. I understood and didn't ask anything further. She asked if I was ready to start the class and I said yes.

Armed with the knowledge that her behaviour was being watched, Risalet crossed a threshold that would change her life.

> I took my books and water bottle, stared at the iron door, and saw something that I will never forget for the rest of my life. The door was opened and the detainees started coming out wearing handcuffs. They walked to the classroom. When I saw them, I could not help but to have tears in my eyes. The police were in the classroom, standing in the back to make sure I was 'safe'. At that point there were no actual desks or chairs. Students sat on the plastic stools. There was a table, chair, and blackboard for me to use. When I saw their faces, I felt so devastated. I prayed to Allah to keep me from crying in front of them. I came to the table in the front without knowing what to do and what do say. Among the people sitting in front of me were elderly men with beards. They looked respectable, just like the kind of elderly people you might see in the mosque.

At this moment the antagonism between parameters of the re-education system and her self-identification reached a moment of crisis. Her double consciousness as a Turkic Muslim, who had been taught her whole life to respect Turkic Muslim elders, and a camp worker who was threatened with detention for showing respect to Turkic Muslims deemed 'extremist' demanded that she make an immediate choice: put on the mask of the Chinese-speaking re-education system which showed 'absolutely no mercy', or reveal her truer self as someone who was taught to treat others with dignity and respect and risk being labelled 'two-faced' (Ala 2018):

> Without thinking I said 'assalamu alaykum' [peace be upon you]. That was the first and last time I said 'assalamu alaykum' during my time there. When I said 'assalamu alaykum', they froze and were all so terrified. I realized I had said something wrong. I introduced myself and started the class. I just stared at the blackboard, and didn't turn back to look at their faces. I couldn't turn around because some detainees were sobbing. Some of the old men's beards were wet from crying. I tried to compose myself. I didn't look back at all during the class. I just kept writing and erasing the content on the blackboard. I finished four different classes, but I felt like it took four years. The detainees were sobbing with me.

Risalet was unable to face the detainees, to witness the immediacy of their suffering directly. Yet, because of her initial identification with them, through the annunciation of a banned Arabic phrase, and her lack of composure, even with her back turned to the detainees it was clear to them that she recognized them as human, as deserving of mercy. In that moment of exposure, her *minkaohan*, urban mask fell away and she was revealed as a Turkic Muslim too.

> I entered my office room during the break. Mayira told me that I should be careful about what I said. She said I should say only 'hello students' (Ch. *xueyuanmen hao*) in Chinese. I went out into the grounds of the compound. There was no camera there. The director of the camp was a Uyghur man named Kadir. He was tall and tan. He said: 'You need to be careful about what you say. You shouldn't say "assalamu alaykum". Saying that can be considered a crime. You could be detained on the spot for saying it. Luckily, today it is me and two other police [officers] on duty.'

Kadir's recognition of the difficulty of the re-education task and their shared Turkic Muslim identification gave Risalet courage to ask a bit more about the detainees.

> I asked, 'Who are those people?'
> He said, 'They are imams and people who worked in the mosques.'
> I said, 'I will be careful next time.'
> He said again, 'You are lucky this time, because I was in the camera room.'

I asked, 'When were those students taken here?'
He replied, 'On 14 February.'
I asked, 'Did they commit any crimes?'
He replied, 'No. They are just religious Uyghurs. You need to be careful. Right above your head in the classroom, there are four cameras.'

In his responses, Kadir pushed Risalet to recognize the detainees as different from them, as religious and thus deserving of punishment. Over and over, he emphasized the force-field of the system and the way it pushed them to show no recognition of the dehumanization of other Turkic Muslims.

Risalet proceeded through this first day of work in the camp in a daze. Eventually the police dropped her off somewhere in the city and she rode buses for hours finding her way home.

My husband was at home and he asked me about my day in the re-education centre. He asked, 'Who were the students?' I cried so hard, explaining everything to him. My husband was shocked. I asked him to keep it a secret. Until now, none of my relatives know.

Over time, Risalet began to acclimate to the stress of performing inhumanity in front of the cameras. But it became increasingly clear to her that a process of dehumanization was unfolding in the camp. Within a week the detainees had their heads shaved. Several weeks later, the classrooms became cells to accommodate hundreds of new detainees. There were so many detainees that they had to take turns sleeping on the concrete floor. The detainees were deeply fearful. Their voices trembled when they answered questions in class. At this point in the interview, Risalet was sobbing, wiping at her face with her hand.

They were all so scared. When I asked something during class, they would not look at my face. At first, there was life on their faces. But after one week, the beards and hair of the men were shaved. At first the female detainees had long hair, but after one week, it was shaved. There was no energy in their eyes. I did not want to look at them. Because every time when I looked at them, I could not help, but be sad. At night, I couldn't sleep. The sound of the iron chains was still ringing in my ears when I tried to sleep.

Over time, the violence she was forced to support and enact effected not just her body but the integrity and dignity of her sense of self. Although she attempted to hide this beneath a 'trustworthy' veneer, eventually this too became impossible. The violence was more than simply a normative response to following the rules, it produced a moral wounding. Violating the entirety of Turkic Muslim detainee personhood resulted in a violation of her own sense of dignity, and self-worth. As Scheper-Hughes *et al.* (2004) note, 'violence can never be understood solely in terms of its physicality – force, assault, or the infliction of pain – alone. The social and cultural dimensions of violence are what gives violence its power and meaning' (cited in Fassin 2013: 130). This type of deep moral violence must be named as such in order for ethno-racialized forms of domination to be challenged and refused.

The trustworthiness mask

In the context of the Xinjiang re-education system, Turkic Muslim police contractors and camp instructors are often treated as though they are simultaneously essential and disposable. Baimurat and Risalet were not permitted to step away from their roles in the system without considerable costs to themselves. The threat of being labelled 'two-faced' always hung over them (Ala 2018). They said that being placed in this position produced an unbearable strain in their lives. Eventually Baimurat was unable to sleep at night. Due to her depression, lack of sleep, and appetite, Risalet's blood pressure dropped to dangerously low levels. She contemplated suicide. She prepared pills beside her pillow to swallow quickly if the police came in the middle of the night. Unable to walk and fearing that she might have a stroke she was admitted to a hospital. Baimurat said that as the system progressed he and his fellow police contractors began to drink alcohol while on duty as a way of coping. Eventually, Baimurat was able to leverage his Kazakhstani citizenship and the threat of international attention to denounce his Chinese citizenship and flee to Kazakhstan. Prior to these institutional interventions in their lives, they were told over and over by authorities that they would be detained if they attempted to refuse the processes of dehumanization they witnessed.

Despite these prohibitions on witnessing, the moments this chapter has described continued to play over and over in Baimurat's and Risalet's minds. When at last they were in a protected space, they felt as though they had no choice but to tell people about them. In those moments of acute subjection, of double consciousness, they recognized the mask of their re-educated 'trustworthy' identity as a police contractor and camp instructor fall away, revealing their Turkic Muslim self-identifications. For Baimurat, the true gravity of his work as a contractor, in placing people in camps, came when he saw lines of Uyghur and Kazakh women, including the elderly and infirm, being loaded onto buses. Perhaps even more importantly, when he saw his co-workers and family members shackled and taken away, he fully realized that his body too could be targeted by the re-education system. Likewise, when Risalet recognized that she was playing a role in the dehumanization of other Turkic Muslims, she was forced to turn away and sob even as the cameras recorded her affective response. She simultaneously recognized that her urban, *minkaohan*, Uzbek identification was overwhelmed by her identification with other Turkic Muslims. Both Baimurat and Risalet were captivated by their Turkic Muslim bodies and the life experiences that constructed them. While it was possible for them to place a 're-educated' mask over their selves, because of the ethno-racialized process of the colonial system, they could not escape the identities that proceeded before them.

These moments of recognition as a process of colonial subject-making resonate with the moments described by Fassin and Althusser, respectively, in which the police hail a citizen, calling them to recognize their normative authority (Fassin 2013; Althusser 2014). Given the racialized aspects of these confrontations they also resonate with a moment described by Frantz Fanon in *Black Skin, White Masks* in which a white French child points to Fanon, an eloquent French speaker and psychiatrist, and declares, 'Look, a Negro!' (Fanon 1967). In his analysis of this moment, Fanon shows how racialization is enacted through assessments of ethno-racial difference itself. An ethno-racialized colonial gaze fixes the identity of the phenotypes and culture of the Other, making it something that cannot be fully overcome as long as a colonial power structure remains in place. No matter how well the colonized speaks the language of the colonizer, which Fanon refers to as a 'white mask' in the French colonial context, the colonized will always be recognized as lacking and potentially Other, or 'two-faced'. Even if the colonized attempt to escape the association of the colonized by mimicking the colonizer and thinking of themselves as unmarked subjects entitled to police and legal protections, these protections can be taken away at a moment's notice. For Baimurat and Risalet the mask of re-educated 'trustworthiness' slipped away when they saw themselves reflected in the eyes of their former co-workers and neighbours.

In his consideration of Fanon's de-colonial framework in the context of colonial India, Homi Bhabha examines the way colonial powers develop intricate strategies of domination (Bhabha 1995). He found that a class of interpreters was essential to a durative transformation of social order that encompassed economic, political, and cultural replacement. In the logic of such a system, the class of interpreters, who moved between the colonized subaltern and the colonial officials, would adapt the forms of cultural distinction and values of the colonizer. Yet, as Bhabha shows, the hybrid figure of the interpreter is never able to fully inhabit this role. Instead the interpreter, or the system janitor as described by Irani, remains an ambivalent figure (Irani 2019). As permitted versions of Otherness they produce 'a partial vision of the colonizer's presence' (Bhabha 1995: 88; Schein 2000). Because of the ethno-racial trace that remains, these interpreters are destined to remain forever stuck in forms of mimicry, and subject to sudden denunciation at the slightest misstep.

Perhaps even more importantly, because of their hybrid position, Turkic Muslim re-education workers are also interrogated by a third type of gaze, beyond that of the self and the colonizer. Because the camp workers are simultaneously being hailed by a racialized police gaze and the gaze of Turkic Muslim detainees, they can also be pulled into moments of human-to-human inter-subjective identification. As Naisargi Dave has argued with regards to animal activists in India, a singular moment of locking eyes with a suffering Other can become a life-changing moment of witnessing (Dave 2014). This moment of intimacy between subjects can expand the self in a way that transcends previous horizons of relational possibility. Dave argues that the suffering Other is brought into the encounter precisely through a shared 'unfreedom'. In recognizing the pain of the Other a new inter-subjective bond can be built. This type of active witnessing demands an inter-subjectivity that emerges from a shared experience of being invited into face-to-face relations as co-creators of experience (Levinas 1979: 198). This immediacy, or true nearness, in contrast to the false intimacy of state power over a subjugated individual is experienced as what Emmanuel Levinas describes as 'living presence' that compels the witness to try and fail and try again to make the pain of the Other matter in the shared experience of life (Levinas 1979: 198).

Moments of shared affective experience are moments in which power is enacted. The profoundly negative experience of being hailed by a colonial gaze demonstrates the racialized power of a colonial state. At the same time moments of active witnessing, of recognizing the self in the Other, and sharing their pain, can also produce forms of de-colonial refusal. These types of moments changed Baimurat's and Risalet's lives forever. They are stories that they will relive and retell until they die. As an ethnographer it is these types of moments that I pay attention to. By collecting and translating them they have the potential to shape the way the world witnesses Turkic Muslim suffering. There is a Uyghur proverb that describes this de-colonial impulse well: 'Drop by drop a lake is formed' (Uy. *tama – tama köl bolar*).

Conclusion

Baimurat's and Risalet's stories are at once normal and exceptional. While perhaps most, if not all, Turkic Muslim camp workers experienced similar moments of extreme stress, the vast majority of them have not been able to step outside of the system. Instead, they have remained embedded in the system, unable to speak or even cry openly. Both Baimurat and Risalet noted that over time certain aspects of violence in the camps became normal. It became more and more difficult to be surprised by what they saw. The normalization of dehumanizing colonial violence appears to be endemic within the camp system. Inside the camps even forms of intense cruelty became part of the ordinary expression of state power. For instance, one former detainee said that Uyghur guards called him and other Turkic Muslim detainees 'animals!' (Kz. *mal!*) over and over again as they beat them with clubs and marched them to the toilet or classroom. A Kazakh man named Erzhan said in an interview that the Uyghur and Kazakh guards told the detainees in his cell: 'You don't have the right to talk, because you are not humans. If you were humans, you wouldn't be here' (Die Zeit 2019). Another former detainee said that one particularly cruel female Uyghur guard would call Han male guards to beat Uyghur female detainees that she recognized. She remembered that the Uyghur guard would say, 'You used to wear a veil, you deserve to be beaten.' She felt like the guard wanted to prove to those in charge that she was even more opposed to Turkic Islamic practice than they were. In general, the structure of the camp and its ethno-racialized processes of dehumanization produced forms of violence that enveloped everyone regardless of their physical and cultural identification. Very few people were able to extract themselves from this force-field and actively witness its effects by expressing their feelings of unmasked pain.

Institutionalized systems which legitimate violence towards ethno-racial minorities are difficult to stop. Once they are designed and put in motion they erode the social worlds they attack. This chapter has argued that the Turkic Muslims who are forced to maintain and implement the re-education system in Northwest China are placed in positions of subjectification. Through their work as police contractors and camp instructors they are pushed into confrontations between their Turkic Muslim selves and the 'trustworthy' mask they are forced to wear. This chapter has shown that, like colonial subjects in other contexts, the double consciousness that they are forced to inhabit as subjects at once complicit in the project and subject to it produces extreme forms of dissonance in their lives. This ambivalence, once recognized, was expressed through extreme forms of stress. During a research trip to Xinjiang in 2018, a Uyghur woman I interviewed told me that many of the police contractors she knew had contemplated suicide. Others told me that their relatives who worked inside the re-education system often cried when they came home at night. Risalet said that after that day crying at the blackboard with her back to the detainees it became impossible to eat bread without thinking about the way the detainees were starving. 'When I saw snow, I couldn't help but cry. Because I was thinking about them. I was thinking that they were freezing in their cells.' The experience of witnessing this suffering changed her. It made her desperate to tell the story of what she witnessed. By uplifting the inter-subjective power of these moments, the broader world may be pushed to witness contemporary colonial violence that is underway in Northwest China.

Notes

1 Risalet's name has been changed to protect her identity.

References

Ala, Memtimin (2018). 'Turn in the Two-Faced: The Plight of Uyghur Intellectuals', *The Diplomat*, 12 October, https://thediplomat.com/2018/10/turn-in-the-two-faced-the-plight-of-uyghur-intellectuals/ (accessed 18 July 2021).
Althusser, Louis (2014). *On the Reproduction of Capitalism: Ideology and Ideological State Apparatuses* (London: Verso).
Amrute, Sareeta (2016). *Encoding Race, Encoding Class: Indian IT Workers in Berlin* (Durham, NC: Duke University Press).
Anand, Dibyesh (2019). 'Colonization with Chinese Characteristics: Politics of (In)security in Xinjiang and Tibet', *Central Asian Survey* 38 (1), 129–147.
Anderson, Amy, and Darren Byler (2019). '"Eating Hanness": Uyghur Musical Tradition in a Time of Re-education', *China Perspectives* (3), 17–26.
Atwood, Christopher Pratt (2004). *Encyclopedia of Mongolia and the Mongol Empire* (New York: Facts on File).
Bhabha, Homi K. (1995). *The Location of Culture* (London: Routledge).
Bovingdon, Gardner (2010). *The Uyghurs: Strangers in Their Own Land* (New York: Columbia University Press).
Brophy, David (2016). *Uyghur Nation: Reform and Revolution on the Russia-China Frontier* (Cambridge, MA: Harvard University Press).
Brophy, David (2017). 'The 1957–58 Xinjiang Committee Plenum and the Attack on "Local Nationalism"', Wilson Center, www.wilsoncenter.org/blog-post/the-1957-58-xinjiang-committee-plenum-and-the-attack-local-nationalism (accessed 18 July 2021).
Byler, Darren (2018). 'Violent Paternalism: On the Banality of Uyghur Unfreedom', *The Asia-Pacific Journal* 16 (24), 1–14.
Dave, Naisargi N. (2014). 'Witness: Humans, Animals, and the Politics of Becoming', *Cultural Anthropology* 29 (3), 433–456.
Die Zeit (2019). 'Ihr seid keine Menschen', www.zeit.de/2019/32/zwangslager-xinjiang-muslime-china-zeugen-menschenrechte/seite-2 (accessed 18 July 2021).
Du Bois, William E. B. ([1903] 1994). *The Souls of Black Folk* (New York and Avenel: Gramercy Books).
Famularo, Julia (2018). '"Fighting the Enemy with Fists and Daggers": The Chinese Communist Party's Counter-terrorism Policy in the Xinjiang Uyghur Autonomous Region', in Michael Clarke (ed.), *Terrorism and Counter-terrorism in China: Domestic and Foreign Policy Dimensions* (Oxford: Oxford University Press), 39–73.

Fanon, Frantz (1967). *Black Skin, White Masks* (New York: Grove Press).
Fassin, Didier (2013). *Enforcing Order: An Ethnography of Urban Policing* (Cambridge: Polity).
Gladney, Dru C. (1996). 'Relational Alterity: Constructing Dungan (Hui), Uygur, and Kazakh Identities across China, Central Asia, and Turkey', *History and Anthropology* 9 (4), 445–477.
Human Rights Watch (2019). 'China's Algorithms of Repression', www.hrw.org/report/2019/05/01/chinas-algorithms-repression/reverse-engineering-xinjiang-police-mass-surveillance (accessed 18 July 2021).
Irani, Lilly (2019). *Chasing Innovation: Making Entrepreneurial Citizens in Modern India* (Princeton: Princeton University Press).
Levinas, Emmanuel (1979). *Totality and Infinity: An Essay on Exteriority*, vol. 1 (Germany: Springer).
Li, Jiarui. (2015) 'The Inbetweeners: Uyghur MinKaoHan and Their Private Lives in Xinjiang' (PhD diss., University of Cambridge).
Millward, James A. (2007). *Eurasian Crossroads: A History of Xinjiang* (New York: Columbia University Press).
Ramzy, Austin, and Chris Buckley (2019). '"Absolutely No Mercy": Leaked Files Expose How China Organized Mass Detentions of Muslims', *New York Times*, 16 November, www.nytimes.com/interactive/2019/11/16/world/asia/china-xinjiang-documents.html (accessed 18 July 2021).
Reddy, Chandan (2011). *Freedom with Violence: Race, Sexuality, and the US State* (Durham, NC: Duke University Press).
Rhodes, Lorna A. (2004). *Total Confinement: Madness and Reason in the Maximum Security Prison*, vol. 7 (Berkeley: University of California Press Press).
Schein, Louisa (2000). *Minority Rules: The Miao and the Feminine in China's Cultural Politics* (Durham, NC: Duke University Press).
Scheper-Hughes, Nancy, Philippe Bourgois, and Richard Perry (eds) (2004). *Violence in War and Peace: An Anthology* (London: Wiley-Blackwell).
Smith Finley, Joanne (2007). '"Ethnic Anomaly" or Modern Uyghur Survivor? A Case Study of the *Minkaohan* Hybrid Identity in Xinjiang', in Ildikó Bellér-Hann, M. Cristina Cesàro, Rachel Harris, and Joanne Smith Finley (eds), *Situating the Uyghurs between China and Central Asia* (London: Routledge), 219–238.
Smith Finley, Joanne (2013). *The Art of Symbolic Resistance: Uyghur Identities and Uyghur-Han Relations in Contemporary Xinjiang* (Leiden: Brill).
Smith Finley, Joanne (2018). 'Uyghur Identities', in Weiping Wu and Mark W. Frazier (eds), *The Sage Handbook of Contemporary China*, vol. 2 (London: SAGE Publications Ltd), 736–759.

Smith Finley, Joanne (2019). 'Securitization, Insecurity and Conflict in Contemporary Xinjiang: Has PRC Counter-terrorism Evolved into State Terror?', *Central Asian Survey* 38 (1), 1–26.

Zenz, Adrian, and James Leibold (2020). 'Securitizing Xinjiang: Police Recruitment, Informal Policing and Ethnic Minority Co-optation', *The China Quarterly* 242, 324–348.

7

Corrective 're-education' as (cultural) genocide: A content analysis of the Uyghur primary school textbook *Til-Ädäbiyat*

Dilmurat Mahmut and Joanne Smith Finley

Introduction

> Two girls (around eight and eleven) are hanging around a musical instrument stall, listening to the stallholder (X) play *dutar*, and chatting to me. I ask them if they like Uyghur music. One says she likes Chinese-language or English-language songs but doesn't listen to Uyghur-language songs. I ask her why not. She says she used to know a Uyghur song when she was little and tries to sing it but can't remember the words. I remark that Uyghur music is beautiful and that she should listen to it. X nods but says that a lot of the kids are like this now. The girl says there isn't a lot of Uyghur music around, and I nod, and observe that there are now next to no Uyghur music *dukan* (kiosks) in the city. X nods. I ask the two girls about their language skills: they say they speak Uyghur best, Chinese second best, and English third best. X concurs and says his three daughters also speak both Uyghur and Chinese fluently. But he adds that he doesn't know how the next generation will be – the ones who are educated in Chinese-immersion kindergartens. (Smith Finley field notes, Döngköwrük, Ürümchi, 6 July 2018)

In a context where Uyghur children in the Xinjiang Uyghur Autonomous Region (XUAR) now have no choice but to attend Chinese-medium schools, where they are immersed in Mandarin Chinese for all but three school hours per week, we may suppose that the Uyghur girl in the above excerpt hears only Chinese-language (and some English-language) songs in the classroom.[1] Her fragmented knowledge of a single Uyghur song likely dates back to her infancy, a time before the onset of the 'People's War on Terror' in 2014 and the new era of Chinese as *tongyong yuyan* (common language of the country) and 'the language of re-educated patriotic Uyghurs' (Byler 2019). Perhaps the song was orally transmitted to her by parents or neighbours, or by a kindergarten teacher. Now, as the father-of-three in this excerpt indicates, fears are growing in the Uyghur community that the recent imposition of Chinese-immersion education from kindergarten level will inflict significant damage on Uyghur children's command of their mother tongue and knowledge of Uyghur culture more broadly.

Since 2012, Xi's Han-majoritarian assimilationist state has reconstructed the Uyghur body, mind, language, religion, and culture as a biological and existential threat to the Chinese nation: all Uyghur individuals are now assumed by default to be potentially disloyal subjects (Roberts 2018; Smith Finley 2019a). This framing of an entire people as a national security threat constitutes a political technology in a hegemonic project – a way for those in power to 'manipulate the concept of security to pursue their goals' (Lemon 2018: 1–2). In this case, the Chinese state has appropriated the lexicon of the 'War on Terror' as a means to label perceived Uyghur opposition as 'religious extremism' and thereby 'generate diplomatic capital for the ongoing repression of Uyghur autonomist aspirations' (Clarke 2018: 32). While the Chinese state hopes to use counterterror rhetoric to persuade external observers of the necessity for 'de-extremification' in Xinjiang, in reality its domestic goal is to use 're-education' ('thought transformation'; 'thought liberation') as a 'final solution' to erase the Uyghur identity (language, culture, religion), perceived as the life force of the (separate) Uyghur nation.

In this chapter, we focus on state attempts to erase and 'invisibilize' the Uyghur culture through the deliberate and systematic replacement of an earlier set of primary school textbooks *Til-Ädäbiyat* (Language and Literature, 1st ed. 2015) with a revised edition in 2018. Through a content analysis of what is present – and what is not – in these revised edition textbooks, we will examine the state's method and intention in transforming the content communicated to Uyghur primary-aged schoolchildren. We do so within the framework of Raphael Lemkin's broad concept of genocide (Lemkin [1944] 2005) and by applying Bradley Campbell's notion of genocide as a means of social control (Campbell 2009).

Lemkin's ([1944] 2005) notion of genocide

In his seminal work, *Axis Rule in Occupied Europe* first published in 1944, Polish jurist Raphael Lemkin developed the term 'genocide' to describe German war crimes aimed at destroying nations (Lemkin [1944] 2005). Crucially, Lemkin saw the cultural destruction of a group as equally important as the physical annihilation of its members:

> The world represents only so much culture and intellectual vigor as are created by its component national groups. Essentially the idea of a nation signifies … original contributions, based upon genuine traditions, genuine culture, and well-developed national psychology. The destruction of a nation, therefore, results in the loss of its future contribution to the world. (Lemkin [1944] 2005: 91)

Lemkin considered genocide to be not necessarily the *immediate destruction* of a nation, but rather the more gradual eradication of 'the essential foundations of the life of national groups, with the aim of annihilating the groups themselves' (Lemkin [1944] 2005: 79). An early draft of the UN Convention on Genocide (1948) by the United Nations Secretariat had originally followed Lemkin's framework, defining genocide as any deliberate act committed with the intention of destroying the language, religion, or culture of a group, such as, for example, prohibiting the use of the group's language or its schools or places of worship. However, the final version of Article 2 of the Convention ended up being a much-reduced version, with no mention of linguistic, religious, or cultural destruction.

Campbell's (2009) theory of genocide as social control of 'deviant' behaviour

In Xinjiang since 2017, the state has enacted a range of policies under the mantle of 'de-extremification' (*qu jiduanhua*) that suggests an ongoing, slow genocide, defined in Lemkin's terms. These include the imposition of Chinese-medium education (in place of the earlier 'bilingual education') and suppression of the Uyghur language and script (Byler 2019); the repression of ordinary, everyday Islamic practices, and imposition of Han Chinese cultural practices in place of Uyghur cultural practices (Smith Finley 2018); mass internment (during which detainees are subjected to physical and psychological torture, and where deaths have occurred as a result of beating, withheld medication, or poor nutrition) (Smith Finley 2019b; Zenz 2019a); coercive birth control including forced abortions and mass sterilizations since 2015 (Zenz 2020); and the forcible transfer of children to securitized orphanages and boarding schools (Zenz 2019b). Each of the above acts may be theorized as a method adopted by the state to control behaviours and practices in the Uyghur community that it perceives as threatening or 'deviant'. We therefore find Campbell's theory of genocide as social control highly applicable to the Uyghurs' situation.[2]

Campbell defines genocide as 'organised and unilateral mass killing on the basis of ethnicity' (Campbell 2009: 153). He notes that it is committed by organized groups, including (but not limited to) governments, armies, and militias. While the available evidence of mass killings in Xinjiang is so far limited to several instances of disproportionate state response to Uyghur protest, here we focus rather on Campbell's notion of control of 'moral deviance'. Rejecting conventional definitions of genocide as 'evil', 'madness', or 'crime', Campbell focuses on the perpetrator's view that *victims* are evil; in this sense, genocide is a response to behaviour defined as 'deviant'. Genocide occurs not when moral evaluations are disregarded by its perpetrators, but rather when they are present and applied: that is, the perpetrator enacts genocide based on their 'moral grievances' against the victim (Campbell 2009: 155).

We find it insightful to compare the 'moral grievances' present in earlier cases of genocide, as analysed by Campbell, with those present in the Xinjiang case. Firstly, perpetrators of genocide often accuse their victims of 'disloyalty'. This was the case, for instance, in Nazi Germany in the 1940s, when Jews were accused of 'disloyalty to the nation'. In contemporary Xinjiang, and particularly in the period following the 2009 Ürümchi demonstration-turned-riot, Uyghurs have routinely been treated as (potentially separatist) 'ingrates', who lack a sense of loyalty to the country and to the Chinese Communist Party (CCP). This perception can be observed in discourses aired in state-sanctioned news mouthpieces, such as the following published on Xinjiang's Tianshan Net regional news website in 2018:

> The masses have thrown supporters of the 'Three Evil Forces' (三股势力 *sangu shili* – extremism, terrorism and separatism), 'agents

of foreign reactionary forces' (境外反动势力的代理人 *jingwai fandong shili de dailiren* – those allied with overseas Uyghur advocacy groups and hostile Western nations), 'rogue advocates of religious extremism' (流窜的宗教极端鼓吹者 *liucuan de zongjiao jiduan guchuizhe*) and 'two-faced persons' (两面人 *liangmianren* – Uyghur officials said to be secretly disloyal to the state) 'into the grave of history'. (Cited in Smith Finley 2019c)

The willingness to simply *eliminate* those Uyghurs who fall into these categories is underlined in the final phrase, even while the state suggests that it is the 'good', hardworking Uyghurs who have demanded and precipitated their disappearance (and not the state). The anonymous author goes on to observe:

Those who criticise our [the CCP's] 'thought liberation' movement are self-evidently 'those who would compete with us for the next generation in the hope of cultivating separatist poisonous grasses' (妄图与我们争夺下一代来培植分裂毒草的人 *wangtu yu women zhengduo xiayidai lai peizhi fenlie ducao de ren*). (Cited in Smith Finley 2019c)

This clarifies the state's intention: in separating Uyghur children from their parents as part of the post-2017 'de-extremification' campaign, they mean to prevent such 'poisoning' of young minds taking place.

Secondly, perpetrators of genocide often believe that victims have 'taken over' or 'infiltrated' the majority culture and society. As detailed by Campbell, in 1940s Nazi Germany, Jews were believed to have 'taken over' German culture; later, in 1994, Tutsis were deemed 'clannish' by Hutus and said to have 'infiltrated' Rwandan society (Campbell 2009: 155). In Xinjiang since 2017, there is no shortage of such observations. Many of them can be found in the 'Xinjiang Uyghur Autonomous Region (XUAR) Regulation on De-extremification' of 30 March 2017 (China Law Translate 2017). To give just two examples: Article 9 (6) prohibits 'extremification' in the form of 'generalizing the concept of Halal, to make Halal *expand into* areas beyond Halal foods, and using the idea of something being non-Halal to reject or *interfere with* others' secular lives'; meanwhile, Article 12 declares: 'De-extremification shall persist in the correct political orientation and direction of public opinion to carry forward the main themes and transmit positive energy; *strengthening resistance to penetration* and the struggle against separatism in the ideological sphere' (China Law Translate 2017, emphasis added).

Other salient points of comparison include perpetrators' perception of genocide victims as 'parasites' who live off the labour of others (more on this below); their perception of the children of genocide victims as a potential future threat; and their tendency to accuse victims of attempted genocide in reverse (Campbell 2009: 155–156). While it may seem implausible, some Han Chinese netizens have claimed that *they* are the victims of an attempted genocide by Muslim perpetrators, pointing to the Han civilian death toll during the 2009 Ürümchi riots or to the local violence occurring in Xinjiang between 2012 and 2015 (Rodríguez-Merino 2019; Smith Finley 2019b). All of the recent developments suggest that the central perception of a 'civilized us' (Han) vs 'backwards them' (Uyghur) dichotomy has become further entrenched in Xi Jinping's new-era Han-majoritarian state (Mahmut 2019).

Corrective 're-education' in Xinjiang since April 2017

If we return once more to the 'XUAR Regulation on De-extremification' (China Law Translate 2017), we see that the state's preferred means of dealing with Uyghur deviance is through a process of 'correction'. This is made explicit through the choice of language in said regulations. Thus, Article 10 states that 'De-extremification shall *correctly (*准确 *zhunque) grasp delineation of* ethnic customs, normal religious activity, unlawful religious activities and extremist conduct'. Article 13 declares that 'De-extremification shall carry out big publicity, learning and discourse … leading believers to *establish correct beliefs (*正信 *zhengxin) positioning'*. In direct reference to the political re-education system then being established in a network of internment camps, we read in Article 14 that 'De-extremification shall complete work on educational transformation … combining ideological education, psychological counseling, *behavioral corrections (*矫正 *jiaozheng)*, and skills training'. Article 35 proclaims that 'Religious groups shall … reject extremist religious ideology, playing a role in de-extremification work, guiding believers to *correctly (*正确 *zhengque) grasp the relationship between law and religion, confirm correct faith (*正信 *zhengxin)'*. Finally, in another implicit reference to extrajudicial internment, Article 46 warns

Corrective 're-education' as (cultural) genocide 187

that 'Where Article 9 of this Regulation is violated, but the circumstances are more minor, the public security organs, together with relevant departments and units, are to *order corrections (改正 gaizheng)*' (China Law Translate 2017, emphasis added).

This language of correction surfaces again in the leaked internal CCP documents that came to be known as the 'Xinjiang Papers' (Ramzy and Buckley 2019). In one document titled 'Tactics from Turpan City for answering questions asked by the children of concentrated education and training school students', translated and published online by *The New York Times*, we see a host of examples. Given the potential for students returning to Xinjiang from other parts of China to '*issue incorrect opinions* on WeChat, Weibo and other social media platforms', the document warns, it will be necessary as soon as students return home to 'carry out direct thought guidance, *remove doubt or misunderstandings*' (Ramzy and Buckley 2019, emphasis added). Moreover, the document continues, students should be grateful that the authorities have taken their relatives away to internment camps and should even 'treasure this chance for free education that the party and government has provided to *thoroughly eradicate erroneous thinking*'. Students' relatives will not be able to 'thoroughly unmask and understand the *reactionary nature* of religious extremism unless they undergo an extended period of standardized study and training that is comprehensive, systematic and behind closed doors, *with correct instruction and guidance* from teachers'. These individuals have been taken away because 'their thinking has been infected by unhealthy thoughts, and if they don't quickly *receive education and correction*, they'll become a major active threat to society' (Ramzy and Buckley 2019, emphasis added). As observed by *Washington Post* journalists, these documents portray a government 'intolerant of deviations from its model-citizen mold' (Knowles *et al.* 2019).

Observations of 'correction' during a 2018 field trip

During a field trip to Xinjiang conducted in June–July 2018, Smith Finley observed and documented many visual examples of religious and cultural 'correction' on the ground (Smith Finley 2018). In this striking photograph (Figure 7.1), which shows a textile banner of a Han Chinese educator teaching Chinese to a mixed-ethnicity class,

Figure 7.1 Textile banner hung outside the Ürümchi No. 1 Primary School, 5 July 2018

the Uyghur (modified Arabic) script has been literally *cut out* from the banner, owing to its connection to Islam, in a move akin to cutting out a cancer. This act of 'disappearing' the Uyghur script reflects a simultaneous process of erasure of online policy documents relating to the earlier People's Republic of China (PRC) state policy of 'bilingual education' (双语教育 *shuangyu jiaoyu*), now being systematically replaced by documents that refer instead to 'national language education' (国语教育 *guoyu jiaoyu*) or Chinese-medium-only education.[3]

Meanwhile, a visit to the Xinhua bookstore in Ürümchi revealed the complete absence of any books teaching Uyghur script to Uyghur children; all that remained was an ageing set of Uyghur phonetics flashcards. On the other hand, a large stand of textbooks and lined exercise books was quite clearly aimed at helping Chinese native speakers to learn Uyghur script. A bookseller confirmed that local Han had begun studying Uyghur since 2017, a date consistent with the onset of 'de-extremification' policies. While the state packages this as a policy to encourage ethnic unity, the bookseller provided a different

Corrective 're-education' as (cultural) genocide

analysis, remarking: 'Han people are not learning Uyghur as a mark of cultural respect; it's a means of control – a way to know what Uyghurs are saying, planning' (Smith Finley, field notes, 6 July 2018). When Smith Finley began to examine a set of six Uyghur-medium textbooks titled *Til-Ädäbiyat* (Language and Literature), the bookseller smiled ironically, and observed that the content was 'new for 2018' (1st ed. 2015). Flicking through one of the textbooks, they found a chapter on Turpan, and gestured at the accompanying picture, which showed Chinese characters engraved into a stone next to an artificial waterfall. While they did not spell out their meaning, they evidently meant to draw attention to the removal of features linked to local Uyghur culture and history, and their replacement with features relating to Han Chinese culture and history.

The above experience immediately recalls the case of Uyghur textbook compiler Yalqun Rozi, who was arrested in 2016 at the age of fifty and later sentenced to fifteen years in prison for 'incitement to subvert state power' (Shepherd 2019). Back in 2001, the Chinese government had asked Rozi to head up a committee in charge of compiling Uyghur literature textbooks for Xinjiang Education Press (XJEP). At the time, he had been in favour. But, following the arrival of new regional Party Secretary Chen Quanguo in 2016, his books were pulled from the shelves and his former colleagues at XJEP disappeared, as did the state officials who had supervised his work. Political meetings were held to denounce the 'problematic textbooks'; it was said they were 'treasonous' and had 'poisoned Uyghurs with ideas of splitting China' (Shepherd 2019). The textbook compilers' crimes were quantified in percentages and keyword frequencies; perhaps the greatest infraction was that, in 200,000 words of text, the word 'China' appeared only four times. And while the permitted upper limit for minority-language sources was 30 per cent, 60 per cent of the material in the textbooks was derived from Uyghur cultural sources. This, it was claimed, constituted state subversion. Yet as Rozi's son, Kamaltürk Yalqun, observed: 'Those textbooks weren't political at all; there were things in there about taking pride in being ethnic Uighurs, and that's what the Chinese government was upset with' (Shepherd 2019). The judgement was made within the frightening new context of 'cultural re-engineering' – a project intended to distance young Uyghurs from their mother tongue and culture, alongside programmes to place them in Chinese-medium orphanages and boarding schools (Leibold, cited in Shepherd 2019).

The leaked Xinjiang Papers contain an internal speech delivered in 2014 by Xi Jinping, in which he exhorts cadres to 'adhere to the daily concentrated study of the national language (Mandarin), law, and skills, [and] make *remedial Mandarin studies* the top priority' (Ramzy and Buckley 2019, emphasis added). Evidently, the state believes that much of the 'correction' required within Uyghur society can be achieved by replacing Uyghurs' mother tongue with the 'national language' (*guoyu*, formerly known as *Hanyu*, or the language of the Han). However, to get there, a linguistic transition period will be necessary. In this chapter, we focus on the correction of Uyghur religion and culture in the revised first edition of a set of Uyghur-medium primary school textbooks titled *Til-Ädäbiyat*.

Content analysis: 'Correction' of *Til-Ädäbiyat*

In this section, we present our findings and analysis of the content of Book 2, Levels 1–6, of the revised first edition of *Til-Ädäbiyat* (Language and Literature) (Xinjiang Education Press Editorial Board 2018).[4] Partway through content analysis, Mahmut discovered that a majority of the texts that we were dealing with appeared to have been translated from texts included in a Chinese-medium primary school textbook of the same name, 语文 (*Yuwen*), published by the People's Education Press (*Renmin jiaoyu chubanshe*). As such, while our analysis had thus far assumed that content had been freshly selected to have a specific influence on, and tell a particular story to, Uyghur pupils, it now evolved to consider the effect on Uyghur pupils of simple transposition of texts intended for Han Chinese pupils. That said, we note that not all texts in the Chinese-medium original were considered suitable for transposition, while some of those that were transposed were adapted in often telling ways.

Finding 1: Han Chinese cultural and social life (Confucian, secular) highlighted; Uyghur cultural and social life (Turkic, Islamic) almost totally absent

Our analysis shows that many of the readings in the textbooks appear to have been translated and adapted from original texts included in the corresponding Chinese-medium textbooks published by the People's Education Press. These readings, created by Han Chinese authors, mostly depict aspects of Han Chinese cultural and social life. To give some examples: *Telewizor Körüsh* (Watching TV) in Book 2, Level 1 (pp. 37–38), shows a Han family's typical routine of TV consumption.[5] Father and son like to watch football matches, while grandma enjoys Peking opera. The focus is squarely on Han Chinese performing arts, reflecting the rise of Han-centric nationalism in recent years under Xi Jinping. Meanwhile, the absence of any mention of Uyghur performing arts in the textbooks mirrors the enforced disappearances of key cultural figures in Uyghur society since 2017 (Harris 2019; UHRP 2019). Two stories, *Dadamning Köktatliqi* (My Father's Vegetable Garden) by Wang Xukui in Book 2, Level 4 (pp. 76–77), and *Bowamning Beghi* (My Grandfather's Garden) by Xiao Hong in Book 2, Level 5 (pp. 18–20), depict rural life in south China, where (unlike in Xinjiang) villagers can grow vegetables in their gardens in all seasons.[6] The image accompanying the second of the two shows an elderly man and his grandson both wearing the straw hats typical of southern Chinese farmers. In Book 2, Level 4, the short story *Beliqlar Qäghizingizgä Üzüp Chiqiwaptu* (The Fish Swam onto Your Paper, pp. 82–84) relates how a girl shouts her amazement at an artist's skill, as he sits in a teahouse and draws fish beside the famous inner Chinese cultural location, the West Lake (*Xihu*) in Hangzhou.[7] With so many lakes in Xinjiang to choose from, one must ask why this reading does not focus rather on one of the region's own famous lakes, such as Sayram Köli or Qanas Köli? Xinjiang's distinctive borderland culture, flora, and fauna are largely absent from the six volumes we analysed, an omission we suggest is indicative of the deliberate, coercive integration of Uyghurs into inner Chinese geography (PRC sovereign territory) and the Chinese national polity.

We found that almost no text features Uyghur traditional culture and society, and only a few texts mention Uyghur names (either people or place). One exception is *Buyluq* (Book 2, Level 2, pp. 35–36), which introduces a village in Turpan.[8] The reading depicts different varieties of grapes grown by the local people and explains how grapes are dried in *chünchä* (a special drying house). Yet the ethnonym 'Uyghur' is not mentioned in the reading. Moreover, while the original Chinese-medium text was accompanied by images of Uyghur men and women (the former wearing beards, the latter headscarves) carrying baskets of grapes and sitting down to eat them, these now outlawed symbols of religion have disappeared from the revised Uyghur-medium version. In their place is a picture of an artificial waterfall, which only seems to highlight the Han settler impact on Turpan, one of the hottest and driest places on earth. The toponym 'Turpan' appears once again on page 91 of Book 2, Level 6, in a section of sentence-making drills alongside three mentions of the traditional Uyghur cuisine *polo* (rice pilaf), while Uyghur *nan* bread appears on page 11 of Book 2, Level 3. However, it is important to note that all three food items – grapes, *polo*, and *nan* – may be said to represent a non-threatening food culture that has long since been co-opted by Han Chinese and is important for ethnic tourism, an industry often dominated by Han Chinese companies (Li and Wall 2008).[9]

Revealingly, in the original Chinese-medium textbook aimed at Han Chinese pupils, we do find a reading about the Uyghurs: 和田的维吾尔*Hetian de Weiwu'er* (The Uyghurs of Khotän, Book 2, Level 6).[10] The reading is accompanied by a photograph of Uyghur stallholders selling *nan* bread at an outdoor market, and includes women wearing headscarves and men sporting beards and *doppa* (traditional Uyghur skull caps). Yet in the corresponding Uyghur-medium textbook that is the focus of our analysis, this reading has (been) disappeared. While an innocent explanation for this omission might be that compilers felt Uyghur school pupils already know all about Uyghur culture and therefore have no need to read this piece, a more cynical conclusion finds that the inclusion of this piece would controvert the current, assimilationist political agenda, which is to eradicate the distinct Uyghur culture and identity.

Where a reading does focus on Xinjiang, the story *Suwadan* (Cottonwood Trees, Book 2, Level 5, pp. 123–125) by Yuan Ying[11] focuses not on the Uyghurs but on the migration of Han pioneers to the region, comparing the valiant process of Han settlement and adaptation to the versatility of cottonwood trees that can 'take root and grow anywhere, withstanding sandstorms, snowstorms, drought, and flood'. The Han Chinese presence in Xinjiang is normalized as a benevolent practice of 'helping' the subaltern Uyghurs to develop to the 'advanced' level of civilization enjoyed by the Han majority. At the same time, Han Chinese are portrayed as strong, adaptable, and indestructible – a description often found on the lips of

Corrective 're-education' as (cultural) genocide 193

Xinjiang Han, who like to boast about the hardy and numerous Han ethnicity.[12] At the same time, only a limited space is dedicated to other ethnic minorities. On pages 125–126 of Book 2, Level 2, a political story relates how Premier Zhou Enlai participated in the Dai ethnicity's Water Splashing Festival in 1961.[13] That this particular example is used is significant, given the frequently discussed tendency of the majority Han to 'exoticize' and 'eroticize' ethnic minority cultures (Gladney 1994; Harrell 1995; Schein 1997). In Book 2, Level 6, there is a special section called *Rānggarāng Örp-Adātlär* (Colourful Customs), which starts with a short introduction to China's fifty-six ethnic groups and their unique (*özigä yarisha*) customs (p. 15), which speaks volumes to the Han preference for colourful and harmless expressions of ethnic minority culture. Tellingly, the sole reading provided for this section (*Kigiz Öydä Mehman Bolush*, Being a Guest in a Felt Yurt) focuses on the hospitality customs of the Mongolian people (pp. 16–18). This selection is especially significant given the Han desire – and state imperative – to represent borderland minorities as welcoming to Han settlers.[14] Meanwhile, a reading about Inner Mongolian people titled 草原 *Caoyuan* (Grasslands), which is included in the Chinese-medium version of the textbook, is missing from the Uyghur-medium version we examined.[15]

While there is next to no content in the textbooks about Uyghur society and culture (or indeed any ethnic minority cultures), a substantial amount of space is given over to readings focused on life and events in foreign countries, particularly from Level 4 onwards. What is noticeable is that most featured countries enjoyed friendly or neutral relationships with China, at least at the time of the textbooks' publication. Second of note is that Turkey, the Central Asian nations, and the majority-Muslim states of the Middle East are all conspicuous in their absence. Evidently, the Chinese authorities do not wish to encourage mutual identifications between Uyghurs and potential linguistic cousins and cultural allies outside the PRC. So we find, for example, a story titled *Dostlar* (Friends) by Va. Osyewa in Book 2, Level 1 (pp. 107–108), which features Russian children on a trip; one about a Russian girl, Sasha, and her brother, Toliya, in Book 2, Level 2 (pp. 19–20), titled *Ana, Män Ajiz Ämäs* (Mother, I Am Not Weak); and another about a Russian male pupil who struggles to understand human evolution in his biology class in Book 2, Level 5 (pp. 15–17): *Baliliqtiki Bayqash* (Childhood Discovery).[16] Russia is presumably considered safe for inclusion because it is China's strategic partner in the Shanghai Cooperation Organisation (SCO), and the two countries have co-operated closely on regional security and energy for two decades. Other countries featured in readings include France, Hungary, Poland, Switzerland, Germany, South Africa, Algeria, the US, Canada, and Finland. At the time of compilation and publication of the 2018 textbooks, China's relations with all but one of these countries (the US) were reasonably good. Relations with France had improved after a low point around the 2008 Olympics, when French pro-Tibet protestors interrupted the progress of the Olympic torch. And China had been pushing for some time its preferred alliance with the world's developing nations in, for example, Latin America and Africa; the inclusion of South Africa here reflects its manoeuvring within BRICS (a bloc of five major emerging national economies: Brazil, Russia, India, China, and South Africa).

A second pattern of note is that the content of some of these readings imparts a strong moral or ideological message, or a political discourse aimed at influencing the pupils' way of thinking about China and its place in the modern world. This goal was no doubt equally important when compiling the Chinese-medium version for the original target audience – Han pupils – as the state seeks to maintain domestic social stability and shore up CCP political legitimacy. For example, several stories reflect China's pragmatic nationalist stance of seeking to learn Western science and technology while rejecting Western culture. Thus, we see positive images of Western scientific innovations (this also links CCP goals back to those of the May Fourth Movement). *Alimlar Häqqidä Hekayilär* (Stories about Scientists, Book 2, Level 6) includes three long texts, of which two focus on Western scientists. *Äsirdin Halqighan Güzällik* by Liang Heng (跨越百年的美丽 A Century of Beauty, Book 2, Level 6, pp. 77–80) is an introduction to Madame Marie Curie, the Polish and naturalized-French physicist and chemist who conducted pioneering research on radioactivity;[17] *Häqiqät 100 Soal Belgisidin keyin Dunyagha Kelidu* (Truth Will Emerge after 100 Question Marks, Book 2, Level 6, pp. 82–84) by Ye Yonglei narrates the tale of several Western scientists who discovered scientific truths after long and tireless enquiries;[18] and *Özi Sinap Körüsh* (Give It a

Corrective 're-education' as (cultural) genocide   195

Try, Book 2 Level 2, pp. 54–55) tells the story of a French scientist's explorations.[19] On a different note, *Yaghach Oyma Satidighan Bala* (A Boy Who Sells Wooden Carvings) in Book 2, Level 3 (pp. 90–92), tells the story of a Chinese tourist in South Africa, conveying the message that African people hold an extremely positive image of China. Such a representation seems to reflect China's preferred self-image – that of the benevolent, paternalistic state 'helping' the African peoples to develop (just as it 'helps' its own borderland subalterns to develop). This ideal self-image is reinforced in a second story in Book 2, Level 3, titled *Junggo Hälqara Qutquzish Ätriti Häqiqätän Qaltis* (Chinese International Aid Group Is Amazing, pp. 93–96). This reading showcases the positive image of China held by Algerians as a result of receiving aid from the Chinese government when Algeria was hit by an earthquake in 2003. In the Chinese-medium original, the goal was likely to suggest to Han children that China nowadays not only enjoys high status in the international community but is also in a superior economic position that allows it to exercise benevolence in lending financial support to countries in need. For the Uyghur children receiving the translated version, there may be an additional message: Uyghurs in Xinjiang should – like the Africans – be grateful for the development assistance (described as 'poverty alleviation' in CCP discourses) they receive from the Chinese central state. In both cases, the CCP clearly hopes to send a message to potentially dissatisfied constituencies (ethnic minority groups; underprivileged Han Chinese) that the strong and powerful Chinese nation can help others in need, and that the CCP has therefore succeeded in making China great on the world stage; this in turn is intended to enhance children's sense of national pride. In a third story titled *Yerim Sham* (Half-Burned Candle, Book 2, Level 5, pp. 27–29) by Ji Xiaojing, a French family tries to hide a secret from the German soldiers during World War Two.[20] Probably, this story is included as it aligns closely with the CCP's anti-imperialist stance; for instance, White Papers on China's 'peaceful rise' and 'peaceful development' frequently claim that China will never take the path of foreign imperialism previously walked by fascist powers such as the Nazis.

It is perhaps telling that when selecting readings about the US, the textbook compilers have used two pieces by Mark Twain, a left-wing American author who was critical of American politics (see e.g. *The*

Adventures of Huckleberry Finn, considered by some to be an indictment of slavery). In Book 2, Level 5, *Pulning Sehri Küchi* (The Magic Power of Money, pp. 93–96) tells a story of materialistic America, and appears to be very much in line with Marxist ideology.[21] Meanwhile, a third piece, *Ölmäs Köz* (Eyes That Don't Die) by American writer Linda Rivers (Book 2, Level 4, pp. 56–57), relates the donation of Linda's mother's cornea after her death.[22] The choice of this reading seems macabre, in the context of ongoing allegations of organ harvesting among Chinese prisoners of conscience – Falungong practitioners and Uyghur re-education camp internees. China has insisted that it banned the use of prisoners' organs for organ donation in 2015, and that voluntary citizen donation is now the only legitimate channel (*China Daily* 2016). An independent tribunal held in London in 2019 found that 'physical acts have been carried out that are indicative of the crime of genocide', but concluded that it could not prove definitively that these acts were carried out with the intention of destroying the group (in whole or in part), rather than merely for profit. It did, however, find unequivocally that these acts constituted crimes against humanity and torture (China Tribunal 2020: 154–156).

Finding 2: The pictures of human characters show only Han cultural elements; Uyghur cultural elements are absent

In the cover images of the six textbooks we examined, the illustrations of human characters display no items of typical Uyghur dress culture, such as *doppa* (skull cap), *kaniway köynäk* (shirt decorated with flowered embroidery at the collar, sleeve, and neckline), and so on. This seems to emphasize the state policy shift from the more conciliatory minority policy of the past to the Han-majoritarian, assimilationist policy of the post-2012 period. Whereas previously ethnic minority material culture was considered harmless and encouraged, where not perceived to be overly religious, any aspect of Uyghur culture is currently perceived and treated as a security threat. We would suggest here that, in the current climate of aggressive Han nationalism, and especially in the context of the post-2017 'de-extremification' campaign, the textbook compilers (themselves Uyghur) did not dare to include images that display distinct Uyghur cultural markers. Thus, the cover pictures depict children in Han Chinese classical dress (Book 2, Level 5) or in modern-day clothing with red pioneer ties (Book

2, Level 4; Book 2, Level 6) or without them (Book 2, Level 1; Book 2, Level 2). This focus reflects the state's desire, post-2009, to link minority groups right back into early Chinese civilization (Tobin 2020). The last book cover depicts foreign children with different racial features, clothed in their own traditional dress style (Book 2, Level 3).

The same is true – with one fascinating exception – of the images accompanying the readings inside the textbooks. In *Quruq Tästäk Kötürgän Bala* (The Boy Carrying an Empty Pot) (Book 2, Level 1, pp. 104–105), one picture clearly shows a king from a Chinese dynasty surrounded by a group of Chinese children sporting traditional Chinese hairstyles and wearing the traditional costume of the period.[23] *Rässam wä Padichi Bala* (The Painter and the Shepherd Boy, Book 2, Level 2, pp. 82–83) narrates the story of a painter and shepherd boy who lived during the Tang dynasty, with all the relevant characters dressed in Chinese-style costumes.[24] *Yultuz Sanaydighan Bala* (The Boy Who Counts Stars, Book 2, Level 2, pp. 110–111) tells the tale of Zhang Heng, a Chinese polymathic scientist and statesman, who lived during the Han dynasty and, again, the appearance of the characters in the picture corresponds with the historical context.[25] *Hekmätlik Hekayilär* (Wise Stories, Book 2, Level 3, pp. 28–31) is accompanied by an image of several ancient Chinese sages, including (apparently) Confucius. Under the theme of *Mehir-shäpqät* (Compassion, Book 2, Level 3, p. 52) we find the image of a mother and a daughter dressed in classical Chinese-style clothing. Finally, the texts borrowed from Chinese classical literature, such as *Yänzi'ning Chu Bägilikigä Älchilikkä Berishi* (Yanzi's Visit to Chu Kingdom, Book 2, Level 5, pp. 30–32), are all accompanied by corresponding figures and landscapes. We argue that these decisions around content are intended to bring about the visual and ideological displacement of the Uyghurs' own, alternative version of regional history and replace it with a state-sanctioned version of Chinese history, which implicitly assumes that Xinjiang – and the Uyghurs who have lived there since AD 845 – have been an integral part of the territory and polity of China 'since time immemorial' (or at least the Han dynasty).

Til Sän'iti (The Art of Language) in Book 2, Level 5, is accompanied by a photograph of individuals in Qing dynasty (Manchu) style clothing (p. 26) and appears to be a still taken from a feature film or TV drama series. We were a little surprised to see this since we had half expected that Qing/Manchu history and culture might – in this Han-majoritarian 'new era' – be totally expelled from the textbooks, being a non-Han, 'barbarian' dynasty. While the TV and film industries in the PRC once frequently featured Manchu dynastic settings, since Xi Jinping came to power, aggressive Han nationalism has resulted in an at least partial eclipse of such products. Certainly, the appearance of just one image depicting Manchu culture does suggest that Manchu-related content has been purposely reduced. On the other hand, its retention may also reflect the authorities' core strategy of familiarizing Uyghur children with the whole, broad sweep of Chinese history, so as to make them feel an integral part of that history (and not part of a separate history, as their Uyghur parents would earlier have taught them, prior to the current era of fear, surveillance, and internment).

On only one page of the six textbooks (Book 2, Level 6, p. 95) did we locate a picture of a group of young students wearing modern clothes and red pioneer ties *but showing typically Uyghur facial characteristics.* Moreover, the girl in the pink dress in this image has her hair dressed in multiple braids, a style unique to Uyghur culture (Figure 7.2).

We were fascinated to find that this picture is *almost* identical to the one which appears on the cover page of the book (Figure 7.3), but with some important differences: the version on the book's cover has been altered to replace the students' deep-set Caucasian eyes (represented with pencil shading in the eye sockets to introduce depth) with the shallow-set eyes typical of Han Chinese and other East Asian peoples. Most visibly, the girl in pink no longer has multiple braids but now sports two regular pigtails. Given the systematic 'invisibilization' of almost all aspects of Uyghur culture elsewhere in the textbooks, we can only speculate that the picture on page 95 has been left in by mistake.

Finding 3: All human characters in texts are Han Chinese, with typical Chinese personal names; Uyghur personal names are largely absent

In a step that goes even further than state ordinances of recent years that proscribe Uyghur names with Islamic roots (Dearden 2017), the human characters in the texts (with the exception of the above-mentioned

Corrective 're-education' as (cultural) genocide 199

Figure 7.2 Picture of a group of Uyghur students, featuring deep-set eyes and Uyghur braids

readings about foreign nationals) almost all have typical Han Chinese names. For example, in *Budruq Qollar* (Chubby Hands), the female protagonist's name is Lanlan (Book 2, Level 1, pp. 34–35).[26] In *Ayning Arzusi* (The Moon's Wish), we find a Chinese girl named Zhenzhen (Book 2, Level 1, pp. 40–41).[27] In *Aptapqa Selinghan Ayagh* (Shoes Placed in the Sunshine), the male character's name is Xiao Feng (Book 2, Level 1, pp. 43–44). Xiongri is the Chinese boy character who stars in *Quruq Tästäk Kötürgän Bala* (The Boy Carrying an Empty Pot) (Book 2, Level 1, pp. 104–105). The story *Obdan Bala* (Good Child) includes many characters, all of whom have Han Chinese names such as Jingjing, Xiaoling, and Xiaomei.[28] In *Yittirgän Närsiliringizni Eliweling* (Pick Up Your Lost Items) it is Mr Zhang and Teacher Tang who teach the children not to litter (Book 2, Level 1, pp. 121–122).[29] A Chinese girl named Xiao Lin tries to modify her raincoat in *Yamghurluq Chapangha Yäl Berish* (Blowing Air into a Raincoat) (Book 2, Level 2, pp. 50–52).[30] In *Äng Chong Kitab* (The Biggest Book), the name of

Figure 7.3 The same picture as that on p. 95 of *Til-Ädäbiyat* (see Figure 7.2, p. 199), but this time depicting a group of Han Chinese students with shallow-set eyes and regular pigtails/ponytails

the male protagonist is Chuanchuan (Book 2, Level 2, pp. 65–66).[31] A boy called Xiao Bing stars in *Oyunchuq Pokiyi Aldidiki Bala* (The Child in front of the Toy Shop Counter, Book 2, Level 2, pp. 88–90). Lingling is the main character in *Ling Ling'ning Räsimi* (Lingling's Drawing, Book 2, Level 2, pp. 94–95).[32] In *U Mening Dostum* (He Is My Friend, Book 2, Level 3, pp. 60–61), Ruanheng is the central character's name, even though a footnote tells us that the original story is not Chinese but rather authored by a foreign national, Cole John. The blind girl who catches a butterfly in *Baharni Tutup Beqish* (Touch of Spring, Book 2, Level 4, pp. 53–54) by Qu Yulou is named Anjing.[33] Finally, *Beshigha Chinä Qoyghan Bala* (The Boy Balancing Bowls on His Head) by Zhao Lihong is about a resilient acrobatic boy who lives in Shanghai (Book 2, Level 6, pp. 113–115).[34]

In none of the readings across the six textbooks we examined does a character with a typical Uyghur name appear, with one sole exception. In *Parasät Gülliri* (Wisdom Flowers, Book 2, Level 6, pp. 110–112) by Sun Yunxiao, a clever Grade 5 female pupil named Märyäm draws on her knowledge to save the lives of five schoolmates from an electric shock, while risking her own safety. In the same story, a Han pupil from the same school called Jiang Xue protects the consumer rights of her schoolmates by contacting the authorities when she suspects that a street vendor is selling contaminated ice creams. The two 'Wisdom Flowers' in this text seem to serve two distinct purposes. First, their actions highlight and promote the spirit of ethnic unity (*minzu tuanjie*) between the Han and Uyghur ethnic groups. Secondly, the tale emphasizes the wisdom and courage of women; this could perhaps be read as a critique of the prevailing patriarchal societies not only in the Muslim world but also in Han China.

In the same way, the ethnonym 'Uyghur' is largely avoided in the textbooks, apart from some rare occasions when the region's name 'Shinjang Uyghur Aptonom Rayoni' (Xinjiang Uyghur Autonomous Region) is used in full (see e.g. Book 2, Level 4, p. 12). On page 21 of Book 2, Level 4, the phrase 'Aptonom Rayonimizda' (in our autonomous region) is used without 'Shinjang Uyghur'. However, most of the time, the shortened name 'Shinjang' is used alone (see Book 2, Level 3, p. 11; Book 2, Level 4, p. 2; and Book 2, Level 5, p. 2). Again, we would suggest the possibility that the region's full name including the ethnonym 'Uyghur' was left in on this one occasion by accident. In general, the pattern of disappearance of the ethnonym 'Uyghur' from the region's name reflects an earlier evolution visible since around 2000 whereby Han state and popular discourses increasingly refer to the region simply as the 'Xinjiang Autonomous Region', erasing 'Uyghur'.

On the other hand, some Uyghur personal names can be found in the practice drill sections. One might ask why these appear here and not in the main readings. We would suggest that whereas many of the readings are evidently borrowed and adapted from the original Chinese-medium textbooks, the drill sections may not be easily transferred from the Chinese-medium to the Uyghur-medium textbooks in the same way. Here, we expect that the Uyghur compilers demonstrated (an albeit limited) agency and purposely included some cautiously selected Uyghur personal names.[35] Some of these drills may have appeared in the earlier

2015 edition of the Uyghur-medium textbook series, while others may have been created anew. Either way, it is noticeable that Han Chinese names do not appear in these drills. One might also ask why the Chinese authorities with oversight over the textbooks' compilation allowed this to happen. One explanation may be that Uyghur personal names are allowed to appear in the practice drills in order to better engage the Uyghur pupils and make them receptive to ideological messaging. That a Uyghur-medium version of the textbooks is still available at all underlines an important practical circumstance: young Uyghur children are currently in linguistic transition between the previous policy era of 'bilingual education' and the new-era policy of 'national language education'. As such, they still require a certain amount of content to be delivered in their mother tongue, at least at the kindergarten and primary school stages. Uyghur children will be unlikely to engage fully with – and absorb – material that seems totally unconnected to them. Thus, if the CCP's ideological goal is to indoctrinate young Uyghur children with the notion that they are an integral part of the Chinese nation and persuade them that no alternative identity is available, then it still needs to use the Uyghur-language channel to do so – at least for now. In order to inculcate Uyghur children with overwhelmingly Han representations of the region's history and culture, they need first to catch the pupils' attention.

Although Uyghur personal names do appear in the practice drills, it is evident that these have been chosen with great caution. Most are common Uyghur names that *lack rich Arab or Islamic roots*. Although some of the names can be traced to Arab roots, for example, Patigül (adapted from Fatima), Aminä, or Alim, these do not have rich religious undertones. Some examples include Adil (Book 2, Level 2, p. 41); Mättursun (Book 2, Level 3, p. 37); Dilnur, Turghun (Book 2, Level 4, pp. 11 and 26; Book 2, Level 5, pp. 25 and 52–53; Book 2, Level 6, pp. 22–23 and 41–42); Güli, Mahmut, Mihray (Book 2, Level 4, p. 71); Gheni (Book 2, Level 5, p. 34); Murat, Dilshat, Örkäsh (Book 2, Level 5, pp. 103–104); Aminä, Ghäyrät, Alim, Zilalä, Polat (Book 2, Level 6, p. 11); Patigül, Almas, Dilyar, Aygül (Book 2, Level 6, p. 12); Äli, Gülnar, Aynur, Alimjan, Qasim, and Ayshäm (Book 2, Level 6, pp. 90–91). The most frequently used names are Dilnur and Turghun, which completely lack Islamic elements and are therefore considered safest for inclusion.

Corrective 're-education' as (cultural) genocide 203

Significantly, those common Uyghur names that have strong Arab or Islamic origins, such as Muhämmäd, Aishä (the name of the Prophet Muhammad's wife), Shähidä, Abdurehim, Abdurahman, or Abdullah, are nowhere to be found. Mahmut (Mahmud or Mahmood in the original Arabic), a common Uyghur name sharing the same root with Muhämmäd, occurs only once (Book 2, Level 4, p. 71).[36] And although Ayshäm, the Uyghurized form of Aishä, is far less politically sensitive in its revised form and one of the most popular female names among the Uyghurs, this too appears only once. Mämät, the Uyghurized form of Muhämmäd, does not appear at all.

The above findings reveal, we argue, a projection of the CCP's preferred national future: one in which all 'good' and loyal Uyghur citizens (and indeed all ethnic minority citizens) speak and write Chinese, familiarize themselves with Han cultural norms, and eventually transition to typical Han Chinese names, as the Hui and Manchu ethnic groups did previously. In highlighting Han Chinese names and proscribing and erasing names with Islamic roots, Chinese authorities seek the coercive secularization of Uyghur children within the framework of the new-era Han-majoritarian assimilationist state. During this transition stage, we find the current textbook compilers operating along a spectrum of personal names, ranging from those considered mainstream, harmless, and religion-free to those that have been outlawed as potentially linked to 'extremist' religious ideologies. Like others in the Uyghur community, they are exercising clear practices of self-censorship in order to protect themselves within an environment of state intimidation and terror.

Finding 4: Texts about animals and nature largely depict elements of inner and coastal Chinese physical geography and ecology; those native to the Xinjiang region are largely absent

As is by now clear, the textbooks under examination make heavy use of translated, adapted versions of original Chinese-medium texts aimed at Han Chinese pupils. Practically no attempt is made to include elements specific to Uyghur cultural experience, and in some cases Uyghur cultural elements that appeared in the original Chinese-medium versions of the textbooks are erased in the Uyghur-medium counterparts.

Whether this happened as a response to a coercive directive from Chinese authorities or was an act of fearful self-censorship on behalf of the Uyghur compilers (and it was likely both), it reflects an intentional 'invisibilization' of the regionally distinct population, culture, and physical geography of the Xinjiang region, and may be construed as an attempt to forcibly integrate borderland Uyghurs with inner China. It is a process previewed in the *Xinjiangban* (Xinjiang Class) programme, which brings Uyghur students to inner China to study under secular conditions in a Chinese-speaking environment, in the hope of fostering their political loyalty and 'inseparability' from Han China (Grose 2019). It is reflected too in the state's recent practice of transferring Uyghurs out of re-education camps in Xinjiang (following 'graduation'), or out of rural villages defined as needing 'poverty alleviation', and into forced labour in factories in inner China (Xu et al. 2020; Zenz 2021b). These redistributions of population are intended both to dilute Uyghur demographic density in Xinjiang (while replacing Uyghurs and other Turkic inhabitants with Han settlers)[37] and to erase their distinct cultural identity, forcibly integrating them into the Chinese polity. In this section, we describe how readings about the natural world focus largely on inner and coastal Chinese landscapes, climates, and ecologies such as lakes, rainy days, fish, monkeys, and Chinese vegetables (pak choi) and fruits (kiwi, flowering quince), while those indigenous to the Xinjiang region such as oases, deserts, snow, and fruits like sweet melon, grapes, walnuts, or pomegranates are largely ignored.

Our first example is found under the theme *Yurtini Sizish* (Drawing Hometowns, Book 2, Level 1, pp. 86–88), where the reading discusses pictures drawn by different children living in different regions of China. While the PRC has fifty-six officially recognized ethnic groups, the children who appear in this text all have Han Chinese names, and none draws a picture depicting the typical natural environment of Xinjiang. Although one child is riding a horse and wearing traditional Mongolian dress, she too has a Chinese name, Qingqing (Book 2, Level 1, p. 88)[38] (see our above point on CCP aspirations towards a nation of standardized Han Chinese names). Later, Book 2, Level 3, begins with the theme *Jälpkar Täbi'ät* (Beautiful Nature), illustrated by a background image of a Daoist painting of mountains and clouds (note that Daoism is a religion indigenous to Han China). This section includes readings focused on typical inner and coastal Chinese natural features, such as *Nelupär* (Lotus Flower, Book 2, Level 3, pp. 7–8)[39] and *Dengiz Astidiki Dunya* (The Undersea World, Book 2, Level 3, pp. 9–10) (note that Xinjiang is completely landlocked). Next, a text titled *Muhit Asrash* (Protecting the Environment) is accompanied by an image of a typical Chinese architectural structure situated on a lake (Book 2, Level 3, p. 15). It is likely that this lake is also situated in inner China, although Han settlers have in recent decades sought to place pagodas and similar structures in places of scenic beauty in Xinjiang, to place the Han Chinese cultural mark on the region's geography. A few chapters later, *Dengizgha Berish* (Going to the Seaside) narrates a story about children playing on a beach (Book 2, Level 3, pp. 46–47). Then, in *Köktarghaq* (Kingfisher, Book 2, Level 3, pp. 107–108), we are introduced to a bird that is not native to the Xinjiang region.[40] On pages 65–67 of Book 2, Level 4, a reading titled *Yeziliqlar* (Country-Dwellers) depicts – and shows a picture of – bamboo groves that are typical of southern Chinese rural regions, but absent in the Uyghur homeland.[41]

As well as the generic scenes of inner and coastal China described above, the textbooks also contain readings focused on specific, named landmarks and scenic spots, all but one of which are located outside of Xinjiang. These include *Qush Arili* (Bird Island), situated on the west side of Qinghai lake (Book 2, Level 2, pp. 38–39); *Yueliangwan*, a story about a village of that name, situated in Guangdong province (Book 2, Level 2, p. 40); and, within a themed section titled *Wätinimining Güzäl Tagh-däryaliri* (Beautiful Mountains and Rivers of Our Motherland, Book 2, Level 4), several readings including Xinjiang's *Tänghritagh* (Heavenly Mountains, Book 2, Level 4, pp. 1–2) by Bi Ye, *Guilin'ning Tagh-däryaliri* (Mountains and Rivers of Guilin, Book 2, Level 4, pp. 5–6) by Chen Miao,[42] and *Alishän Teghidiki Bulutlar* (The Clouds of Alishan Mountain, Book 2, Level 4, p. 7) by Hua Xia. An especially interesting case is *Wätinimiz Näqädär Güzäl* (How Beautiful Our Motherland Is, Book 2, Level 2, pp. 31–33), which depicts the Riyuetan lake in Taiwan.[43] While Taiwan can hardly be described as part of the Chinese motherland (where this is understood to refer to mainland China) and constitutes a contested borderland that has been de facto independent for more than seventy years, the inclusion of this piece seems to embody a subliminal political message – or even warning – to both Han and Uyghur pupils that Taiwan, like Xinjiang, is an 'inalienable part of the territory of the PRC'. It is significant that such strident political messaging is being targeted at children from a very young age, almost like a form of subliminal advertising.

Geographic elements specific to Xinjiang are almost never found in the readings and are only occasionally found in the drill sections. Only from Level 4 do some pieces appear that narrate the geography of Xinjiang, and these are openly politicized in most cases. To return to the above-mentioned text on the *Tängritagh* (Heavenly Mountains), which opens Book 2, Level 4: this is the sole occasion on which an introduction to Xinjiang's natural environment is offered together with a corresponding picture. It is noticeable, however, that the reading is short, and authored not by a Uyghur writer but by a Han writer. Transposed from the original Chinese-medium version, where it appeared under the slightly different title 七月的天山 (*Qiyue de Tianshan*, Heavenly Mountains in July), this reading was probably originally intended to highlight to Han Chinese pupils the vast expanse of the great Chinese nation and engender national pride. In any case, it does not appear to have been purposely included as a familiar geographical feature to encourage regional cultural identification among Uyghur pupils. Rather, authorship by a Han Chinese conveys the message that the Han majority enjoys full authority over these mountains.

Two other readings that relate to contemporary Xinjiang focus on the history of the Silk Road and the *Ghärbiy Yurt* (Western Regions, 西域 *Xiyu*). Book 2, Level 5, begins by briefly introducing Xinjiang's geography, then making a clear connection between the ancient Silk Road and the current Belt and Road Initiative (BRI). Connecting these two serves the apparent purpose of suggesting or 'proving' that Xinjiang has been a part of the Chinese polity 'since ancient times'. This is followed by the reading *Yipäk Yoli* (Silk Road, Book 2, Level 5, pp. 2–5), which tells the story of Zhang Qian, who travelled from China and arrived in the Persian Arsak Kingdom of the Parthian/Arsacid Empire (known to the Chinese as 安息 Anxi) in 115 BC.[44] He is warmly welcomed by the kingdom and the two sides exchange gifts. This event is highlighted as the beginnings of cultural exchange between China and the Western Regions. We would suggest that while such narratives have long appeared in school textbooks in Xinjiang, its inclusion in the present series serves the new, additional purpose of promoting and justifying China's BRI ambitions. The second reading in this section – *Künäs Yayliqidiki Yilqilar* (The Horses of the Künäs Grasslands, Book 2, Level 5, pp. 7–8) – is about Künäs county in Xinjiang's Ili Kazakh Autonomous Prefecture.[45] This piece depicts the magnificent sight of horses running in a thunderstorm, but is authored by a Han writer (Zhou Tao) rather than a Kazakh or Uyghur writer. Like the Tianshan mountains piece analysed above, it showcases the greatness of the Chinese nation, while emphasizing Han Chinese authority over this remote land.

While Xinjiang regional content is scarce, the textbooks do include some introductions to the geography and ecology of foreign countries, in line with the emerging pattern. For example, in the section *Dunyagha Sayahät* (Journey to the World, Book 2, Level 5), there appear several readings about foreign nations. These include *Bashqilarning Huzurlinishi üchün Gül Beqish* (Cultivating Flowers for Others to Enjoy, Book 2, Level 5, pp. 108–110), which teaches pupils about the German people's love of flowers;[46] *Wenitsiyädiki Qeyiqlar* (Boats in Venice, Book 2, Level 5, pp. 111–112);[47] *Pillar bilän Usul Oynash* (Dancing with Elephants, Book 2, Level 5, pp. 115–117), a text about domesticated, trained elephants in Thailand;[48] and *Gollandiyä Täsiratliri* (Memories of the Netherlands, Book 2, Level 5, pp. 118–119). Earlier in the series, *Charwichiliq Döliti* (Nation of Animal Husbandry, Book 2, Level 4, pp. 68–70) similarly introduces the geography of the Netherlands, accompanied by an image depicting typical scenery from the northern European countryside.[49] The emphasis on domestic (inner and coastal) Chinese and international geographies (of politically harmless countries) creates an almost seamless continuum between China and the world, which hopes to underline China's accession onto the world stage and success in – finally – achieving high status in the international community.[50] To access this springboard to the world, pupils learn that they must be loyal and proud citizens of the Chinese nation. In the late 1990s and 2000s, Uyghurs had increasingly tried to fashion their own independent connections with sympathetic cultures of the outside world – especially Turkey, Central Asia, the Middle East, and Moorish Spain – while bypassing Han China (Smith Finley 2013).[51] It is no coincidence, we argue, that these parts of the world, perceived as 'backwards', inferior, and potentially dangerous by the Chinese state, are wholly absent among the readings in this textbook series. Like the Uyghur homeland itself, they are invisibilized, 'disappeared'. The dual message to Uyghur pupils is that the only possible way for them to interact with the outside world is *as a loyal, assimilated member of the decidedly Han-majoritarian Chinese state*, and that the only acceptable cross-border interactions are those with non-threatening, developed, secular nations that do not appear on the list of twenty-six 'sensitive' Muslim-majority countries published by Chinese authorities as part of their ongoing campaign of religious 'de-extremification'.[52]

Finding 5: Han Chinese and foreign/Western literatures highlighted; Uyghur literature and folklore largely absent

From Book 2, Level 5, complex Han Chinese classical literatures start to be introduced. For example, under the theme of *Kilassik Äsärlär* (Classical Pieces) we find *Yänzining Chu Bäglikigä Älchilikkä Berishi* (Yanzi's Visit to the Chu Kingdom, Book 2, Level 5, pp. 30–32);[53] *Pakhalliq Kemide Ya Oqi Yighish* (Collecting Arrows on a Straw Boat, Book 2, Level 5, pp. 55–58), which focuses on the famous Chinese historical figure Zhuge Liang, who lived during the Three Kingdom period;[54] *Bao Gong'ning Eshäkni Sotlishi* (Bao Gong Judging a Donkey, Book 2, Level 5, pp. 60–61), a story about a politician who lived during the Northern Song dynasty; a weighty text (more than five pages long) taken from the famous *Water Margin* about Wu Song, a legendary character in Chinese classical literature who kills a man-eating tiger (Book 2, Level 5, pp. 62–67);[55] and *Ölüm Aldidiki Yan Jiansheng* (Yan Jiansheng on His Deathbed), a classical Chinese literary tale about a wealthy but stingy landlord who can pass away peacefully only after someone has understood his worries about the two wicks in the oil lamp and taken one out (Book 2, Level 5, pp. 91–92).

Investigative journalists have similarly uncovered the teaching of classical Chinese poetry to 'kindness students' in Xinjiang's hastily opened new boarding schools; these are children of doubly detained parents, so-called by Chinese officials to emphasize the party's generosity in making special arrangements for their education. One Han Chinese language teacher at a full-time elementary boarding school in Khotän described the experience of teaching such pupils, who are provided with textbooks, clothes, and a red Young Pioneer scarf, as an opportunity to 'water the flowers of the motherland' (Qin 2019). The imposition on a young and not-yet-literate Uyghur readership of complex classical material that is deeply steeped in a Han Chinese understanding of history reflects disturbing practices that have been documented among

Corrective 're-education' as (cultural) genocide

adults in the re-education camps. There, elderly illiterate Uyghur farmers have been expected to learn classical Chinese pieces such as the Three Character Classic (*Sanzi jing*, a Song dynasty text used to teach children Confucian values) before they can 'graduate' – for most, an almost impossible task (Shih 2018).

From Book 2, Level 6, literary pieces by modern and contemporary Han writers and poets are introduced. Under the theme of *Turmush Ilhamliri* (Life Inspirations), four readings appear: the most interesting of these selections is the first, *Aldirashchiliq* (In Haste, Book 2, Level 6, pp. 2–3) by Zhu Ziqing.[56] The story tells of how swiftly time passes, imparting a didactic message that we must do as much as possible in the time we have. We would suggest that this theme was deliberately chosen to reflect current PRC state discourses that emphasize the need for Xinjiang citizens to embrace secular, economically productive lives: see, for example, the call in a 2018 article posted on regional news website Tianshan Net for pious Uyghurs to cease wasting their days praying and instead work hard to build the socialist economy (Smith Finley 2019c).[57] Indeed, Chinese authorities are now actively fashioning 'generations of docile laborers' by redeploying Uyghurs currently or formerly detained in Xinjiang's internment camps into coerced labour in factories in China's industrial complex (Yi Xiaocuo 2019).

In contrast to the strong emphasis on classical, modern, and contemporary Chinese literature outlined above, not one single reading from Uyghur classical, folk, modern, or contemporary literature may be found in any of the six textbooks, not even a short parable. We would argue that this evidences a deliberate erasure of Uyghur cultural heritage and intention to cut Uyghurs off from their linguistic and cultural roots, thereby disrupting inter-generational identity transmission. While heavily adopting texts from Chinese-medium sources, Uyghur literature sources have apparently not been considered at all. This stands in stark contrast with the content of Uyghur-medium textbooks currently in circulation within the Uyghur diaspora in Turkey. As an example, *Ädäbiyat* (Literature) published by Täklimakan Uyghur Näshriyati (Täklimakan Uyghur Press) gives exclusive attention to Uyghur culture and history. For instance, the reading titled *Güzäl Shärqiy Türkistan* (Beautiful East Turkistan) offers a brief introduction of East Turkistan as the motherland of the Uyghurs, without mentioning

China or Xinjiang, and declares that the Uyghurs are the owners of this land, and have been living there since ancient times (Level 1, pp. 32–33).[58] This openly challenges the Han state's narrative about the territory of Xinjiang.

While Uyghur sources are entirely absent in the revised edition textbooks published by Xinjiang Education Press in 2018, readings about other ethnic minorities originally present in the Chinese-medium version also appear to have been largely excluded. For example, in Book 2, Level 6 (Chinese-language edition, People's Education Press, pp. 30–32), there is a text about Tibetan drama (藏戏 *Zangxi*), accompanied by relevant pictures,[59] but this has (been) disappeared in the Uyghur-medium version.

Instead, a substantial section (thirty-two pages) in Book 2, Level 6, is dedicated to foreign literatures (*Chät'äl Ädäbiyatidin Huzurlinish*, Appreciating Foreign Literature, pp. 44–76), mentioning writers and poets hailing from Western nations including Denmark, Russia, England, the US, and France.[60] The pieces include such famous stories as *Säränggä Satquchi Qizchaq* (The Little Match Girl, pp. 44–49) by Danish author Hans Christian Andersen; *Beliqchi Boway bilän Altun Beliq Häqqidä Chöchäk* (The Tale of the Fisherman and the Fish, pp. 50–57) by Alexander Pushkin, a Russian poet and novelist known for his support of the peasantry and opposition to Tsarist inequalities; *Dengiz Särgärdani Robinzon Kruzo* (Sea Adventurer Robinson Crusoe, pp. 58–65) by English author Daniel Defoe; and *Helen Keller'ning Tärjimihali* (The Biography of Helen Keller, pp. 66–70). This latter piece focuses on Helen Adams Keller – the American author, political activist, and lecturer who was the first deaf-blind person to earn a Bachelor of Arts degree. Keller is famous in China owing to popular perceptions of her resilience and triumph over adversity. Again, we would suggest that this text was chosen because of its underlying message: in line with the CCP's ideological agenda, people (both Han and Uyghur) are urged to work hard and not complain. Finally, some short anecdotes appear in the *Äsläsh wä Kengäytish* (Review and Extension) section about French writer Victor Hugo, English poet Ward (who we surmise to be author and journalist Thomas Humphry Ward, 1845–1926), and American writer Mark Twain. The inclusion of Hugo is noteworthy, given his left-wing socialist credentials and criticism of inequalities in pre-revolution France.

Finding 6: Folk stories are largely selected from Han Chinese sources; Uyghur folk stories are absent

Folk stories that are reproduced in the textbooks are mostly selected from Han Chinese cultural sources. For example, under the theme *Hikmätlik Hekayilär* (Wise Stories) appear two short parables from ancient Chinese folklore: *Qoy Yitkändin keyin Qotanni Ongshash* (Mending the Sheepfold after Losing the Sheep) and *Yol Bashqa, Mänzil Bashqa* (Road and Destination Are Different) (Book 2, Level 3, pp. 28–31). Other typical examples include *Tian Ji'ning Etini Bäygigä Selishi* (Tian Ji Races His Horse, Book 2, Level 3, pp. 34–35), *Kuafu'ning Quyashni Qoghlishi* (Kuafu Chases the Sun), and *Büyük Yü'ning Kälkünni Tizginlishi* (Big Yu Tames the Flood), the latter two appearing in the section *Äpsanä-riwayätlär* (Myths and Legends, Book 2, Level 3, pp. 101–104).

In the case of some folk stories, the reference to the original source or author is withheld. One example is *Bashqilar Oylimighanni Oylang* (Think of What Others Did Not, Book 2, Level 3, pp. 32–33), which tells the tale of three disciples who compete against one another to draw as many camels as possible on a piece of paper. Although the camel is obviously an animal native to the Xinjiang region, this story does not exist in Uyghur folklore (while many other folk stories that do exist in Uyghur folklore are not drawn upon). A second example is *Beliqchining Hekayisi* (Tale of a Fisherman, Book 2, Level 4, pp. 91–93).[61] It is significant that, in the original Chinese-medium version of the textbook, this reading is presented as part of the famous classical Arabian work *A Thousand and One Nights*. In this Uyghur-medium version, however, the Arabian origin of the tale is deliberately omitted, as is the related image. This evidently reflects the authorities' fear of 'Arabization' and their desire to eliminate all Arab cultural elements from the textbooks. Immediately following, a story titled *Mälikä Wenqing'ning Shizang'gha Berishi* (Princess Wencheng's Visit to Tibet, Book 2, Level 4, pp. 94–96) presents a colourful depiction of a Chinese princess sitting in a classic Chinese horse-drawn carriage. The story ends with the ideological message that through this interaction with China, local Tibetans were able to learn farming and other useful techniques.[62] In this way, it seems intended to emphasize both an historical tributary arrangement (Tibetan submission/loyalty to the

Chinese kingdom 'since ancient times') and the inherent subaltern quality of the Tibetan people in comparison with their more advanced and civilized Chinese neighbours.

While the textbook compilers have apparently been instructed to avoid – or have in an act of self-censorship chosen not to include – any traditional Uyghur folk tales, in the Exercises section of Book 4, Level 2 (p. 97), directly after the Tibet story, we find a very brief mention of a published collection of Uyghur folk tales titled *Uyghur Khälq Chöchekliri*, which is recommended as further reading for the students. *A Thousand and One Nights* is also recommended here, but its Arabian origin is again not mentioned.

Finding 7: All selected poems are by Han Chinese authors and translated into Uyghur; works by Uyghur poets are absent

The poems used in the readings are either authored by Han Chinese poets and translated into Uyghur, or else presented as authorless. Texts by Han poets include *Tallar Oyghandi* (The Willow Trees Have Woken, Book 2, Level 1, pp. 27–28) by Xue Ning; *Bahar Käldi* (Spring Has Come, Book 2, Level 2, pp. 122–123) by Jin Bo;[63] *Tuman Basqan Taghliq Shähär* (Foggy Mountain Town, Book 2, Level 3, p. 106) by Pu Huaqing; and *Arzuyum* (My Hope, Book 2, Level 5, pp. 126–127) and *Ularmu Baharning Päyzini Sürsun* (Let Them Enjoy the Spring Too, Book 2, Level 4, pp. 43–44), both by Gao Hongbo.[64] Several of these Han Chinese poems do not even appear in the Chinese-medium version of the textbook, meaning that they have been deliberately chosen for consumption by Uyghur pupils (not just transposed). At the same time, while there exists a vast array of 'safe', apolitical children's poems published by Uyghur poets upon which to draw, not a single piece is present: this only underlines the Chinese authorities' intention to break young Uyghurs from their cultural roots.

Finding 8: Heavy emphasis on political/ideological stories focused on Chinese Communist Party (CCP) moral leadership; Uyghur political history absent

Stories about CCP leaders containing ideological messages – showcasing good, benevolent CCP leadership, or emphasizing the CCP spirit of

Corrective 're-education' as (cultural) genocide

self-sacrifice and selflessness at both national and global levels – are present across the textbook series. Owing to space constraints, we do not analyse individual texts here, but instead highlight one important finding. Throughout these political texts, not a single Uyghur political figure is introduced. This is perhaps not surprising, given the state's evident aim to erase knowledge and memory of alternative Uyghur political histories as well as the distinct Uyghur cultural identity. Yet although the Chinese authorities have long avoided reference to the independent East Turkestan Republic (ETR, 1944–49),[65] the *Üch Wilayät Inqilawi* (Three Districts Rebellion or 三区革命 *Sanqu geming*) that preceded it had in earlier times *been mentioned openly in CCP discourses*. Then, it was officially recognized and hailed as an important part of the CCP's fight against Guomindang forces prior to liberation in 1949. That mention of even this slice of history has gradually become anathema during the period since the 2009 Ürümchi protest-turned-riot signals a distinct change in CCP attitudes to the region's place in PRC national history.

Finding 9: Some Uyghur idioms and proverbs are introduced, but only in the practice drill sections

Owing to the linguistic differences between the Chinese and Uyghur languages, full translation from the original Chinese-medium version of the textbooks has clearly not been possible when creating the practice drill sections. Here, lexical and grammatical rules governing the Uyghur language are introduced along with examples. Those examples include some local place names and Uyghur personal names (as mentioned above) and occasional mention of plants and animals that are native to Xinjiang; see, for example, *qariyaghach* (elm tree); *qarläyilisi* (snow lotus); and *ashköki* (coriander), all found in Book 2, Level 3 (pp. 36–37).

In addition, there are sections that teach the Uyghur language through idioms and proverbs. These linguistic features tend to be specific to individual languages and cultures, thus often cannot be directly translated from the Chinese. There is in general an inextricable connection between language and culture, and nowhere is this more evident than in manifestations of conventionalized language. Idiomatic expressions are 'one of the important and pervasive language uses reflecting culture in real life. Like other types of figurative language, idioms appear to be the natural decoders of customs, cultural beliefs, social conventions, and norms' (Yağiz and Izadpanah 2013). When it comes to language teaching, idioms enable a language learner to understand the thoughts, emotions, and views of the speakers of the target language and to understand the underlying parameters of the language. An awareness of figurative language, particularly idioms, will improve teaching and assist learners to have better communication strategies (Yağiz and Izadpanah 2013). Since the practice drills are crucial for eliciting communication among pupils, the compilers introduce some Uyghur idioms within these sections; as a result, they contain perhaps the most genuinely rich Uyghur cultural elements in the textbooks examined. Featured Uyghur-language idioms include (Book 2, Level 3, pp. 62–63):

- *achköz* (literally, 'hungry eyes' – greedy)
- *aghzi quliqigha yätmäk* (literally, 'mouth reaches ears' – extremely happy, ecstatic)
- *täkhsä kötürmäk* (literally, 'carry a plate' – to be a toady/sycophant)
- *közni yumup achqucha* (in the blink of an eye; in a split second)
- *közigä qarimaq* (literally, 'looking at another's eyes' – to be subordinate to someone)
- *khoriki ösüp qalmaq* (literally, 'to raise the volume of one's snore' – to become arrogant)
- *meghizini chaqmaq* (literally, 'to crack open the kernel' – to enjoy success)
- *qoli ägri* (literally, 'bent arms' – a pilferer)
- *qoli gül* (literally, 'hands are flowers' – dexterous, having skillful hands)
- *purchiqi pishmasliq* (literally, 'one's beans do not cook' – to not see eye to eye with someone)
- *chishini chishlimäk* (literally, 'bite one's teeth' – persevere, be patient)
- *bash kötürmäk* (literally, 'to raise one's head' – to rise up in the world, become famous/powerful)

In the same way, a wealth of published work on proverbs worldwide indicates their function as important cultural repositories for our understanding of past and present; as sanctioning aspects of culture such as religious, economic, social, and political institutions; as reflecting the philosophy, wisdom, and humour of a people; as tools to mould the characters of growing children; and as the embodiment of a culture

Corrective 're-education' as (cultural) genocide

and civilization.[66] As is the case with idioms, foreign language teachers routinely employ proverbs as a means to impart cultural awareness to their students and promote their communicative competence (Richmond 1987). It is presumably for this reason that the compilers introduce some Uyghur proverbs in the drill sections of the six textbooks. Featured proverbs include the following:

From Book 2, Level 2 (p. 26):

- *Dost yighlitip eytar, düshmän küldürüp eytar* (A friend's words will make you cry, an enemy's will make you laugh)
- *Yakhshi söz tashni yarar, yaman söz bashni (yarar)* (A good word can split a rock, a bad word a head)

From Book 2, Level 2 (pp. 79–80):

- *Waqit atqan oq* (literally, 'Time is like a fired bullet' – time flies)
- *Äqil yashta ämäs bashta* (literally, 'Intelligence is not related to age, but to the head' – intelligence depends on one's brain, not age/experience)
- *Oynap sözlisängmu, oylap sözlä* (literally, 'Even if you say it as a joke, think before you speak' – always choose your words carefully)

From Book 2, Level 3 (p. 25):

- *Bilimsizlik namratliqtin yaman* (Lack of knowledge is worse than poverty)
- *Chüshlük ömrüng bolsa, kächlik ozuq tap* (If you can live till noon, you should find food that will last until the evening – i.e. you can never work too hard to prepare for the future)
- *Rastliq – häqliq* (Truthfulness is righteousness)

On pages 79–80 of Book 2, Level 2, a definition of proverb is given, following which dozens of Uyghur proverbs are introduced. This use of proverbs in communicative language teaching undoubtedly showcases Uyghur culture to some extent, and the proverbs are certainly typical, popular, and widely used among the Uyghurs. Yet we would note that roughly half are 'safe' examples that do not embody any Uyghur cultural or Islamic elements. Meanwhile, the other half seem to have been chosen by the compilers – consciously (as a tool of political self-censorship) or unconsciously – for the way in which they can be made to reflect current Chinese government rhetoric and the party's ideological line.[67] Among the plethora of available Uyghur proverbs from which to choose, it is those that can convey the correct ideological message that make up a full half. As the only Uyghur-specific cultural elements in the series, they will have been closely scrutinized by the relevant authorities prior to publication. Key examples include:

- *Üjmä pish, aghzimgha chüsh* (literally, 'Mulberries ripen and drop straight into my mouth' – a sarcastic comment denoting someone who wants to reap benefits without exerting effort; a parasite)
- *Tama-tama köl bolar* (literally, 'Multiple drops make a lake' – patient and sustained hard work leads to success)

Similar examples have been included in Uyghur textbooks since at least the early 1980s. At the current time, their inclusion reflects state discourses aired on regional news websites, in which 'rogue' religious clerics and their pious followers are routinely characterized as parasites, because they spend too much time praying and not enough time being economically productive (Smith Finley 2019c). They also recall comments by Smith Finley's interviewees in 2018 on how Uyghurs are being directed only to work hard now (see note 55).

- *Yalghuz däräkh orman bolmas* (literally, 'A single tree cannot be a forest' – this emphasizes the importance of collective effort; an individual cannot fulfil huge tasks by him/herself)

This example suggests the importance of both ethnic and national unity, the notion that social stability is imperative for China to sustain economic growth and prosperity for all.

The gap-fill exercises that follow the list of proverbs in Book 2, Level 2 (pp. 79–80) also use proverb structures and seem similarly selected to reflect core state ideological imperatives. For instance:

- *Ish ömlüktä, _____.*

Here, the gap should be filled with *küch birliktä* to render the complete proverb 'Success in harmony, strength in unity'.

- *Inaq bolsa äl, _____.*

In the second example, the gap should be filled with *hämmä bolar täl* to produce the completed proverb 'If a nation is in harmony, everything can be obtained'.

- *Qol qolni yusa, _____.*

And, in the final example, the gap should be filled with *qol kelip yüzni yuyar* to render the proverb 'While two hands wash each other, they then wash the face together',[68] which emphasizes the importance of teamwork, unity, and collaboration. In this way, all three examples may be seen to reinforce state discourses promoting ethnic harmony (*minzu hexie*) and ethnic unity (*minzu tuanjie*) and proscribing ethnic splittism (*minzu fenlie*).

Conclusion

The findings suggest that these textbooks were produced in revised form in order to rapidly assimilate Uyghur children into the Han Chinese culture and national polity, which in the 'new era' of Han-majoritarian assimilationism are intertwined. The content of these books is largely transposed and adapted from the corresponding set of Chinese-medium textbooks, which are highly Han-centric. As such, these new Uyghur textbooks largely feature Han Chinese culture, history, natural and geographical features, and touristic attractions specific to Han-dominated inner China, rather than elements related to Xinjiang and Uyghurs. Generally speaking, content about ethnic minorities, not only Uyghurs, is minimized in the Chinese-medium edition, and the Uyghur-medium edition seems to have further erased such content. More specifically, the few Uyghur-related readings that exist in the original Chinese-medium textbooks have been either omitted or heavily modified in the Uyghur-medium textbooks, in order to further 'invisibilize' the Uyghurs within Xinjiang's regional education system. Although certain Uyghur-specific elements can be found in practice drills, such as Uyghur personal names, place names, idioms, and proverbs, these lack Islamic associations and are insufficient for Uyghur pupils to build a positive and strong self-conception about their distinct culture and ethnic group.

The form of 'corrective re-education' we outline in this chapter is very similar to practices that have been taking place in the more than a thousand infamous re-education camps for adults (Zenz 2019a). The only difference is that Uyghur pupils are – so far as we know – spared from physical abuse or torture. However, owing to their very young age, such genocidal practices may affect them much more deeply than their adult counterparts. That Uyghur-medium textbooks are being used in primary school education for Uyghur pupils at all during this coercive assimilationist phase is surprising, and may imply a determinedly pragmatic goal of linguistic transition. Overall, it is very likely that the negative cultural effects of the Uyghur edition textbooks on Uyghur pupils may greatly outweigh their linguistic benefits.

This study further proves that Xi's Han-majoritarian assimilationist state has been intensifying its coercive policies towards the Uyghurs. These revised textbooks expose the ultimate or 'upgraded' aim of the government's two-decade-old 'War on Terror' rhetoric, newly characterized since 2014 as the 'People's War on Terror', which is now to fully erase Uyghur religious and cultural identity. Looking through Lemkin's ([1944] 2005) lens, this is no less than genocide, because destroying the 'essential foundations of the life' of Uyghurs will ultimately end the existence of Uyghurs as a nation. The most recent reports about forced mass sterilizations and abortions among Uyghur women only confirm that the Han-majoritarian state has determined to speed up the earlier process of 'cultural genocide', which it may have deemed too slow.

Notes

1 That Uyghur is currently taught for only three hours per week, i.e. now enjoys the status of a second language, was relayed to Smith Finley in interviews in July 2018 by two primary school teachers in Ürümchi and Kashgar, respectively, and by children aged six to eight years in each location. The three-hour-per-week system is also mentioned in a *China Daily* tweet posted on 2 May 2020, which launched a state propaganda video purporting to highlight the 'wide use' of ethnic minority languages in primary and secondary schools in Xinjiang, and in everyday life: https://twitter.com/ChinaDaily/status/1256463431022137346 (accessed 2 May 2020). However, fieldwork conducted by Hanna Burdorf in Xinjiang in 2019 found that, in some schools at least, Uyghur-medium instruction may have dropped to zero during the early phase of the 'de-extremification' campaign from April 2017.
2 Joanne Smith Finley is grateful to Anna Hayes for drawing scholars' attention to Campbell's theory during the conference 'The Xinjiang Emergency', held at the National Security College, Australian National University, on 3 September 2019.

3 Personal communication, Hanna Burdorf, PhD candidate, Newcastle University, 2019. See also Byler (2019).
4 Smith Finley purchased the Book 2 series of *Til-Ädäbiyat* (Language and Literature, rev. 1st ed. 2018, Levels 1–6) at the Xinhua bookstore in Ürümchi in July 2018 and mailed them back to the UK. Unfortunately, the Book 1 series of the textbook was then not in stock. The authors therefore need to point to an important caveat in respect of our findings: we have no way of knowing what content was included in the Book 1 series. The conclusions we draw here might have looked substantially different had we been able to analyse the Book 1 series as well. That said, given the climate of coercive linguistic and cultural assimilation pervasive in Xinjiang today, we strongly suspect that an analysis of the Book 1 series would have revealed similar results.
5 Original Chinese-medium text online here: www.aoshu.com/e/20090629/4b8bcbdba996d.shtml (accessed 6 July 2020).
6 Original Chinese-medium texts online here: www.aoshu.com/e/20090705/4b8bcc1ff082d.shtml (accessed 6 July 2020) and here: www.aoshu.com/e/20090707/4b8bcc31a7ff5.shtml (accessed 6 July 2020).
7 Original Chinese-medium text online here: www.aoshu.com/e/20090705/4b8bcc1fed949.shtml (accessed 6 July 2020).
8 Original Chinese-medium text online here: www.aoshu.com/e/20090704/4b8bcc149424b.shtml (accessed 6 July 2020).
9 See this song popular among Han: 'Turpan's grapes have ripened!', sung in Chinese by Uyghur musician-comprador Bahargül. The video features alluring Uyghur girls picking grapes in Turpan's grape arbours: https://v.qq.com/x/page/v0025ogra2m.html (accessed 14 August 2021).
10 See www.aoshu.com/e/20090707/4b8bcc336b977.shtml (accessed 6 July 2020).
11 Original Chinese-medium text online here: www.aoshu.com/e/20090707/4b8bcc319133a.shtml (accessed 6 July 2020).
12 Smith Finley, observations from multiple field trips undertaken between 1995 and 2018.
13 Original Chinese-medium text online here: www.aoshu.com/e/20090704/4b8bcc14b3e4f.shtml (accessed 6 July 2020).
14 See Smith Finley (2013: chapter 4) for a contrastive analysis of musician-comprador Bahargül's Chinese-language songs, which seem to invite Han people to 'beautiful Xinjiang', and new folk singer Ömärjan Alim's Uyghur-language song *Mehman Bashlidim* (I Brought Home a Guest), which subverts that theme.
15 This text can be found in the Chinese-medium textbook online here: www.aoshu.com/e/20090707/4b8bcc318b56f.shtml (accessed 6 July 2020).

16 Original Chinese-medium text online here: www.aoshu.com/e/20090707/4b8bcc31aad8d.shtml (accessed 6 July 2020).
17 Original Chinese-medium text online here: www.aoshu.com/e/20090707/4b8bcc3414eda.shtml (accessed 6 July 2020).
18 Original Chinese-medium text online here: www.aoshu.com/e/20090707/4b8bcc342ae8a.shtml (accessed 6 July 2020).
19 Original Chinese-medium text online here: www.aoshu.com/e/20090704/4b8bcc14f012f.shtml (accessed 6 July 2020).
20 Original Chinese-medium text online here: www.aoshu.com/e/20090707/4b8bcc31e1118.shtml (accessed 6 July 2020).
21 Original Chinese-medium text online here: www.aoshu.com/e/20090707/4b8bcc3210192.shtml (accessed 6 July 2020).
22 Original Chinese-medium text online here: www.aoshu.com/e/20090705/4b8bcc1fa3160.shtml (accessed 6 July 2020).
23 Original Chinese-medium text online here: www.aoshu.com/e/20090704/4b8bcc12e5e8b.shtml (accessed 6 July 2020).
24 Original Chinese-medium text online here: www.aoshu.com/e/20090704/4b8bcc1558e4c.shtml (accessed 6 July 2020).
25 Original Chinese-medium text online here: www.aoshu.com/e/20090705/4b8bcc1ce9a31.shtml (accessed 6 July 2020).
26 Original Chinese-medium text online here: www.aoshu.com/e/20090629/4b8bcbdbb1a63.shtml (accessed 6 July 2020).
27 Original Chinese-medium text online here: www.aoshu.com/e/20090629/4b8bcbdbc3ffa.shtml (accessed 6 July 2020).
28 Original Chinese-medium text online here: www.aoshu.com/e/20090704/4b8bcc130a8a0.shtml (accessed 6 July 2020).
29 Original Chinese-medium text online here: www.aoshu.com/e/20090704/4b8bcc128eb96.shtml (accessed 6 July 2020).
30 Original Chinese-medium text online here: www.aoshu.com/e/20090704/4b8bcc1558e4c.shtml (accessed 6 July 2020).
31 Original Chinese-medium text online here: www.aoshu.com/e/20090704/4b8bcc15758e6.shtml (accessed 6 July 2020).
32 Original Chinese-medium text online here: www.aoshu.com/e/20090705/4b8bcc1cdc72d.shtml (accessed 6 July 2020).
33 Original Chinese-medium text online here: www.aoshu.com/e/20090705/4b8bcc1fa0e34.shtml (accessed 6 July 2020).
34 Original Chinese-medium text online here: www.aoshu.com/e/20090707/4b8bcc33281f7.shtml (accessed 6 July 2020).
35 The number of compilers involved in the design of the textbooks is unclear. The publication meta-data tells us that the series was compiled by a group of co-authors (编写组编写 bianxiezu bianxie) but lists only two names: Dilshat Ghopur (editor) and Aygül Hüsän (proofreader).

Corrective 're-education' as (cultural) genocide   221

36 The prominent tenth-century Uyghur scholar Mahmud al-Kashgari, who penned the famous *Dīwān Lughāt al-Turk* (Compendium of the Languages of the Turks) during the Kara-Khanid Khanate (999–1211), is not introduced even briefly.
37 New research published by Adrian Zenz shows how recent Han academic scholarship has advocated a policy of 'population optimization' and 'population rationalization' in Xinjiang. He argues that these recommendations have influenced current policies of Uyghur birth prevention coupled with labour transfer programmes (Zenz 2021b).
38 Original Chinese-medium text online here: www.aoshu.com/e/20090704/4b8bcc12ce51c.shtml (accessed 6 July 2020).
39 Original Chinese-medium text online here: www.aoshu.com/e/20090705/4b8bcc1dba986.shtml (accessed 6 July 2020).
40 Original Chinese-medium text online here: www.aoshu.com/e/20090705/4b8bcc1dbe428.shtml (accessed 6 July 2020).
41 Original Chinese-medium text online here: www.aoshu.com/e/20090705/4b8bcc1fac1f5.shtml (accessed 6 July 2020).
42 Original Chinese-medium text online here: www.aoshu.com/e/20090705/4b8bcc1f57dcc.shtml (accessed 6 July 2020).
43 Original Chinese-medium text online here: www.aoshu.com/e/20090704/4b8bcc148fbf3.shtml (accessed 6 July 2020).
44 Original Chinese-medium text online here: www.aoshu.com/e/20090707/4b8bcc318e454.shtml (accessed 6 July 2020).
45 Interestingly, this reading is not present in the original Chinese-medium version of the textbook. Instead, we find there a reading about building the railroad to Tibet: www.aoshu.com/e/20090707/4b8bcc3192aab.shtml (accessed 6 July 2020).
46 Original Chinese-medium text online here: www.aoshu.com/e/20090707/4b8bcc3213076.shtml (accessed 6 July 2020).
47 Original Chinese-medium text online here: www.aoshu.com/e/20090707/4b8bcc32147ee.shtml (accessed 6 July 2020).
48 Original Chinese-medium text online here: www.aoshu.com/e/20090707/4b8bcc32160a4.shtml (accessed 6 July 2020).
49 Original Chinese-medium text online here: www.aoshu.com/e/20090705/4b8bcc1fb0855.shtml (accessed 6 July 2020).
50 While these revised textbooks were published in 2018, PRC relations with some of the countries previously considered harmless have now soured. For example, the Dutch parliament in February 2021 declared China's treatment of the Uyghurs a 'genocide' (Schaart 2021).
51 See especially Smith Finley (2013: chapter 7) on cultural consumption patterns among the bi- and trilingual urban Uyghur youth during this period.

52 See table 1 in Human Rights Watch (2018: 15).
53 Original Chinese-medium text online here: www.aoshu.com/e/20090707/4b8bcc31d04b5.shtml (accessed 6 July 2020).
54 Original Chinese-medium text online here: www.aoshu.com/e/20090707/4b8bcc31f0888.shtml (accessed 6 July 2020).
55 Original Chinese-medium text online here: www.aoshu.com/e/20090707/4b8bcc3200ca4.shtml (accessed 6 July 2020).
56 Original Chinese-medium text online here: www.aoshu.com/e/20090707/4b8bcc331bbb8.shtml (accessed 6 July 2020). The others are *Bäsh Barmaq* (Five Fingers) and *Qol* (Hand) by Feng Zikai (Book 2, Level 6, pp. 5–7) and *Mahogani Därikhi* (Mahogany Tree) by Lin Qingxuan (Book 2, Level 6, pp. 8–10). Two out of three of the original Chinese-medium texts are online here: www.aoshu.com/e/20090707/4b8bcc332dfc0.shtml (accessed 6 July 2020) and here: www.aoshu.com/e/20090707/4b8bcc3325312.shtml (accessed 6 July 2020).
57 This resonates with what Uyghur respondents told Smith Finley during her visit to Xinjiang in 2018: that the regional authorities 'focus only on work now, forcing Uyghurs to work all hours'. One might surmise that the aim here is to ensure that, with so many hours worked each day, most Uyghurs are left with no time or energy to think about anything else, such as religion or politics.
58 We are grateful to Léo Maillet, a PhD student at the University of Geneva and Center for Turkic, Ottoman, Balkanic, and Central Asian Studies of Paris, for sharing screenshots from this textbook with us. The original copy of the textbook is housed at the Uyghur Institute of Europe. It was purchased from the Satuk Buğrahan Kitabevi at Sumer mah. 29/1 sok no2 A zeytinburn, Istanbul. The inside of that library can be viewed in this short video released in 2016: www.youtube.com/watch?v=MK95mRn7hxE (accessed 14 August 2021).
59 Original Chinese-medium text online here: www.aoshu.com/e/20090707/4b8bcc33588ad.shtml (accessed 6 July 2020).
60 Most of these also appear in the Chinese-medium version here: www.aoshu.com/zlk/dzkb/yw/rjb/lx/ (accessed 6 July 2020).
61 Original Chinese-medium text online here: www.aoshu.com/e/20090705/4b8bcc201a2af.shtml (accessed 6 July 2020).
62 Original Chinese-medium text online here: www.aoshu.com/e/20090705/4b8bcc20036b2.shtml (accessed 6 July 2020).
63 Original Chinese-medium text online here: www.aoshu.com/e/20090705/4b8bcc1d0f240.shtml (accessed 6 July 2020).
64 Original Chinese-medium text online here: www.aoshu.com/e/20090705/4b8bcc1fa027b.shtml (accessed 6 July 2020).

65 While the ETR was rarely mentioned by the government, Uyghurs would of course talk about it privately, and several Uyghur authors wrote and published popular historical novels in the 1980s and 1990s which mentioned East Turkestan openly. At the time, these were all tolerated by the state.
66 See Mahmut and Smith Finley (2017) for an overview of research on proverbs published between the 1950s and the 2000s.
67 Uyghur idioms and proverbs may have long been harnessed by the state for political purposes, such that some Uyghur native speakers have already become desensitized to the process.
68 This appears to be a translation of the original Chinese-language proverb 双手互相洗，手再把脸洗 (*Shuang shou huxiang xi, shou zai ba lian xi*).

References

Byler, Darren (2019). 'The "Patriotism" of Not Speaking Uyghur', *SupChina*, 2 January, https://supchina.com/2019/01/02/the-patriotism-of-not-speaking-uyghur/ (accessed 14 August 2021).

Campbell, Bradley (2009). 'Genocide as Social Control', *Sociological Theory* 27 (2), 150–172.

China Daily (2016). 'China Becomes No.1 in Voluntary Organ Donations in Asia', 16 May, www.ecns.cn/2016/05-16/210664.shtml (accessed 4 June 2020).

China Law Translate (2017). 'Xinjiang Uyghur Autonomous Region Regulation on De-extremification', 30 March, www.chinalawtranslate.com/en/xinjiang-uyghur-autonomous-region-regulation-on-de-extremification/ (accessed 14 August 2021).

China Tribunal (2020). 'Independent Tribunal into Forced Organ Harvesting from Prisoners of Conscience in China', 1 March, https://chinatribunal.com/wp-content/uploads/2020/03/ChinaTribunal_JUDGMENT_1stMarch_2020.pdf (accessed 14 August 2021).

Clarke, Michael (2018). 'China's "War on Terrorism": Confronting the Dilemmas of the "Internal-External" Security Nexus', in Michael Clarke (ed.), *Terrorism and Counter-terrorism in China: Domestic and Foreign Policy Dimensions* (Oxford: Oxford University Press), 17–38.

Dearden, Lizzie (2017). 'China Bans Islamic Baby Names in Muslim Majority Xinjiang Province', *The Independent*, 25 April, https://bit.ly/2TxeqNM (accessed 14 August 2021).

Gladney, Dru C. (1994). 'Representing Nationality in China: Refiguring Majority/Minority Identities', *The Journal of Asian Studies* 53 (1), 92–123.

Grose, Timothy (2019). *Negotiating Inseparability in China: The Xinjiang Class and the Dynamics of Uyghur Identity* (Hong Kong: Hong Kong University Press).

Harrell, Stevan (1995). 'Introduction: Civilizing Projects and the Reaction to Them', in Stevan Harrell (ed.), *Cultural Encounters on China's Ethnic Frontiers* (Seattle: University of Washngton Press), 3–36.

Harris, Rachel (2019). 'Cultural Genocide in Xinjiang: How China Targets Uyghur Artists, Academics, and Writers', The Globe Post, 17 January, https://theglobepost.com/2019/01/17/cultural-genocide-xinjiang/ (accessed 14 August 2021).

Human Rights Watch (2018). '"Eradicating Ideological Viruses": China's Campaign of Repression against Xinjiang's Muslims', September, www.hrw.org/sites/default/files/report_pdf/china0918_web.pdf (accessed 14 August 2021).

Knowles, Hannah, Kim Bellware, and Lateshia Beachum (2019). 'Secret Documents Detail Inner Workings of China's Mass Detention Camps for Minorities', *Washington Post*, 25 November.

Lemkin, Raphael ([1944] 2005). *Axis Rule in Occupied Europe: Laws of Occupation, Analysis of Government, Proposals for Redress* (Clark, NJ: The Lawbook Exchange).

Lemon, Edward (2018). 'Critical Approaches to Security in Central Asia: An Introduction', *Central Asian Survey* 37 (1), 1–12.

Li, Yang, and Geoffrey Wall (2008). 'Ethnic Tourism and Entrepreneurship: Xishuangbanna, Yunnan, China', *Tourism Geographies* 10 (4), 522–544.

Mahmut, Dilmurat (2019). 'Controlling Religious Knowledge and Education for Countering Violent Extremism: Case Study of the Uyghur Muslims in China', *FIRE: Forum for International Research in Education* 5 (1), 22–43.

Mahmut, Dilmurat, and Joanne Smith Finley (2017). '"A Man Works on the Land, a Woman Works for Her Man": Building on Jarring's Fascination with Eastern Turki Proverbs', in Ildikó Bellér-Hann, Birgit N. Schlyter, and Jun Sugawara (eds), *Kashgar Revisited: Uyghur Studies in Memory of Ambassador Gunnar Jarring* (Leiden: Brill), 302–330.

Qin, Amy (2019). 'In China's Crackdown on Muslims, Children Have Not Been Spared', *New York Times*, 28 December, www.nytimes.com/2019/12/28/world/asia/china-xinjiang-children-boarding-schools.html (accessed 14 August 2021).

Ramzy, Austin, and Chris Buckley (2019). '"Absolutely No Mercy": Leaked Files Expose How China Organized Mass Detentions of Muslims', *New York Times*, 16 November, www.nytimes.com/interactive/2019/11/16/world/asia/china-xinjiang-documents.html (accessed 14 August 2021).

Richmond, Edmund B. (1987). 'Utilizing Proverbs as a Focal Point to Cultural Awareness and Communicative Competence: Illustrations from Africa', *Foreign Language Annals* 20 (3), 213–216.

Roberts, Sean R. (2018). 'The Biopolitics of China's "War on Terror" and the Exclusion of the Uyghurs', *Critical Asian Studies* 50 (2), 232–258.

Rodríguez-Merino, Pablo (2019). 'Old "Counter-revolution", New "Terrorism": Historicizing the Framing of Violence in Xinjiang by the Chinese State', *Central Asian Survey* 38 (1), 27–45.

Schaart, Eline (2021). 'Dutch Parliament Declares Chinese Treatment of Uighurs a "Genocide"', Politico, 25 February, www.politico.eu/article/dutch-parliament-declares-chinese-treatment-of-uighurs-as-genocide/ (accessed 7 October 2021).

Schein, Louisa (1997). 'Gender and Internal Orientalism in China', *Modern China* 23 (1), 69–98.

Shepherd, Christian (2019). 'Fear and Oppression in Xinjiang: China's War on Uighur Culture', *Financial Times*, 12 September, www.ft.com/content/48508182-d426-11e9-8367-807ebd53ab77 (accessed 14 August 2021).

Shih, Gerry (2018). 'China's Mass Indoctrination Camps Evoke Cultural Revolution', Associated Press, 18 May, https://apnews.com/6e151296fb194f85ba69a8babd972e4b (accessed 14 August 2021).

Smith Finley, Joanne (2013). *The Art of Symbolic Resistance: Uyghur Identities and Uyghur-Han Relations in Contemporary Xinjiang* (Leiden: Brill).

Smith Finley, Joanne (2018). 'Now We Don't Talk Anymore: Inside the "Cleansing" of Xinjiang', *China File*, 28 December, www.chinafile.com/reporting-opinion/viewpoint/now-we-dont-talk-anymore (accessed 14 August 2021).

Smith Finley, Joanne (2019a). 'Securitization, Insecurity and Conflict in Contemporary Xinjiang: Has PRC Counter-terrorism Evolved into State Terror?', *Central Asian Survey* 38 (1), 1–26.

Smith Finley, Joanne (2019b). 'The Wang Lixiong Prophecy: "Palestinization" in Xinjiang and the Consequences of Chinese State Securitization of Religion', *Central Asian Survey* 38 (1), 81–101.

Smith Finley, Joanne (2019c). 'Uyghur Islam and "De-extremification": On China's "Thought Liberation Movement" in Xinjiang', Focus On, Oxford Islamic Studies Online, www.oxfordislamicstudies.com/Public/focus.html (accessed 14 August 2021).

Tobin, David (2020). *Securing China's Northwest Frontier: Identity and Insecurity in Xinjiang* (Cambridge: Cambridge University Press).

UHRP (Uyghur Human Rights Project) (2019). 'UPDATE – Detained and Disappeared: Intellectuals under Assault in the Uyghur Homeland', 21 May, https://bit.ly/3jB96DH (accessed 14 August 2021).

Yi, Xiaocuo (2019). '"Saved" by State Terror: Gendered Violence and Propaganda in Xinjiang', *SupChina*, 14 May, https://supchina.com/2019/05/14/saved-by-state-terror-gendered-violence-and-propaganda-in-xinjiang/ (accessed 14 August 2021).

Xinjiang Education Press Editorial Board (2018). *Til-Ädäbiyat* [Language and Literature], rev. 1st ed., Book 2, Levels 1–6 (Ürümchi: Xinjiang Education Press).

Xu, Vicky Xiuzhong, Danielle Cave, James Leibold et al. (2020). 'Uyghurs for Sale: "Re-education", Forced Labour and Surveillance beyond Xinjiang', 1 March (Canberra: Australian Strategic Policy Institute), www.aspi.org.au/report/uyghurs-sale (accessed 14 August 2021).

Yağiz, Oktay, and Siros Izadpanah (2013). 'Language, Culture, Idioms, and Their Relationship with the Foreign Language', *Journal of Language Teaching and Research* 4 (5), 953–957.

Zenz, Adrian (2019a). '"Wash Brains, Cleanse Hearts": Evidence from Chinese Government Documents about the Nature and Extent of Xinjiang's Extrajudicial Internment Campaign', *Journal of Political Risk* 7 (11), www.jpolrisk.com/wash-brains-cleanse-hearts/ (accessed 14 August 2021).

Zenz, Adrian (2019b). 'Break Their Roots: Evidence for China's Parent-Child Separation Campaign in Xinjiang', *Journal of Political Risk* 7 (7), www.jpolrisk.com/break-their-roots-evidence-for-chinas-parent-child-separation-campaign-in-xinjiang/ (accessed 14 August 2021).

Zenz, Adrian (2020). *Sterilizations, IUDs and Mandatory Birth Control: The CCP's Campaign to Suppress Uyghur Birthrates in Xinjiang* (Washington, DC: The Jamestown Foundation), https://jamestown.org/wp-content/uploads/2020/06/Zenz-Internment-Sterilizations-and-IUDs-REVISED-March-17-2021.pdf?x86133 (accessed 14 August 2021).

Zenz, Adrian (2021a). Coercive Labor and Forced Displacement in Xinjiang's Cross-Regional Labor Transfer Program: A Process-Oriented Evaluation (Washington, DC: The Jamestown Foundation), https://jamestown.org/wp-content/uploads/2021/03/Coercive-Labor-and-Forced-Displacement-in-Xinjiangs-Cross-Regional-Labor-Transfers-A-Process-Oriented-Evaluation.pdf?x30155 (accessed 7 October 2021).

Zenz, Adrian (2021b). '"End the Dominance of the Uyghur Ethnic Group": An Analysis of Beijing's Population Optimization Strategy in Southern Xinjiang', Central Asian Survey, https://papers.ssrn.com/sol3/papers.cfm?abstract_id=3862512 (accessed 7 October 2021).

8

Predatory biopolitics: Organ harvesting and other means of monetizing Uyghur 'surplus'

Matthew P. Robertson

> Uyghurs are not considered human by the Chinese government. They're like mice being experimented on for research purposes.
>
> Chinese surveillance technology insider
> (Barnwell and Mohammad 2020)

> We were told to go to the family planning office the next morning without eating. I had no choice. I felt as if I was being taken to a slaughterhouse.
>
> Zumrat Dawut (BBC Newsnight 2020)

Every regime shapes the biological lives of its subjects. One way the state does this is through public health projects. Such projects, such as mass vaccinations or anti-smoking campaigns, are carried out to improve, heal, and protect the bodies of the citizenry. The provision of an efficient health care system, state-run or hybrid, is considered a basic indicator of state capacity. But not all therapies can be provided solely by the state. Almost everywhere, organ transplantation is viewed as a 'gift of life' passed between voluntary citizens. The body is seen as inviolable, and the commodification of organs both illegal and taboo. This arrangement is predicated on an understanding of human rights that limits the role of the state to encouraging and facilitating organ donation as an altruistic gift. But what if the state refuses to recognize such limits on its powers, and decides to take the gift instead, eviscerating the organs of those who do not deserve them and making them available (for a price) to those who do?

The organ transplantation industry of the People's Republic of China (PRC) offers up a compelling case study of contemporary biopolitics, where the party-state has allowed and encouraged its agents to harvest organs from prison populations while profiteering from the transaction. Biopolitics is a unifying term for the state's control and regulation of the vital characteristics of its population (Greenhalgh 2009). In the case of China it has been adopted as a lens through which to analyse the one-child policy (Greenhalgh and Winckler 2005), the hukou system (Ye *et al.* 2013), medical accidents (Cooper 2011a), and other intrusions of state imperatives on the biological lives of subjects. Organ harvesting is yet one more case that can be fruitfully seen through a biopolitical lens.

This edited volume deals with the Xinjiang emergency. Here I link the Chinese Communist Party's (CCP) mass incarceration and re-education of Uyghurs with a growing literature on state predation through organ harvesting. I attempt to theorize the political logic of organ harvesting from vulnerable, primarily prison, populations in China, and then to review the evidence and consider the possibility that Uyghur Muslims are now victims of this activity. My primary concern is to clear a space for thinking about coercive organ procurement and transplantation in China that is free from the lurid public descriptions it is often couched within. Bloody depictions of gaping cadavers convey an unreality and horror that inhibits careful thought. To approach human organ harvesting for profit from those we consider innocent is to approach the abject. While it may seem incredible, we can, upon closer inspection, see that coercive organ procurement follows its own internal logic in the context of large-scale political violence and the hyper-marketization of contemporary China. Organ harvesting is a process that is at the confluence of numerous disparate forces. Having recognized those forces, we may be more surprised if organ harvesting did not happen than if it did.

The theoretical motor for this chapter is biopolitics. I first introduce biopolitics as a lens through which to see the Chinese state's relationship to the bodies of its subjects. Next, I review research on China's organ transplantation industry, with a particular focus on the claims that the CCP has harvested the organs from political prisoners before.

Most of these allegations relate to organ harvesting from practitioners of Falun Gong, an indigenous biospiritual cultivation practice that has been forcibly suppressed since 1999. I then examine what we can reasonably infer about China's organ transplantation system at present, before reviewing the evidence that is consistent with Uyghurs being victims of coercive organ procurement. Finally, I attempt to 'de-fetishize' organ harvesting by showing that it can be located firmly within two dominant logics and stages of the CCP's ruling legacy: revolutionary governance and what some scholars have termed 'gangster capitalism' (Holmstrom and Smith 2000; Walker 2006). With PRC medical officials now anticipating China becoming world transplant leader by performing 50,000 transplants annually by 2023 (Liu 2020), a revisiting of the transplant question is timely indeed.

The biopolitical lens

The term biopolitics was coined by Michel Foucault. It was created to capture the modern shift in the logic of government whereby sovereign power begins to operate on the abstraction of the population, rather than over individuals alone. As 'the population' emerges as a political problem in its own right, new categories, metrics, and tools of surveillance and scientific manipulation arise: 'the mortality rate has to be modified or lowered; life expectancy has to be increased; the birth rate has to be stimulated,' and so on (Foucault 2003: 246). The term has now come to encompass substantially all state projects that seek to surveil and manage the biological aspects of human life.

Biopolitical critique implies normative claims and is intended to unveil normative commitments. When established taxonomies, such as conceptualizations of sexual orientation or mental and physical health, are exposed as contingent and historical, power is revealed as the designator of acceptable standards. All such classifications are shown as forms of discipline and regulation. In Foucault's critical chiasmus: 'For millennia, man remained what he was for Aristotle: a living animal with the additional capacity for a political existence; modern man is an animal whose politics places his existence as a living being in question' (Foucault 1978: 143–144).

Biopolitical logic contains a sorting component: which life is to be fostered and promoted, and which (necessarily) demoted. Thus biopolitical 'rationalities and governing technologies are nothing but a vast ensemble of life-sorting and life-adjudicating devices' (Dillon and Neal 2015: 19). Biopolitical choices decide which life matters, and they determine which life must die so that other lives can be augmented. The biopolitical lens thus also determines which forms of life count as life (Lemke 2010: 428).

Biopolitical framing is therefore normative insofar as it exposes the role of state power in intervening in and shaping the population or species. Such exercises of state power rest on modern technology, and may even be a logical conclusion of technological development, in Martin Heidegger's exegesis. Heidegger argues that the exact sciences transform our relationship to the world by turning nature and everything in it into 'standing-reserve', or resources to be exploited. The danger then is that 'man ... comes to the point where he himself will have to be taken as standing-reserve' (Heidegger 1977: 27). Similar perspectives are to be found in the early critical theorists, who claimed that a central danger in the overemphasis on instrumental reason is the creation of a world 'in which nothing exists but prey' (Horkheimer and Adorno 2002: 6).

Predatory biopolitics is one such perverse modernity. In the hands of the predatory biostate, organ transplantation technologies turn human bodies – whether of death row prisoners or enemies of the state – into standing-reserve. Here is an acute irony. In a similar manner to Alexander Kojève's 1957 assessment of the Soviet Union as the only actually capitalist country (Kojève 2001: 118–119), the post-socialist phase of the last great Communist state of the PRC comes to fulfill Marx's own critiques of capitalism as a vampiric force (Marx 1867) that transforms life itself into 'surplus' to be capitalized (Cooper 2011b; Heinrich 2018: 6). The biopolitics of organ harvesting stands in contrast to the spectacle of ritual torture and execution of a failed regicide as depicted by Foucault (2012: 3–6): 'Rather than staging its magnificence, violence conceals itself in shame' (Han 2018: 5). Organ harvesting is carried out in secret, and above all it is practical and profitable.

The growth of organ trafficking in China: Background considerations

China's organ transplantation system unrolled in three broad phases: a quiet period before 2000, the phase of rapid growth, industrialization, and consolidation from 2000 to 2015,[1] and the phase of official reform post-2015. This periodization reflects the CCP's own narratives (difficult to avoid when studying Chinese politics (Unger 2007)) but also genuine reforms in response to external criticism. Structural changes that enhanced central control and oversight corrected some abuses while concealing others.

Until recently, one could not speak of an organ transplantation system in China without speaking of an organ trafficking system. There is now a vast amount of information publicly available about this system and its growth for the last twenty years, but given the issue's long associations with contentious politics, the fact that much of the work is either self-published or produced by lawyers and investigators who are not credentialled by the field of academic China studies, as well as the extreme nature of the allegations of large-scale secret executions for profit, the data has quietly accumulated in a state of benign neglect and permissible ignorance by elite cultural institutions. The standard trajectory for information of this nature is for it to be re-reported by media like *The New York Times*, investigated by human rights organizations, spoken about by governments, and thus enter the popular (and, in particular, elite) imagination as real. This process of social authorization is quite separate from whether or not the claims are actually true. Reflexive scholarship on the issue must first acknowledge its marginal epistemic status: claims of organ harvesting from prisoners of conscience inhabit a liminal zone between recognition and denial – despite the vast body of evidence supporting them.

One explanation for the puzzle as to why such an apparent abundance of evidence has elicited such a muted reaction might be that the evidence, or what can be inferred from it, is weaker than is claimed by advocates. This would assume, however, that decision-making in international human rights NGOs is dominated by normative concerns and that their resource allocation decisions are proportional to the severity and scale of the abuses alleged. These reductionist assumptions are not borne out by scholarship on advocacy organizations which sees them as 'firms' who operate in competition with other advocacy firms, who must cultivate their brand identity, ensure their products suit the human rights market, and maintain their support from specific constituencies (Prakash and Gugerty 2010). Understanding advocacy organizations as firms allows us to entertain the possibility that such processes have been influential in determining how knowledge is produced (or not) on the organ harvesting case. Other scholars argue that major human rights organizations have come to adopt a more expansive definition of human rights, encompassing both economic and social rights alongside traditionally conceived 'natural' rights (Bob 2011; Rhodes 2018). This change in definition of rights, and attendant organizational focus, may ironically have been one factor in the decentring of more straightforward abrogations like organ harvesting.

These arguments suggest that the failure of human rights advocacy organizations – and other elite institutions, such as major media corporations – to take up these claims may have less to do with the evidence itself than with the marginal identity of the primary alleged victims. We can theorize that it is the stigma surrounding the Falun Gong that has in part worked to discourage scholars, journalists, and other organizations from carefully examining their claims of organ harvesting (Clarke 2020a). The reasons for this stigma – a 'spoiled identity' as Erving Goffman put it – likely involve a combination of factors. Among these are presumably Falun Gong's deviance from progressive norms, and the group's unpolished style of communication, often redolent in aesthetic to official mainland propaganda. This is hardly surprising for a group largely socialized in China, where the majority of the diaspora are first-generation migrants. Yet when mainland-style propaganda is combined with High Weirdness and anti-modern Buddhist esotericism, the result is a brand identity that organizations and individuals with progressive political commitments seek to avoid. As sociologist Andrew Junker put it: 'If there is a cautionary lesson in this, it could be told thus: woe be to any people who dare to both reject the hegemonic vision of the CCP and the liberal West's progressive alternative, for the dissenting group faces defamation and violence from the first and mute apathy from the second' (Junker 2019: 7).

While scholarship has begun to show how the seepage from the CCP's anti-Falun Gong campaign impacted a broad swathe of policy areas – including by reshaping the security apparatus (Cook and Lemish 2011; Pan 2020), empowering the rise of Zhou Yongkang (Junker 2019: chapter 3), severely undermined budding rule-of-law efforts (Pils 2006), and coinciding with the inauguration of the CCP's surveillance and censorship state, including the Golden Shield and Great

Firewall (Chase and Mulvenon 2002; EFF 2016)[2] – the significance of these legacies of repression for the Xinjiang case has so far been insufficiently recognized. On the question of a predatory biopolitics targeting Uyghurs, the history of the CCP's anti-Falun Gong campaign is of signal importance.

Much of the received wisdom about China's transplant system held by elites – international human rights NGOs, mainstream media organizations, scholars, and Western governments – is roughly where it was in the 1990s, the last time Human Rights Watch produced a report on the topic. It is confidently 'known' that the almost sole source of organs has all along been death row prisoners (Kirchgaessner 2017). The allegations of Falun Gong practitioners being killed on some significant scale for their organs are seen as marginal (Tatlow 2019), and the burden of proof required to accept the claims is set at an impossible standard (ABC News 2019). Moreover, there is – or was until recently – a readiness to believe the PRC's official narrative of substantial reform in the direction of voluntary donations (Denyer 2017).

When asked by reporters to comment on the allegations of organ harvesting from Falun Gong or other prisoners of conscience, major human rights organizations have disclaimed that it is their job to provide such answers. Such responses seem to conform to what moral philosopher Harry Frankfurt described as 'carefully wrought' utterances where the speaker's intent is 'neither to report the truth nor to conceal it ... [but where] the motive guiding and controlling it is unconcerned with how the things about which he speaks truly are' (Frankfurt 2005: 55) For instance, when Human Rights Watch was asked to respond to the allegations of organ harvesting from Falun Gong, it said that it 'has not substantiated claims that any one community is particularly targeted for this treatment, partly as a result of government-imposed restrictions on research' (van der Made 2019). This response parses the question in such a way as to avoid answering its central concern. The question of organ harvesting is not one of whether 'any one community' has been 'particularly targeted', but whether prisoners of conscience have *also* been preyed upon by the state (along with death row prisoners and any other victims). The public record includes many such responses by elite organizations since the allegations have been made: rather than explaining why they believe the allegations are unsupported, or doing their own research to show that they are, their answers obfuscate the question. Stanley Cohen's work on denial – the wish to be innocent of a troubling recognition – is a generative framework for understanding such responses to disturbing evidence (Cohen 2013: chapter 1). Like the opposite of an availability cascade, where collective beliefs spread in a self-reinforcing manner (Kuran and Sunstein 1998), the ubiquity of denial around organ harvesting has normalized denial and created an ignorance cascade. Many are habituated to the question of organ harvesting remaining indefinitely unresolved.

This outcome is surprising, given that we might expect more epistemic resources to be directed to such a significant question. If organ harvesting does eventually become common knowledge, it may result in an unpleasant epistemological crisis that reconstitutes how a whole chain of events should be interpreted (MacIntyre 1977). The more general lesson is to show us that it is not always a question of evidence that determines how claims are processed, but that every act of judgement first requires 'an act of will' (Fraser 2020). Even in purely deductive reasoning, as the Tortoise demonstrated to Achilles, inference does not just happen – it must be *done* (Carroll 1895; Winch 1990). That such global will is lacking in this case, particularly given the severity of the claims, is an epistemic injustice (Fricker 2007). Organ harvesting is seen as a crime whose truth status is not even worth resolving.

The social fact of this epistemic siloing has significant consequences for grappling with organ harvesting now, in 2021, when the circumstances are at their most tangled and complex. Given that we must traverse over twenty years of history in order to set the scene for what may be happening at present, and to demonstrate how it relates to the CCP's campaign against Uyghurs, this and the following section are a highly truncated summary of what I think we know to date.[3]

Organs without an accounted source

For most of the period since 2000, China's transplantation system has been tightly linked with its security apparatus, and nearly a quarter of authorized transplant hospitals are military or paramilitary (NHFPC

2018). China is also the only country to systematically source organs almost solely from prisoners (Human Rights Watch 1994; Huang *et al.* 2012). As of the end of 2009, the last year for which data of the kind was available, official Chinese sources stated that 101,000 kidneys and 18,000 livers had been procured cumulatively since the beginning of transplantation in China (Chen 2013). These numbers are without doubt major underestimates, but when combined with the absence of voluntary donors serve to establish that the security apparatus was the almost sole provider of large numbers of organs to hospitals. According to three official sources, the total number of voluntary (i.e. non-prisoner) organ donations in China cumulatively as of 2009 was reported as either 120 or 130 (CNN 2009; Beijing Youth Daily 2015; Zhao and Wu 2015).[4] Chinese medical officials say that 'over 90 per cent' or even 'over 97 per cent' of transplants have come from prisoners; this would mean that the remaining 3–10 per cent came from volunteers. But the actual ratio, at least as of the 2009 data, would appear to be closer to 99.7 per cent coming from prisoners and only 0.3 per cent from volunteers (i.e. 360/120,000, assuming each voluntary donor gave three organs) (Zhonghua 2006; Huang *et al.* 2012). No major change in this pattern of organ sourcing took place until recently, though China's transition to voluntary donors is a matter of intense dispute.

Up until 2007, there was no legislation governing China's transplantation sector. The first interim guidelines preceding that legislation were announced two weeks after the Falun Gong organ harvesting claims first surfaced in March 2006 (MOH 2006). Beginning in 1984, the only quasi-legal guidelines for organ procurement from prisoners were the 'Temporary Rules Concerning the Utilization of Corpses or Organs from the Corpses of Executed Criminals', issued under the imprimatur of China's Supreme People's Court, Supreme People's Procuratorate, Ministry of Public Security, Ministry of Justice, Ministry of Health, and Ministry of Civil Affairs (Human Rights Watch 1994). This document, though widely reported, is ostensibly still secret and its legal status has never been publicly clarified by the authorities (Wang 2015). These temporary rules were superseded by the Regulation on Human Organ Transplantation, issued by the State Council in May 2007 (State Council 2007). All of the above shows that until 2015 the authorities did not even claim to have an operating voluntary organ donation system.

An organ transplant surgery can cost tens of thousands of dollars (TV Chosun 2018). In the context of endemic informal payments for services at Chinese hospitals (Müller 2019), there is an obvious incentive for transplant hospitals and surgeons to perform transplants. The use of prisoners as an organ source involves only minimal expenditure for medical examinations. Thus, while some prisoners may be funnelled to labour camps and in-prison sweatshops, a smaller number can be directly monetized via the trafficking of their organs. Access to organ transplants also appears to be one of the medical benefits available to officials in the ranks of the CCP's nomenklatura.

China's transplant system began a phase of sudden and rapid growth in the year 2000, as shown by analysis of official medical reports and speeches by top health care administrators. He Xiaoshun, a leading Chinese surgeon with state ties, told domestic media that the year 2000 was a 'watershed' for China's transplant sector, with liver transplants growing by ten times between 1999 and 2000, and tripling again by 2005 (Su 2010). A team of liver transplant surgeons at a major military hospital in south-west China likened the proliferation of hospitals performing liver transplants post-2000 to 'rising abruptly like spring bamboo after the rain' (Yan et al. 2006). In 2006, Chen Zhonghua, another leading transplant surgeon and director of the Organ Transplant Research Institute at Tongji Hospital in Wuhan, told an official legal publication that 'currently the number of organ transplants taking place in China is too great, and there's a lot of foreign and domestic pressure to come out with regulations' (Guo 2006). Huang Jiefu, a key architect of China's organ transplantation system, in 2006 noted that at least 500 hospitals were performing liver transplants in China (compared to only around 100 in the United States, the report said)[5] and added: 'The number of hospitals carrying out liver, kidney, and heart transplants in China is not too few, but too many'[6] (Guo 2006: 45). Nearly 800 data points from over 400 hospitals also show that the vast majority of new transplant centres, wards, and research labs were constructed soon after the year 2000 (Robertson 2020a). Chinese officials have provided no public explanation for this growth in activity, in particular in addressing where the organs are supposed to have come from at a time when the number of death row executions was in decline and voluntary donations were all but non-existent.

The number of hospitals performing transplants grew from less than 100 in 1999 to nearly 600 in 2004, to a maximum of 1,000 in 2007, according to Chinese media reports. Thousands of new transplant surgeons were trained post-2000, with a total of nearly 10,000 documented transplant personnel by 2014. New patient registrations on transplant technologies grew rapidly after the year 2000, as did the number of hospitals reporting their first ever liver, lung, and heart transplants. (The growth in hospitals reporting new kidney transplants was more modest, because death row prisoners had long been used as a kidney source). In the early 2000s, dozens of hospitals built new transplant research laboratories, wards, or entire buildings. The government also began subsidizing its domestic immunosuppressant industry.

In the post-2000 period transplants also began being performed on demand – a fact that has significant human rights implications. The on-demand nature of organ procurement is shown in PRC annual liver registry reports, which were removed from the Internet after researchers found the information. The 2005 and 2006 versions of these reports show that 29 per cent and 26.6 per cent of all liver transplants (where the timing of surgery was noted) were performed on an emergency, rather than elective basis in 2005 and 2006, respectively (China Liver Transplant Registry 2006, 2007). This means that after the patient presented at hospital with liver failure, a new liver – healthy and with a compatible blood type – was procured within one to three days. The removal of a liver attends the death of the donor. In the absence of a voluntary donation system, this can only plausibly be explained by the pre-screening of prisoners who are executed on demand. The identity of these forced donors, whether death row prisoners, prisoners of conscience, or captives of some other type, has been a central point of contention.

When these findings are combined with a critical analysis of China's claim of organ sourcing from death row prisoners, it becomes clear that the PRC's public narrative is inadequate in accounting for the observations. The official explanation for the source of organs has also shifted over time as international pressure has increased. In 2001, a PRC spokesperson said the claim of organ sourcing from prisoners was 'vicious slander' (Smith 2001). In 2006, this denial was softened to a revised claim that death row prisoners were used 'in only a few cases' (Li 2006). By 2012, the authorities claimed that organs had been coming almost solely from death row prisoners all along (Huang *et al.* 2012). Since 2015, the claim has again been that organs come from voluntary donors only.

While the PRC is highly secretive about its death penalty numbers (Smith 2020), scholars who study the issue agree almost unanimously that the number of official executions in the criminal justice system has been in a long-term decline since the early 2000s (Johnson and Zimring 2009), and that major reforms to the approval process for executions led to a precipitous decline in sentences beginning in 2007 (Liang and Lu 2015). This took place when the PRC Supreme People's Court resumed authority to review and approve every death sentence, rather than leaving the matter in the hands of provincial courts. Judicial insiders told Chinese media outlet Caixin that the drop in executions was so large that they dared not report it, lest the public think they were lying (Dan 2016).

Despite this, China's transplant apparatus continued to grow. In 2007, the largest organ transplantation centre in Asia, a fourteen-storey building, opened at the Tianjin First Central Hospital. It was originally planned to hold 500 transplant beds, but this was expanded to 700 even before it opened. It then reported operating at full capacity, before adding a further 300 beds in 2013 (Editorial Board 2006; Y. Xu 2006; Qu 2014; CBRN 2016). The transplant surgeon leading this expansion, Dr Shen Zhongyang, also founded the transplant centre of the People's Armed Police General Hospital in Beijing (PAP 2006). The combination of patient stay times of one month and full bed capacity suggests the hospital was performing thousands of transplants annually in the post-2007 period. Comments to the media by the head surgeon claiming that he (or more probably, his surgical team) had performed 1,000 liver transplants annually from 2000 to 2014 is further evidence of a large number of transplants taking place at this hospital (Wu *et al.* 2014; Wei *et al.* 2016).

From 2010 to 2012 the People's Liberation Army's 309 Military Hospital, which treats the CCP elite, expanded its transplant bed capacity by 25 per cent, and grew its profits by 800 per cent (309 Military Hospital 2010; Xinhua 2012). Other major transplant centres also expanded, such as the Third Affiliated Hospital of the Sun Yat-sen University in Guangdong, which nearly tripled its transplant beds between 2005 and 2016 (Zhang 2005; Third Affiliated Hospital of Sun

Yat-sen University 2015); while the Shanghai Renji Hospital doubled its transplant beds from 2004 to 2006, then tripled them again by 2016 (D. Xu 2006; Renji Hospital 2016). These are only a few cases which illustrate a much larger trend.

Though it is difficult to reliably estimate the volume of organ transplants implied by all this activity, the available data shows that there is a divergence of an order of magnitude. Death row numbers were, since 2007 and probably earlier, measured in the thousands, but transplant numbers are measured in the tens of thousands. Researchers have adopted a variety of approaches in an attempt to estimate transplant volume. One approach is to extrapolate from limited available data and assume that mandated minimum transplant volumes are upheld. These estimates have suggested transplants in the range of 60,000 to 100,000 annually from the period of 2000 to 2015 (Kilgour *et al.* 2017). Another approach, which I have chosen to adopt, is simply to triangulate official public claims about aggregate transplant volume. This simple, and no doubt highly incomplete, method results in an estimate of at least 30,000 transplants annually in many of the years during the same period (Robertson 2020b).

Whatever the means used, the significant discrepancy in both volume and growth rate between the claimed source (death row inmates) and the actual number of transplants between 2000 and 2015 opens a key question: without a voluntary donation system, where did the organs come from? Officials have proposed their own narrative of organ trafficking, which include rogue doctors operating organ trafficking gangs (Winfield 2018), and voluntary sales of kidneys for iPads and other consumer electronics (BBC News 2011). But such cases do not explain a national system performing tens of thousands of transplants with just weeks and days notice.

Instead, the evidence far more compellingly suggests that the main organ trafficking ring in question has been the civilian hospital system and military-medical complex, which has leveraged its close relationships with the security apparatus to monetize new populations of prisoners as they have become available. In the post-2000 period, based on evidence presented below, the most plausible explanation is that in addition to death row prisoners, the primary source of organs was from practitioners of Falun Gong – a practice that enjoyed official sanction and support in the early 1990s, but that was targeted by the CCP for elimination in July 1999. On the basis of this precedent and in light of a range of other evidence and theoretical expectations, I believe it is highly likely that Uyghurs are also being exploited in this manner.

Organ harvesting as an inferred abuse

The allegations of organ harvesting from Falun Gong emerged in 2006, based on alleged eyewitnesses who made sensational claims of a large crematorium attached to a hospital operating in north-east China. These claims were examined by the US State Department, which failed to find evidence in support of them, and were publicly rejected by the late Chinese human rights activist Harry Wu. It is very likely that this initial presentation of the claims set in motion the subsequent pattern of elite opinion about them. Despite over a decade of elite neglect, the issue has been kept alive for the public by the work of two Canadian lawyers, David Matas and David Kilgour, and later the American investigative journalist Ethan Gutmann, as well as by a number of key NGOs, and the grassroots efforts of the global Falun Gong community. The allegations began receiving belated mainstream recognition in 2019, when they were examined by the former UN war crimes prosecutor Sir Geoffrey Nice, QC, who led a tribunal of experts to reach the judgement that: 'The Tribunal's members are certain – unanimously, and sure beyond reasonable doubt – that in China forced organ harvesting from prisoners of conscience has been practiced for a substantial period of time involving a very substantial number of victims' (China Tribunal 2019a).

This finding rests on inference from two bodies of evidence. The first – evidence that the official explanation is far from adequate in accounting for the observed transplant activity – has been addressed above. This tells us that there is some population from whom organs have been acquired, but does not tell us the identity of that population. For this, positive evidence of organ harvesting from some particular population is required. Below I outline the cumulative evidence that is consistent with Falun Gong practitioners being exploited for their organs. Similar evidence exists for Uyghurs.

Before the CCP's decision to securitize Xinjiang and re-educate Uyghurs, they engaged in a similar eliminationist campaign against Falun Gong. A number of the techniques of 'transformation' being used against Uyghurs were honed over nearly two decades of struggle against Falun Gong. The anti-Falun Gong campaign has been carried out largely extra-legally and circumvented the state and judicial apparatus. It mobilized ad hoc CCP-run security organs to track down believers and subject them to forced ideological conversion, compelling them under pain of torture to renounce their beliefs (Perry 2001; Amnesty International 2015).

Due to the same exclusionary dynamics around organ harvesting, the scale and severity of the overall anti-Falun Gong security campaign is often forgotten. Chinese officials estimated that the Falun Gong population was 70 million by the end of the 1990s (Faison 1999) (the actual number is unclear, though Freedom House estimates the figure to be around 20 million as of 2017 (Cook 2017)). A UN rapporteur in 2006 said that two-thirds of all reported cases of torture were Falun Gong (UN Commission on Human Rights 2006). While official statements about the size of China's national labour camp system would suggest that hundreds of thousands have been imprisoned at any one time, other investigators have referred to Laogai Foundation data, combined with estimates from interviews, and suggested that as many as 1 million have been in custody (Gutmann 2012). As in the Xinjiang case, all such figures are estimates based on a variety of inputs of varying quality, each with a chain of qualifiers attached.

The research on the use of Falun Gong as an organ source includes multiple books and lengthy reports (Matas and Kilgour 2009; Gutmann 2014; Kilgour *et al.* 2017; China Tribunal 2019b). As such, only a brief outline of the key evidence indicative of organ harvesting of Falun Gong practitioners is presented. The primary strands of evidence are as follows. Each of these sets of facts is substantiated by a large base of evidence including, variously, multiple independent eyewitness testimonies, audio recordings, official documents, and more. Many of these documents were examined and are preserved by the UK-based China Tribunal:

(1) Falun Gong detainees report being subjected to unusual blood tests, chest X-rays, and ultrasounds. Refugees report that a bus drives into the labour camp, and only the Falun Gong are called out to be given physical exams and blood tests, without

explanation.[7] In the months that follow, tested prisoners begin disappearing.[8]

(2) There is an extensive catalogue of telephone calls made to Chinese transplant hospitals by investigators outside China posing as potential patients, relatives of patients, and doctors. These investigators have elicited admissions from nurses and doctors that organs are available on demand. In a number of these calls, hospital personnel have stated that the source of the organs is Falun Gong.[9]

(3) China's transplantation sector began its rapid transformation just six months after the campaign against Falun Gong began, at a time when the death row population was going into well-documented decline.

(4) There are many cases of summary cremations of young, healthy detainees who die mysteriously in custody. No information is provided to the family – they simply receive an urn of ashes (Su 2016).

(5) There are documented cases of family seeing the dead with scars indicative of tampering with the body, consistent with organ removal. In one case in Chongqing, the police admitted that the organs were removed immediately after death; local public security officials claimed it was in order to make medical specimens (Ong 2015).

(6) An overlap exists of personnel carrying out the anti-Falun Gong campaign and performing transplants.

The last item – an overlap in personnel engaged in both organ transplantation and anti-Falun Gong work – has been observed in two prominent cases.

The first is the surgeon Dr Zheng Shusen. Dr Zheng is one of China's most well-known liver transplant surgeons and a prominent leader in China's transplantation system, being the chief editor of the leading scientific journal on transplantation, past president of the Chinese Society of Transplantation, vice president of the Chinese Medical Association, and president of Zhejiang Medical University's First Affiliated Hospital. In recent years Dr Zheng co-founded a private hospital with his wife (a leading health official in Zhejiang), which offers organ transplantation as a therapy (Tang 2017). The couple advertise a specialty in short-notice, emergency organ transplants (Hu 2017).

Dr Zheng was also until 2017 the director of the China Anti-Cult Association (CACA) in the province of Zhejiang (Zhejiang University of Water Resources and Electric Power 2010). CACA is a CCP propaganda agency dedicated to the defamation and suppression of Falun Gong. In this role, Dr Zheng has appeared at public events sitting alongside security officials, including secret police, calling for the political struggle against the spiritual practice. In 2009, Dr Zheng wrote in the preface to an anti-Falun Gong book, '"Falun Gong" and similar evil religions are like viruses corroding the organism of humanity, warping the souls of believers, destroying social order, disrupting economic development, and have become a public nuisance to mankind and a cancer on society' (Zhejiang Anti-Cult Association 2009). In 2004, Dr Zheng published a medical paper documenting forty-six instances of 'emergency' liver transplants – that is, where the donor was located within twenty-four to seventy-two hours of the patient's presentation at hospital (Zheng 2005). His position as chief of a provincial anti-Falun Gong agency may offer some explanation as to the source of such organs, given the difficulty of accounting for the rapid sourcing of organs from death row prisoners.

Another official who has served in both capacities – as a career apparatchik in the public security system while moonlighting in the transplant field, rather than the other way around as in Dr Zheng's case – is the disgraced and imprisoned Wang Lijun. Wang was the former police chief of Chongqing and long-time ally of deposed Politburo member Bo Xilai. Wang ran a research project related to organ transplantation when he was Public Security Bureau chief of Jinzhou City, Liaoning Province. Wang's On-Site Psychological Research Centre, a laboratory housed in the same building as the Public Security Bureau, was host to 'thousands' of on-site experiments in organ transplantation, according to the transcript of a 2006 award speech (Dragon Design Foundation 2006). Wang was being given an award by the Guanghua Science and Technology Foundation, a charity that promotes science under the direct leadership of the Communist Youth League, one of the CCP's mass recruitment and mobilization organizations. Photographs on official websites show Wang, dressed in scrubs in his lab, discussing his transplant experiments. Given that there were only thousands of judicial executions annually across the whole of China during these years, Wang's performance of thousands of transplant surgeries in one city and direct involvement in the anti-Falun Gong campaign, suggests that he may also have drawn on non-death row prisoners.

Judgement and epistemology

Reaching an opinion as to the source of the PRC's large supply of human organs requires evaluating competing hypotheses and making a judgement as to which is the most plausible. This process, called abduction, is a common motor of scientific progress and knowledge accumulation. In the present case there are two competing explanations, both involving a national conspiracy of some kind. The first would argue that the death penalty system must have operated at a scale one order of magnitude greater than suggested by extant scholarship, that the underground live donor trafficking industry (involving kidney transplants) has been far more extensive and sophisticated than previously previously thought, and that a vast number of anonymous kidnappings and other opportunistic killings must account for the remainder.

But in this version of events, the PRC's security-medical syndicate would have gone to great lengths to *avoid* utilizing prisoners of conscience in custody. The party's treatment of these populations indicates that there would be no sanctions for their disappearance and death, nor even any means of exercising oversight if they were disappeared by security and medical teams. Refraining from exploiting these vulnerable populations would then have been a moral choice by the security apparatus and medical establishment. It is not possible to disprove this conjecture. But such restraint is not predicted by theoretical expectations as to how power is wielded by state agents and for whose benefit.

The other hypothesis is in my view far more parsimonious: all vulnerable populations have been exploited for their organs, and prisoners of conscience have been exploited for the same reason death row prisoners and innocent citizens have, with the additional proviso that state-led processes of dehumanization, persecution, and the absence of any legal protections have made these populations in fact more vulnerable to such exploitation. This outcome is predicted by the theoretical lens of predatory biopolitics, where the same biopolitical logic that allows the state to reach into the womb, to maintain a system of vast labour expropriation, and to practise settler-colonialist migration, also allows it to directly monetize problem groups via the medical system.

Our knowledge inevitably rests on conclusions arrived at via the exercise of judgement. We judge, in hopefully as rigorous a manner as possible, that some explanation for an outcome is the most plausible; when that explanation becomes socially dominant, we call this judgement 'knowledge'. Due to the nature of the alleged crimes and the attendant secrecy surrounding them, it is not possible in an abstract sense to 'prove' that organ harvesting from prisoners of conscience has taken place on some significant scale. The word 'proof' itself conceals the process of evaluation and judgement that undergirds its meaning. Even with some hypothetical future access to hospital records of transplant operations, coupled with corresponding records of prisoner transfers and confessions from surgeons, we would still need to judge that the records were accurate and the surgeons gave honest witness.

An epistemically hygienic expression of the hypothesis must put the matter in roughly these terms: organ harvesting from prisoners of conscience is the most parsimonious and plausible explanation for (1) the growth of China's transplant system from 2000 onwards; (2) its continued growth from 2007 onwards while the death penalty rate sharply declined; and (3) the unusual medical testing of prisoners of conscience in custody, and range of other positive evidence suggesting the exploitation of these populations. Those who disagree with the allegations must either show errors in the underlying data – in concrete terms, not generalities – or propose a more plausible explanation for that data. Such an explanation must also spell out the theory of state behaviour it is predicated on. Casting doubt on the allegations without doing this work, including by making careless public statements about their epistemic status, conforms to Cohen's definition of denialism.

Current questions about organ sources

The final periodization required to understand China's organ transplantation at present is from 2015 onwards. This date is chosen not for any observable change in practice, but because Chinese authorities announced that on 1 January 2015 they would no longer source organs from death row prisoners. Despite Dr Huang Jiefu, the head of China's transplant system, retreating from the commitment after making it, a further reiteration of the promise was taken as sincere by the international transplantation community. It is currently the official belief of the World Health Organization and The Transplantation Society that China has indeed transitioned to voluntary organ donors only. Dr Huang and his colleagues, erred, however, in their public strategy to substantiate the claims of voluntary donor reform. They appear to have falsified key transplant datasets using a simple mathematical model, and failed to take precautions to prevent the falsification from being discovered. In this section I explain how we can 'know' that the data was falsified, before turning to the relevance of this knowledge for potential organ trafficking from Uyghurs.

Dr Huang presented data of China's alleged reforms at an organ trafficking conference at the Vatican in 2017; it contained data from 2010 to 2016 inclusive, reporting the number of deceased donors, deceased kidney transplants, and deceased liver transplants published by the China Organ Transplant Response System (COTRS). This data, however, conforms almost exactly to a mathematical formula – specifically a quadratic equation. This means that the growth curve is extremely smooth. The finding was reported in the leading medical ethics journal *BMC Medical Ethics* in a study led by the present author and co-authored with a statistician and cardiac transplant surgeon. We then compared China's data to comparable data from fifty countries in the Global Observatory on Donation and Transplantation managed by the World Health Organization and found that China's data was between one and two orders of magnitude smoother than data from every other country, making it a sole, distinct outlier for smoothness of growth. This is an extremely unusual finding, even after controlling for the fact that any rapidly expanding series will exhibit greater 'smoothness', or statistically, a higher R-squared value. There is no reason it should be the case if China's transplant figures were real data formed by the accretion of voluntary deceased organ transplant cases.

The discovery that the COTRS data growth curve was almost exactly a quadratic equation led us to hypothesize that the data was centrally manufactured. To test this hypothesis, we collected and examined Chinese Red Cross data at both the central and provincial levels, to test whether it was internally consistent and consistent with the COTRS. The findings of these analyses substantiated concerns of data falsification, as a wide range of anomalies, inexplicable artefacts, inconsistencies, and apparently forced quotas were found in both central and provincial data. The paper concludes that such anomalies cannot be explained in any other manner than human-directed manipulation, which is consistent with the initial indication.

Following the completion of this initial analysis in April 2018, at the TTS meeting in Madrid in July 2018, the Chinese authorities published the 2017 figure for voluntary deceased donors. This new figure allowed for significant simplification of the original model, so that it could now be explained entirely by a one-parameter quadratic. Given that it is an axiom of statistics and quantitative social science methodology that the more parsimonious a model, the greater its explanatory leverage, this additional finding was significant. The extremely close fit to a general quadratic in the first set of data was already highly problematic for the integrity of China's voluntary donor reform data, but the reduction of that to a far simpler equation gave extremely strong support to the argument that the dataset must have been falsified the entire time. The *BMC Medical Ethics* paper was favourably reviewed by Sir David Spiegelhalter, former president of the Royal Statistical Society, who said that 'the anomalies in the data examined … follow a systematic and surprising pattern', that the fit to quadratic function was 'remarkable', and that 'I cannot think of any good reason for such a quadratic trend arising naturally' (Spiegelhalter 2019).

The paper also documented a number of instances of apparent misclassification of non-voluntary donors as 'voluntary' in medical papers, much lower rates of consent for donation than officials often claim in media reports, and the use of large cash payments to poor rural families to encourage donation. The paper also discussed the intensive secrecy around access to any of the official organ transplant data. The finding of centralized data falsification of purported voluntary donor reforms, and the cessation of organ sourcing from prisoners, is highly significant for evaluating the current status of organ transplantation in China, because it conforms to a pattern. China grew its transplant system precipitously beginning in the year 2000, while claiming that donors were volunteers. As death penalty prisoners declined through the 2000s and in particular after 2007, the system showed no signs of slowing and instead showed rapid expansion. The party-state claimed that death row prisoners were used, yet the number of transplants appears to have dwarfed those that death row prisoners could have supplied. The large body of evidence pointing to prisoners of conscience being exploited for their organs was simply dismissed as political propaganda. Then in 2015, as international pressure continued to grow, Chinese officials announced reforms that would see it rely exclusively on voluntary donors – yet, per the discussion above, we see that this data was simply made up. At present, authorities say they are performing over 20,000 transplants from volunteers annually (Wang 2019). While we are justified in the belief that the data is falsified, we do not know if the figure is an under-report or an over-report. We also do not know how many genuine voluntary donations take place every year.

If we accept the premise that the security-hospital complex colluded to monetize prisoners of conscience before, our theoretical expectation would be that they would do so again. This practice would also comport with other lessons learned from the anti-Falun Gong campaign and applied to the party's policies on Uyghur Muslims (Cook 2019). The final two sections in this chapter discuss the particular vulnerability of Uyghurs to organ harvesting and the evidence that this may be taking place, followed by an attempt to flesh out the overwhelming rationality of predatory biopolitical power in contemporary China.

Uyghur vulnerability to organ harvesting

Since the summer of 2017, Chinese security authorities have embarked on a large-scale campaign of incarceration of primarily Uyghur (though also Kazakh and Kyrgyz) Muslims in the north-western Xinjiang Uyghur Autonomous Region (XUAR).[10] Detainees are held in large facilities where they are subjected to political and religious re-education and 'vocational training' (Human Rights Watch 2017; Shih 2018a). These incarcerations are effected without due process, without the presentation of evidence of any crime, and largely outside the boundaries of Chinese law (Clarke 2018). Estimates of the number of individuals in the centres vary widely but range from hundreds of thousands to nearly two million, with a general consensus of about a million (Shih 2018b). The number of camps is also unknown. Researchers have documented the existence of dozens of camps, but activists have alleged there are far more – upwards of a thousand. The broad range of coercive policies being pursued against Uyghurs in Xinjiang today mirror those used against the Chinese population as a whole when the party was seizing power in China, including regimentation of daily life, struggle sessions, public confessions, displays of loyalty to the party, and incarceration of individuals who constitute perceived threats (including prison sentences of ten-plus years merely for engaging in group worship). There are relatively few reports of deaths of Uyghurs in custody.

Does evidence suggest that Uyghurs and other Muslims subject to coercive state power in Xinjiang or elsewhere in China have been targeted or are vulnerable to being targeted for organ harvesting? I find that while there is less circumstantial evidence to suggest this has taken place than exists surrounding the Falun Gong-related allegations, there are numerous reasons to think such abuses have occurred, continue to occur, or may occur in the future. The evidence supporting this view is as follows.

1. **Widespread, coercive collection of DNA and blood type.** Public security and other authorities in Xinjiang have collected biometric data – including DNA, fingerprints, iris scans, and blood types – of all Xinjiang residents between twelve and sixty-five years of age (Human Rights Watch 2017). Some of this data appears to have been coerced from people, while other collection is done under the aegis of a free physical examination programme – though the participation rates in this ostensibly voluntary programme are so high that researchers suspect coercion (Kuo 2017). The data comes from individual national ID numbers, and the blood type is kept on the IJOP mass surveillance system used to monitor Uyghurs in Xinjiang (Human Rights Watch 2019). Ensuring donor and recipient have compatible blood types is a precondition for successful transplantation, though DNA information can also be used to facilitate donor and recipient matches and ensure better post-transplant outcomes.

    Maya Mitalipova, director of the Human Stem Cell Laboratory at the Whitehead Institute for Biomedical Research at the Massachusetts Institute of Technology, told the China Tribunal that 'scientists have come up with a comprehensive DNA scoring system using many genes to predict long-term success of transplantation' (Mitalipova 2019). This comports with publicly available research (Gautreaux and Freedman 2013; Mesnard *et al.* 2016). While we cannot know if this motivated the collection of DNA data from Uyghurs, improving matching for organ transplantation is one of the purposes to which it could be applied.

2. **Blood tests and physical examinations of individuals consistent with those required for assessing organ health.** Four former Uyghur and Kazakh detainees testified to the China Tribunal that they had blood and urine samples involuntarily taken and were also given ultrasounds. Blood type is a prerequisite for matching for organ transplantation; urine samples may be used for identifying kidney health. These are the same types of targeted examinations that Falun Gong detainees have reported since the early 2000s. Excerpts of their testimonies discussing these tests follow.

Gulbahar Jalilova, a Kazakh businesswoman, stated in her testimony: 'On the night of arrival at the No. 3 prison, I was stripped naked for a medical examination. They took [a] blood sample and urine sample before placing me in a cell. In less than one week, I along with other prisoners with black hoods over our heads were taken to an unknown place, there was medical equipment in the corridor, we were examined and blood samples were taken, and we also had ultrasound tests. We were examined once a week stripped naked. I fainted once when I was in the No. 3 prison, I was taken to the prison hospital where I saw many other prisoners and we all had medical examinations almost daily. In the No. 2 prison, there is a big medical clinic, we were examined regularly [using] blood samples and ultrasound tests. We had injection once every 10 days. On the 27th of August 2018, before I was due to be released, I was taken to a big prison hospital for a check-up' (Jelilova 2019).

Mihrigul Tursun, a Uyghur with family ties in Egypt, stated that she was detained and tortured in April 2017, then detained again in January 2018. She states, 'The authorities handcuffed and placed ankle shackles on me. Also a black hood was placed over my head before I was taken direct[ly] to a hospital. I was stripped naked and put under a big computerised machine. One female and two male officials examined my body while I was still naked and then dressed me in a blue prison uniform' (Tursun 2019).

Omer Bekari, a Uyghur and naturalized Kazakh, stated that he was arrested in March 2017, and released in January 2018. He attested that the following took place soon after his detention: 'I was taken to a medical clinic or a hospital in Pichan, on the 26th of March 2017. I heard the conversation between the medical staff and the police: "There are 2, 3 people in front of you for the urine test, we will let you know when it is your turn to give a sample." They gave me water to drink before taking me to the toilet, insisting that I produce for them a urine sample. About half an hour later, they removed my clothes from above my waist line, [and] the first thing they did was to take blood samples from my arm. Then I was placed on a bed for a full body check, they used ultrasound … applying cold gel, checked my kidneys, then [an] ECG [for my] heart, my lung[s]. I believe they were using ultrasound, as a cold gel was placed on different parts of my body. I was moved from side to side and rolled over from off my back to my chest so that I could be tested back and chest. I believe it is possible that they used different equipment when carrying out their tests' (Bekari 2019). He writes that the physical tests lasted two hours, on that occasion, and were repeated about two weeks later in a hospital, where he was taken to different medical departments for different tests, with a hood over his head the entire time.

Abduweli Ayup, currently a resident of Turkey, says that he was detained in July 2015, during which time he was interrogated via torture in a 'Tiger Chair', after which 'I was taken to a hospital. As I had a hood placed over my head, I don't know which hospital it was. I know they carried out a full body check, X-ray, taking saliva, urine, and blood samples, applying a cold gel before examining different body organs' (Ayup 2019).

3. **Deaths in custody and disappearances.** The total number of deaths of Uyghurs and other victims of the Xinjiang mass detention campaign is unknown. The Xinjiang Victims Database maintained by Eugene Bunin as of early June 2019 identified

sixty-six deaths since 2017, though this is almost certainly incomplete (Shahit.biz n.d.). We were unable to identify instances in which investigations had been launched following these deaths or any officials punished. Given reports of abuses, rape, and torture of detainees (van Brugen 2018; Yeni Şafak 2018; Chao 2019; Imin 2019), it is highly unlikely that wrongful deaths in custody will result in official investigation, oversight, or accountability for those responsible. A climate of impunity is likely to result. No reliable data exists on the number of Uyghurs who have disappeared into the camp system entirely, and we are not aware of any current attempt to systematically track this figure, notwithstanding the difficulties of the exercise. It appears that disappearances are taking place (Ramzy 2019). Ms Tursun, quoted above, says she witnessed nine deaths in her cell of sixty-eight people over three months, and infers from this that the total volume of deaths would likely be far higher across the country (Tursun 2019).

4. **Transfer of detainees by rail around China.** Reports emerged in 2018 that the authorities were secretly transferring up to hundreds of thousands of Uyghurs by rail to prisons and detention facilities in the Chinese interior. These claims are based on first-hand accounts, gathered by overseas Chinese-language media, of guards and others attesting to such transfers (Fang 2018; RFA Staff 2018; Robertson 2018). Related evidence includes large-scale temporary closures of railways in Xinjiang, indicating that rail infrastructure may have been reserved for prisoner transfers during this period. The Victims of Communism Memorial Foundation corroborated these reports, but only via second- and third-hand testimony.[11] Such transfers do not in themselves constitute evidence of additional abuses, though the presence of eligible prisoner donors close to hospitals around China could facilitate coercive organ procurement. New regulations aimed to ensure priority passage for human organs on airlines across China may also facilitate abuses, despite their ostensible purpose being to foster the development of voluntary transplantation in China (CAAC 2016). The appearance of organ transplantation priority lanes at airports in Xinjiang is one development that could be read either way: as evidence of the

development of a voluntary transplantation system (or propaganda meant to create this impression), or as an indication of infrastructure allowing flights of batches of organs from Xinjiang to major cities on the coast (RFA Staff 2017).
5. **The continuation of organ trafficking in China post-2017.** As will be discussed below, substantial evidence suggests illicit organ trafficking has continued in China from 2015 to the present. While we have no data on the scale of this practice at a national level, the available evidence indicates that kidneys and livers were available on short notice – i.e. within weeks, typically – at a number of military hospitals in Beijing as of late 2018. This corroborates the same type of evidence gathered by undercover Korean investigative journalists at the Tianjin First Central Hospital in mid-late 2017 (TV Chosun 2018).
6. **The failure of the official explanation to account for organ transplantation post-2017.** Chinese officials claim that since 2015, voluntary, hospital-based deceased donors have been the only source of organs available for transplant in China. This narrative allows Chinese authorities to explain rapid organ availability at major hospitals by simply asserting that the organs come from the robust and growing voluntary donation apparatus. However, as discussed above, it appears that China's voluntary deceased donation data was falsified at the central level – and thus we do not know what the real transplant figures are. It seems reasonable to infer, however, that the total transplants taking place are *at least* as numerous as those claimed to come from voluntary donors; by 2018 this figure sat at about 18,000 organs from 6,000 donors (Wang 2018).

The above findings must be understood within the context of the entire campaign against Uyghur Muslims in Xinjiang, which appears intended to destroy Uyghurs as a cohesive people. The range of policies under this rubric include mass incarceration and coercive deconversion from Islam, mandatory use of Chinese written and spoken language by children at school, prohibition of the Uyghur language in the public sphere, destruction of mosques, vilification of Uyghur religious beliefs as 'ideological viruses', subsidies and policies encouraging intermarriage between Uyghur women and Han men, incentives for Han settlers to colonize Xinjiang, forced consumption of or injections with unidentified drugs, and more. Biological intrusions and expropriations of Uyghurs – whether forced marriages, mass rape, abortions, sterilizations, or hair and organ harvesting – add yet another dimension to the PRC's 'integration' of the Xinjiang region (Clarke 2011). According to local observers, these policies have effectively changed the face of Xinjiang; their continuation over decades may result in the total effacement of the Uyghur people. Though there are only scattered reports of deaths in custody at present, and no evidence of mass killing, large-scale killing has played an important role in the party's historical campaigns. There are multiple reports of localized massacres of Uyghur villages in Xinjiang by party security forces in years past (Jacobs 2013; RFA Staff 2013, 2014; Beijing 2014).

Given the close resemblance the anti-Uyghur campaign in Xinjiang has to the party's other coercive campaigns through its history – including most recently the anti-Falun Gong campaign, but also the political-ideological mobilization campaigns between the 1940s and 1960s – there are precedents for widespread lethal violence. The global attention this campaign has garnered, and the negative repercussions that open violence would receive, has likely had a moderating effect.

If China is using or has used Uyghurs for organ sourcing, we would expect to find the same evidence we now observe: unusual blood tests or physical exams; transfers of detainees to prisons around China or other means to efficiently transport organs *from* Xinjiang; disappearances of detainees; and continued rapid availability of organs at hospitals. The use of Uyghurs as a source of organs would fulfill multiple needs simultaneously: those who refuse to renounce their beliefs may be disposed of silently and profitably, while civilian and military hospitals with political backing would retain access to fresh organs. The mechanism for using prisoners in this manner is established, and there is an immense demand for organs, which Uyghurs would supply.

It is also possible that while all of the above is strongly suggestive of illicit organ trafficking from Uyghurs, such abuses may not have in fact taken place. As with the evidence on the exploitation of the Falun Gong by organ harvesting, the concept of 'proof' seems elusive – though also inapt. As a technical matter, science does not possess a theory of confirmation (Godfrey-Smith 2009). Knowledge grows via the process of conjecture and refutation; as observations consistent with a theory accumulate, the theory is increasingly supported and adopted as 'true'.

The problem of China's organ transplantation system is one of explanation: organs are evidently coming from somewhere, at some scale, and on demand. As such the organ source must be humans who are being held captive, blood-typed, and ready for execution and procurement (which likely proceed simultaneously). The PRC's attempts at explaining their source of organs turn out, upon inspection, to be false, and so some other population of captives must be relied upon. Aside from other victims, it is clear that Falun Gong and now Uyghurs fit all of the criteria, and there is evidence they are subject to otherwise unusual blood tests and physical examinations. Their bodies are invaded, violated, and treated as state property in numerous other ways. And there is every incentive for the abuse to take place, while there are no constraints or means of stopping it. While we may imagine a variety of truly confirmatory revelations – videos of gruesome surgeries, medical charts of hundreds of thousands of patients, labour camp records showing transfers to hospital authorities, defecting surgeons making detailed admissions – none are feasible without collaboration from insiders, who face obvious risks for themselves and family.

I have concluded that the question of how much evidence one demands before admitting the claim – and as a consequence to begin the next steps of more thoroughly investigating and stopping it – is no longer a question of science but of politics. As this chapter was being prepared, reports emerged of large-scale forced sterilizations and abortions of Uyghur women as well as the harvesting of their hair for resale while in detention. Both phenomena have been carefully documented, involving multiple sources of information independent of one another. There is a bright line separating these acts from organ harvesting, of course, in that the latter involves killing. While similar direct evidence of large-scale organ harvesting from Uyghurs may not yet be at the same level of empirical support, my theoretical account of the CCP's conception of its relationship to the bodies of its citizenry predicts such an outcome.

'De-fetishizing' organ harvesting

For the last fifteen years, claims of extrajudicial killing for organ harvesting have been treated with scepticism in many quarters, in part because it seems so shocking and 'evil'. Both advocates and critics of the hypothesis, each for their own rhetorical purposes, have emphasized the supposedly uniquely depraved aspect of the act. It is my interest here to trouble these assumptions. The use of disposable prison populations as biocapital is not so shocking as to require a fantastic, and effectively impossible at present, standard of proof before it can be thought to be true. I argue that the allegations of organ harvesting should not be thought of as shocking; that while the case might first appear under-determined, it is actually over-determined.

Gary King once quipped, 'You can't throw away all your data and do an analysis – that's called theory' (King 2017). Yet on the question of organ harvesting, it seems that all of the data amassed to date has lacked a robust theoretical account. Theory determines what evidence we look for, what we expect to find, and what we think the evidence we do find means. Convincing theories can have a revolutionary quality, as Barbara Geddes notes in the case of the collective action problem, 'probably the best-known example of a model that simply changed the way we understand the world' (Geddes 2003: 33). Before it was articulated, social scientists were puzzled as to why members of groups did not organize politically. The result of Mancur Olson expressing the collective problem in 1965 inverted expectations of political mobilization: 'We now find it puzzling, and hence worthy of explanation, when large groups do manage to organize in order to press for some public good' (Geddes 2003: 33).

If theory is what the case lacks, then let us theorize. I wish to 'de-fitishize' organ harvesting by showing that the exploitative biopolitical logic that sustains it can be uncovered with reference to Marxian critique – an irony of the case, given that the perpetrators are themselves Communists. Marx's de-fetishizing critique was aimed to show that the supposedly natural character of the commodity form conceals the labour embedded in it. As a later gloss from a popular source put it, rather than the value of, say, a coat being inherent in the coat itself, 'the coat's price comes from its history, the history of all the people involved in making it and selling it and all the particular relationships they had' (Shawn 1997). The fetishism of commodities hides this background.

The confluence of forces that combine to facilitate organ harvesting can also be disaggregated into a series of particular relationships.

At the centre of them is the reform-era hospital system, which was underfunded by the state and thus turned to a fee-for-service, profit-oriented model (Jie 1997; Hsiao 2007; Wang 2014). Hospitals, in general, are incentivized to increase transplants, and surgeons personally and directly profit from each transplant they perform. The medical field in the PRC has been de-professionalized due to political controls exercised by the CCP (Ouyang 2011), and has previously been instrumentalized to perform a range of political tasks that violate the Hippocratic oath, including implementing forced abortions and sterilizations and the pyshiatric confinement of dissidents. Some of the leading transplant surgeons are embedded in the CCP system and hold party rank and titles alongside their entrepreneurial medical roles. They have formed a close compact with both the party-state, which furnishes their livelihood, and the security state, which furnishes the bodies. PRC population management policies in general adopt an instrumental logic towards citizen bodies, whether by expropriation of the migrant labour force (Lim 2017: 258; Zhang 2018), settler colonialism and forced intermarriages (Anand 2019; Tobin 2020: 208), or underground biocapital markets (Anagnost 2006). The state adopts a more extreme relationship to problematic sub-populations, including criminals and political dissidents. Falun Gong practitioners are entirely exempt from the protection of the law (Clarke 2020b: 50), while similar dynamics likely pertain to Uyghurs now; there are no known instances of deaths in custody or disappearances of members of these groups resulting in investigations and punishments. The combination of these factors is a demand for organs able to be met with ready supply. While the voluntary reforms post-2015 complicate this picture, the secrecy and deception surrounding those reforms is highly suggestive of ongoing abuses.

While it is the apparently natural character of the commodity form that obscures the forces that created it, it seems that it is the *unnatural* character of organ harvesting that conceals *its* cold rationality. In Marx's de-fetishizing critique, capital conceals the nature of commodities; in organ harvesting, the state turns its subjects *into* commodities. Because the relation it exposes between the state and the individual is so radical, we have failed to see its logic. If a chief aim of theory is to reduce surprise, this account of the CCP's predatory biopolitics suggests we should be unsurprised by the instrumentalization of PRC political subjects – whether as a slave labour force, or as raw biological products such as hair, plasma, marrow, fetuses, organs, or indeed entire cadavers.

Notes

1 This period could also be helpfully thought of in two parts: the ramp-up from 2000 to about 2007, and the consolidation from 2007 onwards.
2 In a late 2018 interview, a former advertising executive at Baidu informed me that in the early 2000s Baidu was the major contractor with the Chinese government for crawling overseas websites, including pornography sites, 'reactionary' sites, and Falun Gong sites, in order to build a database of banned terms and websites used as part of the party's broader Internet censorship efforts – what eventually became known as the Great Firewall of China.
3 I thank the Jamestown Foundation and the Victims of Communism Memorial Foundation for giving permission to incorporate studies originally published with them in this section.
4 Given the difficulties of reliable official data, it should be noted that the three officials who made this claim were, respectively (per references), Huang Jiefu, former vice minister of health, vice chair of the Health Care Committee of the Chinese Communist Party, and chairman of the China National Organ Donation and Transplantation Committee; Zhuang Yiqiang, deputy general secretary of the Chinese Organ Transplantation Development Foundation; and Chen Zhonghua, director of the Organ Transplant Research Institute at Tongji Hospital in Wuhan, Hebei, and (whether current or former is unclear) vice president of the Chinese Organ Transplantation Society (CUHK 2007).
5 The claim that only 100 hospitals performed transplants in the US in 2006 is difficult to verify in part because the structure of the US Organ Procurement Organization-based organ donation system differs so significantly from China's hospital-based system. In any case, the appearance of the comparison can be read to show that Chinese officials find it a matter of pride to have exceeded US transplant capacity in at least this one manner.
6 Of course, the fact that Huang Jiefu said there were 500 hospitals capable of performing liver transplants does not mean that the number was 500.
7 Interview of Falun Gong practitioner Yin Liping conducted by Matthew P. Robertson in Boston, June 2016.
8 Ethan Gutmann makes extensive documentation of such cases in Gutmann (2014). See also interview of asylee Yu Xinhui: World Focus (2013).

9 See chapter 7 of Matas and Kilgour (2009); an extensive library of calls is also held by the World Organization to Investigate the Persecution of Falun Gong (WOIPFG) on its website. My examination of these recordings and the process by which they were created is available in Robertson (2020c).
10 This section was largely drawn from Robertson (2020a), with thanks to the Victims of Communism Memorial Foundation.
11 A film director was told in 2018 by contacts in the security services in Xinjiang that such transfers had taken place, but they provided no information about their scale. A recently arrived Falun Gong activist stated that he had been in contact with multiple families of detained Falun Gong practitioners in Heilongjiang, who had been told by their detained relatives that the Tailai Prison in Qiqihar had a recent (as of September 2018) influx of thousands of detainees. These accounts match the timeline of the RFA reports (including the prison in question) and offer a form of corroboration from both ends of the transfer process.

References

309 Military Hospital (2010). '器官移植中心简介 – 解放军总参谋部总医院(解放军第309医院)' [Introduction to Organ Transplantation Centre – 309th Hospital of the People's Liberation Army], People's Liberation Army No. 309 Hospital, https://web.archive.org/web/20140417235354/http://www.309yy.com/_Dept/View.aspx?id=3323 (accessed 28 November 2018).

ABC News (2019). 'China "Harvesting Organs from Falun Gong Prisoners"', 17 June, www.abc.net.au/news/2019-06-18/china-harvesting-organs-from-falun-gong-prisoners,-tribunal-says/11219144 (accessed 17 July 2020).

Amnesty International (2015). 'No End in Sight: Torture and Forced Confessions in China', www.amnesty.org/download/Documents/ASA172730 2015ENGLISH.PDF (accessed 1 December 2019).

Anagnost, Ann S. (2006). 'Strange Circulations: The Blood Economy in Rural China', *Economy and Society* 35 (4), 509–529.

Anand, Dibyesh (2019). 'Colonization with Chinese Characteristics: Politics of (In)security in Xinjiang and Tibet', *Central Asian Survey* 38 (1), 129–147.

Ayup, Abduweli (2019). 'Submission for the Independent Tribunal into Forced Organ Harvesting in China', https://chinatribunal.com/wp-content/uploads/2019/04/AbduweliAyup_PD.pdf (accessed 16 July 2021).

Barnwell, Robin, and Gesbeen Mohammad (2020). China Undercover, Frontline, www.pbs.org/wgbh/frontline/film/china-undercover/ (accessed 10 April 2020).

BBC News (2011). 'Chinese Teen "Sells Kidney for iPad"', 3 June, www.bbc.com/news/av/world-asia-pacific-13647438/chinese-teenager-sells-kidney-to-buy-ipad-and-iphone (accessed 14 June 2019).

BBC Newsnight (2020). 'What Is Happening to the Uighurs? Exiled Uighurs Push for "Genocide" Investigation', YouTube, www.youtube.com/watch?v=lZejLYkCZ3c (accessed 17 July 2020).

Beijing, Emily Rauhala (2014). 'China Now Says Almost 100 Were Killed in Xinjiang Violence', *Time*, 4 August, https://time.com/3078381/china-xinjiang-violence-shache-yarkand/ (accessed 20 August 2019).

Beijing Youth Daily (2015). '中国使用死囚器官做移植将成历史' [China's Use of Death Row Prisoners for Transplants Will Become a Thing of the Past], https://web.archive.org/web/20180425212750/http://www.byb.cn/doc_9111.aspx (accessed 25 April 2018).

Bekari, Omer (2019). 'Submission by Omer Bekari for the Independent Tribunal into Forced Organ Harvesting in China', https://chinatribunal.com/wp-content/uploads/2019/04/OmerBekari_PD.pdf (accessed 16 July 2021).

Bob, Clifford (2011). *The International Struggle for New Human Rights* (Philadelphia: University of Pennsylvania Press).

CAAC (2016). '关于建立人体捐献器官转运绿色通道的通知' [Notice on Establishing a Green Channel for Human Donor Transplantation], www.caac.gov.cn/XXGK/XXGK/ZCFB/201605/t20160513_37343.html (accessed 27 December 2019).

Carroll, Lewis (1895). 'What the Tortoise Said to Achilles', *Mind: A Quarterly Review of Psychology and Philosophy* 4 (14), 278–280.

CBRN (2016). '天津市第一中心医院改造项目' [Tianjin First Central Hospital Reconstruction Project], https://archive.is/yAz3W (accessed 21 August 2020).

Chao, Steve (2019). 'Exposed: China's Surveillance of Muslim Uighurs', Al Jazeera, 1 February, www.aljazeera.com/features/2019/2/1/exposed-chinas-surveillance-of-muslim-uighurs (accessed 1 June 2019).

Chase, Michael S., and James C. Mulvenon (2002). *You've Got Dissent! Chinese Dissident Use of the Internet and Beijing's Counter-strategies* (Washington, DC: Rand Corporation).

Chen, Xiaoping (ed.) (2013). 器官移植临床指南 第三版 [Clinical Guidelines for Organ Transplantation, 3rd ed.] (科学出版社 [Beijing: Science Press]).

China Liver Transplant Registry (2006). *中国肝移植注册 2005 年度分析报告* [China Liver Transplant Registry 2005 Annual Analysis Report], 12 February (Hong Kong: Hong Kong University; Zhejiang University First Affiliated Hospital).

China Liver Transplant Registry (2007). *中国肝移植注册 2006 年度报告* [China Liver Transplant Registry 2006 Annual Report] (Hong Kong: Hong Kong University; Zhejiang University First Affiliated Hospital).

China Tribunal (2019a). 'Independent Tribunal into Forced Organ Harvesting from Prisoners of Conscience in China)', https://chinatribunal.com/wp-content/uploads/2019/07/ChinaTribunal_-SummaryJudgment_17June2019.pdf (accessed 16 July 2021).

China Tribunal (2019b). 'Final Judgement Report', https://chinatribunal.com/final-judgement-report/ (accessed 9 December 2020).

Clarke, Donald (2018). 'No, New Xinjiang Legislation Does Not Legalize Detention Centers', Lawfare, www.lawfareblog.com/no-new-xinjiang-legislation-does-not-legalize-detention-centers (accessed 28 December 2019).

Clarke, Donald (2020a). 'Organ Procurement and Extrajudicial Execution in China: A Review of the Evidence', The China Collection, https://thechinacollection.org/organ-procurement-extrajudicial-execution-china-review-evidence/ (accessed 5 September 2020).

Clarke, Donald (2020b). 'Order and Law in China', GWU Legal Studies Research Paper No. 2020-52, http://ssrn.com/abstract=3682794.

Clarke, Michael E. (2011). *Xinjiang and China's Rise in Central Asia: A History* (New York: Taylor & Francis).

CNN (2009). 'China Hopes Organ Donor System Stops Trafficking', 26 August, https://archive.is/SA46A (accessed 25 April 2018).

Cohen, Stanley (2013). *States of Denial: Knowing about Atrocities and Suffering* (Oxford: John Wiley & Sons).

Cook, Sarah (2017). 'The Battle for China's Spirit: Falun Gong', Freedom House, https://freedomhouse.org/report/china-religious-freedom/falun-gong (accessed 2 August 2019).

Cook, Sarah (2019). 'The Learning Curve: How Communist Party Officials Are Applying Lessons from Prior "Transformation" Campaigns to Repression in Xinjiang', *China Brief* 19 (3), https://bit.ly/3AU7FXu (accessed 18 July 2020).

Cook, Sarah, and Leeshai Lemish (2011). 'The 610 Office: Policing the Chinese Spirit', *China Brief* 11 (17), https://jamestown.org/program/the-610-office-policing-the-chinese-spirit/ (accessed 16 July 2021).

Cooper, Melinda (2011a). 'Experimental Republic: Medical Accidents (Productive and Unproductive) in Postsocialist China', *East Asian Science, Technology and Society: An International Journal* 5 (3), 313–327.

Cooper, Melinda (2011b). *Life as Surplus: Biotechnology and Capitalism in the Neoliberal Era* (Seattle: University of Washington Press).

CUHK (2007). 'Current Situation of Organ Donation and Transplantation in China: Presentation by Chen Zhonghua', http://web.archive.org/web/20130123145613/http://www.cityu.edu.hk:80/garc/ARC/ARCfile/SSS/SSS06122007.htm (accessed 10 November 2019).

Dan, Yuxiao (2016). 死刑改革十年录 [Ten Years of Death Penalty Reform], Caixin, https://web.archive.org/web/20170219034238/http://china.caixin.com/2016-12-18/101028169.html (accessed 25 April 2018).

Denyer, Simon (2017). 'China Used to Harvest Organs from Prisoners: Under Pressure, That Practice Is Finally Ending', *Washington Post*, 14 September, https://wapo.st/3wzAoxg (accessed 4 June 2019).

Dillon, Michael, and Andrew W. Neal (2015). *Foucault on Politics, Security and War* (London: Palgrave Macmillan).

Dragon Design Foundation (2006). '现场心理研究中心主任王立军教授在"光华创新特别贡献奖"颁奖典礼上谈话' [Onsite Psychological Research Centre Director Professor Wang Lijun's Speech at the Guanghua Science and Technology Foundation's 'Special Contribution to Innovation' Award Ceremony], 光华龙腾奖 [Soaring Dragon Award], www.ddfchina.org/index.php/Index/content/id/108; www.webcitation.org/65TrM7zHq; http://archive.is/eFUJs; https://web.archive.org/web/20120310013223/http://www.ddfchina.org/index.php/Index/content/id/108 (accessed 28 November 2018).

Editorial Board (2006). '昔日拼搏进取今日重建辉煌' [The Hard Work of the Past Builds Glory for Today], *Chinese Journal of Integrated Traditional and Western Medicine in Intensive and Critical Care*, https://bit.ly/3hxsLmx (accessed 16 July 2021).

EFF (2016). 'EFF to Court: Cisco Must Be Held Accountable for Aiding China's Human Rights Abuses', www.eff.org/press/releases/eff-court-cisco-must-be-held-accountable-aiding-chinas-human-rights-abuses (accessed 18 July 2020).

Faison, Seth (1999). 'In Beijing: A Roar of Silent Protesters', *New York Times*, 27 April, www.nytimes.com/1999/04/27/world/in-beijing-a-roar-of-silent-protesters.html (accessed 28 November 2018).

Fang, Frank (2018). 'Rail Cancellations in Xinjiang Province Boost Concerns about Fate of Imprisoned Uyghurs', *The Epoch Times*, 1 October, https://bit.ly/3k8DCVS (accessed 3 June 2019).

Foucault, Michel (1978). *The History of Sexuality, vol. 1: An Introduction*, trans. Robert Hurley (New York: Pantheon Books).

Foucault, Michel (2003). *'Society Must Be Defended': Lectures at the Collège de France, 1975–1976* (London: Allen Lane).

Foucault, Michel (2012). *Discipline and Punish: The Birth of the Prison* (New York: Vintage Books).

Frankfurt, Harry G. (2005). *On Bullshit* (Princeton: Princeton University Press).

Fraser, Rachel (2020). 'The Will in Belief', *Preprint Manuscript*.

Fricker, Miranda (2007). *Epistemic Injustice: Power and the Ethics of Knowing* (Oxford: Clarendon Press).

Gautreaux, Michael D., and Barry I. Freedman (2013). 'Genotypic Variation and Outcomes in Kidney Transplantation: Donor and Recipient Effects', *Kidney International* 84, 431–433.

Geddes, Barbara (2003). *Paradigms and Sand Castles: Theory Building and Research Design in Comparative Politics* (Ann Arbor: University of Michigan Press).

Godfrey-Smith, Peter (2009). *Theory and Reality: An Introduction to the Philosophy of Science* (Chicago: University of Chicago Press).

Greenhalgh, Susan (2009). 'The Chinese Biopolitical: Facing the Twenty-First Century', *New Genetics and Society* 28 (3), 205–222.

Greenhalgh, Susan, and Edwin A. Winckler (2005). *Governing China's Population: From Leninist to Neoliberal Biopolitics* (Stanford: Stanford University Press).

Guo, Na (2006). '器官移植立法之难' [The Difficulty of Establishing Organ Transplant Legislation], 17 April, 三联生活周刊 [Sanlian Lifeweek Magazine], 45–47.

Gutmann, Ethan (2012). 'How Many Harvested? A Survey-Based Estimate of Falun Gong Murdered from 2000 to 2008', in David Matas and Torsten Trey (eds), *State Organs: Transplant Abuse in China* (Woodstock, ON: Seraphim Editions), 49–67.

Gutmann, Ethan (2014). *The Slaughter: Mass Killings, Organ Harvesting, and China's Secret Solution to Its Dissident Problem* (New York: Prometheus Books).

Han, Byung-Chul (2018). *Topology of Violence*, trans. Amanda Demarco (Cambridge, MA: The MIT Press).

Heidegger, Martin (1977). *The Question Concerning Technology, and Other Essays* (New York: Garland Pub.).

Heinrich, Ari Larissa (2018). *Chinese Surplus: Biopolitical Aesthetics and the Medically Commodified Body* (Durham, NC: Duke University Press).

Holmstrom, Nancy, and Richard Smith (2000). 'The Necessity of Gangster Capitalism: Primitive Accumulation in Russia and China', *Monthly Review* 51 (9), 1–15.

Horkheimer, Max, and Theodor W. Adorno (2002). *Dialectic of Enlightenment: Philosophical Fragments*, ed. Gunzelin Schmid Noerr, trans. Edmund Jephcott (Stanford: Stanford University Press).

Hsiao, William C. (2007). 'The Political Economy of Chinese Health Reform', *Health Economics, Policy, and Law* 2 (3), 241–249.

Hu, Fengsheng (2017). '郑树森当选法国国家医学科学院外籍院士' [Shusen Zheng Elected Foreign Academician of the French National Academy of Medical Sciences], Sina, https://news.sina.cn/2017-12-20/detail-ifypx msq8629756.d.html?wm=3049_0015 (accessed 21 August 2020).

Huang, Jiefu, J. Michael Millis, Yilei Mao et al. (2012). 'A Pilot Programme of Organ Donation after Cardiac Death in China', *The Lancet* 379 (9818), 862–865.

Human Rights Watch (1994). *China: Organ Procurement and Judicial Execution in China*, ed. Robin Munro (New York: Human Rights Watch Asia).

Human Rights Watch (2017). 'China: Minority Region Collects DNA from Millions', www.hrw.org/news/2017/12/13/china-minority-region-collects-dna-millions (accessed 11 June 2019).

Human Rights Watch (2019). 'China's Algorithms of Repression: Reverse Engineering a Xinjiang Police Mass Surveillance App', www.hrw.org/report/2019/05/01/chinas-algorithms-repression/reverse-engineering-xinjiang-police-mass-surveillance (accessed 11 June 2019).

Imin, Tahir (2019). 'Tahir Imin on Twitter', Twitter, https://twitter.com/Uighurian/status/1126494151355375618 (accessed 8 July 2019).

Jacobs, Andrew (2013). 'Over News of Clash, a Shroud of Silence in Xinjiang', *New York Times*, 27 August, www.nytimes.com/2013/08/27/world/asia/over-news-of-clash-a-shroud-of-silence-in-xinjiang.html (accessed 20 August 2019).

Jelilova, Gulbahar (2019). 'Statement of Gulbahar Jelilova for the China Tribunal', https://chinatribunal.com/wp-content/uploads/2019/04/April_Statement-of-Gulbahar.pdf (accessed 16 July 2021).

Jie, Chen (1997). 'The Impact of Health Sector Reform on County Hospitals', *IDS Bulletin* 28 (1), https://bulletin.ids.ac.uk/index.php/idsbo/article/view/2743 (accessed 23 September 2020).

Johnson, David T., and Franklin E. Zimring (2009). 'The Political Origins of China's Death Penalty Exceptionalism', in *The Next Frontier: National Development, Political Change, and the Death Penalty in Asia* (New York: Oxford University Press), 225–286.

Junker, Andrew (2019). *Becoming Activists in Global China: Social Movements in the Chinese Diaspora* (Cambridge: Cambridge University Press).

Kilgour, David, Ethan Gutmann, and David Matas (2017). 'Bloody Harvest/The Slaughter: An Update', 30 April, https://endtransplantabuse.org/an-update/ (accessed 16 July 2021).

King, Gary (2017). 'SICSS 2017 – Guest Lecture by Gary King (Day 2)', presented at the Summer Institute in Computational Social Science, Summer Institute in Computational Social Science, YouTube, www.youtube.com/watch?v=z8h-1av6Emg&t=2161s (accessed 21 August 2020).

Kirchgaessner, Stephanie (2017). 'China May Still Be Using Executed Prisoners' Organs, Official Admits', *The Guardian*, 7 February, www.theguardian.com/world/2017/feb/07/china-still-using-executed-prisoners-organs-transplants-vatican (accessed 14 July 2020).

Kojève, Alexander (2001). 'Colonialism from a European Perspective', *Interpretation* 29 (1), 115–130.

Kuo, Mercy A. (2017). 'Uyghur Biodata Collection in China', *The Diplomat*, 28 December, https://thediplomat.com/2017/12/uyghur-biodata-collection-in-china/ (accessed 11 June 2019).

Kuran, Timur, and Cass R. Sunstein (1998). 'Availability Cascades and Risk Regulation', *Stanford Law Review*, 51 (683).

Lemke, Thomas (2010). 'From State Biology to the Government of Life: Historical Dimensions and Contemporary Perspectives of "Biopolitics"', *Journal of Classical Sociology* 10 (4), 421–438.

Li, Xing (2006). '卫生部驳斥中国随意取死刑犯器官移植的言论' [The Ministry of Health Refutes Claim That China Willfully Transplants Organs from Executed Prisoners], Xinhua News Agency, https://web.archive.org/web/20060416051123/http://news.xinhuanet.com/newscenter/2006-04/10/content_4405862.htm (accessed 21 July 2020).

Liang, Bin, and Hong Lu (eds) (2015). *The Death Penalty in China: Policy, Practice, and Reform* (New York: Columbia University Press).

Lim, Kean Fan (2017). 'Variegated Neoliberalization as a Function and Outcome of Neo-authoritarianism in China', in Cemal Burak Tansel (ed.), *States of Discipline: Authoritarian Neoliberalism and the Contested Reproduction of Capitalist Order* (London: Rowman & Littlefield International), 255–274.

Liu, Huan (2020). '黄洁夫：我国将成世界第一器官移植大国，但有大量器官浪费' [Huang Jiefu: China Will Become the World's Largest Organ Transplant Country, But There's Still a Lot of Organ Waste], *Beijing Daily*, November 20, www.sohu.com/a/433179399_139908 (accessed 7 January 2020).

MacIntyre, Alisdair (1977). 'Epistemological Crises, Dramatic Narrative and the Philosophy of Science', *The Monist* 60 (4), 453–472.

Marx, Karl (1867). 'Economic Manuscripts: Capital Vol. I – Chapter Ten', Marxists.org, www.marxists.org/archive/marx/works/1867-c1/ch10.htm#4a (accessed 10 July 2020).

Matas, David, and David Kilgour (2009). *Bloody Harvest: The Killing of Falun Gong for Their Organs* (Woodstock, ON: Seraphim Editions).

Mesnard, Laurent, Thangamani Muthukumar, Maren Burbach et al. (2016). 'Exome Sequencing and Prediction of Long-Term Kidney Allograft Function', *PLoS Computational Biology* 12 (9), https://doi.org/10.1371/journal.pcbi.1005088.

Mitalipova, Maya (2019). 'Submission of Maya Mitalipova to the China Tribunal', https://chinatribunal.com/wp-content/uploads/2019/06/April_Submission_Maya-Mitalipova.pdf (accessed 16 July 2021).

MOH (2006). '体器官移植技术临床应用管理暂行规定' [Interim Provisions on Administration of Clinical Application of Human Organ Transplantation

Technology], www.moh.gov.cn/mohyzs/s3585/200804/18344.shtml (accessed 1 October 2017).

Müller, Armin (2019). 'Public Services and Informal Profits: Governing Township Health Centres in a Context of Misfit Regulatory Institutions', *The China Quarterly* 237, 108–130.

NHFPC (2018). '178所器官移植医疗机构名单' [List of 178 Medical Institutions for Organ Transplantation], https://web.archive.org/web/20181216133407/http://www.nhfpc.gov.cn:80/zhuz/yzjg/201705/4a3bb274fff6489a91f2a17df3438e54.shtml (accessed 21 July 2020).

Ong, Larry (2015). 'Seeking Justice in a Lawless China', *The Epoch Times*, 6 November, www.theepochtimes.com/mkt_la/seeking-justice-in-a-lawless-china_1891080.html (accessed 28 November 2018).

Ouyang, Wei (2011). 'Governing the Chinese Medical Profession: A Socio-legal Analysis' (PhD diss., University of Edinburgh).

Pan, Jennifer (2020). *Welfare for Autocrats: How Social Assistance in China Cares for Its Rulers* (New York: Oxford University Press).

PAP (2006). '沈中阳' [Shen Zhongyang], https://web.archive.org/web/20060911004348/http://www.wj-hospital.com/expert/wk/gyzzx/173.htm (accessed 21 August 2020).

Perry, Elizabeth J. (2001). 'Challenging the Mandate of Heaven: Popular Protest in Modern China', *Critical Asian Studies* 33 (2), 163–180.

Pils, Eva (2006). 'Asking the Tiger for His Skin: Rights Activism in China', *Fordham International Law Journal* 30 (4), 1209–1287.

Prakash, Aseem, and Mary Kay Gugerty (2010). *Advocacy Organizations and Collective Action* (Cambridge: Cambridge University Press).

Qu, Lulin (2014). '天津市第一中心医院' [Tianjin First Central Hospital], Enorth News, https://archive.is/H1D8F (accessed 1 May 2019).

Ramzy, Austin (2019). '"Show Me That My Father Is Alive": China Faces Torrent of Online Pleas', *New York Times*, 17 February, www.nytimes.com/2019/02/17/world/asia/uighurs-china-internment-camps.html (accessed 11 June 2019).

Renji Hospital (2016). '肝脏外科' [Department of Liver Surgery], www.transplantation.sh.cn/about2.asp?id=1&cid=12; https://web.archive.org/web/20190531012505/http://www.transplantation.sh.cn/about2.asp?id=1&cid=12 (accessed 30 May 2019).

RFA Staff (2013). 'Eleven Killed in Raid on Police Station in Xinjiang', Radio Free Asia, www.rfa.org/english/news/uyghur/shooting-11162013194621.html (accessed 20 August 2019).

RFA Staff (2014). 'Xinjiang Police Open Fire at Protest against Clampdown on Islamic Dress', Radio Free Asia, www.rfa.org/english/news/uyghur/dress-05202014202002.html (accessed 20 August 2019).

RFA Staff (2017). '南航空运活体器官逾500宗 器官来源再受关注' [Renewed Attention over China Southern Airlines Transportation of over 500 Organs], Radio Free Asia, www.rfa.org/cantonese/news/organ-10062017075527.html (accessed 27 December 2019).

RFA Staff (2018). 'Xinjiang Authorities Secretly Transferring Uyghur Detainees to Jails throughout China', Radio Free Asia, www.rfa.org/english/news/uyghur/transfer-10022018171100.html (accessed 11 June 2019).

Rhodes, Aaron (2018). *The Debasement of Human Rights: How Politics Sabotage the Ideal of Freedom* (New York: Encounter Books).

Robertson, Holly (2018). 'Hidden from View: Is China Transferring Uighur Detainees to Far-Flung Prisons?', ABC News, 10 October, www.abc.net.au/news/2018-10-10/is-china-transferring-uighur-detainees-to-far-flung-prisons/10356406 (accessed 11 June 2019).

Robertson, Matthew P. (2020a). 'Organ Procurement and Extrajudicial Execution in China: A Review of the Evidence', Victims of Communism Memorial Foundation, 10 March, www.victimsofcommunism.org/china-organ-procurement-report-2020 (accessed 19 April 2020).

Robertson, Matthew P. (2020b). 'Appendix 4: Data Supplement from VOC Organ Procurement Report Appendices', *Organ Procurement and Extrajudicial Execution in China: A Review of the Evidence*, https://doi.org/10.6084/m9.figshare.11941017.v4.

Robertson, Matthew P. (2020c). 'Authentication and Analysis of Purported Undercover Telephone Calls Made to Hospitals in China on the Topic of Organ Trafficking', VOC China Studies Working Paper 1/2020, https://papers.ssrn.com/abstract=3536155 (accessed 25 February 2020).

Shahit.biz (n.d.). 'Database of Xinjiang Victims', https://shahit.biz/eng/#stats (accessed 1 June 2019).

Shawn, Wallace (1997). 'The Fever', in Wallace Shawn (ed.), *Wallace Shawn Plays 1* (London: Faber and Faber), 162–202.

Shih, Gerry (2018a). 'China's Mass Indoctrination Camps Evoke Cultural Revolution', Associated Press, https://apnews.com/6e151296fb194f85ba69a8babd972e4b (accessed 28 November 2018).

Shih, Gerry (2018b). '"Thank the Party!" Inside China's Muslim Brainwashing Camps', *The Sydney Morning Herald*, 18 May, www.smh.com.au/world/asia/thank-the-party-inside-china-s-muslim-brainwashing-camps-20180517-p4zftn.html (accessed 2 June 2018).

Smith, Craig S. (2001). 'Doctor Says He Took Transplant Organs from Executed Chinese Prisoners', *New York Times*, 29 June, www.nytimes.com/2001/06/29/world/doctor-says-he-took-transplant-organs-from-executed-chinese-prisoners.html (accessed 17 February 2018).

Smith, Tobias (2020). 'Body Count Politics: Quantification, Secrecy, and Capital Punishment in China', *Law & Social Inquiry* 45 (3), 706–727.

Spiegelhalter, David (2019). 'Commentary on "Analysis of Official Deceased Organ Donation Data Casts Doubt on Credibility of China's Organ Transplant Reform" by Matthew P. Robertson, Raymond L. Hinde and Jacob Lavee', submission to the China Tribunal, 19 March, https://chinatribunal.com/wp-content/uploads/2019/06/Commentary-on-Robertson-et-al-Spiegelhalter.pdf (accessed 16 July 2021).

State Council (2007). '人体器官移植条例' [The Regulation on Human Organ Transplantation], www.gov.cn/zwgk/2007-04/06/content_574120.htm (accessed 26 March 2018).

Su, Ling (2010). '器官捐献迷宫' [The Labyrinth of Organ Donation], *南方周末* [Southern Weekend], 25 March, 第A04版.

Su, Yizhou (2016). '中共强行火化冤死者遗体的目的是什么？' [What Is the Communist Party's Goal in Cremating Those Who Have Died Unjustly?], Minghui.org, www.minghui.org/mh/articles/2016/11/25/338146.html (accessed 28 November 2018).

Tang, Mengxia (2017). '与时间赛跑！树兰医院20小时完成8台器官移植手术' [A Race against Time! Shulan Hospital Completes Eight Organ Transplants in Twenty Hours], Zhejiang News, https://zj.zjol.com.cn/news.html?id=638760 (accessed 7 July 2020).

Tatlow, Didi Kirsten (2019). 'Submission to the China Tribunal', https://chinatribunal.com/wp-content/uploads/2019/06/DidiKirstenTatlow_Submission.pdf (accessed 16 July 2021).

Third Affiliated Hospital of Sun Yat-sen University (2015). '肝脏外科-中心介绍' [Liver Surgery – Centre Introduction], www.zssy.com.cn/Home/Detail/GanZangWaiKe?colType=10&colID=10145&pageIndex=1; http://archive.is/1lwit (accessed 1 July 2020).

Tobin, David (2020). *Securing China's Northwest Frontier: Identity and Insecurity in Xinjiang* (Cambridge: Cambridge University Press).

Tursun, Mihrigul (2019). 'Statement of Mihrigul Tursun for the China Tribunal', https://chinatribunal.com/wp-content/uploads/2019/04/April_Statement-of-Mihrigul-Tursun.pdf (accessed 16 July 2021).

TV Chosun (2018). 'The Dark Side of Transplant Tourism in China: Killing to Live' (South Korea: Shin, Duho; Kim, Hyeoncheol), https://vimeo.com/280284321 (accessed 27 November 2018).

UN Commission on Human Rights (2006). 'Report on Torture and Other Cruel, Inhuman or Degrading Treatment or Punishment: Mission to China', 10 March, www.refworld.org/docid/45377b160.html (accessed 19 July 2020).

Unger, Jonathan (2007). 'The Cultural Revolution at the Grass Roots', *The China Journal* 57, http://psc.bellschool.anu.edu.au/sites/default/files/IPS/PSC/CCC/publications/papers/JU_Cultural_Revolution.pdf (accessed 16 July 2021).

van Brugen, Isabel (2018). 'Former Uyghur Inmates Tell of Torture and Rape in China's "Re-Education" Camps', *The Epoch Times*, 15 October, www.theepochtimes.com/former-uyghur-inmates-tell-of-torture-and-rape-in-chinas-re-education-camps_2689053.html (accessed 1 June 2019).

van der Made, Jan (2019). 'Were Human Organs Stolen in 20-Year Conflict between Beijing and Falun Gong?', RFI, http://en.rfi.fr/asia-pacific/20190418-were-human-organs-stolen-20-year-conflict-between-beijing-and-falun-gong (accessed 21 August 2019).

Walker, Kathy Le Mons (2006). '"Gangster Capitalism" and Peasant Protest in China: The Last Twenty Years', *The Journal of Peasant Studies* 33 (1), 1–33, https://doi.org/10.1080/03066150600624413.

Wang, Xiaodong (2018). 'Donation of Organs Continues Rapid Rise', *China Daily*, 25 December, www.chinadaily.com.cn/a/201812/25/WS5c21648ea3107d4c3a00296c.html (accessed 3 June 2019).

Wang, Xiaodong (2019). 'Organ Donation in China Ranks No 1 in Asia', *China Daily*, 9 October, https://archive.is/wip/xeMUD (accessed 5 March 2020).

Wang, Yinchao (2014). 'The Issue of Over-prescription: Drug Prescription Relating to the Government Power in China', www.repository.cam.ac.uk/bitstream/handle/1810/255596/201403-article1.pdf?sequence=1 (accessed 16 July 2021).

Wang, Yinchao (2015). '黄洁夫: 使用死囚器官是历史难堪一页' [Huang Jiefu: The Use of Death Row Prisoner Organs Is an Embarrassing Page in History], China Youth Net [official media of the Communist Youth League of China], http://zhenhua.163.com/15/0313/15/AKJKGOJ5000464BM.html; https://perma.cc/9MPZ-SZ8T (accessed 28 November 2018).

Wei, Yuesu, Xiaoying Wang, and Jianqiang Chen (2016). '沈中阳: 移植希望，让生命坚强' [Shen Zhongyang: The Hope of Transplantation Keeps Life Strong], *Guangming Daily*, http://epaper.gmw.cn/gmrb/html/2011-01/27/nw.D110000gmrb_20110127_1-13.htm; https://archive.is/tlspG; https://perma.cc/6KDA-35AN (accessed 27 November 2018).

Winch, Peter (1990). *The Idea of a Social Science and Its Relation to Philosophy* (New York: Humanities Press).

Winfield, Nicole (2018). 'China Tells Vatican It's Fighting Illegal Organ Transplants', 15 March, Associated Press, https://apnews.com/3501e3d6a0ef4439ac3e1948bd07dd45/China-tells-Vatican-it's-fighting-illegal-organ-transplants (accessed 21 August 2020).

World Focus (2013). '生死之间2013版 (4)：活摘器官真相迟早会在中国大陆大白于天下' [Between Life and Death 2013 (4): The Truth of Organ Harvesting Will Be Revealed in China Eventually], New Tang Dynasty Television, http://ca.ntdtv.com/xtr/gb/2013/10/30/a993590.html (accessed 21 February 2018).

Wu, Hongyue, Zhaoshu Luo, Ying Li et al. (2014). '先驱先行：推动自愿捐献器官立法 记天津市第一中心医院院长沈中阳教授' [The Pioneer: Promoting Voluntary Organ Donation Legislation: Chronicling Tianjin First Central Hospital President, Professor Shen Zhongyang], 中国科技网 [China Technology Net], http://digitalpaper.stdaily.com/http_www.kjrb.com/kjrb/html/2014-12/10/content_286091.htm?div=-1; https://archive.is/CEEQ9; https://perma.cc/AP4U-DSET (accessed 27 November 2018).

Xinhua (2012). '走进全军知名专科中心：解放军第309医院器官移植中心' [Entering the Military's Specialist Realm: The PLA 309 Military Hospital's Organ Transplantation Centre], http://news.xinhuanet.com/mil/2012-02/28/c_122763047.htm; https://archive.is/wLAPm (accessed 6 October 2017).

Xu, Dan (2006). '夏强：肝移植学科的少帅' [Xia Qiang: The Marshal of the Liver Transplantation Department], *People's Daily Online*, http://scitech.people.com.cn/GB/1057/4520977.html; https://web.archive.org/web/20190531011545/http://scitech.people.com.cn/GB/1057/4520977.html (accessed 30 May 2019).

Xu, Yang (2006). '东方器官移植中心昨天投入使用' [The Oriental Organ Transplant Centre Was Put into Use Yesterday], Sina, https://archive.is/PC0hS (accessed 21 August 2020).

Yan, Lunan, Bo Li, Yong Zeng et al. (2006). '提高肝移植手术效果的探讨（单个中心连续 200 例肝移植病例分析）' [Discussion on Improving Liver Transplantation Outcomes (Analysis of 200 Cases of Liver Transplantation in a Single Centre)], 中国肝胆外科杂志 [Chinese Journal of Hepatobiliary Surgery] 12 (5), 292–294.

Ye, J. Z., C. Wang, H. F. Wu et al. (2013). 'Internal Migration and Left-Behind Populations in China', *The Journal of Peasant Studies* 40 (6), 1119–1146.

Yeni Şafak (2018). 'Chinese Internment Camps Are "Torture Centers Worse than Death", Say Survivors', www.yenisafak.com/en/world/chinese-internment-camps-are-torture-centers-that-are-worse-than-death-say-survivors-3468651 (accessed 1 June 2019).

Zhang, Chenchen (2018). 'Governing Neoliberal Authoritarian Citizenship: Theorizing Hukou and the Changing Mobility Megime in China', *Citizenship Studies* 22 (8), 855–881.

Zhang, Lizi (2005). '肝移植走向新时代' [Liver Transplantation Enters a New Era], 健康报 [Health News], www.hbver.com/Article/gyhjqt/gyz/200505/3770.html; https://archive.is/4OpEg (accessed 1 May 2019).

Zhao, Hong, and Ning Wu (2015). '专访黄洁夫：中国器官移植事业光明正大地登上世界舞台' [Exclusive Interview with Huang Jiefu: The China Organ Transplant Field Justly and Honorably Steps onto the World

Stage], Health World, www.cn-healthcare.com/article/20150108/content-468177.html?source=rec; https://perma.cc/X73M-HNRX (accessed 28 November 2018).

Zhejiang Anti-Cult Association (2009). 新时期邪教防治研究学术论文精选 [Selected Academic Papers on Evil Religion Prevention Research in the New Era], ed. Shusen Zheng et al. (Beijing: China Science and Technology Press).

Zhejiang University of Water Resources and Electric Power (2010). '我校2010年反邪教暑期社会实践团荣获省级表彰' [University 2010 Anti-evil Religion Summer Summer Break Social Group Awarded Provincial Honours], www.zjweu.edu.cn/news/37/d5/c455a14293/page.htm; https://archive.is/TrlBf (accessed 14 October 2017).

Zheng, Shusen (2005). '急诊肝移植救治良性终末期肝病 46 例经验分析' [An Analysis of Positive Outcomes in the Experience of 46 Emergency Liver Transplants for End-Stage Liver Disease] (presented at the [第三届国际暨全国肝衰竭与人工肝学术会议论文集] China Medical Association Third International Liver Failure and Artificial Liver Symposium, 浙江大学医学院附属第一医院肝胆胰外科卫生部多器官联合移植研究重点实验室), http://cpfd.cnki.com.cn/Article/CPFDTOTAL-GRZX200503001135.htm (accessed 16 July 2021).

Zhonghua, Chen (2006). '中国首批国际标准化脑死亡自愿无偿器官捐献及成功移植——24位捐献者,106个器官。拯救100例移植病人' [China's First Batch of International Standardized Brain Death Voluntary Unpaid Organ Donation and Successful Transplantation: 24 Donors, 106 Organs, 100 Transplant Patients Saved], 中华医学会第六次全国胸心血管外科学术会议论文集（胸外科分册）[Proceedings of the 6th National Thoracic and Cardiovascular Surgery Conference of the Chinese Medical Association (Thoracic Surgery Volume)], http://cpfd.cnki.com.cn/Article/CPFDTOTAL-ZHYX200611006029.htm (accessed 10 November 2019).

Part III

Domestic and international implications

9

'Round-the-clock, three-dimensional control': The evolution and implications of the 'Xinjiang mode' of counterterrorism

Michael Clarke

Introduction

The Xinjiang Uyghur Autonomous Region (XUAR) of the People's Republic of China (PRC) is now the site of the largest mass repression of an ethnic and/or religious minority in the world today. Researchers estimate that since 2016 over one million people (mostly ethnic Uyghurs) have been detained without trial in the XUAR in a system of 're-education' camps (Zainab 2019; Zenz 2019). Outside of the camps, the region's Turkic Muslim population are subjected to a dense network of hi-tech surveillance systems (including key elements of China's 'social credit' system), checkpoints, and interpersonal monitoring which severely limit all forms of personal freedom penetrating society to the granular level. The objective, as XUAR Chinese Communist Party (CCP) deputy leader Zhu Hailun asserted in 2017, is to ensure that there are 'no cracks, no blind spots, no gaps' in the state's surveillance of the region (Xinjiang Ribao 2017a). The CCP has sought this ambitious and dystopian objective through the imposition of what two theorists at the Xinjiang Police University describe as the 'Xinjiang mode' of counterterrorism which combines the counter-insurgency (COIN) models adopted by the West (primarily the United States) in its 'War on Terrorism' with China's own 'public security' and 'governance' models to, in effect, create a counterterrorism strategy defined by militarization, surveillance, and ideological 'remoulding'. The central objective of the 'Xinjiang mode' is to not only prevent 'terrorism' before it occurs but also to pre-empt its very possibility by identifying and 'remoulding' individuals who display 'abnormal' behaviours.

As others have noted contemporary Xinjiang is a 'carceral state' where everyday life for Uyghurs (and other Turkic Muslim ethnic groups) has become penetrated to the granular level by the state (Byler 2019a; Xiaocuo 2019). Yet, descriptions of the system of surveillance erected in the XUAR as simply the manifestation of a new type of 'police state' only capture part of the story. Surveillance, as Ben Hayes has noted, is one of the 'dominant organizational paradigms of contemporary governance' shared by liberal democratic and authoritarian regimes (Hayes 2012: 167). Surveillance, however, is but 'a means to an end', namely, the 'protection' and 'management' of either the population-at-large or specific segments thereof (Foucault 1977; Jenkins 2012: 162). The case of Chinese counterterrorism in the XUAR reveals the Chinese state's propensity to be much more explicit in its desire – relative to governments in the liberal West – to pursue the active and coercive 'management' of specific segments of its population.

China's counterterrorism policy is in fact highly suggestive of processes of 'high modernism' described by James C. Scott in which the state seeks to legitimate the 'rational design of social order' (Scott 1998: 4) through the centralization, collection, and processing of information. Scott suggested that the imposition of such 'high modernism' tended to correlate with crises (e.g. economic depression, social revolution, or war) and authoritarianism. As we have seen since 9/11, however, the 'threat of terrorism and religious extremism' has stimulated the development of 'new forms of centralized surveillance, monitoring and identification' regardless of regime type (Weller 2012: 61). While legislative oversight and civil society have served as – albeit imperfect – brakes upon the untrammelled imposition of such surveillance in the liberal West, no such barriers have constrained the contemporary Chinese state. Rather, as will emerge below, the Chinese state has been able to instrumentalize the threat of Uyghur 'terrorism' and 'religious extremism' to further a deeper end – the remoulding an entire population's behaviours in the name of cultural assimilation.

Thus the 'Xinjiang mode' is also arguably a 'glocal' phenomena, simultaneously informed by dynamics and practices at the global level – such as the centrality of new surveillance technologies and discourses (e.g. Islamophobia) of the Global War on Terror (GWOT) – and their intersection with local dynamics such as the evolution of new ideologically informed models of 'governance' within the PRC. I argue here that it has been the intersection of technologically enabled surveillance with the CCP's evolving ideological concept of 'social management' that defines the practice and effects of the 'Xinjiang mode' of counterterrorism.

China's colonial project in Xinjiang and Uyghur 'terrorism'

Despite China's contemporary claim that Xinjiang (literally 'new dominion' or 'new frontier') has been 'an inseparable part of the unitary multi-ethnic Chinese nation' since the Han dynasty (202 BC – AD 220), it often remained beyond Chinese dominion due to its geopolitical position as a 'Eurasian crossroad' and the ethno-cultural dominance of Turkic and Mongol peoples (Millward 2007). The Qing dynasty (1644–1911) emperor Qianlong conquered the region in the 1750s, but by the mid-1800s Qing rule was challenged by widespread Turkic-Muslim rebellion. While this rebellion was overcome by a determined Qing military reconquest in 1876–77, and the region created as a province of the empire, it remained a colonial outpost (Kim 2004).

After experiencing significant autonomy from the Republic of China (1911–49), Xinjiang was 'peacefully liberated' by the People's Liberation Army (PLA) in October 1949 and the CCP confronted the question of 'how to run an empire without looking like colonialists' (Millward 2019). Their answer – recognition of the region's twelve non-Han *minzu* (nationality or ethnic group) and implementation of a system of 'national regional autonomy' – in theory, was meant to ensure that 'beneath the supreme central CCP power' the various *minzu* were to stand as equals, their individual culture, language, and practice of religion respected and protected (Millward 2019). In practice, however, this was accompanied by tight political, social, and cultural control, encouragement of Han Chinese settlement, and state-led economic development, backed by the repression of overt manifestations of opposition and dissent by the security forces (Clarke 2011: 120–129).

After the collapse of the neighbouring Soviet Union in 1991 the focus of Beijing's concerns regarding the security of Xinjiang shifted from state-based threats to largely non-state ones driven by the convergence of the Islamic revival in neighbouring Central Asia and Afghanistan and relative weakness of the post-Soviet states (Clarke 2007). This was also compounded by the internal trajectory of Chinese governance in the region which, since the institution of 'reform and opening' under Deng Xiaoping in 1978, had been based on the assumption that delivery of economic development and modernization would ultimately 'buy', if not the loyalty, then at least the acquiescence of the Uyghur (Barabantseva 2009). Under Deng's successor, Jiang Zemin, the question of Xinjiang's economic development assumed national importance under his Great Western Development (GWD) campaign, formally launched in 2000. Under the GWD Xinjiang was envisaged as becoming an industrial and agricultural base and a trade and energy corridor for the national economy. Central to the state's developmental agenda was a focus on a variety of 'mega-projects' such as massive oil and natural gas pipelines and infrastructure developments linking Xinjiang with Central and South Asia and the various subregions of Xinjiang with each other and the interior of China (Becquelin 2004).

While bringing economic development, such projects also created a variety of new socio-economic pressures – encouragement of further Han settlement, rapid urbanization, and environmental degradation – that exacerbated inter-ethnic tensions (Karrar 2017). Xinjiang's GDP surpassed the national average from 2003 onwards but many Uyghurs felt they had not benefitted due to a variety of factors including the concentration of Xinjiang's urban centres and industry in the north of the province; targeting of state investment in large infrastructure projects in which companies have tended to employ Han Chinese; and widening rural–urban disparities (Chaudhuri 2011; Liu and Peters 2017; Cao *et al.* 2018).

This period not coincidentally saw an appreciable increase in Uyghur unrest and militancy. Data collected by the University of Maryland's Global Terrorism Database, for example, records 135 attacks in Xinjiang across the 1992 and 2017 period resulting in 767 fatalities (Global Terrorism Database 2020). However, those figures count as terrorist attacks a number of incidents – such as the 7 July 2009 violence in Xinjiang's capital, Urumqi, which resulted in 184 fatalities – even though they are more accurately defined as inter-ethnic rioting or communal violence prompted by the long-term marginalization of the Uyghur population (Millward 2009; Cliff 2012; Ryono and Galway

2015). Omitting this incident alone decreases the death toll from terrorism in Xinjiang to 583 over the twenty-five-year period.

This data, more significantly, indicates clear peaks and troughs of incidents over this period consistent with a number of qualitative studies of Uyghur militancy that suggest the centrality of an action–reaction cycle between state repression/control and Uyghur resistance (Millward 2004; Clarke 2008; Tschantret 2018; Roberts 2020). Indeed, from 1990 onwards Chinese authorities implemented well-documented periodic 'strike hard' campaigns in Xinjiang against the so-called three evils of 'separatism, extremism, and terrorism' (Becquelin 2000; Hierman 2007). This only increased in intensity after the events of 9/11 as the party-state instrumentalized the threat and discourse of 'global terrorism' to justify and expand its efforts to monitor and control key markers of Uyghur identity such as religious observance/piety. While Uyghur religious expression had of course always been closely managed by the avowedly Marxist–Leninist CCP, post-9/11 it was not only effectively securitized through intense state regulation at the provincial and national levels but also a prompt for major legislative and institutional adaptations such as the passing of China's first national 'anti-terrorism' law in 2015 and the creation of China's National Security Commission (NSC) (Clarke 2010; Castets 2015; Greitens *et al.* 2019/20).

It is clear that 9/11 provided Beijing with the stimulus to reframe its efforts in Xinjiang as 'counterterrorist' rather than simply counter 'separatist' in nature. This began immediately after 9/11, when Beijing released its first documentation of terrorist incidents in Xinjiang, blaming a previously unknown group, the East Turkestan Islamic Movement (ETIM), for 'over' 200 'terrorist incidents' between 1990 and 2001 (Information Office of the State Council of the PRC 2002). A number of high-profile attacks in more recent years, such as the October 2013 SUV attack in Tiananmen Square and the April 2014 Kunming railway station mass stabbing attack, reinforced China's official narrative that it faces a genuine terrorist threat stemming from Xinjiang.

The ETIM, the group Beijing claimed in 2002 as the focal point of Uyghur terrorism, in fact functioned in Afghanistan from 1998 to the early 2000s and established links to al-Qaeda and the Taliban. However, it effectively ceased to function after the death of its leader,

Hasan Mahsum, during a Pakistani military operation in Waziristan in October 2003. A successor group, the Turkestan Islamic Party (TIP), emerged in 2007 and gained some prominence by issuing various threats to attack the 2008 Beijing Olympics (Zenn 2011). However, with the outbreak of the Syrian civil war, the geographical locus of the TIP has shifted to Syria, where evidence emerged over the past year of the group's significant battlefield presence involving potentially hundreds of its fighters with Jabhat al-Nusra (until recently, an al-Qaeda affiliate) (Clarke 2016). Beyond Syria, Beijing has claimed in the past that there may be somewhere between 300 and 500 Uyghurs fighting for Islamic State (IS), primarily in Iraq (Qiu 2014). However, 'entry' and 'exit' data for IS recruits analysed by Nate Rosenblatt at the New America Foundation identified 114 Uyghurs as fighting with the group between 2013 and 2014 (Rosenblatt 2016: 26). The data collected by IS on those Uyghurs suggests that 'not a single fighter in the sample reported to have previously fought in a jihad, suggesting that the sample isn't comprised of seasoned veterans of foreign wars, such as with Uygur separatists in the al-Qaeda-affiliated Turkistan Islamic Party' (Rosenblatt 2016: 26).

The presence of the al-Qaeda-aligned TIP in Syria from 2012 onwards was important in assisting Beijing in its desire to paint Uyghur militancy as intimately interconnected with global 'Jihadist' forces (Clarke 2020). Despite these linkages, however, there is in fact little available evidence of the TIP's direct involvement in attacks in Xinjiang. The TIP has claimed responsibility for a number of high-profile attacks, such as the so-called SUV attack of October 2013 in Tiananmen Square, but, Jacob Zenn notes, 'only a 2011 hit-and-run attack in Kashgar' has been 'credibly proven' to have been organized by the group from Afghanistan (Zenn 2018). Chinese state media, however, leveraged the presence of Uyghurs in Syria to argue that Beijing's hard-line in Xinjiang was warranted. The English-language tabloid *Global Times*, for instance, published an editorial on 12 August 2018 asserting that China's hard-line approach in the region had prevented it from becoming 'China's Libya' or 'China's Syria' (*Global Times* 2018). Prior to institution of China's hard-line, it continued, 'young people were brainwashed by extremist thoughts and manipulated by terrorist organizations', resulting in terrorist attacks not only in Xinjiang but also 'in places such as Tiananmen Square of Beijing and Kunming Railway Station' (*Global Times* 2018).

China's counterterrorism policy: From 'strike hard' to 'enduring peace'

It was in this period of heightened official concern with the threat of terrorism to Xinjiang that China's form of 'preventive' counterterrorism took shape. Of particular note was the development of a new strategy based on the integration of traditional Maoist 'mass line' mobilization and social control with new forms of technologically enabled surveillance and policing. The roots of this approach to terrorism took shape from the late 1990s onwards. In the wake of the events of 9/11, then Chinese president Jiang Zemin launched a round of 'strike hard' (*yan da*) campaigns domestically and declared support for the US GWOT. The acceptance by the international community of Chinese assertions that it too faced a terrorist threat in the XUAR – illustrated by the George W. Bush administration's listing of the ETIM as an 'international terrorist organization' (subjecting it to international sanctions) in September 2002 – provided cover for Beijing to initiate a number of legal and institutional changes that began China's instrumentalization of 'terrorism' as a means of repression in the XUAR (Millward 2004; Clarke 2008; Roberts 2012).

'Strike hard' campaigns had been widely used throughout China previously and focused upon achieving accelerated arrests, trials, and sentencing of a range of criminal offences such as drug trafficking and prostitution (Trevaskes 2007). In Xinjiang, however, the 'strike hard' campaigns focused almost exclusively on repression of the 'three evils' – 'separatism, extremism, and terrorism'. In parallel, Beijing moved quickly to amend the 1997 Criminal Law of the PRC in December 2001 (Ministry of Foreign Affairs of the PRC 2001). The amendments to the Criminal Law established a range of offences including funding of 'terrorist organizations', theft of 'ammunition or explosives', and disturbance of 'social order' as crimes violating 'state security' (Clarke 2010). The changes to the Criminal Law also significantly increased the punitive measures for such crimes. Coupled with annual 'strike hard' campaigns these changes resulted in accelerated conviction, sentencing, and execution of Uyghurs for 'crimes' against 'state security' over the next few years (Human Rights Watch 2005). In the run-up to the Beijing Olympics in 2008, for instance, 1,300 Uyghurs were arrested for 'endangering state security' and charged for offences related the 'three evil forces' (CECC 2009).

This period also saw significant institutionalization of China's relatively under-developed counterterrorism bureaucracy (Reeves 2016). Two key organizations were created in the wake of 9/11. The first was China's National Counter-Terrorism Working and Coordinating Small Group (NCTWCSG), designed to coordinate all terrorist-related activities within the Ministry of Public Security (MPS), the People's Armed Police (PAP), and the People's Liberation Army (PLA) at the provincial, autonomous region, municipal, city, and county levels. Along with the establishment of the Anti-Terrorism Bureau in 2002 under the MPS and an Office of the NCTWCSG within the Anti-Terrorism Bureau, the party-state also established special police units to address the threat of terrorism. The PAP also set up special counterterrorism forces within its special police units in a number of major cities, including Beijing (Scot Tanner 2018: 39–41).

However, it was the inter-ethnic violence in the region's capital or Urumqi on 5 July 2009 (referred to in China as the 7/5 Incident) that served as a major spur to crucial changes in the CCP's thinking about how best to secure its colonial project in Xinjiang (Millward 2009; Ryono and Galway 2015). The 7/5 Incident, in which officially 194 people were killed over two days of inter-ethnic violence, convinced influential leaders that the twin strategies of 'national regional autonomy' and state-led economic development upon which Chinese governance had rested since 1978 had exacerbated rather than assuaged long-standing sources of disgruntlement with the Chinese state.

The CCP's immediate response to the 7/5 Incident was focused on replacement of senior party figures in Xinjiang (including Urumqi CCP secretary Li Zhi and long-serving Xinjiang CCP chairman Wang Lequan), deployment of the PAP and special police units to the XUAR, and a renewed focus on 'stability maintenance' and economic development (Ramzy 2010). In this latter regard, then president Hu Jintao, at the first Central Xinjiang Work Forum (XJWFI) of the CCP, held 17–19 May 2010, unveiled a 'Xinjiang support package' including targeted central government investment and infrastructure spending. The objective, according to Hu, was to achieve 'leapfrog development' of the region that would lift its GDP to the national average by 2015 and thus contribute to 'ethnic unity' and 'social stability' (Jia and Zhe 2017; Wong 2010).

The new XUAR CCP chairman, Zhang Chunxian, thus embarked on what was dubbed a 'two-handed' policy in the region of both 'hard' and 'soft' measures focused on 'stability maintenance' work and improving 'people's livelihood' that would consolidate the party's 'grassroots infrastructure' throughout the region (Lianhe zaobao 2011). However, it was under Zhang's tenure that 'a staged security build-up, which included not only highly trained SWAT teams and People's Armed Police units in urban areas but also the stationing of at least one uniformed police officer in each rural village' was undertaken (Leibold 2019: 3). This was the first step towards the implementation of a 'tiered yet socially inclusive policing profile' increasingly reliant 'on low-skilled, high-paid Uyghur foot soldiers' (Zenz and Leibold 2019). Unsurprisingly, after 2009 official public security spending increased rapidly, with much of this soaked up in introduction of high-definition surveillance cameras across public spaces in Xinjiang, including in mosques (*China Daily* 2010).[1] By the next year at least 40,000 high-definition 'Eagle-Eye' surveillance cameras equipped with 'riot-proof' casings were fitted on buses, in schools, and in shopping centres, as well as on the streets of urban areas to increase police presence in key places, vital sectors, and public areas (Qiang 2014; Famularo 2018: 58).[2]

Efforts to improve socio-economic conditions, meanwhile, were increasingly framed around the Partnership Assistance Programme (PAP) that sought to 'match up' under-developed townships and prefectures with 'developed' counterparts in inner China, resulting in the transfer of cadres, commodities, and financial and technical assistance, the provision of financial and in-kind incentives from the state for labour-intensive and/or resource-oriented firms to relocate to Xinjiang, and the establishment of 'special economic zones' in cities such as Kashgar (Yue 2010; Li 2018: 17–26; Song *et al.* 2019). Much of this investment, however, was 'channelled through domestic Chinese companies and state entities' into projects that did not 'benefit the broader local population', with the result that such capital 'hopped' between the developed east and the XUAR 'without generating much lasting benefit' (Steenberg and Rippa 2019: 6).

Significantly, however, Zhang's era of 'two-handed' policy was also accompanied by a transition in how the CCP conceived of the relationship between development, identity, and security. For much of the post-Mao era the party's strategy in Xinjiang had rested on the assumption that development would resolve its 'Uyghur question' by breaking down the traditional cultural, religious, and social ties that underpinned Uyghur identity and thus secure the region. After 7/5, however, economic development per se was viewed as no longer sufficient. Rather, the question now was: what obstacles prevented development from achieving the goal of integration and what should the party do about it? An answer emerged from the debates about a so-called second generation of ethnic minority policy after 2009 (Leibold 2013). Party-affiliated scholars such as Ma Rong, Hu Angang, and Hu Lianhe argued that the 'first generation' of policy – based on ethnic equality and 'national regional autonomy'– had solidified ethnic boundaries, ethnic elites, and notions of 'separateness' (Leibold 2018a). The direction of ethnic minority policy since has demonstrated that their conclusion has been that there is something intrinsic to Uyghur identity that blocks the path to the party's vision of modernization, and hence, integration. Advocates of 'second-generation' policy therefore argued that ethnic policy must discard the nominal pluralism and preferential policies of the past in favour of an approach that explicitly sought the 'mingling', 'fusing', or 'standardization' of ethnic groups with a supra-national conception of the Chinese 'state-nation' (*zhongguo minzu*) (Leibold 2018a). The means through which this was to be achieved included political, economic, and cultural measures such as 'eliminating group-differentiated rights and obligations to ensure the equality of all citizens'; increasing 'economic interaction and ties between ethnic minority regions and the rest of the country'; and 'increasing ethnic mobility, co-residence, and intermarriage and promoting Putonghua, bilingual, and mixed-ethnic schooling' (Leibold 2013: 13–16).

In March 2012, however, Xi Jinping (then vice president) rebuked Zhang's 'two-handed' approach. Meeting with Zhang and the Xinjiang delegation to the National People's Congress (NPC) Xi noted not only that 'Xinjiang work' held a 'particularly important strategic position in the overall work of the party and the state' but that they must 'unswervingly insist on both development and stability' and 'hold high the banner of unity' (Song 2012). Xi's emphasis on the centrality of 'stability' and the party's leadership over society – hallmarks of his subsequent tenure as chairman of the CCP and president of the PRC – were also reflected in institutional changes including the downgrading of the State Ethnic Affairs Commission (SEAC) and State Administration for Religious Affairs (SARA) in favour of the United Front Work Department (UFWD) of the CCP and the creation of the NSC in November 2013 (Leibold 2018a). In October 2014, the NSC also established a National Anti-Terrorism Intelligence Centre to strengthen anti-terrorism intelligence gathering in order to boost its counterterrorism, pre-emptive and preventive, capabilities (Ji 2016: 190). The SEAC, as Taotao Zhao and James Leibold document, was gradually downgraded as the locus of ethnic minority governance after 2009 as provincial level 'UFWD offices assumed primary responsibility for ethnic work in ethnic minority regions, with SEAC officials left to follow the direct lead of their Party counterparts' (Zhao and Leibold 2020: 491).

The NSC meanwhile, created as a party and not state body, prioritized 'political' and 'homeland' security, institutionalizing the conflation of regime security with that of national security (Lampton 2015). The fact that both Meng Jianzhu, secretary of the CCP Political and Legal Affairs Commission, and XUAR party chief Zhang Chunxian were 'initially identified as sitting in the NSC' also spoke to its domestic and Xinjiang-oriented priorities (Cabestan 2017: 117). In 2018, a little more than half a year after assuming his role as MPS vice minister, Shi Jun was reassigned vice minister of the UFWD, and in 2019 appointed head of the Office of the Central Xinjiang Work Coordination Group (XWCG) (Caixin 2019). The multiple portfolios of the current head of the Central XWCG in the UFWD and the MPS further indicates the dominance of security officials in the official policy-formation agenda in Xinjiang (Batke 2018).

The need for the reinforcement of party guidance and control over ethnic minority governance was underlined by a number of violent incidents in or connected to Xinjiang in 2013 and 2014 including the so-called SUV attack in Tiananmen Square on 28 October 2013 and the Kunming railway station attack of 1 March 2014 that officials blamed on 'radicalized' Uyghurs (Roberts 2013; Clarke 2015). Such incidents contributed to Xi's decision after a Politburo meeting on 19 December 2013 that the CCP would abandon Zhang's 'two-handed' policy in Xinjiang. State media reported that the party's 'prime task' in Xinjiang would now be the pursuit of 'social stability and an enduring peace' (Jingjie 2014). As would become clear over the following two years, 'enduring peace' in Xinjiang would be pursued through reinvigoration of Maoist 'mass line' forms of party mobilization, implementation of new forms of technological surveillance, and intensive 'de-extremification' work, including 'concentrated re-education training' of those deemed to be at risk of 'extremism'.

Xi Jinping himself provided further details of what the pursuit of 'social stability' and 'enduring peace' would entail, at the second Central Xinjiang Work Forum (XJWFII) on 28–29 May 2014 (Xinhua 2014). Specifically, Xi emphasized that the focus of the current struggle in Xinjiang was to severely crack down on violent terrorist activities under the socialist rule of law, and to strengthen the defense and governance capabilities of the masses, build a wall of iron and steel, and a network that stretched from 'heaven to earth'. Xi stated that the issue of national unity was the 'lifeline of the people' and one that would propel the dream of the 'great rejuvenation of the Chinese nation'. Xi also stressed the importance of strengthening inter-ethnic contact, exchange, and mingling; the need to 'actively guide religion to adapt to socialist society'; economic development, to improve the people's livelihoods; the critical role of the Xinjiang Production and Construction Corps (XPCC) in maintaining stability and border maintenance; the importance of 'strengthening ideological and political work'; and called for the building of 'grassroots party organisations into a strong fighting fortress for serving the masses, maintaining stability, and opposing separatism' (Leibold 2014; Xinhua 2014).

The new policy strategy under Xi, as noted by James Leibold, called for 'two potentially contradictory courses in Xinjiang' (Leibold 2019). Party directives were, on the one hand, oriented towards greater migration by Uyghurs into regional cities like Urumqi as well as to coastal city centres like Shanghai and Beijing, in line with the policy of inter-ethnic mingling (*jiaorong*). On the other hand, the policy would also see the party's security apparatus redoubling its hold in Xinjiang through a deeper penetration of the daily lives of Xinjiang residents, hence serving towards the imperatives of 'stability maintenance' (*weiwen*) and which, relatedly, entailed not only the use of stability enhancing mechanisms but the exercise of disciplinary power, as exemplified by the work of 'standardizing of human behaviour' (*guifan rende xingwei*) articulated by Hu Lianhe in his 2010 speech on the 'scientific view' of stability (Leibold 2018a).

Zhang Chunxian flagged mass mobilization when he announced in February 2014 that 200,000 CCP cadres would be 'walking the mass line' through their rotation into 9,000 different 'grassroots' villages and communities (chiefly in rural southern Xinjiang) in order to 'aid and assist' ordinary citizens over the next three years and 'win the hearts' of the Uyghur people (Li 2014; Xinjiang Ribao 2014). The security function of such 'mass line' work, however, was underlined by regular visits to the region by then minister for public security Guo Shengkun. On one such visit in August 2014, for example, Guo was quoted as telling a 'symposium' of 'armed police officers and soldiers, grassroots cadres and masses' that it in order to 'severely crack down on violent terrorist activities' it was 'necessary to vigorously strengthen intelligence and information work and overall social prevention and control' (Boxun xinwen 2014).

However, it was after further violence in May and July 2014 that then XUAR CCP leader Zhang Chunxian voiced the starkest rhetoric yet exhorting a meeting of the XUAR Party Committee to fight a 'people's war against terrorism' that would not only 'cut weeds' but also 'dig out the roots' of extremism (Jacobs 2014). This resulted in accelerated arrests and trials of suspected 'terrorists' – including public, mass sentencing rallies of Uyghur suspects – and ongoing sweeps of Uyghur neighbourhoods and mosques in search of potential militants and their weapons (Koplowitz 2014). From this point onwards cadres sent to the 'grassroots' became 'frontline soldiers' in the 'people's war against terrorism'. 'Winning the hearts' of the Uyghur people was jettisoned in favour of identifying 'radical or deviant elements' in their jurisdictions (Leibold 2019: 4). Significantly, it was in late 2014 and early 2015 that such 'deviant elements' were first subjected to 'education transformation work' in a small number of localities. In Yining County, for example, 'twenty villages' carried out 'education transformation work for key personnel' where 'lecturers were hired to explain policies and legal knowledge to the students of all ethnic groups'. After 'nine days of training' the 'trainees' had become 'deeply aware of the harmfulness of religious extremism' (Xinjiang xingnong wang 2015).

These trends of heightened mass line and technological surveillance combined with ideological 're-education' of those defined as potential 'extremists' were accelerated in 2016 under the new XUAR CCP chairman, Chen Quanguo. Chen had in fact implemented a policing system of 'grid style management' during his previous role as party leader in Tibet (2011–15) that segmented 'urban communities into geometric zones' policed by 'convenience' police stations connected to CCTV cameras and police databases enabling greater surveillance capabilities (Zenz and Leibold 2017a). In Xinjiang, Chen implemented 'grid management' and integrated it with the CCTV surveillance systems established under his immediate predecessor, resulting in a multi-tiered policing system based on exponential recruitment of contract police officers to man 'convenience' police stations (Zenz and Leibold 2017b, 2019). Additional surveillance measures – including compulsory fitting of GPS trackers in motor vehicles, use of facial recognition scanners at checkpoints and major public amenities, and installation of 'nanny apps' that wipe smartphones of so-called subversive material – were also implemented under Chen's watch (Radio Free Asia 2017; Coca 2018). This data is then fed into the Integrated Joint Operations Platform (IJOP) – an app used by XUAR public security – to report 'activities or circumstances deemed suspicious' and to prompt 'investigations of people the system flags as problematic' (Human Rights Watch 2019). The purpose of such a system was explicitly detailed by Chen in a speech on 18 August 2017 in which he gave instructions for the 'party, government, military, police, soldiers, and civilians' of the XUAR to implement 'comprehensive, round-the-clock, and three-dimensional prevention control' in order to 'deny *any* opportunity to hostile forces and violent terrorists' to undermine the region's 'stability' (Xinjiang Ribao 2017b, emphasis added). Stability, Chen asserted, 'overrides everything' across 'all departments, at every level' (Xinjiang Ribao 2017b).

Seeing like a party-state: 'Social management' and counterterrorism

The methodology that has been central to the pursuit of this 'comprehensive, round-the-clock, and three-dimensional prevention control' has been the concept of 'social management'. Samantha Hoffman notes that 'social management' embodies an effort to optimize 'interactions vertically (within the Party), horizontally (between agencies), and holistically, between the Party and society' in order 'to improve governance capacity to shape, manage, and respond to social demands' (Hoffman 2017). It ultimately seeks to enhance the 'legibility' of citizens and to make them pliable subjects to be engineered and thus controlled by the state (Scott 1998). As James C. Scott reminds us, the 'utopian, immanent, and continually frustrated goal of the modern state' has been 'to reduce the chaotic, disorderly, constantly changing social reality beneath it to something more closely resembling the administrative grid of its observations' thereby rendering citizens and the spaces in which they inhabit more legible and responsive to central control (Scott 1998). Crucially, surveillance is of course but 'a means to an end', namely, the 'protection' and 'management' of either the population-at-large or specific segments thereof (Jenkins 2012: 162).

The 'security state' erected in Xinjiang under the tenures of XUAR CCP chiefs Zhang Chunxian and Chen Quanguo has permitted the party-state to undertake 'social sorting' on a large scale. 'Social sorting', in Jenkins' conception, seeks the 'identification and ordering of individuals in order to "put them in their place" within local, national and global "institutional orders"', and to thus ascribe to them particular penalties, constraints, or sanctions according to their categorization (Jenkins 2012: 160). The function of such surveillance is thus not simply to make potential 'deviants' visible but rather 'to permit an internal, articulated and detailed control' that 'would operate to transform individuals' by taking 'a hold of their conduct, to carry the effects of power right to them, to make it possible to know them, to alter them' (Foucault 1977: 172). In fact, this is what has occurred to large numbers of Xinjiang's Uyghur population. The end to which such means are deployed is not simply to increase the party-state's 'legibility' of this population but also to manufacture the consent of the Uyghurs and enable it to actively mould and shape those individuals into 'productive' and pliable citizens.

The CCP's project of making of Uyghurs 'legible' has been highlighted in its recommitment to expand the security presence throughout the region (including enhanced surveillance capabilities), and by means of the legalization and institutionalization of ideological and political 'thought' work on its citizens. It has been well documented that technological innovation has been harnessed to monitor and control the region's Turkic Muslim populations. Here, the use of facial recognition and iris scanners at checkpoints, train stations, and petrol stations, collection of biometric data for passports, and mandatory apps to cleanse smartphones of subversive material has now become a fact of everyday life (Byler 2019a; Daly 2019; Ma 2019; Mozur 2019; Grauer 2021). The data collected is then aggregated by an app used by security personnel, the IJOP, to report 'on activities or circumstances deemed suspicious' and to prompt 'investigations of people the system flags as problematic' (Human Rights Watch 2019).

That such surveillance is but a means to an end, however, is confirmed by a closer examination of the legislative and discursive architecture that has been erected to support the security state in Xinjiang. Legislatively, there have been a number of shifts at the national and provincial level here. First, in December 2015 the NPC passed China's first national 'anti-terrorism' law, providing an expansive and ambiguous definition of terrorism that further enables the state to criminalize a wide array of actions. The law states that terrorism is:

> Any advocacy or activity that, by means of violence, sabotage, or threat, aims to create social panic, undermine public safety, infringe on personal and property rights, or coerce a state organ or an international organization, in order to achieve political, ideological, or other objectives. (Xinhua 2015)

Second, the XUAR government announced in March 2017 so-called de-extremification regulations that reveal the state's objective to categorize and punish those it defines as 'deviant' and 'abnormal'. These regulations not only defined 'extremification' as 'speech and actions under the influence of extremism, that imbue radical religious ideology, and reject and interfere with normal production and livelihood' but also explicitly identified fifteen 'primary expressions' of 'extremist thinking', including 'wearing, or compelling others to wear, gowns with face coverings, or to bear symbols of extremification', 'spreading religious fanaticism through irregular beards or name selection', and 'failing to perform the legal formalities in marrying or divorcing by religious methods' (China Law Translate 2017). This, Joanne Smith Finley argues, amounted to a criminalization of 'all religious behaviours, not just violent ones', leading 'to highly intrusive forms of religious policing' that violate and humiliate Uyghurs (Smith Finley 2018). Such legislation demonstrates that for the CCP 'extremism' is now identified to be inherent to everyday markers and practices of the Uyghur profession of Islam.

China's White Paper of 16 August 2019 on 'Vocational Education and Training in Xinjiang' (Information Office of the State Council of the PRC 2019), meanwhile, highlighted the core objective of the CCP to define and regulate Uyghur values, beliefs, and loyalties so that they become 'useful' subjects for maintaining the regime's political security (Klimeš 2018). While defining 'terrorism and extremism' as 'common enemies of human society' and Xinjiang as the 'main battlefield of China's fight against terrorism', the document asserted that the state must not only deal with 'terrorist crimes in accordance with the law' but also '*educate* and *rescue* personnel infected with religious extremism and minor crimes' in order to treat 'both symptoms and the root causes' of religious extremism (Information Office of the State Council of the PRC 2019, emphasis added). Through 'education and training', the document concludes, the training centres will promote 'development' and 'increase the people's overall income' and help Xinjiang 'achieve social stability and enduring peace' (Information Office of the State Council of the PRC 2019).

The ideology and practice of such 'education and training', however, reveals it to be less than benign. All of these facilities are underpinned by the logic of 'transformation through re-education' (*jiaoyu zhuanhua*) – a concept whose lineage blends elements of traditional Chinese statecraft and state socialism of the Leninist–Stalinist and Maoist variants with the CCP's more recent racialized politics of exclusion. In the first instance, as James Leibold has noted, both traditional Chinese statecraft and the major variants of state socialism have held a 'paternalistic approach that pathologizes deviant thought and behavior, and then tries to forcefully transform them' (Leibold 2018b). Under Stalin, the Soviet state went to great lengths to propagandize the *gulag* as a transformative 'reforging' of former 'class enemies' into ideologically committed Soviet citizens (Draskozy 2012). Vyachslav Molotov, one of Stalin's key lieutenants, asserted in 1931, for example, that the *gulag* 'accustoms them [class enemies] to labor and makes them useful members of society' (cited in Vinokour 2018). Once the CCP had achieved power, it too instituted a system of extrajudicial 'remoulding through labor' (*laogai*) and 're-education through labor' (*laojiao*) camps where the goal was to 'transform' the prisoner (usually defined as a 'class enemy') and achieve their 'reform and rehabilitation' (Fu 2005). By the late 1990s the CCP drew on these precedents to develop the concept of 'transformation through re-education' in response to a series of new political and social challenges such as the rise of the Falun Gong spiritual movement and drug addiction. A key element in the repression of the Falun Gong was the implementation of 'legal education centres', where detainees were 'forced to watch propaganda videos, sing patriotic or pro-Communist Party (CCP) songs, and "repent"', while recalcitrants were 'subject to various forms of physical coercion and torture' and dedicated believers described as 'addicts' (Cook 2019).

The key elements of this discourse of 'transformation through re-education' have been markedly intensified in Xinjiang. Of particular note is how the language of pathology has now permeated official statements and rhetoric regarding the purpose of the system. From government officials describing Uyghur 'extremism and terrorism' as a 'tumour' to the equation of religious observance to an 'illness', the CCP's discourse frames central elements of Uyghur identity as pathologies to be 'cured' (Dooley 2018). That such pathologizing of Uyghur identity guides official policy was made plain by a CCP Youth League official's justification of 're-education' in October 2017. 'Being infected by religious extremism and violent terrorist ideology', the official asserted, 'is like being infected by a disease that has not been treated in time, or like taking toxic drugs'. Even after completing the 're-education process', the official continued, individuals 'must remain vigilant, empower themselves with the correct knowledge, strengthen their ideological studies ... to bolster their immune system against the influence of religious extremism and violent terrorism, and safeguard themselves from being infected once again' (Radio Free Asia 2018). This thus explicitly frames the Uyghur population as a 'virtual biological threat to the body of society' (Roberts 2018). The ultimate 'cure' for this biopolitical threat, as stated in an internal CCP document of March 2018, is to 'break their lineage, break their roots, break their connections, and break their origins' (Government Information Public Platform of Kashi 2018).

Conclusion

The CCP, as demonstrated above, has actively sought to manage and reshape the behaviours of the Uyghur population through a security and surveillance apparatus that makes them 'transparent' to the gaze of the state and hence eminently controllable. This, as two theorists at the Xinjiang Police University argued in 2016, amounted to the emergence of a 'Xinjiang model' of counterterrorism that would combine what they defined as the 'war model' of counter-insurgency adopted by the US military in Iraq and Afghanistan with China's own 'public security model' and 'governance model' (Wang and Shan 2016). The 'public security model' was built on 'the construction of the anti-terrorism intelligence system' – embodied in 'grid management' and technological surveillance initiatives noted above – which would provide security forces with 'the ability to obtain information on signs, tendencies ... related to violence and terrorism' and thereby enhance 'social prevention and control capabilities' (Wang and Shan 2016). The 'governance model', in turn, focuses on the long-term 'resolution of ethnic and religious ideological issues' that give rise to 'extremism' and 'terrorism'. Here, Wang and Shan asserted that as religious 'extremism' is an 'ideological' problem it must be solved 'by ideological methods' (Wang and Shan 2016: 25). This entailed sustained 'education' of the population in order to 'reject the brainwashing of distorted religious views' and thereby increase their 'immunity to extreme terrorism' (Wang and Shan 2016: 25).

In a key passage, Wang and Shan reveal that a central objective of the 'Xinjiang model' is to undermine what the state sees as a fundamental root cause of terrorism in Xinjiang: religion. 'Extreme religion', Wang and Shan assert, 'attempts to change the true face of national culture and block exchanges and fusion among all ethnic groups' and as such the party's 'cultural guidance' must assist 'people of all ethnic groups' to 'move closer to secularization and modernization'. The central implication, as Darren Byler notes, is that 'there must be an acceleration of "the deep fusion" of Chinese culture in Xinjiang' in order to eliminate terrorism (Byler 2019b). That this 'deep fusion' is to remain the core objective of the CCP in Xinjiang for the foreseeable future there is now of little doubt. Indeed, Xi Jinping's report to the CCP Central Symposium on Xinjiang-related work on 26–27 September 2020 stated not only that the party's Xinjiang policy is '100 per cent correct' but that it remained critical that 'education on the sense of Chinese identity should be incorporated into the education of officials and the younger generation in Xinjiang as well as its social education' in order to 'let the sense of Chinese identity take root in people' (Xinhua 2020).

Yet it is the intersection of discourses of 'prevention' and 'uplift' that arguably defines the CCP's contemporary repression in Xinjiang as a form of 'high modernist' ideology of social control (Scott 1998: 4). The 'Xinjiang mode' of counterterrorism, as detailed above, has sought to enhance the state's capacity to not only interdict and punish acts the CCP defines as 'terrorism' but to develop capabilities through which to prevent the possibility of 'terrorism' in the first instance. The evolution of the discourse and practices of the 're-education' system, in turn, resonate with historical precedents from traditional Chinese statecraft through to the totalitarian experiments of state socialism under Stalin and Mao Zedong that have sought to not simply punish but remake or 'remould' individuals and whole categories of population deemed too 'deviant' according to state-defined norms.

The CCP's mass interment of an estimated one million Uyghurs (and other Turkic minorities) in facilities whose stated primary function is 're-education' or 'vocational training' also makes them consistent with the defining characteristics and functions of concentration camps throughout history. As Andrea Pitzer reminds us, concentration camps throughout history are defined by the 'removal of certain populations from one area to house them somewhere else' and the exclusion of a target population from 'society with all its accompanying rights, relationships and connections to humanity', while removal and exclusion is often justified as a preventive measure 'to keep a suspect group from committing future crimes' or as 'part of a civilizing mission to uplift supposedly inferior culture and races' (Pitzer 2019: 5–8).

China's 17 September 2020 White Paper on 'Employment and Labor Rights in Xinjiang' is revealing in this respect. It notes that many parts of Xinjiang have remained 'impoverished' as 'terrorists, separatists and religious extremists have long preached that "the afterlife is fated" and that "religious teachings are superior to state laws", inciting the public to resist learning the standard spoken and written Chinese language, reject modern science, and refuse to improve their vocational skills, economic conditions, and the ability to better their own lives'

(State Council Information Office of the PRC 2020). This has caused 'local people' to have 'outdated ideas', 'suffer from poor education and employability', and have 'low employment rates and incomes' (State Council Information Office of the PRC 2020). The provision of 'education and training' for all social classes of Uyghurs, as a number of researchers have demonstrated, points towards an attempted 'proletarianization' of such populations into a 'docile yet productive lumpen class' via a clear linkage between the 're-education' system and forms of forced labour (Byler 2019c; Xu *et al.* 2020; Zenz 2020). Here, Uyghurs are either compelled to work as low-skilled labour in factories directly connected to 're-education' centres or, upon their 'release', in closely proximate 'industrial parks' where companies from throughout China have been incentivized to relocate to (Rickleton 2019). This is something the September 2020 White Paper tacitly acknowledges by noting that the state has in fact been actively 'promoting capital, technology and knowledge-intensive advanced manufacturing industries and emerging industries' as well as 'labor-intensive industries such as textiles and garments, shoes and accessories' into Xinjiang to provide 'key groups' such as 'surplus rural labor' with employment (State Council Information Office of the PRC 2020).

The White Paper thus illustrates the intersection between concern for the 'welfare' of subject populations and the desire to eradicate 'defective' elements of Uyghur cultural identity and marks the CCP's objective in Xinjiang as inherently settler colonial in nature. Although the intersection of these two opposed dynamics may seem counterintuitive, the history of the subjugation of indigenous populations throughout the globe suggests otherwise. The removal of Aboriginal children from their families by the Australian government, for instance, as Robert van Krieken (2010: 142) notes, was consistently justified in terms of 'welfare' and the 'interests' of these peoples themselves. For administrators of 'Aboriginal affairs', van Krieken argues, Aboriginal culture was perceived to be 'inherently flawed, fragile and basically worthless, producing only illness, disease, drunkenness, filth and degenerancy' and as such removal of Aboriginal children was a means to provide such subjects with the *possibility* of becoming 'civilized' and assimilated citizens (van Krieken 2010: 145). Detaching Aboriginal children from their familial and communal ties, and thus preventing cultural reproduction of Aboriginal identity, was thus seen by 'most

White Australians' as 'evidently synonymous with civilization and progress itself' (van Krieken 2010: 145).

The convergence of 'prevention' and 'uplift' thus provide a means through which the party can – to paraphrase American general and founder of the Carlisle Indian Industrial School, Richard H. Pratt – 'kill the Uyghur, but save the man'. The 'Xinjiang mode' has served as an important instrument in this context through which the party-state has sought to enhance its capacity to not only surveil and control Xinjiang, but to discipline in the Foucauldian sense individuals according to the party-state's norms. Taken as a whole, the system of pervasive surveillance – both of the 'mass line' and technologically enabled varieties – combined with the practices of 're-education' in XUAR demonstrates the dystopic potentialities of 'high modernist' ideologies of social control.

Notes

1 Chinese state media (e.g. *China Daily* 2010) reported that official public security expenditures in Xinjiang rose by 87.9 per cent from 1.54 billion yuan in 2009 to 2.89 billion yuan in 2010 (US$423 million).
2 These measures represented a continuation of the 'Skynet project', a nationwide surveillance system which began in 2005 during the Hu Jintao era, designed to monitor, deter, and control a range of undesirable behaviour, including crime, dissent, and criticisms of the party-state.

References

Barabantseva, Elena (2009). 'Development as Localization: Ethnic Minorities in China's Official Discourse on the Western Development Project', *Critical Asian Studies* 41 (2), 225–254.
Batke, Jessica (2018). 'Central and Regional Leadership for Xinjiang Policy in Xi's Second Term', *China Leadership Monitor* 56, www.hoover.org/sites/default/files/research/docs/clm56jb.pdf (accessed 19 February 2019).
Becquelin, Nicolas (2000). 'Xinjiang in the Nineties', *China Journal* 44, 65–90.
Becquelin, Nicolas (2004). 'Staged Development in Xinjiang', *The China Quarterly*, 358–378.
Boxun xinwen (2014). '公安部长郭声琨年内第三次赴新疆调研反恐', 6 August, www.boxun.com/news/gb/china/2014/08/201408062003.shtml (accessed 28 July 2018).

Byler, Darren (2019a). 'Ghost World', *Logic Magazine*, 1 May, https://logicmag.io/china/ghost-world/ (accessed 19 May 2019).
Byler, Darren (2019b). 'Preventative Policing as Community Detention in Northwest China', *Made in China Journal*, 25 October, https://madeinchinajournal.com/2019/10/25/preventative-policing-as-community-detention-in-northwest-china/ (accessed 17 November 2019).
Byler, Darren (2019c). 'How Companies Profit from Forced Labor in Xinjiang', *SupChina*, 4 September, https://supchina.com/2019/09/04/how-companies-profit-from-forced-labor-in-xinjiang/ (accessed 11 September 2019).
Cabestan, Jean-Pierre (2017). 'China's Institutional Changes in the Foreign and Security Policy Realm under Xi Jinping: Power Concentration vs. Fragmentation without Institutionalization', *East Asia* 34 (2), 113–131.
Caixin (2019). '中央统战部副部长侍俊任中央新疆工作协调小组办公室主任' [Central UFWD Vice Minister Shi Jun Appointed Head of the Office of the Central Xinjiang Work Coordination Group], 26 March.
Cao, Xun, Haiyan Duan, Chuyu Liu et al. (2018). 'Digging the "Ethnic Violence in China" Database: The Effects of Inter-ethnic Inequality and Natural Resources Exploitation in Xinjiang', *China Review* 18 (2), 121–154.
Castets, Rémi (2015). 'The Modern Chinese State and Strategies of Control over Uyghur Islam', *Central Asian Affairs* 2 (3), 221–245.
CECC (2009). 'State Security Cases from Xinjiang Appear to Surge in 2008', 16 April, www.cecc.gov/publications/commission-analysis/state-security-cases-from-xinjiang-appear-to-surge-in-2008 (accessed 3 August 2020).
Chaudhuri, Debasish (2011). 'Minority Economy in Xinjiang: A Source of Uyghur Resentment', *China Report* 46 (1), 9–27.
China Daily (2010). 'Xinjiang Security Funding Increased by 90 Percent', 13 January, www.chinadaily.com.cn/china/2010-01/13/content_9311035.htm.v (accessed 20 March 2020).
China Law Translate (2017). 'Xinjiang Uyghur Autonomous Region Regulation on De-extremification', 30 March, www.chinalawtranslate.com/en/xinjiang-uyghur-autonomous-region-regulation-on-de-extremification/ (accessed 30 June 2020).
Clarke, Michael (2007). 'The Problematic Progress of "Integration" in the Chinese State's Approach to Xinjiang, 1759–2005', *Asian Ethnicity* 9 (3), 261–289.
Clarke, Michael (2008). 'China's "War on Terrorism" in Xinjiang: Human Security and the Causes of Violent Uighur Separatism', *Terrorism and Political Violence* 20 (2), 271–301.
Clarke, Michael (2010). 'Widening the Net: China's Anti-terror Laws and Human Rights in the Xinjiang Uyghur Autonomous Region', *International Journal of Human Rights* 14 (4), 542–558.

Clarke, Michael (2011). *Xinjiang and China's Rise in Central Asia: A History* (London: Routledge).
Clarke, Michael (2015). 'China and the Uyghurs: The "Palestinization" of Xinjiang?', *Middle East Policy* 22 (3), 127–146.
Clarke, Michael (2016). 'Uyghur Militants in Syria: The Turkish Connection', *Terrorism Monitor* 14 (3), https://bit.ly/3ioDeAf (accessed 21 March 2020).
Clarke, Michael (2020). 'Uyghur Militancy and Terrorism: The Evolution of a "Glocal" Jihad?', in Tom Smith and Kristen Schulze (eds), *Exporting Global Jihad Vol. 2: Critical Perspectives from Asia and North America* (London: I.B. Tauris), 74–98.
Cliff, Thomas (2012). 'The Partnership of Stability in Xinjiang: State–Society Interactions following the July 2009 Unrest', *China Journal* 68, 79–105.
Coca, Ninthin (2018). 'China's Xinjiang Surveillance Is the Dystopian Future Nobody Wants', Engadget, 22 February, www.engadget.com/2018/02/22/china-xinjiang-surveillance-tech-spread/ (accessed 5 April 2019).
Cook, Sarah (2019). 'The Learning Curve: How Communist Party Officials Are Applying Lessons from Prior "Transformation" Campaigns to Repression in Xinjiang', *China Brief* 19 (3), https://bit.ly/36Kbws7 (accessed 25 May 2019).
Daly, Angela (2019). 'Algorithmic Oppression with Chinese Characteristics: AI against Xinjiang's Uyghurs', https://strathprints.strath.ac.uk/71586/1/Daly_GISW2019_Algorithmic_oppression_Chinese_characteristics_AI_against_Xinjiang_Uyghurs.pdf (accessed 19 March 2020).
Dooley, Ben (2018). '"Eradicate the Tumours": Chinese Civilians Drive Xinjiang Crackdown', Yahoo News, 26 April, www.yahoo.com/news/eradicate-tumours-chinese-civilians-drive-xinjiang-crackdown-051356550.html (accessed 3 June 2018).
Draskozy, Julie (2012). 'The *Put* of *Perekovka*: Transforming Lives at Stalin's White Sea-Baltic Canal', *The Russian Review* 71 (1), 30–48.
Famularo, Julia (2018). '"Fighting the Enemy with Fists and Daggers": The Chinese Communist Party's Counter-terrorism Policy in the Xinjiang Uyghur Autonomous Region', in Michael Clarke (ed.), *Terrorism and Counter-terrorism in China: Domestic and Foreign Policy Dimensions* (Oxford: Oxford University Press), 39–73.
Foucault, Michel (1977). *Discipline and Punish: The Birth of the Prison* (London: Penguin).
Fu, Hualing (2005). 'Re-education through Labour in Historical Perspective', *The China Quarterly* 184 (December), 811–830.
Global Terrorism Database (2020). 'Xinjiang Keyword Search', National Consortium for the Study of Terrorism and Responses to Terrorism (START), University of Maryland, www.start.umd.edu/gtd/search/Results.aspx?search=Xinjiang&sa.x=48&sa.y=4 (accessed 11 September 2020).

Global Times (2018). 'Protecting Peace, Stability Is Top of Human Rights Agenda for Xinjiang', 12 August, www.globaltimes.cn/content/1115022.shtml (accessed 1 May 2019).

Government Information Public Platform of Kashi (2018). 'Notice on Printing and Distributing the "Responsibility Plan for the Key Points of Inspection Work in Kashgar Region in 2018"', 6 March, http://kashi.gov.cn/Government/PublicInfoShow.aspx?ID=2851 (accessed 19 September 2020).

Grauer, Yael (2021). 'Revealed: Mass Chinese Police Database', *The Intercept*, 29 January, https://theintercept.com/2021/01/29/china-uyghur-muslim-surveillance-police/ (accessed 13 February 2021).

Greitens, Sheena Chestnut, Myunghee Lee, and Emir Yazici (2019/20). 'Counterterrorism and Preventive Repression: China's Changing Strategy in Xinjiang', *International Security* 44 (3), 9–47.

Hayes, Ben (2012). 'The Surveillance-Industrial Complex', in Kirstie Ball, Kevin Haggerty, and David Lyon (eds), *Routledge Handbook of Surveillance Studies* (London: Routledge), 167–175.

Hierman, Brent (2007). 'The Pacification of Xinjiang: Uighur Protest and the Chinese State, 1988–2002', *Problems of Post-Communism* 54 (3), 48–62.

Hoffman, Samantha (2017). 'Managing the State: Social Credit, Surveillance and the CCP's Plan for China', *China Brief* 17 (11), https://jamestown.org/program/managing-the-state-social-credit-surveillance-and-the-ccps-plan-for-china/ (accessed 16 October 2018).

Human Rights Watch (2005). 'Devastating Blows: Religious Repression of Uighurs in Xinjiang', 1 April, www.unhcr.org/refworld/docid/42c3bcf20.html (accessed 14 October 2020).

Human Rights Watch (2019). 'China's Algorithms of Repression', 1 May, www.hrw.org/report/2019/05/01/chinas-algorithms-repression/reverse-engineering-xinjiang-police-mass-surveillance (accessed 23 March 2020).

Information Office of the State Council of the PRC (2002). 'East Turkistan Terrorist Forces Cannot Get Away with Impunity', 21 January, www.china.org.cn/english/2002/Jan/25582.htm (accessed 18 March 2020).

Information Office of the State Council of the PRC (2019). 'Full Text: Vocational Education and Training in Xinjiang', Xinhua, 16 August, www.xinhuanet.com/english/2019-08/16/c_138313359.htm (accessed 3 September 2019).

Jacobs, Andrew (2014). 'China Says Nearly 100 Killed in Week of Unrest in Xinjiang', *New York Times*, 3 August, www.nytimes.com/2014/08/04/world/asia/china-says-nearly-100-are-killed-in-week-of-unrest-in-xinjiang.html?_r=5 (accessed 1 October 2019).

Jenkins, Richard (2012). 'Identity, Surveillance and Modernity: Sorting Out Who's Who', in Kirstie Ball, Kevin Haggerty, and David Lyon (eds), *Routledge Handbook of Surveillance Studies* (London: Routledge), 159–166.

Ji, You (2016). 'China's National Security Commission: Theory, Evolution and Operations', *Journal of Contemporary China* 25 (98), 178–196.

Jia, Cui, and Zhu Zhe (2010). 'Xinjiang Support Package Unveiled', *China Daily*, 21 May, www.chinadaily.com.cn/china/2010-05/21/content_9874981.htm (accessed 8 December 2020).

Jingjie, Yang (2014). 'Xinjiang to See "Major Strategy Shift"', *Global Times*, 9 January, www.globaltimes.cn/content/836495.shtml#.UtS1ivaFZ0Q (accessed 7 April 2019).

Karrar, Hassan (2017). 'Resistance to State-Orchestrated Modernization in Xinjiang: The Genesis of Unrest in the Multiethnic Frontier', *China Information* 32 (2), 183–202.

Kim, Hodong (2004). *Holy War in China: The Muslim Rebellion and Khanate in Chinese Central Asia, 1864–1877* (Stanford: Stanford University Press).

Klimeš, Ondřej (2018). 'Advancing "Ethnic Unity" and "De-extremization": Ideational Governance in Xinjiang under "New Circumstances" (2012–2017)', *Journal of Chinese Political Science* 23 (3), 413–436.

Koplowitz, Howard (2014). 'China Uighur Conflict: Gang Knife Attack in Xinjiang Blamed on Islamic Terrorists', *International Business Times*, 29 July, www.ibtimes.com/china-uighur-conflict-gang-knife-attack-xinjiang-province-blamed-islamic-terrorists-1642368 (accessed 24 May 2020).

Lampton, David (2015). 'Xi Jinping and the National Security Commission: Policy Coordination and Political Power', *Journal of Contemporary China* 24 (95), 759–777.

Leibold, James (2013). 'Ethnic Policy in China: Is Reform Inevitable?', *Policy Studies* 68 (Honolulu: East-West Center), https://scholarspace.manoa.hawaii.edu/bitstream/10125/30617/ps068.pdf (accessed 14 February 2020).

Leibold, James (2014). 'Xinjiang Work Forum Marks New Policy of "Ethnic Mingling"', *China Brief* 14 (12), https://jamestown.org/program/xinjiang-work-forum-marks-new-policy-of-ethnic-mingling/ (accessed 11 November 2019).

Leibold, James (2018a). 'Hu the Uniter and the Radical Turn in China's Xinjiang Policy', *China Brief* 18 (16), https://jamestown.org/program/hu-the-uniter-hu-lianhe-and-the-radical-turn-in-chinas-xinjiang-policy/ (accessed 11 November 2019).

Leibold, James (2018b). 'Mind Control in China Has a Very Long History', *New York Times*, 28 November, www.nytimes.com/2018/11/28/opinion/china-reeducation-mind-control-xinjiang.html (accessed 13 November 2019).

Leibold, James (2019). 'The Spectre of Insecurity: The CCP's Mass Internment Strategy in Xinjiang', *China Leadership Monitor*, 1 March, www.prcleader.org/leibold (accessed 29 May 2020).

Li, Yuhui (2018). *China's Assistance Program in Xinjiang: A Sociological Analysis* (Lanham: Rowman & Littlefield).

Lianhe zaobao (2011). '张春贤治疆凸显'两手政策' [Zhang Chunxian Highlights His Two-Handed Policy in Governing Xinjiang], 21 July, www.zaobao.com.sg/special/report/politic/cnpol/story20110721-139990 (accessed 16 April 2020).

Liu, Amy H., and Kevin Peters (2017). 'The Hanification of Xinjiang, China: The Economic Effects of the Great Leap West', *Studies in Ethnicity and Nationalism* 17 (2), 265–280.

Ma, Alexandra (2019). 'China Uses an Intrusive Surveillance App to Track Its Muslim Minority', Business Insider, 11 May, www.businessinsider.com.au/how-ijop-works-china-surveillance-app-for-muslim-uighurs-2019-5?r=US&IR=T (accessed 6 February 2020).

Millward, James (2004). 'Violent Uyghur Separatism in Xinjiang: A Critical Assessment', *Policy Studies* 6 (Honolulu: East-West Center).

Millward, James (2007). *Eurasian Crossroads: A History of Xinjiang* (New York: Columbia University Press).

Millward, James (2009). 'Does the 2009 Urumchi Violence Mark a Turning Point?', *Central Asian Survey* 28 (4), 347–369.

Millward, James (2019). 'Reeducating Xinjiang's Muslims', *New York Review of Books*, 7 February, www.nybooks.com/articles/2019/02/07/reeducating-xinjiangs-muslims/ (accessed 26 June 2020).

Ministry of Foreign Affairs of the PRC (2001). 'Amendment III to the Criminal Law of the PRC', Adopted at the 25th Meeting of the Standing Committee of the Ninth National People's Congress, 29 December, www.fmprc.gov.cn/eng/wjb/zzjg/jks/jkxw/t208622.htm (accessed 12 March 2020).

Mozur, Paul (2019). 'One Month, 500,000 Face Scans: How China Is Using A.I. to Profile a Minority', *New York Times*, 14 April, www.nytimes.com/2019/04/14/technology/china-surveillance-artificial-intelligence-racial-profiling.html (accessed 9 February 2020).

Pitzer, Andrea (2019). *One Long Night: The Global History of Concentration Camps* (New York: Back Bay Books).

Qiang, Wu (2014). 'Urban Grid Management and Police State in China: A Brief Overview', China Change, 12 August, https://chinachange.org/2013/08/08/the-urban-grid-management-and-police-state-in-china-a-brief-overview/ (accessed 10 February 2020).

Qiu, Yongzheng (2014). 'Turkey's Ambiguous Policies Help Terrorists Join IS Jihadist Group: Analyst', *Global Times*, 15 December, www.globaltimes.cn/content/896765.shtml (accessed 4 October 2018).

Radio Free Asia (2017). 'Vehicles to Get Compulsory GPS Tracking in Xinjiang', 20 February, www.rfa.org/english/news/uyghur/xinjiang-gps-02202017145155.html (accessed 11 April 2019).

Radio Free Asia (2018). 'Xinjiang Political "Re-education Camps" Treat Uyghurs "Infected by Religious Extremism": CCP Youth League', 8 August, www.rfa.org/english/news/uyghur/infected-08082018173807.html (accessed 13 September 2018).

Ramzy, Austin (2010). 'A Year after Xinjiang Riots, Ethnic Tensions Remain', *Time*, 5 July, http://content.time.com/time/world/article/0,8599,2001311,00.html (accessed 23 February 2019).

Reeves, Jeffrey (2016). 'Ideas and Influence: Scholarship as a Harbinger of Counterterrorism Institutions, Policies, and Laws in the People's Republic of China', *Terrorism and Political Violence* 28 (5), 827–847.

Rickleton, Christopher (2019). 'From Camps to Factories: Muslim Detainees Say China Using Forced Labour', AFP, 4 March, https://sg.news.yahoo.com/camps-factories-muslim-detainees-china-using-forced-labour-041047367.html (accessed 9 October 2020).

Roberts, Sean R. (2012). 'Imaginary Terrorism? The Global War on Terror and the Narrative of the Uyghur Terrorist Threat', March (Washington, DC: PONARS Working Paper).

Roberts, Sean R. (2013). 'Tiananmen Crash: Terrorism or Cry of Desperation?', CNN, 31 October, https://edition.cnn.com/2013/10/31/opinion/china-tiananmen-uyghurs/index.html (accessed 13 October 2020).

Roberts, Sean R. (2018). 'The Biopolitics of China's "War on Terror" and the Exclusion of the Uyghurs', *Critical Asian Studies* 50 (2), 232–258.

Roberts, Sean R. (2020). *The War on the Uyghurs: China's Campaign against Xinjiang's Muslims* (Manchester: Manchester University Press).

Rosenblatt, Nate (2016). 'All Jihad Is Local: What ISIS' Files Tell Us about Its Fighters', New America Foundation, Washington, DC, July.

Ryono, Angel, and Matthew Galway (2015). 'Xinjiang under China: Reflections on the Multiple Dimensions of the 2009 Urumqi Uprising', *Asian Ethnicity* 16 (2), 235–255.

Scott, James C. (1998). *Seeing Like a State: How Certain Schemes to Improve the Human Condition Have Failed* (Princeton: Princeton University Press).

Scot Tanner, Murray (2018). 'China's Response to Terrorism' (Washington, DC: CNA), www.cna.org/CNA_files/PDF/IRM-2016-U-013542-Final.pdf (accessed 5 May 2019).

Smith Finley, Joanne (2018). 'Islam in Xinjiang: "De-extremification" or Violation of Religious Space?', *Asia Dialogue*, 15 June, https://theasiadialogue.com/2018/06/15/islam-in-xinjiang-de-extremification-or-violation-of-religious-space/ (accessed 4 September 2018).

Song, Jianhua (2012). '习近平参加新疆团审议 强调坚持稳定压倒一切' [Xi Jinping Participates in Xinjiang Delegation Review], *Zhongguo xinwen wang*, 12 March, reprinted in https://news.qq.com/a/20120312/000209.htm (accessed 15 August 2020).

Song, Tao, Weidong Liu, Zhigao Liu et al. (2019). 'Policy Mobilities and the China Model: Pairing Aid Policy in Xinjiang', *Sustainability* 11 (13), 3496.

State Council Information Office of the PRC (2020). 'Full Text: Employment and Labor Rights in Xinjiang', 17 September, http://english.scio.gov.cn/whitepapers/2020-09/17/content_76712251_6.htm (accessed 1 October 2020).

Steenberg, Rune, and Alessandro Rippa (2019). 'Development for All? State Schemes, Security, and Marginalization in Kashgar, Xinjiang', *Critical Asian Studies* 51 (2), 274–295.

Trevaskes, Susan (2007). 'Severe and Swift Justice in China', *British Journal of Criminology* 47, 23–41.

Tschantret, Joshua (2018). 'Repression, Opportunity, and Innovation: The Evolution of Terrorism in Xinjiang, China', *Terrorism and Political Violence* 30 (4), 569–588.

van Krieken, Robert (2010). 'Cultural Genocide in Australia', in Dan Stone (ed.), *The Historiography of Genocide* (London: Palgrave Macmillan), 128–155.

Vinokour, Maya (2018). '2+2=5: On the White Sea-Baltic Canal and Totalitarian Pipe Dreams', *Los Angeles Review of Books*, 27 September, https://lareviewofbooks.org/article/225-white-sea-baltic-canal-totalitarian-pipe-dreams/# (accessed 8 April 2019).

Wang, Ding, and Dan Shan (2016). '反恐研究与新疆模式' [Studies on Anti-terrorism and the Xinjiang Mode], 情报杂志 [Journal of Intelligence] 35 (11), 20–26.

Weller, Toni (2012). 'The Information State: An Historical Perspective on Surveillance', in Kirstie Ball, Kevin D. Haggerty, and David Lyon (eds), *Routledge Handbook of Surveillance Studies* (London: Routledge), 57–63.

Wong, Edward (2010). 'China Announces Development Plan for Xinjiang', *New York Times*, 29 May, www.nytimes.com/2010/05/29/world/asia/29china.html (accessed 3 May 2020).

Xiaocuo, Yi (2019). 'Recruiting Loyal Stabilisers: On the Banality of Carceral Colonialism in Xinjiang', *Made in China Journal*, 25 October, https://madeinchinajournal.com/2019/10/25/recruiting-loyal-stabilisers-onthe-banality-of-carceral-colonialism-in-xinjiang/ (accessed 15 March 2020).

Xinhua (2014). 'Xi Jinping: Expanding the Size of Xinjiang Ethnic Minorities to the Mainland', 29 May, www.xinhuanet.com//politics/2014-05/29/c_1110926294.htm (accessed 7 August 2019).

Xinhua (2015). 'China Adopts First Counter-terrorism Law in History', 28 December, www.xinhuanet.com/mil/2015-12/28/c_128574674.htm (accessed 14 August 2019).

Xinhua (2020). 'Xi Stresses Building Xinjiang Featuring Socialism with Chinese Characteristics in New Era', 26 September, www.xinhuanet.com/english/2020-09/26/c_139399549.htm (accessed 17 November 2020).

Xinjiang Ribao (2014). '张春贤同志对各级干部深入基层'访民情惠民生聚民心'活动提出明确要' [Comrade Zhang Chunxian Put Forward Clear Requirements for the Activities of Cadres at All Levels Going to the Grassroots Level to 'Visit the People and Benefit the People's Livelihood and Gather People's Hearts'], 5 March, www.xjdaily.com.cn/special/2014/06/1027136.shtml (accessed 17 November 2020).

Xinjiang Ribao (2017a). 'Zhu Hailun zai Akesu diqu zhaokai jiceng ganbu zuotanhui' [Zhu Hailun Convenes a Grassroot Cadre Forum in the Aksu Region], 20 April, http://news.sohu.com/20170420/n489632907.shtml (accessed 13 November 2020).

Xinjiang Ribao (2017b). 'Chen quanguo jiu zuo hao dangqian xinjiang wending gongzuo zuochu pishi zhu qi fankong weiwen de tongqiangtiebi quebao quan jiang shehui daju hexie wending' [Chen Quanguo Gave Instructions on Doing the Current Stability Work in Xinjiang: Build a Copper Wall and Iron Wall to Fight Terrorism and Maintain Stability to Ensure the Overall Harmony and Stability of Xinjiang], *Renming wang*, reprinted in http://xj.people.com.cn/n2/2017/0819/c186332-30628706.html (accessed 20 March 2018).

Xinjiang xingnong wang (2015). '新疆伊宁县: 开展"去极端化"集中教育"' [Yining County, Xinjiang: Carrying Out 'De-radicalization' Intensive Education], 12 January, www.agri.cn/DFV20/XJ/dfzx/dfyw/201501/t20150113_4331764.htm (accessed 5 December 2019).

Xu, Vicky Xiuzhong, Danielle Cave, James Leibold et al. (2020). 'Uyghurs for Sale: "Re-education", Forced Labour and Surveillance beyond Xinjiang', 1 March (Canberra: Australian Strategic Policy Institute), www.aspi.org.au/report/uyghurs-sale (accessed 17 May 2020).

Yue, Hu (2010). 'Hand in Hand: China Unveils a Partner Assistance Program to Propel Xinjiang toward Economic Prosperity and Social Stability', *Beijing Review* 23 (10 June), www.bjreview.com.cn/Cover_Story_Series_2010/2010-06/07/content_277589.htm (accessed 16 February 2020).

Zainab, Rana (2019). 'China's "Political Re-education" Camps of Xinjiang's Uyghur Muslims', *Asian Affairs* 50 (4), 488–501.

Zenn, Jacob (2011). 'Jihad in China? Marketing the Turkistan Islamic Party', *Terrorism Monitor* 9 (11), https://jamestown.org/program/jihad-in-china-marketing-the-turkistan-islamic-party/ (accessed 14 March 2019).

Zenn, Jacob (2018). 'The Turkistan Islamic Party in Double-Exile: Geographic and Organizational Divisions in Uighur Jihadism', *Terrorism Monitor* 16 (17), https://jamestown.org/program/the-turkistan-islamic-party-in-double-exile-geographic-and-organizational-divisions-in-uighur-jihadism/ (accessed 23 July 2021).

Zenz, Adrian (2019). '"Thoroughly Reforming Them towards a Healthy Heart Attitude": China's Political Re-education Campaign in Xinjiang', *Central Asian Survey* 38 (1), 102–128.

Zenz, Adrian (2020). 'Coercive Labor in Xinjiang: Labor Transfer and the Mobilization of Ethnic Minorities to Pick Cotton', Center for Global Policy, December, https://cgpolicy.org/briefs/coercive-labor-in-xinjiang-labor-transfer-and-the-mobilization-of-ethnic-minorities-to-pick-cotton/ (accessed 6 February 2021).

Zenz, Adrian, and James Leibold (2017a). 'Chen Quanguo: The Strongman behind Beijing's Securitization Strategy in Tibet and Xinjiang', *China Brief* 17 (12), https://jamestown.org/program/chen-quanguo-the-strongman-behind-beijings-securitization-strategy-in-tibet-and-xinjiang/ (accessed 3 October 2019).

Zenz, Adrian, and James Leibold (2017b). 'Xinjiang's Rapidly Evolving Security State', *China Brief*, 14 March, https://jamestown.org/program/xinjiangs-rapidly-evolving-security-state/ (accessed 17 August 2019).

Zenz, Adrian, and James Leibold (2019). 'Securitizing Xinjiang: Police Recruitment, Informal Policing and Ethnic Minority Co-optation', *The China Quarterly* 242, 324–348.

Zhao, Taotao, and James Leibold (2020). 'Ethnic Governance under Xi Jinping: The Centrality of the United Front Work Department and Its Implications', *Journal of Contemporary China* 29 (124), 487–502.

10

The effect of Xinjiang's virtual lockdown on the Uyghur diaspora

Ablimit Baki Elterish

Introduction

Uyghurs living outside China began to lose contact with their loved ones in Xinjiang[1] from towards the end of 2016. By July 2017, many thousands in the Uyghur diaspora have been made to be unable to communicate with families in China. Phone calls are unanswered. Text messages are rejected – a clear indication that the senders are blocked or phone contacts of loved ones have been deleted. Many Uyghurs whose calls are answered have been asked not to call again. Some revert to using emojis – strange facial expressions rather than words when communicating with their relatives abroad. This virtual lockdown of Xinjiang is causing harmful effects on the Uyghur diaspora who have families, friends, or businesses in China. It has severed almost all people-to-people communication between Uyghurs living in China with those living abroad.

Why are Uyghurs living abroad not able to talk to their families in China? China's state media claims that Uyghurs are free to talk with their relatives living outside China. But in reality, Uyghurs in Xinjiang have been virtually locked down from the outside world. One obvious reason for this is that there is something that Xinjiang does not want the outside world to know about – the unprecedented sweeping crackdown in Xinjiang. The crackdown, allegedly a counter-extremism measure, includes implementation of mass surveillance, mass incarceration, and mass detention policies that target Turkic minority groups, primarily Uyghurs, in a vast network of internment camps (Human Rights Watch 2018). More than one million Turkic people are being detained in these internment camps without formal charges (Amnesty International 2018; Raza 2019; Smith Finley 2019). This includes large numbers of the Uyghur, Kazakh, and Kyrgyz cultural elite: intellectuals, artists, business people, and writers. The government does not provide official reasons for their detention, or even confirmation that individuals have been detained, and most families have chosen not to speak out because of fear.

The internment camps in Xinjiang

The structure and operation of the internment camp system in Xinjiang is being kept secret from the general public. China's state media initially denied the existence of any internment camps, but later insisted that these facilities are 're-education centres' (再教育中心), or 'vocational and professional training centres' (职业技能培训中心) like 'boarding schools' (寄宿学校). In reality, these facilities were officially established as political thought transformation centres – 'de-extremification education and transformation centres' (去极端化教育转化中心). However, scholars of the subject, including Roberts (2018) and Smith Finley (2019), describe these as 'concentration camps' based on the massive evidence discovered by international media organizations such as WSJ, CNN, and BBC following rare access to some facilities, and testimonies given by some eyewitnesses. It is not known how long the internment camps in Xinjiang will operate. Official documents and satellite images show that many of Xinjiang internment camps are continuously running (Sudworth 2018). Uyghurs in the diaspora refer to these internment camps as *jaza lagirliri* (punishment camps). Many members of the diaspora believe Uyghurs in Xinjiang are being collectively punished for their ethnic identity, harbouring 'politically incorrect ideas' or 'strong religious views', being Muslims, or being 'two-faced persons'. The internment camp system is seen by many in the Uyghur diaspora as an attack on the entire Uyghur population, their culture, and their religion.

The feelings of being severed from contact with their loved ones in Xinjiang have been exacerbated by the constant exposure to heartbreaking reports of the treatment of Uyghurs in Xinjiang in the media: reports of mass detention, mass disappearance, mass surveillance, banned Uyghur language from schools and religious activities, forced inter-ethnic marriages between Uyghurs and Han, forced celebration of Han festivals, forced labour in factories, destruction of mosques and graveyards, collection of extensive biometric data such as DNA samples, organ harvesting, sudden deaths of well-known Uyghur figures, forced birth control and sterilization of Uyghurs, secret transfer of Uyghur detainees to prisons in inner China, and other measures amounting to what has been globally reported as 'genocide'. The prolonged loss of contact coupled with constant tragic news reports from Xinjiang are causing a variety of psychological and psychiatric problems among Uyghurs living outside China. This chapter will investigate the effects of Xinjiang's virtual lockdown on the Uyghur diaspora. It argues that the virtual lockdown of Xinjiang and the internment camps are human-made disasters, which have a huge impact on the everyday life, work, and studies of the Uyghur diaspora living across the world.

The theory of collective trauma

This study is framed through the concept of collective trauma. The term collective trauma refers to psychological reactions to traumatic events affecting an entire society (Hirschberger 2018). Traumatized people show many different and mixed symptoms. These include fear, sadness, anxiety, depression, guilt, anger, grief, crying, fatigue, confusion, despair, feelings of helplessness, suicidal thoughts, forced isolation, sleeping difficulties, and concentration difficulties (Pearlman and Saakvitne 1995). Most research on collective trauma is focused on the effects of past traumatic events such as the Great Depression, the Holocaust, and the 9/11 attacks because they are generally considered to be prototypical twentieth- and early twenty-first-century human disasters.

As a human-made disaster, the internment camps in Xinjiang are unparalleled in many respects. Firstly, a complete blanket targeting of the entire Uyghur population is unprecedented. Security crackdowns in Xinjiang have been implemented for decades. However, previous crackdowns targeted selective members of the Uyghur population. But this time, the sweeping crackdown (全覆盖) targets all Uyghurs. Secondly, the crackdown relies on a wide range of new technology such as high-tech surveillance to monitor and control the activity of the Uyghur population. Thirdly, the duration of the crackdown is exceptional. Earlier 'strike hard' campaigns were relatively limited in duration and periodically renewed. However, the current crackdown is more prolonged with no stated end in sight. Lastly, the traumatic experiences of the Uyghur diaspora caused by this disaster are unparalleled. The crackdown happening in Xinjiang is mostly observed through mass media reports by the Uyghur diaspora with only a limited number of first-hand eyewitnesses.

Are the internment camps in Xinjiang comparable to some of the past traumatic events in other parts of the world? The Uyghur diaspora say that what is happening to the Uyghurs in Xinjiang at present is 'a tragedy befallen us' (*beshimizgha kelgen apet*). Many news reports have already started to link the internment camps in Xinjiang to the Holocaust (Forth 2020). In their view, Xinjiang practises ethnic cleansing through its internment camp system. Some reports even claim that the world's promise of 'Never Again' is already being broken in Xinjiang (21wilberforce 2019).

Dimensions of collective trauma

This study will investigate the effects of Xinjiang's virtual lockdown and internment camps on Uyghurs living outside China. Semi-structured interviews were conducted with sixty-one Uyghur individuals. There are thirty-eight males and twenty-three females, all living outside China, ranging from twenty-five to sixty years old. Half of the interviewees have lived in their host countries for around five years. Some have lived abroad for about ten years, and others for around twenty years. This study does not use the real names of interviewees in order to follow the principles of research ethics. Only fictitious first names are used to equate their actual names.

Face-to-face interviews were conducted in Turkey and the UK from the end of 2018 to 2020. Online interviews were conducted from the beginning of 2019 to 2020. Fieldwork was originally conducted using

Table 10.1 Dimensions of collective trauma among the Uyghur diaspora

Dimensions	Symptoms
Psychological	Fear, sadness, anxiety, depression, anger, crying, sleep problems, concentration difficulties, depression
Family	Separation, grief
Social	Suicidal ideation, community withdrawal

face-to-face interviews only. Given the Uyghur diaspora's geographical spread across the globe, the sample's representativeness was enhanced using online interviews with Uyghurs in Canada, the US, Australia, and Europe. Research suggests that online interviews provide a useful complement to the traditional face-to-face interviews, particularly in qualitative or interpretive studies (Curasi 2001). From the beginning of 2019, the reaction to the virtual lockdown of Xinjiang began to change drastically among the Uyghur diaspora as they became more anxious to find information about their loved ones due to long-term loss of contact. Many Uyghurs began to use social media to speak out about their missing or detained family members in Xinjiang. This increasing outspokenness also offered more insightful data for this study as more people were willing to be interviewed. All interviewees for this study were selected regardless of their diaspora status in their host countries. The final interviewees consisted of Uyghurs living in Turkey, Canada, the US, Australia, and across Europe. Face-to-face interviews were conducted in Uyghur only. Online interviews took place either in Uyghur or in English according to the preference of the interviewees. The interview questions focused on the effect of the long-term loss of contact with their loved ones in Xinjiang. The most frequently mentioned themes associated with the focus of this study were coded and arranged for analysis. Using the theory of collective trauma, a variety of psychological symptoms are analysed in three dimensions: psychological, family, and social (see Table 10.1).

The psychological dimension of collective trauma

Although the symptoms of the psychological dimension of collective trauma can affect and damage bodily functions, the source of the injury is psychological (Aydin 2017: 127). The interview results will show that the effects of Xinjiang's virtual lockdown on the Uyghur diaspora are predominantly psychological, including fear, sadness, anxiety, depression, anger, crying, sleep problems, and concentration difficulties.

Fear is the most common symptom of collective trauma among the Uyghur diaspora. According to researchers (Silver *et al.* 2002), traumatized people fear for their own safety as well as their loved ones. The disaster occurring in Xinjiang certainly creates feelings of fear among the Uyghur diaspora. The interview results show that there is a widespread of fear among Uyghurs living in exile: fear of something bad that has happened or is happening to their loved ones, fear of returning to China, fear of being sent back to China, fear of being harassed by the police from China, and fear of using real names on social media.

Fear of something bad that has happened or is happening to their loved ones

The most common fear that Uyghur exiles felt is that something terribly bad has happened or is happening to their family members in China. This fear comes from their assumptions based on prolonged loss of contact, and on frequent news reports of various kinds of harsh mistreatment of Uyghurs in Xinjiang.

Askar, aged thirty, is from the UK. He fears that his family members in Xinjiang have been taken into the *jaza lagirliri*. Askar describes the scale and level of fear as something he has never thought he would experience. By the middle of 2017, Askar had completely lost contact with his families and friends. Askar's elderly parents-in-law, who were just ordinary farmers, kept in touch for a bit longer but the most shocking and heart-breaking moment came when they stopped greeting in the usual way of saying 'assalamu alaykum' (Arabic, peace be upon you). Although this is the religious greeting, non-religious people would use it naturally as a cultural form of greetings to each other. By the beginning of 2018, Askar had completely lost contact with everyone back home. Askar says the news is getting worse day by day. This has made him believe that his extended family members and friends have been interned (Askar, male, living in the UK for fifteen years; interviewed in June 2019).

Erkin, a young Uyghur man living in Turkey, fears that something bad may have happened to his father-in-law: 'I have not heard from my father-in-law, a well-known artist, since November 2018. My wife and I are fearful every day that something worse may have already happened to him or is happening to him' (Erkin, male, living in Turkey for five years; interviewed in March 2019).

The Chinese government maintains that 'students' in the 'vocational and professional training centres' learn Mandarin Chinese, law, and job skills. However, many Uyghur elites, like Erkin's father-in-law, are Mandarin-speaking professionals who do not require any vocational or professional training. Furthermore, in many cases, they were only casually observant in their religious practice. Actually, these are the very ideal Uyghurs promoted by the party-state. But unfortunately, these Uyghurs have not been spared from being sent to the *jaza lagirliri*.

Fear of returning to China

The fear of returning to Xinjiang is especially common among young Uyghur students. For many people studying or living abroad, returning home is taken for granted and something to look forward to, but this is something fearful for Uyghurs from Xinjiang. News reports of Uyghur graduate students going missing upon returning to China have exacerbated their fears.

Mahire, aged twenty-six, came to the UK to pursue postgraduate studies at a London-based university. Upon successful completion of her degree, she decided to apply for asylum in the UK in order to remain as a refugee. She is certain she will be taken away as soon as she arrives in China because she studied an Islamic-related subject for her degree (Mahire, female, living in the UK for nearly three years; interviewed in May 2019).

Another student, Kadir, aged twenty-nine, also came to study at the postgraduate level in the UK. According to Kadir, he lost direct contact with his family back in Xinjiang. He would occasionally talk with his mother who could use a WeChat account belonging to a Han friend in the same town in Xinjiang. His mother repeatedly told him to continue his studies as long as possible and not to think about coming back home. He believed this was coded language warning him not to return to China to endanger himself (Kadir, male, living in the UK for four years; interviewed in May 2019).

Fear of being sent back to China

Uyghurs living in the Middle Eastern and Central Asian countries are afraid that one day they may be forcibly sent back to China. While numerous North American and European countries have criticized China's policy in Xinjiang, Muslim-majority countries in the Middle East and Central Asia have been relatively silent to the plight of the Uyghurs. The increased financial ties of these Muslim-majority countries with China have made the Uyghur diaspora believe these are no longer safe countries for them.

Subi, aged fifty, had established a successful business in Dubai. From the end of 2018, he started to transfer his business to the UK, fearing that one day he would be sent back to China where three of his relatives are imprisoned for sending money to him to assist his business in Dubai (Subi, male, living in the UK for one year; interviewed in May 2019).

Another young Uyghur man interviewed shared the same kind of fear. After learning in the news that the Egyptian authorities were arresting and sending Uyghur students back to China in the summer of 2017, Irfan managed to travel to Turkey from Egypt. He believed, like thousands of Uyghurs, that Turkey is a haven for Uyghurs. However, closer economic relations between China and Turkey made him fearful of being sent back to China because Turkey has become indebted to China like most of the Muslim world. Irfan wanted to move to a European country where he and his family could settle down peacefully and permanently (Irfan, male, aged twenty-five, living in Turkey for one year; interviewed in May 2018).

Fear of being harassed by the police from China

Many Uyghurs abroad feel unsafe and they live in fear of being harassed by the Chinese police. Reports of harassment of Uyghurs living overseas have been well documented and circulated in mainstream media. Zumret, aged thirty-five, described her experiences:

I have been constantly harassed by the police from back home in China. They kept calling me to provide personal information of the Uyghurs in my city. They threatened me to co-operate with them and if I don't, all my relatives will be harmed. It's very frustrating. (Zumret, female, living in Canada for fifteen years; interviewed in May 2019)

Abdul, aged thirty-three, a Uyghur man who had lived in the US for eight years, thought he had been forgotten by the police in China. Nevertheless, he became struck with fear when the local police from Xinjiang demanded proof of his identity and evidence of his employment from his parents via a mutual contact he still maintains in China: 'My contact with my parents is indirect through a third person in another Chinese city. One day, I received a message that the police in Xinjiang asked my parents to send them a picture of me in front of my company sign, holding my passport photo page in one hand and holding that day's newspaper showing the date in another. This made the hair on the back of my neck standing up' (Abdul, male, interviewed in May 2019).

Fear of using real names on the Internet

There is also fear of using real names on the Internet, especially on social media. China's sophisticated Internet censorship system monitors criticism of the government not only from people within China but also abroad. Many Uyghurs do not use their real names on social media platforms such as Facebook and Twitter when they comment on Uyghur issues due to extreme fear and self-censorship.

A Uyghur woman from Germany, aged forty-three, is afraid of using her real name on Facebook: 'Being a Uyghur person with relatives already detained in the *jaza lagirliri*, I always have an urge to express my opinions whenever I see a discussion about the Uyghur issues on Facebook. But I am so frightened to use my real name because of the exponentially growing strength of China's Internet army with more sophisticated surveillance technology. In my understanding, China's long arms can reach anywhere in the word' (Akide, living in Germany for twenty years; interviewed in December 2019).

These fears were shared by another Uyghur man in the US: 'I have deactivated my Facebook account because I realized someone was watching my online activity. My Chinese passport was going to expire and my application to renew my passport was rejected by the Chinese Consulate saying the Xinjiang side did not approve it. Not long after this, I received an indirect message from my mother in Xinjiang asking me to stop talking nonsense on the Internet (*torda qalaymiqan sozlime*). I only used Facebook to express my dissatisfaction about the treatment of the Uyghurs in Xinjiang' (Kuresh, aged thirty-five, living in the US for fifteen years; interviewed in October 2019).

Overwhelming sadness

Like fear, sadness is another common symptom associated with collective trauma. The Uyghur diaspora, in general, have an intense feeling of sadness. They often compare their 'good old days' to present times as they imagine the potential things that have happened or are happening to their loved ones in Xinjiang. Although it is common for people to have distressing thoughts, images, and feelings like these for short periods of time, a long-term sadness leads to depression which can trigger trauma (Fivush and Buckner 2000).

A Uyghur woman who formerly worked as a tourist leader for visitors from Australia to visit Urumqi, Turfan, and Kashgar during the summer seasons described her sad feelings. She explained why she feels extremely sad when she sees pictures and videos of empty streets and bazaars of Kashgar and Urumqi posted recently online. Her heart sinks when she compares her old pictures taken during her visits there. 'Streets and bazaars were crowded with happy and friendly shoppers and tourists. But where have they all gone?' she asked (Gulshen, aged thirty-nine, female, living in Australia for eighteen years; interviewed in May 2019).

Being unable to contact family members for such an extended period of time has increased the intensity of sadness among many in the Uyghur diaspora. Shohret's experiences were representative of the Uyghur diaspora whose feelings of sadness changed gradually over time. 'The happiest moment of my life brought the saddest moment. I came to study at a university in the US in 2015. My parents were planning to come to my graduation in 2017. But their passports which have US visas on them have been confiscated like all Uyghurs in Xinjiang. I lost contact with my parents in July 2017. After two months, I learned that my parents were taken to the *jaza lagirliri*. During my graduation ceremony, everyone around me was super happy. They could hug their parents. They could video call or text anyone they wanted to. But for me, not knowing whether my parents are alive is killing me,' he said. 'My graduation day became one of the worst days in my life.' Shohret maintains that his parents do not need 'vocational or professional training'. 'My father is a businessman. He went to Chinese school. Therefore, he can speak native-level Chinese. He has more Han Chinese friends than Uyghurs,' he said (Shohret, aged twenty-six, male, living in the US for three years; interviewed in June 2019).

Aliye, aged forty-five, is a Uyghur woman in the UK. She said that she becomes very sad whenever she watches her child's wedding video from Xinjiang. 'My sister, her husband, and my brother-in-law were all taken and imprisoned. Whenever I miss them, I just watch a video of the wedding of my son in Urumqi. Seeing so many familiar faces at the wedding party is a great comfort, but I just start to cry again each time I see the video,' she said (Aliye, female, living in the UK for two years; interviewed in May 2019).

The Uyghur diaspora often emotionally struggle when encountering news reports comparing the internment camps in Xinjiang to Nazi concentration camps from the Second World War. A Uyghur woman in the UK reported that she is deeply saddened when she reads stories comparing the treatment of the Uyghurs in Xinjiang to the treatment of the Jews in Nazi concentration camps. 'I cannot help crying when I read some news articles that compare Uyghur concentration camps to Nazi concentration camps. This has led me to watch films about the Nazi concentration camps. When I see shocking footages of the Nazi concentration camps, I cannot imagine what my family and friends are going through. We don't deserve to be treated like this in the twenty-first century' (Zubeyre, aged thirty-eight, female, living in the UK for six years; interviewed in March 2019).

Anxiety

Research in social psychology and clinical psychiatry suggests that people who have experienced traumatic events are more likely to suffer from anxiety (Muldoon *et al.* 2019). The interviews conducted show that the current situation of internment and family separation of Uyghurs in Xinjiang is the main cause of anxiety among the Uyghur diaspora. Like fear and sadness, there has been an increase in anxiety among the Uyghur diaspora. A Uyghur woman living in Norway describes how her long-term experience of being unable to talk with her mother elevated her anxiety levels: 'Loss of contact with my mother dragged on for three years and I still have no word of my mother's whereabouts. My anxiety mounted when my relatives deleted me from their phones' (Bahar, aged forty, female, living in Norway for ten years; interviewed in February 2020).

A Uyghur man from the UK reported how he has been plagued by anxiety over the past few years: 'It has been three years now since I last spoke to my parents. Not knowing their health and well-being is slowly pushing my anxiety to an abyss of depression. I am struggling to do my job. My brain is under constant worry. Having bad dreams every day is nothing unusual. To make it worse, the spread of the coronavirus has made my anxiety even worse. Why using such torture?' (Yusuf, aged sixty, male, living in the UK for twenty years; interviewed in July 2020).

Another Uyghur man living in Germany explained that not having any information about his father is causing him excessive levels of anxiety. 'I constantly worry too much about my father. He is a well-known researcher. He has written over twenty books on Uyghur culture and Arabic textbooks. I believe he is now in prison. Learning my father was detained, I tried to carry out my online campaign both on Facebook and Twitter to find information about him. One day in March 2019, I suddenly received a video call from my detained father via WeChat. My father demanded me to stop my campaign. This has made me feel extremely worried about him. I simply cannot imagine what he had been through and under what pressure or threat he was obliged to video call me' (Osman, aged thirty-four, male, living in Germany for seventeen years; interviewed in June 2019).

Anger

Research on emotional reactions during and after trauma finds that feelings of anger are common symptoms (Amstadter and Vernon 2008). Many in the Uyghur diaspora are angry at the lack of information about their loved ones for such a long period of time. Some furiously demand answers from the Chinese authorities.

Askar felt extremely angry when his sister in Xinjiang asked him to stop calling home in the future: 'I have an absolute sense of anger growing in my mind day by day. I stopped calling my siblings in *weten* after my youngest sister asked me not to call anyone out of the blue. Who told them not to talk with a son, daughter, or a brother, or sister, just because they live in a foreign country?' (Askar, aged forty-one, male, living in the UK for nine years; interviewed in June 2019).

Patigul, a Uyghur woman in France, expressed her anger and frustration of having to make group video calls in order to talk to her parents. 'I am very angry that my parents are not allowed to talk to me. I had a baby in 2017 and I wanted my parents to see their first grandchild. As we are afraid to talk to each other directly on the phone, I had to ask a former Han classmate in Shanghai to help. I video call my classmate who in turn places another video call to my parents. By using several phones at the same time, my parents were finally able to see their grandchild,' she said (Patigul, aged thirty-four, female, living in France for two years; interviewed in December 2018).

Some in the Uyghur diaspora direct their high level of anger at the Chinese government. 'I haven't been able to contact with my family ever since I left China in 2016. I don't know where my family are. I don't even know whether they are alive or they have already passed away. Chinese government, where are my family?!' a Uyghur man in Turkey asked (Rahman, aged twenty-seven, living in Turkey for two years; interviewed in 2018).

Many in the Uyghur diaspora have mixed feelings of fear, sadness, and anger. Nursiman, a Uyghur woman in Finland, said: 'My father and my brother were taken to the *jaza lagirliri* during the last week of Ramadan in 2017. Eid used to be the happiest day when we gather together with families and friends, paying respect to the elders and showing love for the young.' Nursiman continued: 'But the Eid of the past three years has lost those meanings. I only have tears, fear, and anger' (Nursiman, aged thirty-five, female, living in Finland for nine years; interviewed in February 2020).

Depression

Research on public mental services suggests that suffering from prolonged symptoms of trauma induces depression (Bob *et al.* 2010;

Vitriol *et al.* 2014). Uyghurs living abroad tend to experience serious symptoms of depression. Some in the Uyghur diaspora have already manifested certain depressive behaviour as a result of a long-term psychological problem.

Memetjan reported that he is experiencing some possible symptoms of depression. 'I have mixed feelings of fear, sadness, anger, and anxiety, and this is having a major effect on my mental health. I looked up the symptoms of self-depression through the NHS website for the first time in my entire life, and sadly I can tick of a majority in the list. I pretend everything is normal at work and gradually I have become quiet at my workplace,' he said (Memetjan, aged forty-six, male, living in the UK for twenty years; interviewed in June 2019).

Hasan in Holland described the experience of a young Uyghur man in his city. A twenty-two-year-old Uyghur man died in Holland in early 2019. How he died was not clear. Living in the country for a year and half, this man, just like thousands of other Uyghurs living in the diaspora, was going through severe depression because he was unable to find any information regarding his parents for a long time. He could not help thinking every day about what his parents were going through. Not being able to contact any family members and being alone in a new and very unfamiliar social environment added to his stress and anxiety. Finally, he could not take it any longer. None of his family members or relatives had any idea that this man had died, and they would probably not know for a long time. His death is a window into what the Uyghur diaspora experience when they cannot contact their loved ones back home (Hasan, aged fifty-six, male, living in Holland for twenty-five years; interviewed in July 2019).

Sleeping difficulties are traditionally considered as secondary symptoms of trauma (Hefez *et al.* 1987). However, recent studies on post-traumatic stress disorder (PTSD) find that sleeping difficulties are, in fact, a core feature and response to trauma (Spoormaker and Montgomery 2008). Lack of sleep or poor sleep subsequently has a tremendous negative influence on people's ability to concentrate and stay focused during the day (Medic *et al.* 2017).

Kahar, aged thirty-nine, a Uyghur IT worker in a UK-based company, described why he has sleeping and concentration difficulties. 'I think too much about my relatives back home in *weten*. Probably because of this, sometimes I cannot sleep, because I just feel I cannot help, and sometimes I cannot sleep well. I wake up frequently in the middle of the night. This is affecting my work. I feel tired at work. I cannot stay focused at work a lot of the time. I am beginning to lose hope because the news about the Uyghurs is getting worse. Luckily, I have a family member here in the UK and I can talk with them,' said Kahar (Kahar, male, living in the UK for fifteen years; interviewed in May 2019).

Family and social dimension of collective trauma

There are two major symptoms of trauma in the family dimension of collective trauma among the Uyghur diaspora: separation and grief. All members of the Uyghur diaspora have suffered from emotional difficulties due to separation from family because they are unable to visit or communicate with them. Furthermore, some Uyghur families have suffered from the loss of loved ones in China under these circumstances.

Separation

Family separation is a growing symptom of collective trauma among the Uyghur diaspora. Research on family separation and refugee mental health shows that a long period of family separation is harmful to the psychological health of family members (Lobel 2020). For many Uyghur families enduring family separation for extended periods is felt not just as trauma, but also as torture.

Many members of the Uyghur diaspora are struggling after separation from their families. The intensity of this situation is reflected in various accounts of the interviews. Meryem's account is one example: 'My husband went back to *weten* to sort out some business matters in May 2017. Since then, he has disappeared. I live here in Istanbul with my daughter not knowing what to do. Although I get help from my neighbours from time to time, I strongly have a sense of complete loss of something so valuable in my life. I dare not to think about what might have happened to my husband' (Meryem, aged thirty-two, female, living in Turkey for four years; interviewed in December 2018).

Abdul, aged twenty-eight, described his separation from his family in Xinjiang as torture. 'Where is my family? Why can't we communicate? What is my crime to be separated from my family? What wrong did they do to be disconnected from their son and brother?' he asked. 'I feel terribly bad for what I have to go through. No parent or child deserves family separation,' Abdul continued (Abdul, male, living in Norway for five years; interviewed in June 2019).

Grief

Some Uyghur diaspora families have had to deal with the loss of their loved ones during the time when they are forcibly separated. The death of a family member is certainly experienced as traumatic. For Uyghur diaspora families who have experienced the loss of family members in China, it can be more traumatic. Due to the lack of information as a result of the loss of contact, there is significant uncertainty about the cause of death of family members. Bereaved Uyghur families wonder why and how this has happened; whether they had been taken to the *jaza lagirliri* where they might have suffered psychologically or physically; and whether their deaths could have been prevented.

According to Uyghur tradition, a death in the family is not just felt by the individual family but is experienced by the whole community. All people from the community, far and near, including neighbours, friends, relatives, or even strangers, come to help and comfort a bereaved friend or families.

One Uyghur man in the UK described how he learned of his mother's death: 'In November 2017, my mother died. This bad news reached me after a few days via a contact in a different town in China. My siblings urged my contact to tell me again and again not to try to come back. I feel I am still in mourning. I will have to live with this kind of feeling till one day I can return and visit her grave and give it a loud cry' (Rustam, aged fifty, male, living in the UK for fifteen years; interviewed in March 2019).

It is common for a death in the family to be followed by another such as when a husband or wife dies and the other follows. But suffering two deaths in the same family in a short period of time when the virtual lockdown of Xinjiang is still in place is felt as something hard to believe or process by the Uyghur diaspora.

Shakir in the UK described his cumulative grief: 'Two months after my mother's funeral in March 2019, my father died in May. On both occasions, my sister, the only person that I can talk with on a regular basis, asked me not to come back. I wanted to know how they died but I just cannot ask. I feel guilty for not being able to be on the bedside of my parents when I was needed. And I feel extremely bad for being unable to attend their funerals' (Shakir, aged thirty-nine, male, living in the UK for thirteen years; interviewed in May 2019).

Murat, aged fifty, reported that he could not understand the cause of death of his two younger brothers: 'My two younger brothers passed away within seven months of one another. As far as I am aware, they didn't have any health issues. Their deaths came so sudden that I cannot get over from accepting it' (Murat, male, living in the UK for twenty-three years; interviewed in May 2018).

Research on PTSD shows that people who have experienced traumatic events are at a higher risk of suicidal ideation (Luo 2011; Reisman 2016). One Uyghur woman in Canada reported why she had suicidal thoughts: 'I'm Uyghur Canadian. I have been constantly harassed by the police from back home in China. They threatened me to co-operate with them. If not, all of my relatives will be harmed. It's very frustrating, and my frustration is leading to suicidal thoughts' (Rizwan, aged forty-one, female, living in Canada for fifteen years; interviewed in May 2019).

Withdrawal from community is another symptom in the social dimension of collective trauma. Maintaining strong community bonds is beneficial to psychological well-being (Kawachi and Berkma 2001), while withdrawal from community can trigger depression (Charuvastra and Cloitre 2008). There are many Uyghurs in the diaspora throughout the world who have chosen to distance themselves from interacting with fellow Uyghurs in their own community. Some have explicitly notified the community before their withdrawal and some have simply disappeared from any community network or community activities.

One Uyghur man in the UK explained his reason for deciding to leave the community group chat and activities. 'My wife is stuck in *weten* with our young child. My mother-in-law was taken to a *jaza lagiri*. I try not to meet or communicate with any other Uyghurs anywhere in the world. I have limited access to talk with my wife and I don't want to lose contact with her completely just because of my activity in the UK' (Tayir, aged thirty-seven, male, living in the UK for thirteen years; interviewed in May 2019).

Conclusion

This study focused on the effects of Xinjiang's lockdown on the Uyghur diaspora. Using the theory of collective trauma, this study investigated three dimensions of collective trauma among Uyghurs living abroad: psychological, family, and social. Semi-structured interviews were conducted to collect data among Uyghurs living in Turkey, North America, Australia, and Europe.

The interview findings show that the virtual lockdown of Xinjiang has caused and is still causing an enormous psychological and psychiatric effect on Uyghur diaspora. Members of the Uyghur diaspora are fearful and sad. They live with anxiety. They are crying and they are angry. Some are feeling depressed and others are having sleeping and concentration difficulties. In addition to the psychological effect, Xinjiang's virtual lockdown has made Uyghur families fall apart. The deaths of family members occurred in Xinjiang during this period of time means that the bereaved families of the Uyghur diaspora have to live in grief without being able to attend the funerals of their loved ones. Lastly, the virtual lockdown of Xinjiang is causing some in the Uyghur diaspora to have suicidal thoughts, while others have chosen to live in isolation away from their Uyghur community.

The effect of the virtual lockdown of Xinjiang is not on isolated individuals, but on all Uyghurs, living abroad and in China as well. The Uyghur diaspora, like diasporas of other origins, are scattered in many parts of the world, but they are mainly spread out in Turkey, Canada, the US, Australia, and Europe. Therefore, the experiences that the Uyghurs living in these countries are going through are representative of the entire population of the Uyghur diaspora. Indeed, the symptoms of trauma can manifest in different ways but when all Uyghur, no matter whether they live abroad or in China, are targeted and directly affected by this human-made disaster, this virtual lockdown of Xinjiang can be seen as the collective punishment (Darcy 2003, 2010) of the Uyghur people.

The effect of the virtual lockdown of Xinjiang indicates the severity of it on Uyghurs living abroad. Some studies find that lack of communication with family, friends, neighbours, and community is harmful to people's psychological well-being, and loss of contact with family and other people is a risk factor for developing depression (Ozbay *et al.* 2007). Xinjiang's virtual lockdown has affected the psychological health and well-being of the Uyghur diaspora since many of them reported to be suffering from various symptoms of trauma. In some cases, Uyghurs in the diaspora are at a higher risk of developing a mental health condition. Some in the diaspora are obviously coping with depression.

The effect of the virtual lockdown of Xinjiang on the Uyghur diaspora is unlike any the world has ever seen. Lockdown in Xinjiang is not new. Internet access and mobile phone text messaging across Xinjiang were shut down after the Urumqi riots in July 2009 for nearly a year. Even so, Uyghurs in Xinjiang were allowed to use the officially authorized telephone at the post office to make international phone calls. But the lockdown in Xinjiang this time is not physical, but virtual, and this is still ongoing. Internet access, Chinese social media apps such as WeChat, and phone call services are all in place, but it is the fear of using any of them, WeChat in particular, to communicate with anyone abroad, that has been widely instilled among the Uyghurs (Byler 2019).

Notes

1 *Weten*, motherland, is a Uyghur term that many Uyghurs living outside China use to refer to their ancestral land.

References

21Wilberforce (2019). '"Never Again" Is Happening Again in China', One We Stand, 10 September, https://21wilberforce.org/never-again-is-happening-again-in-china (accessed 13 January 2021).

Amnesty International (2018). 'China: "Where Are They?" Time for Answers about Mass Detentions in the Xinjiang Uighur Autonomous Region', 24 September, www.amnesty.org/en/documents/asa17/9113/2018/en/ (accessed 13 January 2021).

Amstadter, Ananda B., and Laura L. Vernon (2008). 'Emotional Reactions during and after Trauma: A Comparison of Trauma Types', *Journal of Aggression, Maltreatment and Trauma* 16 (4), 391–408.

Aydin, Ciano (2017). 'How to Forget the Unforgettable? On Collective Trauma, Cultural Identity, and Mnemotechnologies', *Identity: An Introductional Journal of Theory and Research* 17 (3), 125–137.

Bob, Petr, Jiri Raboch, Michael Maes et al. (2010). 'Depression, Traumatic Stress and Interleukin-6', *Journal of Affective Disorders* 120 (1–3), 231–234.

Byler, Darren (2019). 'I Researched Uighur Society in China for 8 Years and Watched How Technology Opened New Opportunities Then Became a Trap', The Conversation, 18 September, https://bit.ly/3iq1kuf (accessed 13 January 2021).

Charuvastra, Anthony, and Marylene Cloitre (2008). 'Social Bonds and Post-traumatic Disorder', *Annual Review of Psychology* 59, 301–328.

Curasi, Caroline Folkman (2001). 'A Critical Exploration of Face-to-Face Interviews vs. Computer-Medicated Interviewing', *International Journal of Market Research* 43 (4), 1–13.

Darcy, Shane (2003). 'Punitive House Demolitions, the Prohibition of Collective Punishment, and the Supreme Court of Israel', *Penn State International Law Review* 21 (3), 477–507.

Darcy, Shane (2010). 'Prosecuting the War Crime of Collective Punishment: Is It Time to Amend the Rome Statute?', *Journal of International Criminal Justice* 8 (1), 29–51.

Fivush, Robin, and Janine P. Buckner (2000). 'Gender, Sadness and Depression: The Development of Emotional Forces through Generated Discourse', in Agneta H. Fishcher (ed.), *Gender and Emotions: Social Psychological Perspectives* (Cambridge: Cambridge University Press), 232–253.

Forth, Aidan (2020). 'The Ominous Metaphors of China's Uighur Concentration Camps', The Conversation, 20 January, https://theconversation.com/the-ominous-metaphors-of-chinas-uighur-concentration-camps-129665 (accessed 13 January 2021).

Hefez, Albert, Lily Metz, and Peretz Lavie (1987). 'Long-term Effect of Extreme Situational Stress on Sleep and Dreaming', *American Journal of Psychiatry* 144 (3), 344–347.

Hirschberger, Gilad (2018). 'Collective Trauma and the Social Construction of Meaning', *Frontiers in Psychology* 9, 1–14.

Human Rights Watch (2018). '"Eradicating Ideological Viruses": China's Campaign of Repression against Xinjiang's Muslims', 9 September, www.hrw.org/report/2018/09/09/eradicating-ideological-viruses/chinas-campaign-repression-against-xinjiangs (accessed 13 January 2021).

Kawachi, Ichiro, and Lisa F. Berkma (2001). 'Social Ties and Mental Health', *Journal of Urban Health* 78 (3), 458–467.

Lobel, Lea-Maria (2020). 'Family Separation and Refugee Mental Health: A Network Perspective', *Social Networks* 61, 20–33.

Luo, Feijun. (2011). 'Impact of Business Cycles on US Suicide Rates, 1928–2007', *American Journal of Public Health* 101 (6), 1139–1146.
Medic, Goran, Micheline Wille, and Michiel E. H. Hemels (2017). 'Short- and Long-term Health Consequences of Sleep Disruption', *Nature and Science of Sleep* 9, 151–161.
Muldoon, Orla T., S. Alexander Haslam, Catherine Haslam et al. (2019). 'The Social Psychology of Responses to Trauma: Social Identity Pathways Associated with Divergent Traumatic Responses', *European Review of Social Psychology* 30 (1), 311–348.
Ozbay, Fatih, Douglas C. Johnson, Eleni Dimoulas et al. (2007). 'Social Support and Resilience to Stress: From Neurology to Clinical Practice', *Psychiatry (Edgmont)* 4 (5), 45–40.
Pearlman, Laurie Ann, and Karen W. Saakvitne (1995). *Compassion Fatigue: Coping with Secondary Traumatic Stress Disorder in Those Who Treat the Traumatized* (New York: W.W. Norton & Co.).
Raza, Zainab (2019). 'China's "Political Re-education" Camps of Xinjiang's Uyghur Muslims', *Asian Affairs* 50 (4), 488–501.
Reisman, Miriam (2016). 'PTSD Treatment for Veterans: What's Working, What's New, and What's Next', *Pharmacy and Therapeutics* 41 (10), 623–627.
Roberts, Sean R. (2018). 'The Biopolitics of China's "War on Terror" and the Exclusion of the Uyghurs', *Critical Asian Studies* 50 (2), 232–258.
Silver, Roxane C., E. Alison Holman, Daniel N. McIntosh et al. (2002). 'Nationwide Longitudinal Study of Psychological Responses to September 11', *Journal of the American Medical Association* 288 (10), 1235–1244.
Smith Finley, Joanne (2019). 'Securitization, Insecurity and Conflict in Contemporary Xinjiang: Has PRC Counter-terrorism Evolved into State Terror?', *Central Asian Survey* 38 (1), 1–26.
Spoormaker, Victor I., and Paul Montgomery (2008). 'Disturbed Sleep in Post-traumatic Stress Discourse: Secondary Symptom or Core Feature?', *Sleep Medicine Review* 12, 169–184.
Sudworth, John (2018). 'China's Hidden Camps', BBC News, 24 October, www.bbc.co.uk/news/resources/idt-sh/China_hidden_camps (accessed 27 July 2021).
Vitriol, Veronica, Alfredo Cancino, Kristina Weil et al. (2014). 'Depression and Psychological Trauma: An Overview Integrating Current Research and Specific Evidence of Studies in the Treatment of Depression in Public Health Services in Chile', *Depression Research and Treatment* (February), 1–10, https://doi.org/10.1155/2014/608671.

11

'Window of opportunity': The Xinjiang emergency in China's 'new type of international relations'

David Tobin

Introduction

Xi Jinping presented China's approach to international relations at the 19th Party Congress in a 'new era' of the Great Revival (*weida fuxing*): 'Dissatisfied' China will preserve sovereignty but reform a Western colonial-built order using new norms of 'mutual respect, fairness, and justice' (Xi 2017a, 2017b). In the era of China's rise, politically connected public intellectuals[1] have consistently argued for 'anti-hegemonic' Chinese international relations (IR) approaches to reverse 'national humiliation' and de-colonize world order. Leading intellectuals narrate China's identity as a 'new type of superpower', using consent and harmony to organize domestic politics and world order, contrasted against Western coercion and conflict (Hu 2012; Zhang 2012). Critical political scientists describe political challenges in democracies (terrorism, financial crises, and declining incomes) as evidence that *we* live in an 'age of anxiety' (Eklundh *et al.* 2017). However, China's foreign policy narratives celebrate Xi's 'new era' as a reshaping of world order with a 'new type of International Relations' (Xi 2013). Nevertheless, global euphoria amongst Chinese elites is embedded in anxieties that ethnic minority identities are 'colonial manipulations' that threaten state sovereignty, which has culminated in 'fusion' (*jiaorong*) ethnic policies to secure China's identity and the

Great Revival. Xi's 'justice'[2] narrative reflects intertwined anxieties regarding Western colonial desires to convert China and the idea that ethic minority identities run counter to the Great Revival's historic 'mission'. State sovereignty is the basis of 'mutual respect' and starting point of a 'new type of international relations', which considers 'pressure' regarding China's frontier policies as formal 'intervention' (Song 2019: 66).

China's ethnic politics and foreign policymaking are institutionally inseparable, though their shared goals are ordinarily overlooked in policy analysis.[3] World order and ethnic politics are explicitly linked in universal ethnic unity textbooks for Xinjiang's cadres, high school and university students, which teach the Great Revival of the Chinese people, singular, as the basis of 'national strength' in international relations (MOI 2009). This chapter asks: how are ethnic policy in Xinjiang and China's foreign policy interlinked in the Great Revival? It argues that ethnic and foreign policymaking are intertwined strands of the Chinese Communist Party's (CCP) national narrative, embedded in racial anxieties, which drive its 'anti-hegemonic' 'mission' towards mono-ethnic national identity and global power.

Mainstream IR's consensus is that no single power leads world order alone in the twenty-first century.[4] China's foreign policy thinkers conceptualize contemporary global power shifts as liberal hegemony's decline, enabling non-Western states to reshape world order with new values (Yan 2018: 5). *Global* IR conceptualizes twenty-first-century world order as complexes of crosscutting orders, an emerging decentred world without a hegemonic state (Buzan 2011; Acharya 2014: 653; 2017: 278–280). As these shifts have unfolded, China's official self-identification transformed from Mao's global revolution (1949–78), to Deng's reform-era status quo,[5] to Xi's (2017a) 'trailblazing' combination of the 'visible hand' of state-planning and 'invisible hand' of the market. The Belt and Road Initiative (BRI) and Asian Infrastructure Investment Bank (AIIB) are presented as China's flagship foreign policy projects, combining plan and market, focused on South–South relations (Acharya 2017: 278). Following the 2008 financial crisis, the 'China model' expanded public expenditure and state control, framed by its philosophical proponents as China's 'indigenous values' of unity and harmony, opposed to Western division and conflict (Pan 2009). However, the 'China model' is less clear on its development model than its narratives of cultural politics, which resists 'Westernization' per se, ordinarily associated with but not limited to economic liberalization and democratization (Breslin 2011: 1343; Callahan 2013: 90). Global power shifts and domestic identity debates led Chinese relational IR theorists to conclude that China's rise has produced an 'identity dilemma' through contradictions between adoption of European thought (sovereignty and nationalism) and Chinese traditions of unity and harmony (Qin 2006: 11). China's 'identity dilemma' emerges alongside a related Western 'identity crisis' as its hegemony is challenged (Qin 2006: 12; Yan 2018: 1). Many leading foreign policy commentators responded by framing China's predicament as the time for 'East Asia to become East Asia' (Wang 2014a: 19–20). China's 'new type of international relations' emerged through these debates but this chapter will show how its hybrid approach reinforces, rather than challenges, the nationalist and ethnocentric logics of Western hegemony.

China's revival sparked what Yongjin Zhang (2012) called 'China anxiety' and Zhang Weiwei (2012), 'China shock'. There is widespread *cultural* anxiety amongst Western IR theorists and policymakers that China will reshape world order according to its own illiberal values (Reus-Smit 2017: 881). China anxiety reflects Eurocentric narratives in mainstream IR, which constitute world order as culturally neutral, highlighting non-Western factors in support of existing theory while dismissing alternatives as un-parsimonious (Hobson 2007: 93; Acharya 2014: 648; Ling 2014: 1–3). China's revival, in principle, challenges the assumed cultural neutrality and technical superiority of the West.[6] Alternatively, Postcolonial IR draws from mainstream IR and non-European sources to 'provincialize Europe' and 'globalize Asia',[7] analysing the interconnections between the ongoing reproduction of world orders and multiple modernities.[8] However, China's rise is frequently subsumed into binarizing IR debates as a threat to world order *or* a de-colonizing (or business) opportunity. This threat/opportunity binary framing overlooks how China's racialized state violence in Xinjiang represents the interweaving of Chinese theories and practices with Western values of ethnic nationalism and sovereignty.

This chapter shows that China's interlinked approach to IR and ethnic politics seeks to de-colonize world order by securing and homogenizing Chinese identity. Securing identity attributes authenticity, consistency, and indisputability of specific national narratives towards what Brent Steele (2007) famously termed 'ontological security', rather than reflecting objectively existing shared self-identification. IR's 'emotional turn'[9] developed from analysis of how those identities, and IR's related meta-narratives, build on unproblematized emotional politics, most notably fear and anxiety. However, the 'emotional turn' has overlooked legacies of colonialism in non-Western affective politics (Ling 2014). Anxious relations between the US and China are structured by desires for stable identities within fixed East–West binaries. The CCP's understanding of an individualist US perpetuating Western cultural hegemony through democracy and containment narratives and the US foreign policy narrative that collectivist China seeks to build an authoritarian world order are mutually constitutive mirror images in their shared vision of IR as a competition between fixed, singular national identities under material anarchy. The chapter's methodology builds on Acharya's (2014) *Global* IR as 'disciplinary area studies' but analyses China's Great Revival narrative as an embedded component of world order rather than an alternative to Western hegemony. It rejects binary thinking and draws from postcolonial approaches that examine how world order and national identity narratives circulate between global and local levels, making them indistinguishable (Darby and Paolini 1994: 382; Hobson 2007: 107). China's foreign policy narratives constitute East–West oppositional identities and explain state violence against Xinjiang's in-between peoples as securing China from colonialism. However, China's racial anxieties are rooted in the same attachments to fixed, relational identities (ontological security), enabling violence to fix and secure itself from objects of fear, namely, Xinjiang's non-Chinese identities.

The chapter's first section analyses Great Revival euphoria, which narrates cultural unification of China's peoples in overcoming colonial humiliation and returning to a position of global power. Western decline is officially described as a 'window of opportunity' for China to pursue 'fusion' policies in Xinjiang to guarantee China's identity and revival. The second section shows how Great Revival euphoria is embedded in domestic ethnic anxieties that Xinjiang's identities are colonial manipulations and security threats, which must be modernized and assimilated to secure *Zhonghua minzu*.[10] Influential 'second-generation' ethnic policy thinkers, including Hu Angang (2012) and Ma Rong (2012), helped shift policy from nominal cultural pluralism towards assimilation, arguing that China must build a unified 'race-state' (*guozu*) to survive in a world order of cultural competition under material anarchy. 'Fusion' policy includes extra-legal internment camps and practices of inter-generational separation to transform the identities of Xinjiang's Turkic-speaking, Muslim peoples towards the Great Revival. The chapter argues that China resists global cultural inequality but deploys racialized narratives that bifurcate the world into advanced and backwards, the underlying narrative that enables and produces this inequality. The CCP resists global 'hegemonism' but inverts its logics inwards, categorizing and valuing groups according to contribution to China's Great Revival. The CCP's anti-hegemonism seeks to propel China to the top of a racialized order of states and secure the fixed ontology of the Great Revival by colonizing 'backwards' peoples within its borders.

China's Great Revival euphoria

This section analyses how the CCP's Great Revival euphoria guides China's intertwined approaches to ethnic politics and IR, narrating cultural unification of China's peoples in overcoming colonial humiliation and returning to global power. For those who celebrate the Great Revival, 'it is a good time to be Chinese' (Callahan 2013: 1). The consensus in China's public political debates since the US invasion of Iraq and 2008 financial crisis is that the West is declining and China is subsequently rising. Public intellectuals explain Western failures alongside China's rapid growth, arguing that world order has entered a 'post-American century'.[11] China's leaders describe world order in a transitional juncture under 'new conditions' of Western decline, offering an unparalleled strategic 'window of opportunity' for transformation.[12] However, revival euphoria is mutually constituted by anxieties about Westernization and domestic instability. Politically influential thinkers, such as Hu Angang (2012), argue that China, a 'new type of superpower', orders the world by attraction and consent instead of Western coercion and assimilation, resting on unproblematized occidentalist logics of fixed East–West binaries. Xi Jinping's signature slogan, the 'China Dream' of the Chinese people's Great Revival in becoming a culturally unified, 'strong and prosperous nation' (*fuqiang daguo*), again is a culmination of these popular narratives. The Great Revival narrates China's peoples uniting as *Zhonghua minzu*, rising to reverse humiliation, and returning to their rightful position of global power. Prior to Xi's rise, former diplomat Zhang Weiwei (2012) emphasized China's uniqueness and superiority, writing that 'China is a unique civilization-state', representing unbroken, unified history. China's cultural nationalism attempts to resolve, what Qin Yaqing (2006) termed China's 'identity dilemma' by fixing '5,000 years' of *Zhonghua minzu* identity and re-representing the socialist 'new China' as an ephemeral phase in China's grand telos. Postcolonial anxieties, where dreams of the past, present, and future mimetically reconstruct what happened elsewhere ('we are as good as') (Krishna 1999: xix), constitute the Great Revival's euphoric progress beyond 'backwardness'. However, the Great Revival narrates sovereignty, nationalism, and markets as ephemeral tools preserving China's exceptionally unbroken identity. Anxious euphoria regarding unknowable futures is tightly narrated in this fixed identity, constituting difference and spontaneity outside teleological inevitability as national security threats. What Hannah Arendt (1958) termed the 'rectilinear course' of Western teleological history that makes humans superfluous and what Walter Benjamin (1979) called, a 'depraved mysticism', circulate in the telos of *Zhonghua minzu*, which displaces anxieties about the future with concrete threats of Westernization and national disintegration.

The consensus in Chinese IR that world order is in transition is explained through the disintegration of the historical conditions of post-1945 liberal hegemony, world war, and totalitarianism (Song 2019; Yan 2018; Xi 2017a). Moral realist Yan Xuetong (2019) argues that China has risen because its political system is more capable of reforming itself through these rapidly changing global conditions than the US system. This transition is considered the natural 'rationalization' of world order as Xi Jinping's policy represents balance of 'oriental wisdom' and 'progress' of world order towards a 'community of destiny' (Song 2019: 65–66). China's public intellectuals borrow from reflective psychoanalysis of Western anxieties about Eastward power shifts to dismiss criticism of policy or its ethnocentrism as 'China threat theory' (Pan 2004: 307; Sun 2018). Similarly, Xi (2015) warned a US audience, including Henry Kissinger, that anxiety of Western hegemonic state's strategic miscalculations regarding peaceful emerging powers threatens world order in a self-fulfilling 'Thucydides trap'. US realists' psychoanalysis of China's foreign policy as 'strategic autism' (Friedberg 2014: 136–137), the inability to comprehend why self-perceived defensive policies are interpreted offensively by others, is mirrored in these popular Chinese perspectives on world order. US trade protectionism and 'inward' identity politics are diagnosed as symptoms of 'strategic anxiety disorder' and 'hegemon anxiety'.[13] These diagnose the US in denial of reality that Chinese approaches to international relations are the 'new normal', irrationally behaving as if the world is unchanged since the Cold War, which traps itself in self-perpetuating anxiety (Kong 2015: 71). 'Hegemon anxiety' and 'China threat' emerge through denial of identity change, triggered by declining incomes and institutional trust (Sun 2018; Yan 2018). Chinese IR describes US 'containment strategy' as colonial domination by a threatened great power, while US foreign policy thinkers see relative decline as an opportunity for China to impose illiberal, Eastern values (Pan 2004: 308; Lieberthal and Wang 2012: 7). These relational anxieties interact in Xi's euphoric 'new era', which identifies China as 'trailblazing' guarantor of world order, threatened by a declining, self-destructive hegemon.[14]

The US and China's shared relational anxieties are historically contingent but rooted in longer-term narratives of world order. China's nineteenth-century intermediate position between active 'core' and backward 'periphery', first described by Stalin as 'semi-colonialism', is routinized in official Chinese discourse, to characterize colonialism's impact on China's historical trajectory despite never being fully colonized. The Manchu state (1644–1911) ceded sections of key port cities, Tianjin, Shanghai, and Qingdao, to European powers during a century of 'national humiliation' (1839–1949), who 'opened' China by gunboat diplomacy. Western world order narratives anxiously imagined China's position as an exotic intermediate role, in-between the threatening 'Second World' and cultureless Third World of the undeveloped 'dark continent'. Renan categorized China as 'a worker race' while Immanuel Kant described a society of 'ridiculous grotesqueries' in its cosmic ritual (Césaire 1972: 4; Kant 2011). China was anxiously positioned as an indeterminate mystery between Western civilization and the contagious threat of anarchy, derived from the 'primitive' inferior races in the tropics, which the 'civilized' white race must halt through 'rational' administration (Henderson 2013: 85). Nevertheless, China's anxiety that the West seeks total domination shaped how it navigated its integration into a European-led world order, resonating in claims that criticisms of trade practices or assimilation in Xinjiang are unbroken ideological Western traditions. Mao and Deng's socialist narratives of China's anti-imperial national resistance circulate in new hybrid forms of culturalist exceptionalism under Hu Jintao (2002–12) and Xi (2012–present), that explain adopting capitalist practices and the Western principle of sovereignty as exceptional resistance to Western capitalism.[15] Western anxieties about China's rise focus on market access and human rights but have grown and morphed into fear as China becomes less exotic and increasingly familiar through the practices of sovereignty, nationalism, and markets. The CCP responds to these criticisms and scholarly critique as the continuation of colonialism countered by the Great Revival, continuing cycles of self-fulling and mutually reinforcing anxieties.

China, the modern world's first postcolonial great power, is identified by the party-state as a non-Western, anti-hegemonic state. Behind this inter-state animosity, conceptual binaries of East–West and backwards–modern that constituted Western colonial thought circulate in China's international relations theories and practices. Realists such as Yan Xuetong (2018) and Wang Yiwei (2014a) describe how China's revival, based on Eastern identity, precipitated a Western 'identity crisis', grappling with Eastward shifts in material and cultural power. Qin Yaqing's relational IR turns this question inwards, framing the Great Revival as an interrelated 'identity question', sparked by contradictions between Western revolutionary narratives deployed to resist Western hegemony and traditional Eastern harmonious thought that China must resolve (Qin 2006: 11). The relational IR school uses 'Chinese dialectics', drawn from Daoist philosophy, to theorize the world through deeply interconnected, constitutive relations between phenomenon, rather than discrete billiard-ball variables of Western positivism (Qin 2007; 2016: 20–21). 'Chinese dialectics' is the harmonious opposite to the extreme 'dialectics of conflict' of 'radical Westerners', from Hegel to Robert Cox; the Eastern 'light' to the Western 'darkness' (Qin 2016: 26–27). 'Chinese dialectics' conceive identity as relational and ever-changing, familiar themes to all students of critical IR. Yet, like orientalism, these occidentalist logics rely on opposition between preconceived identities of East and West prior to interaction, ontologically stabilizing and fixing these identities, while invisibilizing hybridity and interstitiality. Central Asian identities within China are constituted as threats when this binary is securitized in narratives of insurmountable civilizational difference or clash of civilizations. Similarly, pacifist

'East–West dialogue' delimits its potential by excluding hybridity, and minorities, prior to interaction, simply reinforcing or reversing predominant binary hierarchies (Hutchings 2011: 644–645). Clash of civilizations and inter-civilizational dialogue proceed within the same civilizational boundaries that delimit interaction in IR, strictly proceeding between ethnic majority representatives of East and West, usually the CCP and the US. This relational geopolitical ordering tends to invisibilize or constitute Turkic-speaking, Central Asian Muslim identities within China as threats.

Although Chinese relational IR inadvertently preserves these underlying colonial-built binaries, mainstream Chinese IR anxiously focuses on more blunt framings of China's rise as a 'threat' to global order *or* 'opportunity' for Western gains in traditional IR debates.[16] The CCP's realist-tinged approach to IR is not simply anti-Western, rather it demands Western recognition of China's exceptional difference. Anglophone IR tends to frame China's foreign policy as moving towards a less risk-averse and more assertive position.[17] However, Chinese sources explain this position in relational terms, namely, that risks associated with foreign policy to expand China's influence have lowered with Western decline, particularly US trade protectionism.[18] Political leaders[19] and leading theorists[20] routinely describe 'new conditions' of Western decline as an historically unprecedented 'window of opportunity' to transform world order, resolve 'identity crises' faced by 'West and East', and 'for East Asia to become East Asia'. In English-language outlets, the CCP frames critiques of its pursuit of global influence under a 'new type of International Relations', particularly the BRI, as a colonial mindset or 'new Cold War' but its documents for internal consumption describe its aims as helping China to 'surpass the West' (NDRC 2015).[21] Although official and scholarly BRI narratives begin with 'twin concerns' of surplus capital and 'neighbourhood' relations, these authors explicitly relate them to grand strategy of reforming world order using exceptional values.[22] China's revival euphoria and postcolonial anxieties are mutually constitutive in desires for recognition as culturally exceptional and technically equal or superior to the West but they do not challenge underlying principles of sovereignty and nationalism.

Xi's (2018) 'new era' is officially described through the policy narrative of 'awareness of future danger' (*youhuan yishi*), which aims to alleviate anxiety about unknown futures by 'preparing for future dangers in advance' (*fangfan fengxian*). The party-state and Chinese intellectuals construct foreign policy within this cultural problematic of *youhuan yishi*, from issues of surplus capital to regional security and ethnic relations (LJX 2018: 4–5; Sun 2018). Xi's *youhuan yishi* narrative contrasts the 'prospering', 'courageous', and 'active' East from the 'declining', 'cowardly', and 'passive' West (Xi 2017a, 2018). However, this focus on risk constitutes perpetual dangers of Westernization to the East, heightening the anxieties it claims to alleviate. *Youhuan yishi*, first translated by Perry Link (1992) as 'worrying mentality', is described by Gloria Davies (2008) as the most 'important general principle for Anglophone readers to grasp' in understanding Confucian tradition and Chinese critiques of contemporary authoritarianism (Davies 2008: 16). Callahan (2013) calls it 'patriotic worrying' because public intellectuals deploy it to offer different policy paths but contain their arguments within the cultural problematic of strengthening the Chinese state and unifying identity. However, Xi's party-state has co-opted the history of *youhuan yishi*, by linking Confucian traditions of worrying about the cosmos (*youtianxia*) to worrying about party and nation (*youdang youguo*) in China's inevitable yet anxious revival. Leading foreign policy analysts today build arguments on anxiety narratives by focusing on insecurity, including 'preparing for danger in peacetime' (*ju'ansiwei*) to contrast the self-defeating narcissism of Western anxiety's focus on individual comfort ('hesitant, difficult slackers') against the East ('firm, brave pioneering communists'), building a new global 'community of destiny' (Wang 2014b; 2018: 10; Wei 2018).

Revival euphoria is constituted by China's historico-cultural anxieties in relations with Western anxieties. The anxiety of 'anti-hegemonism' and aversions to the idea of Westernization do not reject concrete practices of sovereignty, nationalism, or even racism, but reflect desires for Western recognition of China's unique civilization and its right to global power. China's foreign policy narratives alleviate these anxieties by 'preparing for future dangers in advance' but constructing a fixed Eastern identity constitutes the inevitably opposed West as a threat, perpetuating that anxiety and heightening ontological insecurity. The 'rectilinear course' of China's teleological history alleviates anxieties by fixing and giving meaning to identity but displaces anxieties about the future with concrete fears of Westernization and national disintegration.

The next section turns to how revival euphoria is always coupled with ethnic anxieties and fears that interstitial minority identities threaten China's Chineseness, justifying violence to secure and fix its non-Western identity.

China's domestic ethnic anxiety

This section analyses how the Great Revival is constituted by ethnic anxieties, which frame Xinjiang's peoples as sources of identity instability and threat to China's rise, rationalizing 'modernization' and assimilation. Xi's euphoric narratives interweave the optimism of a return to national glory and pessimistic warnings of national collapse (Callahan 2013: 16). In official and scholarly ethnic policy narratives, 'patriotic worrying' about China's revival emerges in explanations of security and state violence in Xinjiang and Tibet (LJX 2018: 4–5; Sun 2018). Following the ethnically targeted violence between Turkic-speaking Uyghurs and the Han ethnic majority in July 2009, the party-state described China's 'ethnic unity' (*minzu tuanjie*) and shared national identity as 'zero-sum political struggles of life or death' manipulated by Western 'enemies of China' (XEP 2009: 15). The euphoric revival and anxieties about national collapse are mutually constitutive narratives that have been displaced by fear of ethnic groups who do not identify as *timelessly* Chinese. As Western anxiety grows with China's increasingly familiar methods of capitalist development and colonial violence, the party-state's anxiety regarding unknown futures similarly morphs into fear of Uyghur identity and cultural difference as they become more clearly known. Xinjiang, once a 'barren wasteland' in nineteenth-century courtly debates over the region's worth to empire (Millward 2007: 126), remained a culturally empty object in the CCP's geopolitical 'strategic chess game' against Western colonialism, following its 'peaceful liberation' (Zhou 1950: 63). However, Uyghurs no longer represent *tabula rasa* in the twenty-first century because their identities are present and *known* as Turkic and Islamic, between East and West, threatening the timeless ontological security of China's Great Revival. *Zhonghua minzu*, a fixed national subject moving in rectilinear historical progression, is secured by the CCP's narratives of teleological national history (Duara 1995: 4). Narrating China as a timelessly fixed Eastern nation constitutes interstitial and hybrid identities as perpetual potential sources of threat. The CCP's focus on risk and danger produces perpetual anxiety and insecurity by seeking to secure a fixed, Han-centric Chinese self with state violence. Cycles of violence between Han, Uyghurs, and the state have culminated in mass extra-legal internment camps to secure and fix the unfixable.

Chinese scholarship tends to frame anxiety (*jiaolü*) as an historico-cultural phenomenon, a disorder sparked by transition from *Chinese* plan to *Western* markets[23] or the driving force behind China's reversal of 'national humiliation'.[24] 'Postcolonial anxiety' demands progress beyond a backward past and in 'opening and reform-era' China, nineteenth-century resistance to the Manchu state and European imperialism has been reimagined through Stalin's 1931 slogans that 'backward nations get beaten' and 'we don't want to become backward again' (Wang 2014c: 8; Zhu 2017: 89). However, China's postcoloniality refers to itself as much as to the West (Fiskesjö 2017: 6). *Hanzu*, China's ethnic majority ethnonym, is a semantically hybrid intercultural translation of race, travelling across Europe and Asia, before being reimagined in contestations between biological and cultural conceptualizations of Chinese identity in the early twentieth century (Chow 2001: 48). Official Chinese occidentalism has no history of dominating the West but aims to discipline Chinese identity within the PRC's contemporary territory (Chen 2002: 3). Louisa Schein (2000) conceptualized domination of non-Han populated territories as 'internal orientalism'. More recent postcolonial literature considers 'nothing peculiarly Western' about colonialism, which is based on asymmetries of power between groups, framing China's frontier policies as 'Chinese colonialism' (Anand 2019: 135–136). Conceptualizing colonialism as peculiarly Western conceals how settler colonialism in Xinjiang persists in binaries of modern/backwards and security/danger, shaping what Michael Clarke (2007) termed Xinjiang's 'problematic integration' because it belongs to China but is never fully Chinese.[25] China's euphoria and anxieties are rooted in intertwined narratives of resistance to European colonialism and settler colonialism on China's frontiers that require the party-state to resist colonialism through perpetual colonization of Xinjiang.

Like Henderson's (2013) postcolonial reading of early Western IR, racism in China's ethnic politics is 'hidden in plain sight'. Morgan's (2005) theory of cultural evolution that justified European settlement of the Americas by evaluating and ranking identity according to levels of material development tops universities' anthropology course-guides, celebrated as the CCP's unique 'historical materialist' approach to ethnic relations (Pan 2008). Popular representations of 'ethnic minorities'[26] as inalienable but exotic and primitive components of China relationally narrate the Han majority as modern and superior (Schein 2000: 130). Official textbooks for cadres and universities position Turkic identities as passively super-structural to material base ('animal husbandry'), contrasted against the active, unbroken Han 'frontier building culture' (*tunken wenhua*)[27] in Xinjiang (SEAC 2009: 24–55, 80–97). Official narratives of China's national history organize ethnic relations through colonial binaries between the Han's 'active spirit', driving China's unity and 'fusion' by developing Xinjiang, and the 'simple, uncomplicated assistance of ethnic minority armies' (SEAC 2009: 87). The 'new China', which originally intended to sweep away tradition and majority chauvinism, is now narrated as a continuation of timeless 'historical progress', which binds the Central Plains and the 'frontier' in 'economic complementarity' (*jingji hubu*) and always 'supply minorities with everything they need for daily living' (State Council 2009a: 6; XEP 2009: 66). The 'frontier' is included in China as dependent and its identities anxiously narrated as backwards since ancient times *and* progressing since 'peaceful liberation' (State Council 2009b: 4). In these official narratives, ethnic minorities cannot progress, let alone survive, without Han settler culture because 'if the settlers were to leave, they would … fall back into barbarism' (Fanon 2001: 37).

China's postcolonial anxieties are redirected inwards in constructions of ethnic minorities, blamed for China's unstable identity and 'backwardness'. China's political and intellectual establishment consensus since the mid-1950s was that China is a multi-ethnic state, contrasted against Western 'one-nation-one-state' as incompatible with China's national conditions and traditions (Pan 2008). Minority identities were positioned as historical leftovers of colonial manipulation and class exploitation from earlier stages of development, which will naturally disappear with economic progress (Shijian Bianjibu 1965: 213). 'Anti-hegemonism' adapts colonial binaries to traditional hierarchies of civilization and barbarism (*hua/yi*), conceptualizing settler colonialism and transformation of non-Han as a struggle against Western colonialism. During Hu Jintao's leadership, the CCP explicitly rearticulated China as built through '5,000 years' of 'fusion' (Hu 2006: 632). In the 1950s, minority anthropologists, such as Jian Bozan, warned that timeless 'fusion' was a Han chauvinist narrative that conceals China's own history of class conflict and ethnic oppression, and will promote Western-style assimilation of China's many peoples (Jian 1960: 14–21). In the era of China's rise, the CCP's ethnic politics has explicitly shifted away from cultural pluralism towards 'contact, communication, fusion' (*jiaowang, jiaoliu, jiaorong*), which has intensified under Xi Jinping's security-first approach (XUAR 2018). The notion of 'separatist history'[28] conceals China's pluralistic history, securitizing a fixed mono-ethnic *Zhonghua minzu* and prosecuting minority authors who do not identify with 5,000 years of 'fusion' as threats to China's national security.[29] Social anthropologists, trained in China's historical materialist approach, including Bao Shengli (2011), accused those arguing for 'fusion' of promoting Westernization and Han chauvinism, warning that China should 'not repeat the same mistakes as the West'. However, 'second generation' of ethnic policy commentators Hu Angang and Lianhe Hu (2012) and Ma Rong (2018) vocally claimed victory in these debates as the CCP promotes assimilation in Xinjiang towards unifying Chinese identity and becoming a 'new type of superpower'.

Xinjiang's cultural absence ('barren wasteland') in nineteenth-century Chinese imperial narratives was displaced by the CCP's nominal cultural pluralism of fifty-six *minzu* before anxiety about culturally indeterminate barbarians gave way to fear of the ethnic Other. The CCP's postcolonial meta-narratives were disrupted with knowledge that Xinjiang's Turkic and Islamic identities have their own historical presence in-between East and West and they became framed as threats to China, the unbroken, non-Western, anti-hegemonic civilization. Ethnic unity education texts, universalized following July 2009 and a precursor to official explanations of internment camps, teach that Uyghurs are 'not a Turkic *minzu*' and 'not an Islamic *minzu*', because these identities are 'colonial manipulations', which *only* 'the inside/outside Three Evils' (separatism, terrorism, and extremism) could believe (XEP 2009: 55; State Council 2019). The attributive, 'inside/outside', links Uyghur identity as a group with perceived external threats of Islamic terrorism and Western colonialism. Since Xi's rise to power and appointment of regional party chief, Chen Quanguo, 'fusion' and 'de-extremification' (*qujiduanhua*) campaigns have intensified as solutions to the 'ethnic problem' (*minzu wenti*) (Roberts 2018: 246–250). Xi's speeches and the 19th Party Congress documents effectively de-recognized minority identities by conspicuously avoiding the 'ethnic minorities' (*shaoshu minzu*) concept, which structured all ethnic policy narratives from 1949 to 2009.[30] Policy narratives now almost exclusively use *minzu* in reference to what can only be translated as the Chinese race (*Zhonghua minzu*).[31] 'Fusion' and its exceptional security policies began under Hu and are logically consistent with long-term ethnocentric national narratives that conceive Uyghur identity as existentially destabilizing and in need of 'modernization'. Ethnic policy is embedded in old narratives of 'patriotic worrying' (*youhuan yishi*) and 'dealing with dangers in advance' (*fangfan fengxian*), which aim to eliminate the 'thought' at the root of terrorism (XUAR 2018; State Council 2019). However, Uyghur Turkic and Islamic identities are now explicitly treated as 'ideological viruses' and 'sickness of the heart' (Roberts 2018: 232), the historical leftovers from colonialism and roots of contemporary terrorism. Xi's announcement to the 2017 National People's Congress that Xinjiang's peoples must be tightly and homogeneously 'held together like pomegranate seeds'[32] represents a formal policy shift with far-reaching human consequences but is tragically familiar to readers of *minzu* theory and its denouncements of Han chauvinism.

Since 2017, the CCP has sought to alleviate fear of ethnic difference by eliminating and converting Turkic and Islamic identities through mass extra-legal internment in Xinjiang's camp system. Official narratives explaining these methods of isolation and conversion, traditionally associated with European colonialism and Fascism, intertwine geopolitical strategy and ethnic politics, describing world order's transitional juncture as a 'critical stability period' and 'window of opportunity' while the BRI expands outwards and the West turns inwards (XUAR 2018). Approximately one million people were interned without trial in 'education and transformation training centres' by 2018 (Zenz 2018: 1).[33] China's extra-legal internment camp system reflects the party-state's semantically hybrid politics, which interweave Western and Chinese political narratives. Ma Rong (2007) famously rejected ethnicity as a Western concept, reasserting China's exceptional civilizational identity of 'teaching without discrimination' (*jiaohua*). This conceives non-Han barbarians not as culturally different but behind the Han's cultural progress, becoming Chinese through attraction, the binary opposite of Western ethnic assimilation (Ma 2007: 7). *Jiaohua* circulates in the camp system's conceptualization as 'transformation education', advertised in public relations videos, which illustrate 'vocational training' benefits of learning Mandarin and chanting praise to Xi Jinping.[34] The CCP uses methods of European settler colonialism by isolating ethnic Others identified as threats to state-building, including the Cherokee and West Australian Aboriginal peoples, but adapts these to Chinese traditions of harmony and peaceful attraction by attempting to convince Uyghurs they have always been Chinese but behind the Han's level of teleological development.

The CCP's attempted conversion of identities in Xinjiang is based on implicit notions of Han superiority that have resurfaced in its cultural nationalism throughout the era of China's rise, and intensifying following application of this lens to explain the 2009 violence as rooted in Uyghur identity. The camp system does not target individuals accused of legally defined crimes or for political resistance but targets the group per se, which requires arbitrary selection of victims. Like the German camp system, classification of inmates is an organizational measure but the institution's essential principle is its arbitrary, extra-legal selection of victims to distinguish them from the safe ethnic majority and to deprive them of the right to rights (Arendt 2017: 450–451). Their identities become superfluous obstacles of the teleological progress of the Great Revival. CCP Secretary of the XUAR Justice Department, Zhang Yun, explained that Uyghurs must be targeted as a group and 're-educated' because 30 per cent are 'extremists' and the remaining 70 per cent are vulnerable to extremism.[35] The official 'Population Data Collection Form',[36] now collected using automatic AI-driven facial recognition technology,[37] determines individuals' danger level, bureaucratically collating scores by 'religion', 'holding a passport', 'having foreign contacts', and 'relatives in detention'. There are some patterns to this targeting but the categorization of Uyghurs as 'safe, average, and unsafe' indicates how the 'average' Uyghur is not 'safe' and always a potential threat, thus justifying camps to isolate their social existence entirely outside the law. Reasons given to released detainees include religious extremism and inciting Pan-Turkism but also not greeting officials appropriately, not watching state television, not smoking, wanting to travel abroad, using WhatsApp Messenger, or being of the 'untrustworthy generation' born in the 1980s or 1990s.[38] Conditions in camps[39] include cramped rooms without sanitation, poor nutrition, daily renunciations of Islam, praise for Xi Jinping for bowls of gruel, widespread rape by guards, and torture for crying or using Uyghur language. Uyghurs and other Turkic-speaking Muslims are targeted 'in advance' as potential threats and can be tortured for innocuous expressions of emotion or cultural difference, which are irreducible to counterterrorism, anti-separatism, or Islamophobia. Camps place peoples outside the law and render their identities and existence as superfluous obstacles to historical progress, creating perpetual anxiety that anyone could be next and that anything can happen. State violence in Xinjiang targets Turkic-speaking and Islamic peoples as inferior groups whose existence threatens China's superior identity as a fixed, non-Western civilization.

Claudia Card's (2003) notion of genocide as 'social death' builds on Arendt's (2017) proposition that camps represent the same inexorable doom for individual humans as nuclear annihilation for the human race because they deprive them of social meaning and cultural reproduction. The party-state's promotion of social death as 'fusion' is crystallized in mass 'inter-generational separation' through secured, state-run 'centralised boarding facilities' to raise and educate approximately 100,000 Uyghur children, 'happily growing up under the loving care of Party and government'.[40] Family separation, as practised by European state-builders in North America and Australia, prevented cultural transmission through language and family education. The Xinjiang Work Report (XUAR 2018) explains 'fusion' polices as 'anti-hegemonism' but describes camps and 'boarding facilities' as defeating the 'foundations of separatism', Turkic and Islamic identities, '*forever*'. The CCP's postcolonial anxieties about backwardness and relative global power disparities are turned inwards, blaming Uyghurs and enabling the elimination of peoples' identities and rendering their existence superfluous as defeating colonialism. The Great Revival is a teleological mission that enables state violence against the in-betweenness and Otherness of Uyghurs and other peoples in Xinjiang as a form of peace and 'justice' to secure China's Eastern identity and comfort its anxieties because 'happiness is the most important human right' (State Council 2019). 'Fusion' policies, specifically the camp system and inter-generational separation, seek to eliminate interstitial identities because they disrupt China's fixed identity in the CCP's geopolitical ordering of the world into harmonious East and colonial West.

Conclusion

China's Great Revival and domestic anxieties are mutually constitutive dimensions of the CCP's 'anti-hegemonism' narrative that pursues reform of world order and ethnic assimilation as historical progress. This chapter has shown how the CCP's approach to IR and ethnic politics are interlinked, semantically hybrid repetitions of sovereignty and nationalism, which emerge from and reinforce the colonial logics of world order. The CCP reverses 'national humiliation' by fixing *Zhonghua minzu* identity in a world order of Eastern and Western civilizations, rising to its apex by using state violence to eliminate 'backward' identities in-between East and West, defined as an internal, sovereign matter. The chapter's first section showed how the CCP narrates relative Western decline as a 'window of opportunity' to de-colonize world order and advance the Great Revival towards becoming, yet always being, a unified, non-Western civilization-state. The second section showed how domestic anxieties about China's unknown futures have morphed into fear of 'backward' ethnic minority identities between East and West, which must be isolated and converted in camps to secure China's Chinese identity. The CCP's challenge to global inequality tragically replicates the colonial practices that produced this inequality in a 'new age'.

Xi's (2017a) preparation for danger narratives emphasize self-sacrifice and 'patriotic worrying', constituting China's ontological security by starkly contrasting itself against Western individualism and racism. However, in responding to anxiety by fixing national identity as a security matter, the CCP justifies state violence against ethnic Others as progress, transforming China into a state that resembles how CCP narratives identify the West. The US and China's anxieties about unknown futures of status decline and cultural disintegration as they navigate a world order in transition have both turned to romantic, mono-ethnic visions of the past that are paradoxically reactionary and progressive ('make American great *again*' and 'Great *Revival*'). Neither 'East–West dialogue' nor 'clash of civilizations' between the exceptional collectivist East and individualist West can secure minority peoples from limitless, arbitrary violence because their existence between and outside East and West disrupts the ontological security of these mutually constituted binaries. Interstitial voices must be included to counter the mutually reinforcing orientalism–occidentalism, which conceives world history through East–West binaries and international relations as competition between unified, singular actors representing this timeless binary.

With adoption of sovereignty and nationalism, China has become demystified in Western narratives but its increasing familiarity exacerbates anxieties, which morph into fear of China's rise. The CCP responds by reinforcing the colonial geopolitical ordering it nominally resists by seeking to 'surpass the West' and eliminate non-Han identities. Uyghurs and other Turkic-speaking Muslims are narrated as culturally empty barbarians attracted to Chinese civilization or as security threats but this identity–security framing is a conscious effort to assimilate in-between peoples who understand China's presence as colonialism.[41] The CCP's formal ethnic policy shift from nominal cultural pluralism towards racial assimilation ('fusion') conceives China as a Han nation-state in global competition for power with other nation-states. However, fixing a plurality of identities as timelessly singular perpetuates anxiety and insecurity because identity is never singular or fixed, and will, therefore, require more state violence to eliminate identities in-between East and West.

Notes

1 See Callahan (2013) on the party-state and public intellectuals' interrelated narratives.
2 See Xi (2014, 2015, 2016, 2017).
3 Domestic and foreign policymaking is made by the Politburo Standing Committee.
4 See Ikenberry and Lim (2017); Keohane and Colgan (2017); Mearsheimer (2010).
5 See Zhang (1991); Armstrong (1993).
6 See Barkawi and Laffey (2002: 123); Acharya (2017: 271).
7 See Chakrabarty (2000); Darby (2004: 31).
8 See Darby (1998); Barkawi and Laffey (2002); Acharya (2014).
9 See Crawford (2000); Mercer (2014); Koschit *et al.* (2017); Solomon (2017).

10 *Minzu* is officially translated as ethnicity but following the CCP's 'fusion' policy shift, official documents use *Zhonghua minzu* (Chinese race) and generally avoid using the 'ethnic minorities' (*shaoshu minzu*) concept.
11 See Hu (2012); W. Zhang (2012); Yan (2013, 2018); Wang (2014b).
12 See Xi (2017a, 2017b); NDRC (2015).
13 See Kong (2015); Lin (2018); Sun (2018).
14 See NDRC (2015); Xi (2013, 2015, 2017a).
15 See Callahan (2013) on China's cultural exceptionalism since Hu Jintao.
16 See Shambaugh (1996); Mearsheimer (2010); Ikenberry (2014).
17 See Buzan and Lawson (2014); Ferdinand (2016: 955).
18 See Yan (2013); Wang (2014b); NDRC (2015).
19 See NDRC (2015); Xi (2017a, 2017b).
20 See Qin (2006); Wang (2014b); Yan (2018).
21 See Xi (2015, 2017a, 2017b).
22 See Callahan (2016); Zheng and Zhang (2016).
23 See Xin *et al.* (2009); Tian (2012).
24 See Zhu (2017); Wang (2018); Wei (2018).
25 Following incorporation of the 'Western Regions' (*xiyu*) into the Manchu state, it was renamed 'new frontier' (*Xinjiang*) in 1884. Uyghurs reject this as a colonial name and call their homeland 'East Turkestan'.
26 The term minority refers to official Chinese thought. Uyghurs and Tibetans object to the term, spatially conceptualizing the relevant territory as 'East Turkestan' and 'Tibet', not 'China'.
27 Literally translated as 'station troops to open up wasteland culture'.
28 See XEP (2009).
29 China's 'anti-separatism' laws convict Uyghur scholars for life (e.g. Ilham Tohti), consistent with definitions of separatism as forms of thought on identity and history (XEP 2009: 50).
30 Xi's (2017) 19th Party Congress speech only used the *shaoshu minzu* concept once to refer to minority cadre recruitment. Conversely, Xi used the Chinese race (*Zhonghua minzu*) forty-three times, twenty-seven instances collocating with the Great Revival.
31 See Ma's (2018) interpretation of these narratives as the end of cultural pluralism and victory for the 'second generation'.
32 See *China Daily* (2017).
33 By April 2020, some camps closed but others have expanded, while video evidence shows population transfers to standard prisons without trials.
34 See Tursun (2018); *Telegraph* (2019).
35 See CHRD (2018).
36 See Chin (2019).
37 See Human Rights Watch (2019).

38 See XVD (2018).
39 See Human Rights Watch (2018); Tursun (2018); Mauk (2019); Mahmut (2020).
40 See Zenz (2019).
41 See Bovingdon (2010).

References

Acharya, Amitav (2014). 'Global International Relations (IR) and Regional Worlds', *International Studies Quarterly* 58, 647–659.

Acharya, Amitav (2017). 'After Liberal Hegemony: The Advent of a Multiplex World Order', *Ethics and International Affairs* 31 (3), 271–285.

Anand, Dibyesh (2019). 'Colonization with Chinese Characteristics: Politics of (In)security in Xinjiang and Tibet', *Central Asian Survey* 38 (1), 129–147.

Arendt, Hannah (1958). 'The Modern Concept of History', *The Review of Politics* 20 (4), 570–590.

Arendt, Hannah (2017). *The Origins of Totalitarianism* (London: Penguin).

Armstrong, David (1993). *Revolution and World Order: The Revolutionary State in International Society* (Oxford: Oxford University Press).

Bao, Shengli (2011). 'Ye Tan Zhongguo ke Jinyibu Wanshan Minzu Zhengce' [Discussion on Progressing the Perfection of *Minzu* Policy], Chinese Communist Party News Online, 28 October, http://theory.people.com.cn/GB/16057587.html (accessed 9 April 2019).

Barkawi, Tarak, and Mark Laffey (2002). 'Retrieving the Imperial: Empire and International Relations', *Millennium* 31 (1), 109–127.

Benjamin, Walter (1979). 'Theories of German Fascism', *New German Critique* 17, 120–128.

Bovingdon, Gardner (2010). *The Uyghurs: Strangers in Their Own Land* (New York: Columbia University Press).

Breslin, Shaun (2011). 'The China Model and the Global Crisis', *International Affairs* 87 (6), 1323–1343.

Buzan, Barry (2011). 'A World without Superpowers: A Decentred Globalism', *International Relations* 25 (1), 3–25.

Buzan, Barry, and George Lawson (2014). 'Capitalism and the Emergent World Order', *International Affairs* 20 (1), 71–91.

Callahan, William A. (2013). *China Dreams: 20 Visions of the Future* (Oxford: Oxford University Press).

Callahan, William A. (2016). 'China's Asia Dream: The Belt Road Initiative and the New Regional Order', *Asian Journal of Comparative Politics* 1 (3), 226–243.

Card, Claudia (2003). 'Genocide and Social Death', *Hypatia* 18 (1), 63–79.
Césaire, Aimé (1972). *Discourse on Colonialism* (London: Monthly Review Press).
Chakrabarty, Dipesh (2000). *Provincialising Europe: Postcolonial Thought and Historical Difference* (Princeton: Princeton University Press).
Chen, Xiaomei (2002). *Occidentalism: A Theory of Counter-discourse in Post-Mao China* (Lanham: Rowman & Littlefield).
Chin, Josh (2019). 'Twelve Days in Xinjiang: How China's Surveillance State Overwhelms Daily Life', *Wall Street Journal*, 19 December, www.wsj.com/articles/twelve-days-in-xinjiang-how-chinas-surveillance-state-overwhelms-daily-life-1513700355 (accessed 28 March 2020).
China Daily (2017). 'Cherish Ethnic Unity, President Tells Xinjiang', 11 March, www.chinadaily.com.cn/china/2017twosession/2017-03/11/content_28515253.htm (accessed 28 March 2020).
Chow, Kai-Wing (2001). 'Narrating the Nation, Race, and National Culture', in Kai-Wing Chow (ed.), *Constructing Nationhood in Modern East Asia* (Ann Arbor: University of Michigan Press), 47–85.
CHRD (Chinese Human Rights Defenders) (2018). 'China: Massive Numbers of Uighurs and Other Ethnic Minorities Forced into Re-education Programs', 3 August, www.nchrd.org/2018/08/china-massive-numbers-of-uyghurs-other-ethnic-minorities-forced-into-re-education-programs/ (accessed 28 March 2020).
Clarke, Michael (2007). 'The Problematic Progress of "Integration" in the Chinese State's Approach to Xinjiang, 1759–2005', *Asian Ethnicity* 8 (3), 261–289.
Crawford, Neta C. (2000). 'The Passion of World Politics: Propositions on Emotion and Emotional Relationships', *International Security* 24 (4), 116–156.
Darby, Phillip (1998). *The Fiction of Imperialism: Reading between International Relations and Postcolonialism* (London: Cassell).
Darby, Phillip (2004). 'Pursuing the Political: A Postcolonial Rethinking of Relations International', *Millennium* 33 (1), 1–32.
Darby, Phillip, and A. J. Paolini (1994). 'Bridging International Relations and Postcolonialism', *Alternatives* 19, 371–397.
Davies, Gloria (2008). *Worrying about China: The Language of Chinese Critical Inquiry* (Cambridge, MA: Harvard University Press).
Duara, Prasenjit (1995). *Rescuing the Nation: Questioning Narratives of Modern China* (Chicago: University of Chicago Press).
Eklundh, Emmy, Emmanuel-Pierre Guittet, and Andreja Zevnik (2017). 'Introduction: The Politics of Anxiety', in Emmy Eklundh, Emmanuel-Pierre Guittet, and Andreja Zevnik (eds), *Politics of Anxiety* (Lanham: Rowman & Littlefield), 1–14.

Fanon, Frantz (2001). *Wretched of the Earth* (London: Penguin Books).
Ferdinand, Peter (2016). 'Westward ho – the China Dream and "One Belt, One Road": Chinese Foreign Policy under Xi Jinping', *International Affairs* 92 (4), 941–957.
Fiskesjö, Magnus (2017). 'The Legacy of the Chinese Empires: Beyond the West and the Rest', *Education About Asia* 22 (1), 6–10.
Friedberg, Aaron (2014). 'The Sources of Chinese Conduct: Explaining Beijing's Assertiveness', *The Washington Quarterly* 37 (4), 133–150.
Henderson, Errol A. (2013). 'Hidden in Plain Sight: Racism in International Relations', *Cambridge Review of International Affairs* 26 (1), 71–92.
Hobson, John (2007). 'Is Critical Theory Always *for* the White West and Western Imperialism?', *Review of International Studies* 33, 91–116.
Hu, Angang (2012). *Zhongguo 2020: Yige Xinxing Chaoji Daguo* [China 2020: A New Type of Superpower] (Zhejiang: Zhejiang People's Press).
Hu, Angang, and Lianhe Hu (2012). 'Di Er Dai Minzu Zhengce: Cujin Minzu Jiaorong Yiti he Fanhua Yiti' [The Second Generation of *Minzu* Policies: Promoting *Minzu* Fusion and Prosperity in an Organic Whole], China Ethnicity and Religion Online, 10 April, www.mzb.com.cn/html/Home/report/293093-1.htm (accessed 28 March 2020).
Hu, Jintao (2006). 'Zuohao Xinshiqi Minzu Gongzuo he Zongjiao Gongzuo' [Doing Good *Minzu* Work and Religious Work in the New Era], in CCP Central Committee Document Research Office (ed.) (2010), *Xinjiang Gongzuo Wenxian Xuanbian* [Xinjiang Work: Selected Documents] (Beijing: CCP Central Committee Party Literature Publishing House), 632–637.
Human Rights Watch (2018). 'Eradicating Ideological Viruses: China's Campaign of Repression against Xinjiang's Muslims', 19 September, www.hrw.org/report/2018/09/09/eradicating-ideological-viruses/chinas-campaign-repression-against-xinjiangs (accessed 28 March 2020).
Human Rights Watch (2019). 'China's Algorithms of Repression', 1 May, www.hrw.org/report/2019/05/01/chinas-algorithms-repression/reverse-engineering-xinjiang-police-mass-surveillance (accessed 28 March 2020).
Hutchings, Kimberley (2011). 'Dialogue between Whom? The Role of the West/Non-West in Promoting Global Dialogue in IR', *Millennium* 39 (3), 639–647.
Ikenberry, John (2014). 'The Rise of China and the Future of Liberal World Order', Chatham House Lecture, 7 May, 1–9.
Ikenberry, John, and Darren Lim (2017). 'China's Emerging Institutional Statecraft: The AIIB and Prospects for Counter-hegemony', Brookings Institution, Project on International Order and Strategy.
Jian, Bozan (1960). 'Guanyu Chuli Zhongguoshi shang de Minzu Guanxi Wenti' [On the Question of How to Deal with *Minzu* Relations throughout Chinese History], in Wulin Peng et al. (eds) (2013), *Zhongguo Jindai Minzushi*

Yanjiu Wenxian [Research Documents on China's Ethnic History] (Beijing: Social Science Academic Press), 14–31.

Kant, Immanuel (2011). *Observations on the Feeling of the Beautiful and Sublime* (Cambridge: Cambridge University Press).

Keohane, Robert, and Jeff Colgan (2017). 'The Liberal Order Is Rigged – Fix It Now or Watch It Wither', *Foreign Affairs* May/June, 36–44.

Kong, Xiangyong (2015). 'Tazhe xiangxiang yu Meiguo de Jiaolǜ' [The Imagining of Others and American Anxiety], *Meiguo Yanjiu* [America Research] 4, 69–88.

Koschit, Simon, Todd H. Hall, Reinhard Wolf et al. (2017) 'Discourse and Emotion in International Relations', *International Studies Review* 19 (3), 481–508.

Krishna, Sankara (1999). *Postcolonial Insecurities: India, Sri Lanka, and the Question of Nationhood* (Minneapolis: University of Minnesota Press).

Lieberthal, Kenneth, and Jisi Wang (2012). 'Addressing US-China Strategic Mistrust', John L. Thornton China Center Monograph Series, 4.

Lin, Limin (2018). 'Meixifanglǜ he Xianrun Zhanluexing Jiaolǜ' [Why Is the US/West Sliding into Strategic Anxiety?], *Renmin Luntan* [People's Forum] July, 36–38.

Ling, Lily (2014). 'Decolonizing the International: Towards Multiple Emotional Worlds', *International Theory* 6 (3), 578–583.

Link, Perry (1992). *Evening Chats in Beijing: Probing China's Predicament* (New York: W.W. Norton & Co.).

LJX (Lingdao Juece Xinxi) [Leader's Policy News] (2018). 'Dahao Xinshidai Kaojuan Zuodao Sange Yiyiguanzhi' [Answering the Examination of the New Era with the Three Consistents] 18, 4–5.

Ma, Rong (2007). 'A New Perspective in Guiding Ethnic Relations in the 21st Century: Depoliticization of Ethnicity in China', The University of Nottingham China Policy Institute, Discussion Paper 21.

Ma, Rong (2012). 'Dangqian Zhongguo de Minzu Wenti de Zhengjie yu Chulu' [The Crux and Solution to the Ethnic Problem in Contemporary China], China Ethnicity and Religion Online, www.mzb.com.cn/html/Home/report/293002-1.htm (accessed 10 April 2020).

Ma, Rong (2018). 'Xi Jinping Tongzhi Jinqi Jianghua Zhudao Woguo Minzu Gongzuo de Fangxiang' [Comrade Xi Jinping Guides the Direction of our Country's *Minzu* Policy], *Journal of the Central Institute of Socialism* 3 (213), 121–126.

Mahmut, Rahima (2020). 'Surveillance and Repression of Muslim Minorities: Xinjiang and Beyond', SOAS, YouTube, 7 March, www.youtube.com/watch?v=rRgUg2P-l3I (accessed 28 March 2020).

Mauk, Ben (2019). 'Weather Reports', *The Believer*, 1 October, https://believermag.com/weather-reports-voices-from-xinjiang/ (accessed 25 August 2020).

Mearsheimer, John J. (2010). 'The Gathering Storm: China's Challenge to US Power in Asia', *Chinese Journal of International Politics* 3 (4), 381–396.

Mercer, Jonathan (2014). 'Feeling like a State: Social Emotion and Identity', *International Theory* 6 (3), 515–535.

Millward, James (2007). *Eurasian Crossroads: A History of Xinjiang* (London: Hurst and Company).

MOI (Ministry of Information, Theoretical Department) (2009). *Lilun Redian Mianduimian* [Face-to-Face Hot Theory Topics] (Beijing: People's Publishing Press).

Morgan, Lewis (2005). *Ancient Society* (New York: Adamant Media Corporation).

NDRC (National Development and Reform Commission) (2015). 'Vision and Actions on Jointly Building Silk Road Economic Belt and 21st-Century Maritime Silk Road', http://english.www.gov.cn/archive/publications/2017/06/20/content_281475691873460.htm (accessed 28 March 2020).

Pan, Chengxin (2004). 'The China Threat in American Self-imagination', *Alternatives* 29, 305–331.

Pan, Jiao (ed.) (2008). *Zhongguo Shehui Wenhua Renleixue/Minzuxue Bainian Wenxuan* [Selected Works of 100 Years of Chinese Social and Cultural Anthropology/*Minzu* Studies] (Beijing: Intellectual Property Publishing House).

Pan, Wei (2009). *Zhongguo Moshi* [China Model] (Beijing: Peking University Press).

Qin, Yaqing (2006). 'Guoji Guanxi Lilun Zhongguo Xuepai Shengcheng de Keneng he Biran' [The Possibility and Inevitability of the Formation of a Chinese School of IR Theory], *Guoji Guanxi Lilun* [International Relations Theory] 3, 7–13.

Qin, Yaqing (2007). 'Why Is There No Chinese International Relations Theory?', *International Relations of the Asia-Pacific* 7, 313–340.

Qin, Yaqing (2016). 'Guoji Zhengzhi Guanxi Lilun de Jige Jiading' [Several Hypotheses on Relational Theories of International Politics], *Guoji Guanxi Lilun* [International Relations Theory] 10, 19–28.

Reus-Smit, Christian (2017). 'Cultural Diversity and International Order', *International Organization* 71, 851–885.

Roberts, Sean R. (2018). 'The Biopolitics of China's "War on Terror" and the Exclusion of the Uyghurs', *Critical Asian Studies* 50 (2), 232–258.

Schein, Louisa (2000). *Minority Rules: The Miao and the Feminine in China's Cultural Politics* (Durham, NC: Duke University Press).

SEAC (State Ethnic Affairs Commission) (2009). *Xinjiang Wenhua Zhishi Duben* [Xinjiang Cultural Knowledge Study Guide] (Beijing: People's Publishing Press).

Shambaugh, David (1996). 'Containment or Engagment of China? Calculating Beijing's Responses', *International Security* 21 (2), 180–209.

Shijian Bianjibu [Practice – Editorial] (1965). 'Bixu Bawo Minzu Wenti de Jieji Shizhi' [We Must Grasp the Class Essence of Ethnic Problems], in Jiao Pan (ed.) (2008), *Zhongguo Shehui Wenhua Renleixue/Minzuxue Bainian Wenxuan* [Selected Works of 100 Years of Chinese Social and Cultural Anthropology/*Minzu* Studies] (Beijing: Intellectual Property Publishing House), 213–221.

Solomon, Ty (2017). 'Rethinking Productive Power through Emotion', *International Studies Review* 19 (3), 497–500.

Song, Xiaofeng (2019). 'Xinxing Guoji Guanxi: Neihan, Lujing yu Fanshi' [New Type of International Relations: Content, Path, Model], *Xinjiang Shehui Kexue* [Xinjiang Social Sciences] 2, 65–71.

State Council (2009a). *Zhongguo de Minzu Zhengce yu ge Minzu Gongtong Fanrong Fazhan* [China's Ethnic Minority Policy and the Common Prosperity of all Ethnic Groups] (Beijing: People's Publishing Press).

State Council (2009b). *Xinjiang de Fazhan yu Jinbu* [The Progress and Development of Xinjiang] (Beijing: People's Publishing Press).

State Council (2019). 'The Fight against Terrorism and Extremism and Human Rights Protection in Xinjiang', March, www.xinhuanet.com/english/2019-03/18/c_137904166.htm (accessed 28 March 2020).

Steele, Brent J. (2007). *Ontological Security in International Relations: Self-identity and the IR State* (London: Routledge).

Sun, Haizhao (2018). 'Meiguo de Zhanlue Jiaolǜ yu Guoji Xingshi' [US Strategic Anxiety and the International Situation], *Beijing Ribao* [Beijing Daily], 24 April.

Tian, Xianyun (2012). 'An Analysis of Anxiety-Related Postings on Sina Weibo', *International Journal of Environmental Research and Public Health* 14 (775), 1–10.

Telegraph (2019). 'One Minute Felt like a Year: A Day in the Life of Inmates in the Xinjiang Internment Camps', 26 March, www.telegraph.co.uk/news/2019/03/26/dispatch-day-life-inmate-xinjiang-internment-camps/ (accessed 28 March 2020).

Tursun, Mihrigul (2018). 'Congressional-Executive Commission on China: Testimony of Tursun Mihrigul', 28 November, www.cecc.gov/events/hearings/the-communist-party%E2%80%99s-crackdown-on-religion-in-china (accessed 28 March 2020).

Wang, Taozheng (2018). 'Lixingzixin, Ju'ansiwei, Tigaobenling: Guanche Luoshi Shijiuda Jingshen Ying youde Jingshenzhuangtai' [Rational Self-confidence: Preparing for Danger in Peacetime, Improving Skills], *Zhonggong Shijiazhuang Shiwei Dangxiao Xuebao* [Central Party School Journal of the Shijiazhuang Municipal Party Committee] 20 (4), 4–10.

Wang, Yiwei (2014a). 'Zhongguo Zhoubian Gonggong Waijiao de Wenming Fudan' [Civilizational Burdens of China's Peripheral Diplomacy], *Gonggong Waijiao Jikan* [Journal of Public Diplomacy] 4, 15–20.

Wang, Yiwei (2014b). 'Sichouzhilu Gonggongjiao de Shiming' [Mission of Silk Road Public Diplomacy], *Gonggong Waijiao Jikan* [Journal of Public Diplomacy] 7, 10–15.

Wang, Yiwei (2014c). 'Great Power Security Concept in the Age of Globalisation', *Frontiers* 6, 6–13.

Wei, Jikun (2018). 'Xi Jinping Xinshidai Youhuan Yishi Lunxi' [Analysis of Awareness of Future Dangers in Xi Jinping's New Era], *Socialism Studies* 2 (138), 12–18.

XEP (Xinjiang Education Press) (2009). *50ge 'Weishenme': Weihu Guojia Tongyi, Fandui Minzu Fenlie, Jiaqiang Minzu Tuanjie Duben* [The 50 Whys: Protecting National Unification, Opposing Ethnic Separatism, Strengthening Ethnic Unity Study Book] (Wulumuqi: Xinjiang Education Press).

Xi, Jinping (2013). 'Xi Jinping Calls for the Building of New Type of International Relations', 23 March, www.fmprc.gov.cn/mfa_eng/topics_665678/xjpcf1_665694/t1024781.shtml (accessed 28 March 2020).

Xi, Jinping (2014). 'Central Conference Relating to Foreign Affairs Was Held in Beijing', 29 November, www.fmprc.gov.cn/mfa_eng/zxxx_662805/t1215680.shtml (accessed 28 March 2020).

Xi, Jinping (2015). 'Speech on China-US Relations in Seattle', 23 September, http://news.xinhuanet.com/english/2015-09/24/c_134653326.htm (accessed 1 December 2019).

Xi, Jinping (2017a). 'Speech at Opening of Belt and Road Forum', 14 May, http://news.xinhuanet.com/english/2017-05/14/c_136282982.htm (accessed 28 March 2020).

Xi, Jinping (2017b). 'Report at 19th CPC National Congress', 3 November, www.xinhuanet.com//english/special/2017-11/03/c_136725942.htm (accessed 28 March 2020).

Xin, Ma, Yu-Tao Xiang, Zhuo-Ji Cai et al. (2009). 'Generalised Anxiety Disorder in China: Prevalence, Sociodemographic Correlates, Comorbidity, and Suicide Attempts', *Perspectives in Psychiatric Care* 45 (2), 119–127.

XUAR (Xinjiang Uyghur Autonomous Region Government) (2018). '2018 nian Xinjiang Weiwuer Zizhiqu Zhengfu Gongzuo Baogao' [Xinjiang Uyghur

Autonomous Region Government's 2018 Work Report], 2 March, http://cn.chinagate.cn/reports/2018-03/02/content_50636629.htm (accessed 15 April 2020).

XVD (Xinjiang Victims Database) (2018). https://shahit.biz/eng/ (accessed 15 April 2020).

Yan, Xuetong (2013). 'New Values for New International Norms', *China International Studies* (January/February), 15–28.

Yan, Xuetong (2018). 'Chinese Values vs. Liberalism: What Ideology Will Shape the International Normative Order?', *The Chinese Journal of International Politics* 11 (1), 1–22.

Yan, Xuetong (2019). 'What Made China's Rise Possible?', *Global Times*, 19 May, www.globaltimes.cn/content/1150626.shtml (accessed 26 May 2020).

Zenz, Adrian (2018). 'Thoroughly Reforming Them towards a Healthy Heart Attitude', *Central Asian Survey* 38, 102–128.

Zenz, Adrian (2019). 'Break Their Roots: Evidence for China's Parent-Child Separation Campaign in Xinjiang', *Journal of Political Risk* 7 (7).

Zhang, Weiwei (2012). *Zhongguo Chudong* [China Shock] (Shanghai: Shanghai People's Press).

Zhang, Yongjin (1991). 'China's Entry into International Society', *Review of International Studies* 17, 3–16.

Zhang, Yongjin (2012). 'China Anxiety: Discourse and Intellectual Challenges', *Development and Change* 44 (6), 1407–1425.

Zheng, Yongnian, and Chi Zhang (2016). 'The Belt Road Initiative and China's Grand Diplomacy', *China International Studies* (January/February), 52–63.

Zhou, Enlai (1950). 'Renzhen Shixing Dang de Minzu Zhengce' [Earnestly Implement the Party's *Minzu* Policy], in CCP Central Committee Document Research Office (ed.) (2010), *Xinjiang Gongzuo Wenxian Xuanbian* [Xinjiang Work: Selected Documents] (Beijing: CCP Central Committee Party Literature Publishing House), 63.

Zhu, Jianjun (2017). 'Bujiaolǔ ye shi Aiguo' [Not Being Anxious Can Also Be Patriotic], *Jingcai Wenzhai* [Wonderful Digest] 276, 89.

Index

abduction 244
abortion 218, 255, 257
abuses against the Uyghurs 117–118, 252–257
　facilitation of 252
Acharya, Amitav 330
advocacy organizations 231–232
African peoples 195
al-Qaeda 105–106, 112
Althusser, Louis 156
Amnesty International 40
Anand, Dibyesh 157
Andersen, Hans Christian 210
anger 317–319
animals and nature 203–208
Anti-Rightist Campaign (1957) 17, 36–37, 51–52, 101
Anti-Terrorism Bureau 282
anxiety 316–317
Apter, David E. 130
Araoz, Gustavo 71–72
Arendt, Hannah 332, 343
Aristotle 229
art 39
artificial intelligence (AI) 155
Asian Infrastructure Investment Bank (AIIB) 328

assimilation 2, 8, 18–19, 22, 38–42, 73, 92–103, 107, 110, 182, 217–218, 276, 337, 340–342, 345
　forced 95, 97
　incentivized 103, 107
Atran, Scott 5
Australian Aborigines 295–296
authoritarian regimes 64
autonomy, regional 277
Ayup, Abduweli 251

Balandier, Georges 3, 9
Bao Shengli 340
'barbarians' 345
beards 17, 36, 139
Bekari, Omer 251
Belt and Road Initiative (BRI) 7, 68, 91, 129, 328, 335, 341
Benjamin, Walter 332
Bhabha, Homi 158, 175
bin Laden, Osama 105–107, 110
biometric data 249
biopolitics 228–230, 256–257
　predatory 230, 233, 257
blacklisting 131
Bo Xilai 243

book burnings 43
bookstores 42, 188
Bowles, Devin 64
Brophy, David 1
Bunin, Eugene 47, 251–252
Bush, George W. 281
Byler, Darren (author of Chapter 6) x, 14, 21, 45

cadres, treatment of 39–40
Callahan, William A. 336
Campbell, Bradley 21–22, 63–64, 78, 80, 182–185
capitalism 230
Cappelletti, Alessandra 7
Card, Claudia 343
Catris, Sandrine (author of Chapter 2) x, 16–17
censorship 314
Chanisheff, Soyüngül 45, 48, 52
Cheek, Timothy 51
Chen Quanguo 2, 18, 36, 38, 41, 47, 49, 51, 55, 77–78, 115, 189, 288–289, 340
Chen Zhonghua 236
Chiang Kai-shek 5, 39
children, treatment of 12, 15, 42, 165, 184, 186, 253, 295, 343
'China model' 328
China Organ Transplant Response System (COTRS) 246
'China threat' 333
China Tribunal 241
Chinese Communist Party (CCP) 2–3, 6, 12–25, 53, 55, 65–66, 73, 79, 91, 101, 114, 184, 187, 194–195, 203, 212–213, 228–229, 231, 239–240, 249, 255, 257, 273–279, 287–295, 328–331, 334–345
 Central Committee 44, 49, 134
 officials of the *nomenklatura* 236
 roles of 130–131
Chinese thinking about Xinjiang 91–93, 98, 116
citizenship 173
'civilising mission' 92–93, 97–100

Clarke, Michael (editor of present book and author of Chapters 1 and 9) xi, 23–24, 182, 338
'clash of civilizations' 335, 344
Cliff, Thomas 109–110
Cohen, Stanley 234, 245
collective action problem 256
collective trauma 308–315, 317, 320–322
 dimensions of 309–315, 320–322
 theory of 308–310, 323
colonialism 3–4, 8–10, 18, 21, 37, 42, 91–96, 117, 154–158, 174–177, 338, 341
 contiguous 95–96
 definition of 3
 European 92–93
 'internal' 8
 standard forms of 94
 types of 8–10
 Western conception of 3–4
 'colonies of settlement' and 'colonies of exploitation' 9
concentration camps 61–63, 78, 80–81, 294, 307, 316
Confucianism 132, 134, 336
conquest of Uyghur homeland by China 99
content analysis 182, 190–217
contractors in Xinjiang 162–165, 173–174
corporal punishment 145
counterterrorism measures 3, 14, 92–94, 107–109, 112, 116, 128, 182, 272, 275–288, 293
COVID-19 pandemic 144–145, 317
Cox, Robert 334
creeping genocide 61–62, 65, 69, 81–82
crime 53
criminal law, changes to 281
Crossley, Pamela 4
cultural genocide 2, 15, 18–20, 51, 54–55, 62–63, 74, 90–94, 98–99, 103–105, 114–116, 128, 218
 definition of 62

Index

cultural practices 182–184, 189–192, 196–198, 217–218
    distinctively Uyghur 36, 81, 107
Cultural Revolution (CR) 16–17, 73, 101, 135
    legacy of 36–51, 54–55

Daoist philosophy 334
Dave, Naisargi 175
Davidson, Lawrence 62–63, 74, 97
Davies, Gloria 336
Dawes General Allotment Act (US, 1887) 96–97
Dawut, Zumrat 227
death sentences 236, 244–247
deaths
    in custody 251–254, 257
    of family members 321–323
    through mass killing 254
de-colonization 101
de-extremification 183–188, 290
Defoe, Daniel 210
dehumanization 21, 46–47, 62, 72, 80, 98, 117–118, 155–156, 160, 172–177
Deng Xiaoping 6, 278, 328, 333–334
denial of abuses 234, 245
depression, feelings of 318–319, 323–324
detainees 80, 135–136, 141, 155–156, 166–167, 171–176, 183–184, 248, 252, 275, 307–308, 341
'Develop the West' campaign (2000) 107
developmentalism 6–8
diaspora communities, Uyghur 24, 306–311, 315–324
    lost contact with homeland 306–308, 319
Di Castro, Angelo Andrea 70
Di Cosmo, Nicola 4
differentiation of peoples 4
digital authoritarianism 77–78
Dillon, Michael 230
'disappearances' 37, 40, 47–48, 54

DNA records 249–250
dress 199–200, 312
Du Bois, William E. B. 162

Eastern Turkestan Islamic Movement (ETIM) 106–108, 279–281
Eastern Turkestan Republics (ETRs) (1933–1934 and 1944–1949) 65, 100–101
economic value of Xinjiang 91, 98
elite individuals and institutions 4, 17, 232–233
Elterish, Ablimit Baki (author of Chapter 10) xi, 24
embeddedness 144, 176
ethnic anxiety 337–344
ethnic distinctions 64
ethnic minorities 275, 284–285
    opposing each other 160–161
ethnic politics 328–329, 345
ethnography 176
ethno-nationalities 161
evidence of abuses 231–234, 255–256
exploitation 4, 9, 244–245, 248
'extremism' 93, 110–118, 127, 140

falsification of data 246–248, 255
Falun Gong 12, 23, 137, 229, 232–235, 239–244, 248–250, 254–257, 292
Fan, Maureen 74
Fanon, Frantz 174–175
Fassin, Didier 156–160
fear on the part of Uyghurs 311–315, 318–319
Feierstein, Daniel 63, 69, 79–80
folk stories 211–212
foodstuffs 45, 53
forced donation of organs 237, 240
forced labour 14, 36, 47–48, 81, 134–135, 145, 209, 295, 308
foreign policy 328–332, 336
Foucault, Michel 229–230
'four olds' 40
France 96

Frankfurt, Harry 233
Freedom House 241
Freeman, Joshua 52
'frontier of defense' or 'frontier of settlement' 109–110
frontier regions of China 95–102, 339
'fusion' policies 341–345
future prospects 55

'Gang of Four' 38, 50, 55
gap-fill exercises 216–217
Geddes, Barbara 256
genocide 18, 61, 72, 97, 103, 107–108, 115–117, 182–186, 218, 343
   definition of 15–16, 63–64, 82, 90, 183–184
   perpetrators of 184–186
   physical 63, 65, 81
   prevention of 64
   as a process 63, 65, 80–81
   as social control 64, 184
   structural factors in 65
   warning signs of 61–62, 81
   see also creeping genocide; cultural genocide
gentrification 76
Gladney, Dru C. 8–9
Global Observatory on Donation and Transplantation 246
Global Terrorism Database 278
Global Times 280
Global War on Terror (GWOT) 78, 104–105, 117, 182, 218, 277
Goffman, Erving 232
Great Leap Forward 101
Great Revival of China 24–25, 330–331, 337, 341–344
   euphoria associated with 331–337
Great Western Development (GWD) plan 7, 278
greetings, traditional 41
grief 320–321
Grose, Timothy A. (co-author of Chapter 5) xi, 13, 19–20, 42

Guantanamo Bay 104
'gunboat diplomacy' 333
Gutmann, Ethan 240

Halal foods 185
Han Chinese 5–7
   dominance of 19, 198–199, 203–208, 217, 339, 345
   portrayal of 192–193
   settlement in Xinjiang 50, 101–102, 109, 161
Hanzu 338
harassment, fear of 313–314
Harrell, Stevan 138
Hayes, Anna (author of Chapter 3) xi–xii, 16, 18
Hayes, Ben 276
He Xiaoshun 236
Hechter, Michael 8
Hegel, G. W. F. 334
hegemony 329–333, 336
Heidegger, Martin 230
Henderson, Errol A. 338
historical perspective 208–209, 338–339
Hoffman, Samantha 289
Holocaust, the 117, 309
home life 42
Hopkins, Benjamin D. 95
Hoshur, Memtimim 41, 46
hospital system 257
Hu Angang 284, 330–331, 340
Hu Jintao 282, 334, 339–341
Hu Lianhe 284, 287, 340
Huang Jiefu 236, 245–246
Hugo, Victor 210
human rights 19, 55, 73, 92, 104–106, 157, 227, 231–232, 237, 343
Human Rights Watch 137, 233
Hundred Flowers Campaign 51
Hutus 185

Id Kah 44–45, 78
identity 22, 294, 329–332, 345
ideological messages 194
idioms 213–214

Index

immersion 182
imprisonment 37, 47–48, 54–55, 141–142
  reasons given for 40
indigenous peoples 93–103, 114–117, 295
  elimination of 10
indoctrination 142, 145
infrastructure projects 7, 278
Integrated Joint Operations Platform (IJOP) 114
integration of Xinjiang into China 7–8, 91, 99–103, 254
intellectuals 51–55, 113–115, 307
  public 331–332, 336
intelligence 285
intention of Chinese policies 11–12
international law 90–91
international relations (IR) 327–335, 344
  new type of 327–329, 334–335
  and Xinjiang 329–331
Internet resources 314–315, 324
internment camps 1, 35–37, 47, 54, 115–116, 142, 145, 163, 186, 209, 294, 307–308, 316, 331, 338, 341–343
  as subjectification spaces 165–173
interpreters, role of 175
intersubjectivity 175
'invisibilization' of the Uyghurs 22
Irani, Lilly 155
Iraq, invasion of (2003) 105–107
Islam 66, 79
Islamic State (IS) 280
Islamophobia 79

Jacobs, Justin 100
Jailova, Gulbahar 250
jaza lagirliri, the 311–315, 318, 321
Jian Bozan 340
Jiang Zemin 278, 281
judgement, need for 245
Junker, Andrew 232
junxian system of administration 5

Kant, Immanuel 333
Kashgar 66–78, 81–82, 107–108
Kashgar Dangerous House Reform Programme (KDHRP) 18, 61–62, 69–82
Kazakh groups 65
Keller, Helen 210
Kerimi, Abdurräshid Haji 41–45, 48
Kilgour, David 240
King, Gary 256
Kissinger, Henry 332
Kojève, Alexander 230
Kuldja 103
Kunming railway station incident (2014) 113
Kuomintang 39

'labelling' 131, 140–141, 160
labour camps 133–137
labour expropriation 245
language issues 8, 14–15, 41, 46, 110, 142, 181–183, 190, 213–214, 218, 253
Laogai Foundation 241
Leibold, James co-author of Chapter 5) xii, 12–13, 19–20, 42, 92, 285–286, 291
Lemkin, Raphael 15–16, 63–64, 82, 90, 182–183, 218
Lemon, Edward 182
Levinas, Emmanuel 175–176
Levine, Mark 63, 81
liberalization policies in China 102
Link, Perry 336
literature 208–211, 338
Little Red Book 17, 36, 45
Liu, Tianyang 68
liver transplants 236
Li Zhi 282
laojiao system 136
localness, natural 62–63
loyalty 45, 51–52, 129, 158, 184

McDonell, Stephen 74–77
MacGregor, Isabelle 64
McMillen, Donald 51, 53
Mahasum, Hasan 279–280

Mahmut, Dilmurat (co-author of Chapter 7) xii, 21–22
Manchu state 333
Mao Zedong (and Maoism) 6, 36–38, 41–46, 49–55, 129–131, 137, 286, 291, 294, 328, 333–334
  images of 17
  marginalization of the Uyghurs 7–8
Ma Rong 284, 330, 340–341
marriages, forced 308
Marx, Karl 23, 230, 256–257
'mass line' mobilization 281, 286–288, 296
Matas, David 240
Mechanical Turk network 155
medical examinations 250–251
mega-projects 7, 278
Mekhsum, Memetjan 52
Meng Jianzhu 285
mental health 320, 324
Merzbacher, Gottfried 71–72
Michell, George 66
militancy, Uyghur 278–279
Millward, James 4–5
mingling, inter-ethnic 286
minzu 6–7
Mitalipova, Maya 249–250
mobile phones 324
Molotov, Vyachslav 291
Mongolia 4, 7, 99, 161
Morgan, Lewis 338–339
mosques 44–45, 73, 78
Muslim communities 20, 104–105
Muslim-majority countries 313

names of Uyghurs 198–203, 314
'nanny apps' 288
National Counter-Terrorism Working and Coordinating Small Group (NCTWCSG) 282
national identity 328
National People's Congress 341

nationalism 52–55, 138, 345
Native Americans 96–99, 116–117
Nazi regime 63, 80, 184–185, 195, 316
Neal, Andrew W. 230
New York Times 73
Newby, Laura 4
Nice, Sir Geoffrey 240
9/11 attacks 103–104, 117, 279
Noakes, Stephen 135–136

Olson, Mancur 256
Olympic Games (Beijing, 2008) 108, 110, 280
organ harvesting 22–23, 227–234, 240–245, 248–258
  background considerations 230–234
  de-fetishizing of 255–258
  as an inferred abuse 240–244
  Uyghur vulnerability to 248–255
Osterhammel, Jurgen 3, 9

Pan, Jennifer 132
Partnership Assistance Programme (PAP) 283
party-state system 35, 37, 54, 137, 145, 228, 247, 257
passports, confiscation of 315
paternalism 12
pathologizing of cultural difference 20, 129, 143–145, 292
Peng Zhen 39
'People's War on Terror' 36, 114–115, 138
Perdue, Peter C. 4
physical appearance of Uyghurs 199–200
Pitzer, Andrea 294
pluralism, cultural 340
poetry 208–209, 212
police units and police action 156, 164, 282–283, 288, 313–314
political crimes 341
Polo, Marco 66
postcolonial values 116

Index

post-traumatic stress disorder (PTSD) 319
power relations 157
Pratt, Richard H. 296
pre-emptive action 79
pressures, socio-economic 7, 278
'prisoner of war' status 104
prisoners of conscience 245, 248
Production and Construction Corps (Bingtuan) 136
'Project Beauty' 111, 139
proof, concept of 254, 256
propaganda 12, 35–36, 54, 75, 232, 243, 248
protectionism 333, 335
proverbs 213–216
psychiatric confinement 257
psychological problems and psychological treatment 143, 323–324
public health projects 227
public-private partnership model 109
Pushkin, Alexander 210

Qin Yaqing 332, 334
Qing Empire 3–5, 99–100, 277

racialization 158–159, 174–177
racism 338
railways, temporary closure of 252
rebellions 4–6, 100
Red Cross 246
Red Guards 17, 36, 39–43, 46–50
Reddy, Chandan 155–158
re-education system 11–22, 40, 80, 115, 248, 128, 134–145, 154–157, 162, 167–177, 182, 186–187, 217, 275, 286, 291, 295, 307, 341
 Uyghurs and Kazakhs working in 162–165
religion and religious behaviour 15, 36, 42–44, 47, 111–112, 290–291
resistance by Uyghurs 11
rights 341, 343

Rivers, Linda 196
Roberts, Sean R. (author of Chapter 4) xii–xiii, 7, 13, 16–19, 78–79, 292, 307
Robertson, Matthew P. (author of Chapter 8) xiii, 22–23
Rosenblatt, Nate 280
Rozi, Yalqun 21–22, 189
rules and regulations on transplantation 235–236

sadness, feelings of 315–319
Saich, Tony 130
samples of blood and urine 250
Sautman, Barry 8–9
Sauytbay, Sayragul 47
Saypedin, Eziz 39, 52
Schein, Louisa 338
Scheper-Hughes, Nancy 173
Schluessel, Eric 100
Schneider, Julia C. 4
school textbooks 22, 115, 182, 189–192, 201, 217–218
Scott, James C. 20–21, 129, 276, 289
Second World War 316
secularisation 15
self-censorship 215
self-rule for Xinjiang 65, 102
separation from families 185, 320–327, 343
separatism 51–54, 65, 103, 107, 113–114, 184, 340
settler colonialism 2–3, 10–11, 14, 16, 19, 90–99, 102–109, 116, 245, 295, 339
sexual abuse 15
Seydin, Iminjan 40
Shahidi, Burhan 39–40, 46
Shan, Dan 293
shared experience 175–176
Shawn, Wallace 256
Shawn, Zhang 44, 47
Shen Zhongyang 238
Shi Jun 285
'shrines of the soul' 16
silence in the streets 35

Silk Roads 66, 69–70
sleep disturbance 319–320
smartphones 290
Smith Finley, Joanne (co-author of Chapter 7) xiii–xiv, 21–22, 36, 44, 79, 161, 187, 189, 216, 290–291, 307
social conditions 129, 135–136
social control 21, 64, 78, 80, 184, 281, 293–296
social engineering 59, 63, 73, 75, 101–102
'social management', concept of 288–289
social media 40, 47, 54, 310, 314, 324
'socialism with Chinese characteristics' 25
sources of human organs 234–241, 244–248, 254–255
Soviet Union 100–102, 230
Spain 96
special economic zone (SEZ) status 68
Spieglehalter, Sir David 247
'stabilization' of Xinjiang 7, 285–286, 291
Stalin, Joseph 12, 291, 294, 333, 338
state-building 2
state power 156, 158, 162, 230
Steele, Brent 329–330
sterilizations 218, 255, 257
'strike hard' campaigns 281
students 52–53
subjectification 157
suicide 322–323
Sun Yatsen 5
'surrogate colonization' 5
surveillance systems 1, 24, 35, 37, 48, 77–78, 81, 108, 110, 116, 131, 136, 141, 145, 155–156, 164, 275–276, 281–283, 286–290, 296, 308, 314
suzhi 132–133, 138
Syrian civil war 112
'systematic environmental transformation' 10

Taotao Zhao 285
targeting
 for organ harvesting 249
 of populations 127, 131–132, 136–141, 145
 of Uyghurs 308–309
terrorism, definition of 105, 290
'terrorism' label 19, 92–94, 98, 104–118, 140, 159
therapeutic intervention 144
'thought work' 129–130
'three evils' 279, 281
Thum, Rian 44, 99
Tian Shan report (2015) 143
Tiananmen Square incident (2013) 112
Tiananmen Square incidents (1989) 102
Tibet 4, 7, 77–78
Tobin, David (author of Chapter 11) xiv, 24–25
Tohti, Ilham 113–114
Tong Mingkang 71–74
torture 12, 15, 104, 135, 142, 183–184, 217, 230, 241, 292, 343
totalitarian regimes 64
traditions, Uyghur 41
trafficking in human organs 253–254
transfer of detainees around China 252
'transformation through education' policy 12, 292
transplantation of human organs 227–228, 231, 236–248, 253–257
 alleged reforms of 246–248, 257
 in emergencies 242–243
 official failure to account for 253
 system for and growth of 231, 236, 238–239, 245, 247
Transplantation Society, The 246
Troops, Stanley 9–10
trustworthiness 157, 160, 163, 172–177
truth, nature of 255

Index

Turkestan Islamic Party (TIP) 108–112, 280
Turkey 313
Turkic Muslim rebellion (1866–1877) 4
Turkic peoples 36–40, 47, 50, 54–55, 154–155, 159–162, 174–177, 276–277, 307
Tursun, Mihrgul 47, 250–252
Tutsis 185
Twain, Mark 195–196, 210

uniqueness of China 331–332
United Nations 15, 63, 82, 90, 105–106, 116, 183, 241
  Educational, Scientific and Cultural Organization (UNESCO) 69
United States (US) 95–99, 103–106, 116–117, 293, 330–335
'upstream' factors 64
Urumqi 108, 137
  railway station incident (2014) 113
  riots in (2009) 184, 186, 278–279, 282, 324, 341
Uyghurs
  'good' and 'bad' 114–115
  perceptions of 161

van Krieken, Robert 295–296
veiling 17, 36, 139
Veracini, Lorenzo 9–10, 94–95
Victims of Communism Memorial Foundation 252
violence 42, 54, 78–79, 108–113, 140, 155–156, 172–173, 176–177
  practised by the state 92, 344–345
  social and cultural dimensions of 173
vocational training internment centres (VTICs) 35
  see also internment camps
voluntary organ donation 246–247, 253

Wang Enmao 50
Wang Lequan 282
Wang Lijun 243–244
Wang, Ding 293
Wang Yiwei 334
Ward, Thomas Humphry 210
'warlord colonialism' 5
WeChat 324
'weeds' 47, 80, 129, 131, 287
Westernization 328–332, 336, 340
White Papers 13–14
Wines, Michael 75
witnessing 176–177
Wolfe, Patrick 10, 14
Work Forum (2010) 109–110
Work Forum (2014) 113
World Health Organization 246
World Heritage list 70, 72
world order 328–335, 341–343
Wu, Harry 240
Wu Dianting 74
Wu Guang 43, 46–47
Wu Han 38–39
Wu Lili 73–74

Xi Jinping 2, 11, 14, 18, 22, 25, 35–36, 45, 49–51, 55, 62, 79, 91–92, 113, 129, 137–138, 190, 284–286, 293, 327–328, 331–337, 340–341, 344
Xinjiang Daily (newspaper) 38–39, 42, 142–143
'Xinjiang model', the 276–277, 293, 296
'Xinjiang Papers', the 187, 190
Xinjiang treated differently from other Chinese provinces 49
Xunzi 134

Yan Xuetong 332, 334
Yang, Mayfair 133
Yongjin Zhang 329
Yuan, Ying 192
Yuan, Zhenjie 68

Zakir, Shöhrät 141, 143
Zenn, Jacob 280
Zenz, Adrian 47, 80
'zero-24' policy 80–81
Zhang Chunxian 138, 283–289
Zhang Weiwei 329, 332
Zhang Yun 341

Zhe Wu 52
Zheng, Shusen 242–243
Zhou Enlai 39, 50
Zhou Yongkang 232
Zhu Hailun 24, 275
Zhu Weiqun 138